Inside the
Norton Utilities™
Revised and Expanded

Rob Krumm

Introduction by Peter Norton

Brady

New York   London   Toronto
Sydney   Tokyo   Singapore

Brady

Simon & Schuster, Inc.
15 Columbus Circle
New York, NY 10023

Distributed by Prentice Hall Trade

Manufactured in the United States of America

3 4 5 6 7 8 9 10

Library of Congress Cataloging-in-Publication Data

Krumm, Rob, 1951-
　　　Inside the Norton Utilities / Rob Krumm. -- Rev. and expanded.
　　　　　p.　cm.
　　　1. Utilities (Computer programs) 2. Norton utilities (Computer programs)
I. Title.
QA76.76.U84K78　1989
005.4'3--dc20　　　　　　　　　　　　　　　　　　　　89-48590

ISBN 0-13-468406-0

For information about our audio products, write us at:
Newbridge Book Clubs, 3000 Cindel Drive, Delran, NJ　08370

Dedication

If she is Snow White, then I must be Grumpy.

Acknowledgement

I wish to extend my thanks to Brad Kingsbury, John Socha, and the people at Peter Norton Computing for their cooperation and advice.

Limits of Liability and Disclaimer of Warranty

Trademarks

Contents

Preface

Why Read This Book?

The highest compliment I can give to the programs discussed in this book, the Norton Utilities Advanced Edition 4.5, the Norton Commander 3.0, the Norton Editor 1.3 and the Norton Guides 1.0, is that I never use a computer without having them available. If I have to go to another location I make sure I take them with me. These programs comprise a basic toolkit that enables you to deal effectively with any MS-DOS based computer system.

The purpose of this book is to serve as a companion guide to the programs from Peter Norton Computing. While many of the features of the Norton programs can be used without much guidance at all, almost any user can benefit from a deeper understanding of the structure and benefits provided by the hundreds of operations, techniques and procedures that can be performed with these programs.

The information in this book, with the exception of Part V, is written in the form of a step by step guide to perform a wide range of operations. Each and every keystroke needed is documented and annotated to explain the reason behind the operations. The book contains hundreds of screen shots which illustrate exactly how the computer screen will look when you are performing the operations.

The book is organized in five major sections containing a total of 14 chapters.

Section I: Fundamental Concepts

This section is an introduction to the fundamental concepts that underlie both DOS and the Norton Utilities programs. This section is useful for user who want to learn or refresh their memory about the basic concepts and terminology involved in the use of MSDOS computers.

Section II: Batch Files

This section teaches the reader how to create and use DOS batch files. The batch files created in this section range from simple utilities to complete menu systems. The power of batch files is combined with the power of the Norton Utilities programs to create enhanced batch files that display a sophisticated user interface beyond what you would normally exexpect from batch file operations.

Section III: Everyday Tasks

This section shows how the Norton Utilities programs are used to increase productivity in everyday computer tasks.

Section IV: Survival Skills

This section details the use of the Norton Utilities programs to recover erased, formatted or damaged data from hard and floppy disks. The section explains what can go wrong with disks and how the Norton Utilities programs enable you to correct or prevent loss of data.

Section V: Other Programs

This section discussed three applications besides the Norton Utilities which are available from Peter Norton Computing: The Norton Commander, The Norton Editor, and The Norton Guides.

It is my sincere hope that this book helps you get the most of the Norton Utilities, a package of programs that making life with a computer system much easier.

Rob Krumm

Introduction

It is a true pleasure for me on behalf of all my colleagues at Peter Norton Computing to introduce this official guide to the whole assortment of utility software that we publish. Rob Krumm first wrote about The Norton Utilities in 1986 in *Getting the Most from Utilities on the IBM PC*. Since then we've gotten to know each other better, and our mutual respect and friendship have grown steadily.

While he was writing this book, Rob practically became part of the family at Peter Norton Computing. That's why you see on the cover, not just Rob and me, but my good friend and colleague, Brad Kingsbury. Brad Kingsbury has played a key role in developing The Norton Utilities, and he is one of the most gifted and original software developers working today. The whole Peter Norton team worked closely with Rob to make this book a definitive guide not only to both versions of The Norton Utilities, but also to The Norton Commander. The Norton Editor, and the newest members of our product line, The Norton Guides.

Why did The Norton Utilities become such popular software? Well, industry wisdom has it that software becomes standard either by providing superior capabilities or by solving problems that were previously unsolvable. In 1982, when I sat down at my PC to write Unerase, I was solving a common problem to which there was no readily available solution. Since then we've added to Unerase utilities to deal with common traps and pitfalls of computer operations. At Peter Norton Computing we've steadily expanded and improved these utilities to help you understand and control the computer better. With these products you control the whole environment beneath individual applications to manage your files, arrange your hard disk effectively, and to get yourself out of emergency situations caused by an accidental erase or delete command.

When I wrote *Inside the IBM PC* in 1984 I began with these words:

> This is the beginning of a marvelous voyage of discovery into the secrets, wonders, and mysteries of the IBM Personal Computer and the family of computers that has grown up around it.

That book and the subsequent books have been one part of the shared voyage of discovery that I and millions of readers have undertaken. The growing family of utility products from Peter Norton Computing has been the other part. Now, for the first time, Rob Krumm brings the two streams together to the benefit of both the readers and the more that one million users of Norton Utility software. Rob has created the one book that should accompany every copy of our utility software. I recommend it unhesitantly to everyone who has read one of my books or used any Peter Norton Computing software.

Peter Norton

Section I

Fundamental Concepts

The purpose of Section I is to provide the reader with a basic understanding of the concepts used throughout this book. These concepts underlie many of the operations and techniques discussed in this book that involve the use of the Norton Utilities, the Norton Commander, the Norton Editor, and the Norton Guides.

Since each section contains a complete hands-on, step-by-step sequence of commands that addresses the specific topics being discussed, it is not strictly necessary to read Chapter 1 of Section I in order to perform the operations related to those topics. However, this section provides some background information that explains the basis upon which MS-DOS computers operate, the understanding of which is crucial to the education of any computer user. While there are many good books about MS-DOS on the market, the information supplied in this section is valuable for two reasons:

1. The information is presented to provide a conceptual basis for the operation of the Norton Computing programs discussed in this book. It is designed to touch on important themes and concepts that will be expanded upon in other sections of the book.

2. By using the facilities of the main Norton Utilities programs, this section includes a hands-on exploration of how disks store data. Because the Norton Utilities program enables you to display information that DOS is not capable of displaying, the reader can gain insight into the structure and use of disks, which would not be

possible if the subject of the book were limited to MS-DOS alone.

For readers who want to skip this section and jump into specific operations right away, cross references to the information contained in this section are provided in various places throughout the book, where allusions to these concepts are made.

1

Memory Versus Storage

It is not uncommon for people to become disoriented by the kind of technical language they encounter when beginning to work with computers. Language is not necessarily technical because it contains strange new words, although there are some terms that are specific to computers. The majority of the problems with computer terminology arise from the use of some very ordinary words. The difference is that in a technical field, these words have a specific, narrow meaning, as opposed to their broader, more general usage.

The most important terms in a computer-oriented vocabulary consist of some very ordinary words borrowed from the general lexicon. It is possible to start with the general meaning of these words and by some reflection arrive at a meaning approximating their technical use in terms of computers. The two most important terms to understand are **memory** and **storage** (albeit, information storage).

To demonstrate, let's begin with a simple question: "What are the dates of the Mexican-American War?" There are two ways to respond to this question. If you know the dates, you can answer the question. But if you don't know the dates what options do you have? The most obvious option is to seek out some resource, such as an almanac or encyclopedia, and look up the information. Once the information is found, you can answer the question.

The process just described is a common, everyday experience, which contains the outline of the distinction between what is meant by computer memory and computer storage. When the question is asked, the first step to finding the answer is to check to see if that information resides in your personal memory. What characteristics does that memory possess?

First, there is easy access. The information stored in your memory is easy to retrieve. In fact, it seems to take little or no effort to access that information; it simply pops out.

However, not everyone can answer the question from memory--perhaps they have never been exposed to the information. More likely, they knew the information at one time but the information is no longer in their memory. What does this tell you about the nature of memory? This tells you that memory is

3

subject to change, the second characteristic. The set of information contained in your memory today is different from what it contained 10 years ago or will contain 10 days from now.

This ability to change the contents of your memory is beneficial because it allows you to get rid of obsolete information and learn new information that is of greater significance at the moment. Implicit in this idea is a third characteristic of memory. There would be no advantage to a changeable memory unless there was, at the same time, a limit on the total amount of information the memory could hold. It is because of this limit that it is an advantage to discard some information in favor of other information.

Of course, human memory is not well understood. The exact limit of information is difficult to judge and some people claim humans remember everything from womb to grave, in some hidden form. But as a practical matter, we accept the characteristics of memory as:

1. Fast access

2. Changeable

3. Limited in capacity

What happens when you don't know the information and must seek additional information in a book? What sort of "memory" lies in a book?

To answer this question you can compare the information "stored" in a book, on an audio or video tape, in a photograph, and so on, with the characteristics associated with memory.

Begin with access, the first characteristic. Reading material from a book takes longer and is harder to do than simply remembering it. Also, the information stored in the book is useless by itself and becomes useful only once it has been read (that is, placed, even temporarily, into someone's memory). Information stored in books, tapes, and so on serves the purpose of providing information for memory. Without transferring the information to a memory, the stored data has no meaning.

Is stored information subject to change in the same way that memory is? The answer is no. In fact, the purpose of storage is to create a permanent reservoir of information. You would not expect ink to fade from a page in the way that the date of the Mexican-American War fades from your memory. Of course, permanence is a relative concept. Catastrophic events can destroy books or even words engraved in stone. But excluding such events, stored data is intended to be permanent.

The final characteristic is capacity. When considering stored information, it is clear that it is designed to be unlimited. (Unlimited, here, refers more to an economic definition than some cosmic infinity.) For stored information to be practical, a readily available, inexpensive medium of storage is needed. For a long time, paper was the obvious choice. Today, electronic devices, such as computers, use a nonpaper form of storage that serves the same purpose.

You can see that memory and storage are really reverse images of each other. The memory is fast, changeable, and limited, while the storage is slower, permanent, and unlimited.

This relationship between memory and storage applies to computers as well as human activity. Computer memory is hard to picture because it is usually not visible to the person using the computer. The memory consists of banks of memory chips located on the computer's main circuit board, or on expansion boards. The specific function of these chips is to hold information that is of immediate use to the computer.

Chips that perform this memory function are often referred to as **RAM**, which stands for ***Random Access Memory***. Random access refers to the method by which the computer retrieves information from memory chips. The term random, often misunderstood technically, has a common connotation of disorganization and haphazardness. However, in the computer context, random has come to mean that there exists multiple ways of accessing data, as opposed to a single order.

A good analogy can be made by exploring the differences between a novel and an encyclopedia. The novel is meant to be read from beginning to end. Starting in the middle or skipping around to different parts would be a misuse of the novel and would fail to get the point across. When a system is designed to be read from beginning to end, with a single beginning and end point, it is referred to as a sequential access system.

The encyclopedia, on the other hand, is designed to be read in small pieces, not from beginning to end. Reading the encyclopedia from beginning to end does not have an advantage over reading all the selections in some other order, dictated by your information needs. Since the encyclopedia can be read in an almost infinite number of sequences, it would be considered a random access system.

The duration of human memory is uncertain, while the RAM used in microcomputers has a very definite duration cycle. The RAM holds information as long as there is a constant supply of power to the computer. When this supply is cut off, on purpose when you turn the machine off or by accident when there is a power failure, all the information in the memory is lost.

> *Operations such as rebooting or resetting your computer will also wipe out the memory.*

It is for this reason that it is necessary to have a means of storing information. Computers can recognize a wide variety of stored information from many different devices including tapes, disks, optical character readers, and paper punch cards. In today's microcomputers, disks of varying types and capacities are almost the exclusive means of storing data.

Remember that no matter what a disk looks like, hard or floppy, internal or external, local or remote network, they all serve the same function of storing information. The information on the disk cannot be used until it is loaded into the computer's memory, in the same sense that information in a book is meaningless without a person to read it, that is, to load the information into human memory.

The advantages of stored information are many. For example, because memory can be changed easily, you can place different groups of information into the memory to conform to a specific task that you want to perform. When you are finished, the same memory can then be loaded with different information for another task. This ability gives both humans and computers much greater flexibility than would be possible with memory alone.

The terms **internal** and **external** memory are also used to refer to memory and storage. The difference in terminology is not important. What is important is to keep in mind the characteristic differences between the two types of information. Computer operations often involve a complex series of memory and storage operations. Keeping the distinction in mind will be helpful in understanding these tasks.

Data and Programs

So far, the term information has been used to describe the material stored in memory or on disk. Information falls broadly into two categories. The two categories appear in language as **verbs** (action words) and **nouns** (words that represent objects). This distinction quite naturally flows through into computer languages and structures.

When a computer works with information it can be action-oriented, that is, give instructions for operations, or object-oriented, contain data that describes things. When a series of instructions are grouped together, it is referred to as a program.

Computer programs are verb-oriented because they are meant to carry out actions or operations. Today, most people purchase programs designed by other people, rather than creating the programs themselves. Some programs provide means by which the user can create new actions, that is, verbs, by pasting the program's original verbs together in a new way. Such user-defined commands are often called macros.

On the other hand, computer memory and storage can also record data about people, places, financial transactions, American history, and so on.

Like the pages of a notebook, disks can record either kind of information. Disks can hold programs as well as data. The same is true of the internal memory of the computer. In fact, it is always the case that the memory is holding some verbs (programs) and some objects (data). Data such as this is usually entered by the people using the computer, although it is becoming more common to purchase some standard reference text such as dictionaries in disk-based format.

Computer operations are always a combination of verbs acting on objects.

Disk Type

Disks play a crucial role in computer systems. They are the repositories for the accumulated information, verbs and objects, in the computer system.

There are primarily two types of disks used in computers today, **hard disks** and **floppy disks**. The key distinction between the **hard** and **floppy** disk is that the hard disk contains nonremovable media, while a floppy disk system haas two parts, a disk drive and a removable disk.

The **floppy disk** got its name because it is made of a soft plastic called mylar. The disk is flexible enough to "flop" once it is removed from the drive. Hard disks are constructed of rigid aluminum disks. But the important distinction between the disks is that hard disks are fixed into the disk drives and cannot be removed. In fact, "hard disks" are factory-sealed units, whose capacity is fixed when manufactured. Today, the average hard disk has a capacity of more than 20,000,000 characters and some disks boast capacities in the area of 100 or 200 million characters.

The floppy disk is characterized by its ability to be removed from the drive and replaced with another disk. The capacity of each disk, which has an average of 360,000 characters, is much smaller than that of a hard disk. However, the advantage is that the disk can be removed and replaced with another.

Today, 3.5 inch hard plastic disks have become more popular. These disks are not "floppy" but are classified as floppy disks because they are removable.

On the other hand, special drives allow you to insert and remove cartridges with capacities of 20,000,000 characters. These are called removable hard disks because they have so large a capacity.

It might be better to classify disks as fixed or removable, but the traditional names are hard to shake. The key to remember is that all disks, regardless of their type, serve the same purpose--to store information, programs, and data, so that it can be loaded into the memory when needed.

> *The distinction is a bit fuzzier because there are disk storage systems that have removable hard disk cartridges. These cartridges typically hold 10 or 20 megabytes or more, and can be removed from the drive in a similar manner to floppy disks. However, these systems are not nearly as common as the standard hard and floppy disks.*

Speed of Access

Another distinction between disks classified as hard and floppy is the speed at which the data is accessed. Hard disks characteristically have a much higher rate of transference of data between the disk and memory. Hard disks are usually ten or more times faster than floppy disks. As with most technical specifications, you can measure the speed of a device in many ways. Disks can be timed for transfer rate, latency, seek time, and access time. Each measures one part of the operation necessary to move information between the memory and the disk.

One key number that helps provide some indication of the differences in the performance between hard and floppy disks is the number of rotations per minute (RPM). A record player spins an LP at 33.3 RPM. A floppy disk drive spins a disk at 300 RPM. When your car idles, it turns the crankshaft at about 1000 RPM. A hard disk rotates at 3600 RPM. It is that faster rotation speed that gives the hard disk much of its improved performance.

A Primer on Binary and Hexadecimal Numbers

The following section is provided for those readers that would like some background on the different types of notations used to express values in computers. The key is in remembering that decimal, binary, and hexadecimal numbers are different ways of expressing the same thing. The only variations are the forms in which the values are written. Since this is the case, understanding these numbering systems is a much simpler task than it sounds.

Number Systems

Why hexadecimal numbers? Why binary numbers? The answers to those questions might be found by asking a more direct question: Why decimal numbers?

There is no special mathematical reason why a decimal system, i.e., a numbering system based on ten digits--0,1,2,3,4,5,6,7,8,9--should be used instead of some other numbering system. The reasons are historical, cultural, and perhaps partly biological.

Most people are acquainted with another system of numbering, the system of roman numerals, which works very differently from the one used every day. In the roman numeral system each digit has an exact value, no matter where it appears. For example, in the Roman number II each I has a value if 1. The value of the number is arrived at by adding together each digit.

$$1 + 1 = 2$$

In a roman numeral system, when a new digit is added, its position is irrelevant. The value of the number results from adding the values together.

$$1 + 1 + 1 = 3$$

> *Today, it is common to use IV as a roman numeral for 4, and VI for 6. This is a modern practice. The Romans used IIII for 4, and either IV or VI would have represented 6.*

In the decimal system, the orders in which the numbers appear, is quite significant. For example 123, has a very different value from 321 or 132. Why is order so significant?

The reason is that the order in which the numbers are sequenced tells you their place value. Place value is something most people take for granted, since it was learned early in their education. When you look at a number, you obtain its value by performing both addition and multiplication. First, each numeral is multiplied by its place value and then all the values are added together to arrive at the total value of the number.

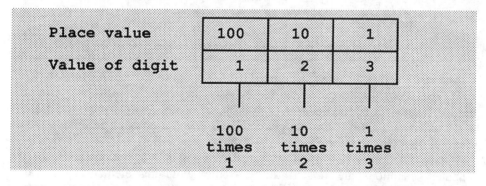

The concept of place values is based on the total number of digits used in a numbering system. There are ten numbers, 0, 1, 2, 3, 4, 5, 6, 7, 8, and 9, in the decimal system. The first place value is the ones place. The value of each of the following places is determined by multiplying by 10. Thus the values for place go from 1 to 10, 100, 1000, and so on.

But why must there be exactly ten digits? Why not 9 or 11? There actually is no reason why you couldn't construct a number system with any number of digits, as long as you had at least two. Thus, the simplest number system would be one that contained only two digits, 1 and 0. Such a system is called a binary system. In a binary system the place values are determined by multiples of two, since there are only 2 digits. Thus, the value of each place doubles as you go to the left.

128	64	32	16	8	4	2	1

For example, if you wanted to write the number 27 in binary notation you would need to have one group of 16, plus one group of 8, plus one group of 2, and finally 1 group of 1.

$$16+8+2+1$$

To write a binary number you would place a 1 in the place value location where you wanted to add the value, and a zero in the place value locations where you did not want the value added.

128	64	32	16	8	4	2	1
			1	1	0	1	1

The result is that the binary number 11011 is equal to the decimal number 27.

If your computer documentation requests the value of 100, be sure to question whether it is 100 decimal or 100 binary. Both systems share the 1 and the 0 characters, thus it is easy to get confused if you are not clear about which system of notation the information is describing.

Binary notation is very good at expressing computer operations because all computer operations are related to electronic switching elements. Like all switching mechanisms, computer operations have only two possible states, open or closed. These states can be represented by 0 for open and 1 for closed. A binary number has a direct one-to-one correspondence with the switch settings.

Binary digits, often referred to as "bits," are more cumbersome to read and write than decimal numbers. In many cases, an exact correspondence with the actual bits is not needed. You can summarize the value of long binary numbers by using the decimal values, which are shorter and easier to read. The decimal system is a higher level numbering system because it can represent larger values in fewer digits.

Decimal numbers have one disadvantage. Because they are based on a system of ten digits, there is no quick, simple way to convert between binary and decimal notation. It would be much simpler if the high-level numbering system was a multiple of 2, which 10 is not. Because of this, computer scientists have tended to adopt systems that use the increment of 2 closest to 10-8 (octal notation) or 16 (hexadecimal notation).

In microcomputers, hexadecimal notation is the most widely used system. Since hexadecimal notation requires 16 digits and there are only 10 digits in the decimal system, it is necessary to add or invent some additional numbers. The traditional answer to this problem is to use the letters A, B, C, D, E, and F as the six additional numbers.

Table 1-1 Decimal, Hexadecimal and Binary Digits

Decimal	Hexadecimal	Binary
0	0	0
1	1	1
2	2	10
3	3	11
4	4	100
5	5	101
6	6	110
7	7	111
8	8	1000
9	9	1001
10	A	1010
11	B	1011
12	C	1100
13	D	1101
14	E	1110
15	F	1111

The hexadecimal system allows you to represent all of the binary numbers from 0 to 1111, with a single digit. Even more significantly, you can easily convert binary numbers to hexadecimal numbers. Below is an example of a Binary number:

10110011

The first step in converting to hexadecimal is to break the number into groups of four digits each.

Decimal	11	3
Binary	1011	0011

You can then match each four-digit group with a hexadecimal digit.

Binary	1011	0011
Hexadecimal	B	3

Thus the hexadecimal number for 10110011 is B3. There is no quick conversion to the decimal number. To translate a hexadecimal number to a decimal number you must go through the process of multiplying each hexadecimal digit by its place value.

	16	1
Hexadecimal	B	3

Since B in hexadecimal notation stands for 11, the calculation is (11 times 16) + (3 times 1) which equals 179. You can see why going from binary to hexadecimal, or hexadecimal to binary, is much simpler than decimal conversion.

Bits, Bytes, and Words

Special types of notation, such as hexadecimal, are employed because they make references to actual computer data, simpler and more direct, after you have gotten used to switching back and forth between different numbering systems.

In MS-DOS systems, and in most microcomputers, data is referred to in three ways. The smallest unit of data is the bit. A **bit** cannot be divided into a smaller unit because it represents a single switch setting inside the computer. All computer data is composed of bits.

Normally, **bits**, representing single switches, are too small to be meaningful on the human level. When you work with a computer you are concerned with letters, numbers, and other characters. The unit used to represent a single character is a **byte**. The **byte** is composed of eight bits, which together are used to represent a single character, such as the letter **A**.

A byte is often said to be equal to the amount of space needed to store a single character. This is true, but it can be misleading. Many applications, such as spreadsheets or word processing programs, always store information with additional data about its location, type, or format. For example, storing the number 1 in a spreadsheet cell will use up much more than a single byte because the spreadsheet program also records data about its location and format.

In some instances it is common to use a unit of measure called a **word**. The term word has no grammatical meaning. Rather, it refers to 2 bytes of information taken together as a unit.

In the next chapter, the concepts discussed above will be put to use to explore the way disks operate. The Norton Utilities program will be used to see the operation of disk storage in a way not possible with DOS commands alone.

A Primer on Disk Structure

Disks, both hard and floppy, are organized in roughly the same way. The only difference between disks is the amount and number of the features that they share in common. All disks are divided into basic units of storage, called **sectors**. The amount of information stored on a disk is determined by the number of sectors that a disk contains. In theory, the size of the sector can vary quite a bit. In practice, however, there is a remarkable conformity among MS-DOS computers. Each sector contains **512** bytes of information.

Disk sectors are created by dividing the disk into a series of concentric circles called **tracks**. The number of tracks on a typical floppy disk is 40, while a 20 megabyte hard disk will usually have over 600 (614 and 615 are common track numbers for 20 megabyte hard disks).

To create the sectors a disk is divided a second time, this time radially, by cutting the tracks into sections. A floppy disk will usually have nine sectors on each track, while a hard disk will have seventeen sectors on each track.

In addition, a disk will have two sides, top and bottom, numbered 0 and 1.

Hard disks actually consist of several disks stacked on top of one another, with space left between. A typical 20 megabyte disk drive contains two disk plates, sides 0 through 3.

When a disk uses both sides and/or one or more plates, DOS uses the term *cylinder* to represent all the tracks that fall in the same vertical plane. For example, suppose you have a floppy disk that has 40 tracks on the top and 40 on the bottom, a total of 80 tracks. Because the tracks are on opposite sides of the same disk, DOS views the disk as having 40 pairs (top and bottom) of matched tracks. Each pair in this case is a *cylinder*. Hard disks often use four or more surfaces to store data. A cylinder consists of all the tracks that align vertically. A cylinder is an important concept in hard disk operation because it represents an exact physical location on the disk. Once positioned to a given cylinder, the disk can read all the data on any of the surfaces, at a high rate of speed. Moving to a different cylinder causes a delay in the transfer of data. The number of cylinders is usually equal to the total number of tracks on each disk surface.

You can calculate the total amount of space on a disk by multiplying the following:

sectors times track times sides by 512

For example, a floppy disk with 9 sectors per track, 40 tracks, and two sides would be:

9 times 40 times 2 times 512 = 368,640

The capacity is referred to as 360K (kilobytes) per disk.

A hard disk with 17 sectors per track, 614 tracks, and 4 sides would have a capacity of:

17 times 614 times four times 512 = 21,377,024

This would be referred to as a 20 megabyte disk.

In order to keep track of the information on the hard disk, each sector is given a unique number. The first sector is 0, the second 1 and so on. A 360K disk will have 720 sectors, number 0-719. A 20 megabyte hard disk will have over 41,000 sectors.

The tracks and sectors are created by a process called formatting, which makes use of a special computer program called **FORMAT**. You cannot use a disk, hard or floppy, before it has been formatted.

When the format command is run, a disk will be divided into the proper number of tracks and sectors. In addition, those sectors must be numbered for identification purposes. Also, the format program checks the integrity of the disk to make sure that all the sectors will correctly accept data. If a defect is found, the sector is marked as unusable.

The formatting process is a complicated one. It actually consists of two separate operations called **low-level** and **high-level** formatting. Low-level (physical) formatting consists of placing electronic marks in the disk to imprint the physical locations of the tracks and sectors. Once the marking has taken place, the high-level formatting organizes the sectors, which are all alike, into separate and distinct functions. This second type of formatting is called high-level or logical formatting.

In MS-DOS computers, the two-stage formatting of floppy disks is implemented with a single command, FORMAT. The same command, when applied to a hard disk, will perform only the high-level formatting. The assumption is that the low-level or physical formatting of the hard disk has already been done.

Usually, low-level formatting of hard disks is something the average user is never faced with. Suppose you wanted to perform a low-level format on your hard disk. How would you do it? The supplier of the hard disk will usually provide a program that performs the low-level format. IBM includes the program as part of the diagnostic disk. If you are using a compatible computer you may find that the program for formatting is not on a disk but built into the ROM on the hard disk controller card. To run this program you will have to use the DEBUG program to access the location in the memory where the program is stored. The typical address of a hard disk device is C800, such as with the popular Western Digital controller supplied with many hard disks.

The Role of DOS

The high-level or logical disk formatting brings in the concept of the operating system. To understand what an operating system does, return to the analogy used to discuss memory and storage. If disk storage space is roughly analogous to a book, a disk drive is a kind of library in which data can be stored and then later retrieved.

As with a library, a record must be kept of which books are stored in the library and where they are located. A library without this type of organization is possible but not practical. The ancient library in Alexandria was reputed to have the finest collection of books in the world. But the scholars who gathered there seldom referred to the wisdom stored in the volumes. The reason is that there was no formal method of organization. You could store information, but there was no organized retrieval system, such as that used in modern libraries.

The same principles apply to disk storage. There must be a master librarian in the computer system, responsible for keeping track of the data stored on the disk. The job requires constant attention because computers can save and then revise data very quickly. The master program that takes care of these library operations, as well as other crucial computer tasks, is called the operating system. The acronym **DOS** stands for *Disk Operating System,* which implies the type of storage device that will be used. **OS** is often used to stand for *Operating System* as well, usually on computers that use different types of storage devices.

When DOS prepares a disk, it builds new structures out of the sectors created by the low-level format, during the high level formatting process. The first sector on the disk is called the **boot** sector. Then two other groups of sectors are set aside to hold information about the files stored on the disk. These two groups form a *card catalog* for the disk. The two groups of sectors are called the **File Allocation Table** (FAT) and the **Directory**. In this book, you will use the Norton Utilities program to explore the structure of these areas, in detail.

Once the areas of the disk needed for the **card catalog**-the Allocation Table and the Directory-have been set aside, the rest of the disk is grouped into *data clusters*. A **data cluster** is the name given to the basic unit of storage on a disk. What is the difference between a cluster and a sector? Why are clusters needed?

The purpose of the cluster is to create a minimum allocation unit for data storage. Minimum allocation units are quite a common idea. For example, when you go to the market, you cannot buy just one egg. Instead, the eggs are packaged in a minimum size carton that defines the minimum allocation unit.

The DOS librarian also has to consider what is the efficient minimum unit for disk storage. The amount of space defined as a cluster will vary in proportion to the size of the disk. On floppy disks, DOS usually allocates two sectors to each cluster.

$$512+512 = 1024$$

This means that the minimum allocation unit is 1024 bytes of space. For example, if you want to save a file with only 5 bytes, DOS will allocate 1024 bytes for that file.

On a hard disk, the total capacity is much larger, so it makes sense to increase the cluster size. Typically, a hard disk will use a cluster size of 4 sectors, 4 times $512 = 2048$.

Once DOS has formatted a disk, it is ready to receive data. It now has a structure in which to store data and record information about the data so that it can be retrieved. As part of the system, DOS requires that all data be given a "name." The name, like a title of a book, is the logical handle by which a specific block of information can be located.

DOS recognizes three levels of organization in names for data, forming a hierarchy. For example, when you write an address on an envelope there are three parts that define the exact location:

1. State

2. City

3. Street

The largest unit is the state. Within the state is city and within city is the street. This type of system allows you to use the same street but in different cities or states. For example, the addresses below use the same street name, but are clearly different because they are located in a different city and state.

Pine Street, Philadelphia, PA
Pine Street, Walnut Creek, CA

The address breaks down into a structure with three distinct parts: city, state, zip code.

Street	City	State
Pine Street,	Philadelphia,	PA
Pine Street,	Walnut Creek,	CA

The DOS logical naming system uses volumes, directories, and filenames. Below is a typical name for a file:

c:\dos\ansi.sys

The name really consists of three parts. Each part corresponds to one of the three organizational levels recognized by DOS.

Volume	Directory	File Name
c:	\dos\	ansi.sys

A volume in DOS, an easy unit to think about, is one disk drive, hard or floppy. A directory is a unit that is smaller than a disk but larger than a file. It is a kind of file folder in which groups of related files can be gathered together.

In DOS, volumes contain directories, and directories contain files. On low-volume disks, such as floppies, most users skip the directory level of organization. But it important to remember that DOS creates at least one directory on each formatted disk called the root directory.

Note also the punctuation that DOS uses to identify the organizational parts:

C: Volumes are single letters with a colon.

\   The backslash is used to mark off a name of a directory. If no name is used with the \, the root directory is assumed.

The table summarizes the terms used to describe storage space.

Table 1-2 DOS Storage Terms

Sector	Smallest unit of data storage, e.g., 512 bytes
Cluster	A group of one or more sectors
Track	A circle of data sectors on a disk
Side	A disk surface, top or bottom
Cylinder	All of the tracks in the same vertical plane

Commands in DOS

The major functions of DOS take place behind the scenes. When you run programs such as word processors, spreadsheets, or databases, DOS performs a variety of tasks behind the scenes that allow those programs to operate.

As a computer user you are not exposed to the details of those operations. However, the decision about what disk, directory, and filename should be used for storing data are up to you. In addition, the tasks of maintaining this data library require you to manually enter specific instructions to DOS.

These instructions cover a wide range of operations from erasing old files, making duplicates, creating directories, copying programs from floppies to hard disks, to making backups of data.

In addition, it is your instructions that tell DOS to load and execute programs. In short, whether you like it or not, you will have to issue instructions to the operating system.

Most people approach DOS commands and operations as if they were a list of specific commands to memorize. But a better way to look at DOS is as a language consisting of verbs and objects.

Grammar

Computer languages and command environments, like human languages, have a fundamental structure from which all the commands can be constructed. DOS works with six basic elements:

1. Commands

2. Delimiters

3. Parameters

4. Options switches

5. File specifications / wildcards

6. Input/output devices

The most important rule is that all DOS entries must begin with a command. While every DOS command begins with a command word, it is usually followed by one or several of the basic elements above.

DOS commands are really the verbs of the DOS language. They represent the basic actions that DOS can perform and are divided into two major classifications:

1. **Internal Commands.** These commands are contained in the memory of the computer at all times when the DOS prompt is displayed. Because these commands are internal, no special disks or files need be present in the computer to execute an internal command.

2. **External Commands.** These commands are really small computer programs that are stored in disk files until they are needed. External commands are loaded each time they are requested and are erased from memory when the command is finished.

Both types of commands have their advantages and disadvantages. Internal commands are always available because they reside in the memory whenever DOS is active. However, internal memory is limited in a computer. If you increase the number of DOS commands that are resident in the memory of the computer, you decrease the amount of room that can be used for programs and their data.

External commands occupy internal memory only when they are being executed. Otherwise they reside in the external storage medium like other programs and data files. External commands make efficient use of the internal memory, but they are slower to execute than internal commands because they must be loaded into the internal memory each time they are used. In addition, the external commands must be stored on disk space that is immediately available to the computer or these commands cannot be executed. On floppy disk systems, where storage is limited, this can be a problem.

Internal Commands

Internal commands are the ones that are always available when the system prompt is displayed. Naturally, they are the commands that you will need to use most frequently. Examples:

Table 1-3 Typical Internal DOS Commands

BREAK	Frequency of Ctrl-break checks
CHDIR or CD	Changes active directory
CLS	Clears screen
COMMAND	Invokes the command interpreter
COPY	Transfers data from one device to another
CTTY	Change standard console device
DATE	Displays/sets system date
DIR	Lists filenames
ERASE or DEL	Deletes files
MKDIR or MD	Creates directory
PATH	Sets search path
PROMPT	Sets DOS prompt
REM	Displays a remark
RENAME or REN	Renames a file
RMDIR or RD	Removes empty directory
SET	Creates a text variable
TIME	Displays/sets system time
TYPE	Displays file contents
TYPE	Displays files contents
VER	Displays DOS version number
VERIFY	Verify during copying
VOL	Displays the disk volume name

The commands listed above have one thing in common. They can be executed at any time that you see the DOS system's prompt. There is no need for any special disk to be present.

There are a number of internal commands that operate from DOS batch files (IF, GOTO, etc.). These commands are discussed in Section II of this book which is about writing batch files.

External Commands

External commands are not kept resident in the memory of the computer but are loaded from files stored on the disk when you request them. Thus if you ask for an external command and DOS cannot find the corresponding program file on the disk, the command will not operate. In order to access external commands you must make sure that they are available by copying the files from the DOS systems disk onto the disks you are using. Put another way, the DOS external commands are optional. Experience and need will indicate which external commands you require. Hard disk users often copy all the external command files onto the hard disk. Examples are:

Table 1-4 DOS External Commands

ASSIGN	Swap drive designations
ATTRIB	Set file attributes
BACKUP	Backup hard disk
CHKDSK	Check disk integrity
COMP	Compare files
DISKCOMP	Compare floppy disks
DISKCOPY	Duplicate floppy disk
EDLIN	Line editor program
FASTOPEN	Speed up file opening on networks
FDISK	Create disk partitions
FIND	Search /screen output
FORMAT	Prepare disks for data
GRAPHICS	Set print screen for graphics
MODE	Select output, screen modes
MORE	Pause screen display output
PRINT	Print text files
RECOVER	Recover damaged files
REPLACE	Replace existing files
RESTORE	Restore backup files
SHARE	Network lock routine
SORT	Sort screen output
SUBST	Create a substitute drive
SYS	Copy system files
TREE	List directories
XCOPY	Copy whole disks and directories

Most external commands function like programs in that they load into memory only when they are executed and release the memory they use once the command has completed. However, there are some DOS commands that remain in memory for the duration of the session once they are loaded. These commands are called TSR (terminate and stay resident) because they remain in memory after you have executed the command. For example, the APPEND command is used to establish a search path for data files. When used APPEND is loaded and remains in memory until the computer is rebooted.

Parameters and Delimiters

Parameters are additional pieces of information added to commands, and fill the same role in DOS commands that the object does in human languages. Parameters indicate what will be effected by the command. For example, the command DEL deletes a file from the disk. However, simply entering DEL as a command to DOS is incomplete. DOS needs to know what you want to delete before it can carry out the command. To create a valid command you would have to supply a filename. Example:

DEL FORMAT.COM

The command has two parts: DEL is the command; FORMAT.COM is the parameter.

Notice that there is a space between the command and the parameter. The space is an important part of the grammar of DOS; commands must be separated from their parameters by such delimiters. The space, in this instance, serves to delimit or punctuate the command. Without the delimiter the command would not be interpreted properly.

File Specification and Wildcards

There are times when you will find it advantageous to refer to files in a more general way. When you issue a command you may want to refer to more than one file at a time, so that the command entered can act upon more than one file.

For example, suppose there were 50 files on a disk that needed erasing. You might enter 50 commands, one to erase each file. However, the most convenient way would be to use a **wildcard**. The purpose of DOS wildcards is to refer to a group of files with a single command. DOS recognizes two special characters as wildcards: **?** and *****.

The * is even more general than the ?. An * used in a filename indicates that any character beginning at that position and continuing to the end of the filename

or extension, is acceptable. For example, entering   *.PAY would refer to all
files with a PAY extension.

MARY.PAY
MORRIS.PAY
JOE.PAY
SUE.PAY
WALTER.PAY
SAM.PAY

If you entered M*.PAY you would get:

MARY.PAY
MORRIS.PAY

When * is used, DOS does not care how many characters follow the
specified characters. One of the most common wildcards is *.*. When *.* is
used, it tells DOS to use all the files contained in a directory. Most DOS
commands and many programs allow you to enter file specifications with
wildcard characters.

Options and Switches

Options affect how a command is carried out. They function as adverbs do in
human languages, modifying the action of the command verb. Not all
commands have options, but those that do may have several. Options can be
inclusive or exclusive of each other, depending upon the command. If options are
inclusive, they will function at the same time and produce a combined effect.
The usual form for an option is a slash followed by a letter. DIR also has a /P
option that pauses the listing when the screen is filled. This makes it easier to
read the directory display. The command below shows how two options can be
used at once.

DIR/W/P

The number of options varies with each command. Also, some commands
have no options at all. The options entered with / are also called "switches"
because they turn on or off various features of the command.

Disk Partitions

When the IBM XT was first released it contained a 10 megabyte hard disk. At the time, this was one of the largest drives available as standard equipment on a microcomputer system. Because the XT was adapted from the original two-floppy-drive PC design, the hard disk was treated as a third drive added to a floppy drive system. Thus, the hard disk was assigned the letter C, while A and B drives were reserved for the floppy drives.

Today, hard disk systems are the standard but the drive designations still reflect the early development decision that made drive C the first hard disk.

Another limitation built into DOS (Versions 2.0 through 3.3) was a limit to the capacity of any one hard disk to 32 megabytes. When 10 and 20 megabyte drives were common, this limit was not significant. But today when 40 megabyte drives are the most common drives sold with new computers, the limitation becomes a real problem. The solution used is to create DOS partitions.

A *partition* is a physical section of the hard disk consisting of a specified number of tracks that is marked off from the rest of the disk. For example, suppose that a hard disk has 614 cylinders. You could divide the disk into several partitions, each with a specific number of cylinders allocated to each partition.

There are two reasons for creating partitions.

1. **Multiple Operating Systems.** Some users want to have additional operating systems, such as UNIX, installed on the disk. Partitions make it possible to store multiple operating systems on the same disk. Note that you can only run one operating system at a time, despite the fact that they are both stored on the same disk.

2. **Extended DOS Partitions.** You can divide the disk into several *logical* drives, all running under DOS. A *logical* drive is one that DOS treats as a separate drive, e.g. D:, E:, F:, etc., but that actually resides on a single physical disk drive with a large capacity. This method is typically used to divide a disk that is larger than 32 megabytes, into drives C:, D:, E:, etc.

When a hard disk is partitioned into logical drives, the C: drive from which the computer actually boots, is called the *primary* drive. All the other logical drives are *extended* drives.

> *The term primary refers to the fact that this partition contains the partition table information that DOS uses to keep track of the partition setup on the disk. The name primary does not imply anything about the size of the partition. The primary partition can be as small as a single cylinder, if desired.*

Partitions are **hard** designations. This means that changing the partition setup on a disk erases the data stored on the disk. The best time to create partitions is just after formatting, before you begin to place programs and data on the disk. Partitions can be defined using the DOS program, FDISK. Many manufacturers supply a special program that formats and partitions the hard disk, in a single step.

Pathnames

If a disk has more than one directory, the path refers to the name of the file and the names of the directory and/or subdirectories that contain the file. Pathnames are needed to locate files that may be stored in various directories. When you instruct the computer to use a file on the disk, the computer has to know what directory to look in. If you don't correctly identify the file and its pathname, the computer won't find the file. The term full pathname refers to the complete name of a file and the directories in which it is contained. For example:

\ACCOUNT\PAYROLL\WORKERS.88

This means that there is a file WORKERS.88 stored in the PAYROLL subdirectory of the ACCOUNT directory. Note that the pathname lists the items in descending order, generally with the filename coming last. The drive can be added to the pathname. Below is an example of the full drive and pathname of a file.

C:\ACCOUNT\PAYROLL\WORKERS.88

File Types

There are two basic types of files stored on computer disks.

1. **Binary Files**. Binary files are long sequences of numbers that contain coded information to be read directly by the computer. The microprocessor in your computer contains enough information to break the number sequence codes and interpret them as commands and/or data. Most programs are provided in the binary form. By convention, files that are program files carry either a COM or EXE extension.

   Binary program files are microprocessor-specific. This means that a program written for an IBM PC will run only on a computer that has the same decoder set as the IBM.

If data is stored in a binary file it is likely that only the program and computer it was designed to operate with can understand the data.

2. **ASCII Files.** ASCII stands for the American Standard Code for Information Interchange. The purpose of this code is to create files that are stored in a format common to many different programs and computers.

Storage in ASCII format is usually less compact than binary storage. However, the advantage is that ASCII provides a common basis for the interchange of information.

As a computer user you will want to be aware of which programs work with ASCII files. Programs that can read and write ASCII files can exchange information with other programs that do the same. Programs that use only their own specially coded binary files are much more limited in terms of sharing information.

ASCII provides 128 standard representations. The 128 ASCII characters include all the characters shown on the normal keyboard, plus characters that represent special keys, such as [Esc], ↵, and [Tab].

A file that is standard ASCII format means that any program reading standard files can read and understand the information contained in that file. Therefore, the terms ASCII file, DOS text file, text file, and ASCII standard file, refer to the same thing.

The IBM PC and compatible computers have a built-in character set that consists of 256 characters. The additional characters are often displayed on the screen by programs that form the lines and boxes seen so often in screen displays. Other additional characters are those such as the accented e and the Greek letters used in mathematics. The entire set of 256 characters, the 128 ASCII characters, and the 128 other characters displayed by the IBM PC is referred to as the extended character set.

All the 128 standard ASCII characters can be represented with only seven bits. You can confirm this by calculating the number of possibilities with seven bits. Each bit can have only two options, ON or OFF. A seven-bit number can be arranged in 2 to the seventh power, or 128, different ways.

But the eight-bit structure used by the IBM PC allows you to represent data with eight bits. That means there are 2 to the eighth power, or 256, possible arrangements.

The Norton Utilities program has much in common with DOS commands. You will notice that the entry of Norton Utilities instructions work just about the same way as DOS commands using parameters, option switches, and file specifications.

Setup for Working with This Book

In order to create a detailed, hands-on, interactive book about the Norton Utilities programs, it is necessary to make some assumptions about the computer you are working with. Inevitably, these assumptions will make some of the exact procedures presented in this book vary with the results on your computer, since you may be using a different version of DOS, or some other item.

This book assumes that you are working with a MS-DOS computer that has at least one hard and one floppy disk drive. The type of monitor you have is not particularly significant. The parts of the book that deal with menu batches assume you are working with a single color (black and white, if you have a color system).

The assumption is made that you are using a version of **DOS 3.3**, which is currently the most common version of DOS. Earlier versions, or users with DOS 4.0, should be able to carry out all the operations in the remainder of this section, but keep in mind that there will be differences in the exact size and location of some files. These differences are noted in the text and should not cause you undue confusion.

The Norton Utilities Advanced Edition Version 4.5

The book also assumes that you have a copy of the Norton Utilities Advanced Edition Version 4.5. Section V deals with other products from Norton Computing: the Norton Commander, the Norton Editor, and the Norton Guides. You will probably want to read these sections even if you don't have the programs. The information contained in them is useful in learning about other programs from Peter Norton Computing.

The Norton Utilities Advanced Edition Version 4.5 is supplied on three disks. If you are using the 3.5 inch version, there are only two disks. The files contained on these disks are:

Disk 1 of 3, 6 files

READ.ME	Text file with updated information
FR.EXE	The Format Recover program
NDD.EXE	**The Norton Disk Doctor program**
NU.EXE	The main Norton Utilities program
NU.HLP	Help file for main Norton Utilities program
INSTALL.EXE	**Installation program**

Disk 3 of 3, 22 files

DS.EXE	The Directory Sort program
DT.EXE	The Disk Test program
FF.EXE	The File Find program
NCC.EXE	**The Norton Control Center program**
NCD.EXE	The Norton Change Directory program
NI.EXE	The Norton Integrator
QU.EXE	The Quick Unerase program
SD.EXE	The Speed Disk program
SF.EXE	**The Safe Format program**
UD.EXE	The Unremove Directory program

Disk 3 of 3, 22 files

BE.EXE	**The Batch Enhancer program**
DI.EXE	The Disk Information program
FA.EXE	The File Attributes program
FD.EXE	**The File Date program**
FI.EXE	The File Information program
FS.EXE	The File Size program
LD.EXE	The List Directories program
LP.EXE	The Line Print program
TM.EXE	The Time Mark program
SI.EXE	The System Information program
TS.EXE	The Text Search program
VL.EXE	The Volume Label program
WIPEDISK.EXE	The Wipedisk program
WIPEFILE.EXE	The Wipefile program
FILEINFO.FI	File Information data file
MARY	Sample for batch Beep command
BEDEMO.BAT	Batch Enhancer demonstration program
BEDEMO.DAT	Batch Enhancer demonstration data
MENU.DAT	Sample menu with Batch Enhancer
MAKE-TUT.BIN	Binary File for Unerase Tutorial
MAKE-TUT.BAT	Batch file for Unerase Tutorial
TUT-READ.ME	Text on Unerase Tutorial

The filenames listed in *bold* print are programs added to the 4.5 version, which were not in the 4.0 version of the utilities. The Unerase Tutorial referred to is the one included in the Norton Utilities manual. This book includes a section on unerasing and recovering files that is different from the supplied tutorial.

Installing the Norton Utilities Programs

Generally speaking, the Norton Utilities programs do not require specialized installation. You can use the DOS COPY or XCOPY commands to copy files from the floppy disks supplied with the program to your hard disk. The command below copies all the files from the floppy disk in drive A to a directory named \DOS on drive C:.

copy a:*.* c:\dos ↵

Each of the programs consists of a single file with an EXE extension, with the exception of the main Norton Utilities program (NU.EXE), which uses the file NU.HLP to supply on line help. Keep in mind that the NU.EXE program can be run without the help file. The only difference is that on line help will not be available.

However, Version 4.5 of the Norton Utilities programs is supplied with an install program, INSTALL.EXE. The program automatically copies the program files into the a hard disk directory of your choice, performing the same basic function as the DOS command shown above. However, the installation program was included in Version 4.5 for three other reasons.

1. **Older Versions.** If you have Version 3.1 or earlier of the Norton Utilities programs installed on your hard disk, you will find that copying the files supplied on the Version 4.5 disks to your hard disk will not properly install the new programs.

    The reason illustrates an interesting point about DOS, which is also related to new versions of DOS as well. DOS program files can have either a **COM** or an **EXE** file extension Many of the programs supplied in the 3.1 or earlier versions were COM files. Beginning with Version 4.0, the file types were changed to EXE files.

> *The difference between a COM program file and an EXE program file is a technical one that is seldom important to a person using the program. When a program is stored in a COM file it is loaded into memory in the same sequence in which it is stored on the disk. The data loaded into the memory is an exact duplicate of the file on the disk. An EXE file allows the program to load information into memory in a different order and location than it is stored on the disk. The program contains special commands that indicate where in memory the program should be placed. Typically, this means that the program expands as it is loaded. This is why a program that takes up 200K on the disk requires 512K of memory to operate.*

This created a problem when Version 4.0 files were copied to the same directory as the older Norton Utilities files. The copying process did not overwrite the older COM files because the new versions had EXE extensions. For example, the 3.1 version File Find programs was FF.COM, while the 4.0 version was FF.EXE.

While it is perfectly all right with DOS to store these two files in the same directory, DOS does have a problem in executing the programs. Because only the filename without the extension is entered, e.g., FF, which file, FF.COM or FF.EXE, will be executed? The answer is that DOS always selects the COM file first. The result is that although you have copied the new files to your hard disk, the older files continue to execute when you enter commands.

In order to prevent this problem with Version 4.5, the INSTALL program searches for the existence of previous versions of the Norton Utilities programs. If found, you are given a chance to back up and/or erase the older files before the new files are copied. This procedure protects you from having both a COM and EXE version of the same program in the same directory.

2. **AUTOEXEC.BAT.** The installation program adds a command to the AUTOEXEC.BAT file in the root directory of the boot drive that automatically creates the file necessary for **unformatting** the hard drive. The command issued is **FR /SAVE**. This command uses the Format Recover command to create a data file, **FRECOVER.DAT**, that can be used to recover your data should the hard disk be accidentally reformatted. Also, the Main Norton Utilities program (NU), the Unremove Directory (UD), and the Quick Unerase (QU) programs can operate more effectively if the **FRECOVER.DAT** is present. By placing this command in the AUTOEXEC.BAT file, you can ensure that a new **FRECOVER.DAT** file is created each time you turn on (or boot) your computer.

3. **Safe Format.** A new program added to the 4.5 version is the Safe Format program. This program is designed to replace the DOS FORMAT program which is often the cause of accidental erasures of disks. As part of the installation process you can select to rename the DOS FORMAT program XXFORMAT and copy the Norton Utilities Safe Format program as FORMAT. This means that whenever the command FORMAT is issued the Safe Format program runs. If you choose not to substitute Safe Format for the DOS format command you can still use Safe Format by entering SF to run the Safe Format program.

Running the Install Program

To install the program, place disk 1 of 3 in the floppy drive, usually drive A. You can run the install program in one of two ways. If you are currently logged into a hard disk, you can enter

a:install ↵

You can also run the program from the floppy drive by entering

a: ↵
install ↵

The result in either case will be the same. The first screen that appears is a warning about when you should **not** install the Norton Utilities. Figure 1-1 shows the text of the warning message.

```
   Do not install the Norton Utilities on your hard disk
   if it has been accidentally formatted or currently has
     erased files you intend to UnErase, since you might
      overwrite the erased files with the Norton Utilities
   themselves. If you have erased files to recover on your
   hard disk, run the Utilities from a floppy disk, recover
        the files, then proceed with the installation


              Do you wish to continue?

                    Yes    No
```

Figure 1-1 Installation program opening screen.

The warning is related to installing the programs after you have erased files, either by using the DOS DEL or FORMAT commands, that you wish to recover. Proceeding to install the programs could possibly overwrite data that remains in disk sectors that are part of the files you want to recover. In this situation, you are advised to run the programs from a floppy disk. This procedure is discussed in Chapter 11. If you select **Yes** by pressing ↵, the next screen, Figure 1-2, outlines the 6 steps of the installation procedure. Entering ↵ tells the program to begin the installation process.

```
This installation will go through the following steps:

1. Find any old copies of the Norton Utilities.
2. Ask where you would like to install the new Utilities.
3. Backup or delete old copies of the Utilities, as you choose.
4. Copy new Norton Utilities files to the directory you
   specified.
5. Ask if you want us to change your AUTOEXEC.BAT file for you.
6. Ask if you want us to make our Safe Format program your
   default FORMAT program.

            At any step along the way, you may Cancel
               the installation and return to DOS.

            Continue installation     Return to DOS
```

Figure 1-2 Outline of installation procedure.

The next screen asks you to select the floppy drive, A or B, in which the program's disks will be found. When you have selected the correct floppy drive, the program will then search for existing copies of the Norton Utilities programs. If they exist, you will be prompted to make a backup copy and/or erase the files.

Note that the new files will be copied to the same disk and directory in which the existing copies of the Norton Utilities were found.

If there are no current copies of the Norton Utilities on the hard disk, then the install program will insert the **C:\NORTON** as the directory for the programs.

> *Since the **C:\NORTON** directory is the default, this book assumes you have installed your copy of the programs in that directory. However, on my own computers I like to place the Norton Utilities programs into a directory called **\DOS**, which contains both the DOS program files and the Norton Utilities file. This is a reflection of my own personal preference to place the DOS and Norton Utilities programs in a single group. Placing all the utility programs in a single directory means that you need open only a single path in order to gain access to all utility programs.*

The next series of screens will copy the data from each of the disks (three in 5.25 inch format and two in 3.5 inch format) onto the specified disk and directory.

After the files have been copied to the hard disk, the Install program then asks if you want to substitute the Safe Format program for the DOS FORMAT program (Figure 1-3). Selecting **OK** will cause the DOS FORMAT program to be renamed XXFORMAT.EXE, and the SF.EXE program copied to the name FORMAT.EXE. This will cause the Safe Format program to run each time you enter the FORMAT command.

```
We will now rename any and all executable files on your
            path named FORMAT.* to XXFORMAT.*
        Then we will copy SF.EXE to FORMAT.EXE.

   Ok     Skip to Next Step    Return to DOS
_____

                    EXPLANATION
    This step makes the Norton Safe Format program your
  default FORMAT command. You may still invoke any other
  FORMAT procedures that you had by typing XXFORMAT.
```

Figure 1-3 Screen explains installation of Safe Format.

The next screen explains the procedure by which the Safe Format command is placed into the AUTOEXEC.BAT file as shown in Figure 1-4. The AUTOEXEC.BAT is automatically executed each time the computer is turned on or rebooted. This procedure helps ensure that you have the best chance to recover formatted disks or erased files and directories.

```
We will now copy C:\AUTOEXEC.BAT to C:\AUTOEXEC.BAK
                    Then we will add
                       D:\NORTON
  your path statement and add FR /SAVE to your AUTOEXEC file.

   Ok    Skip to Next Step    Return to DOS
_____

                      EXPLANATION
   In this step, we save your old AUTOEXEC.BAT file and then
       add the Norton Utilities directory to your path
                 if it wasn't there already.
    it lets you invoke The Norton Utilities from any directory.
   We also add the command FR /SAVE to your AUTOEXEC file.
  This saves the information needed to recover your hard disk
             in case it is accidently formatted.

In addition to placing the files on the hard disk, you must have
access to the files. This means that a PATH should be opened to
the \DOS directory using the DOS command PATH. To check the open
                   paths, if any, enter
```

Figure 1-4 Screen explains installation of Format Recover program.

It is a good idea to allow this change to the AUTOEXEC.BAT to be made.

When you have completed the AUTOEXEC.BAT modification, the last screen, in the install program is displayed (Figure 1-5). When you exit the screen, you will return to DOS but the active directory will be the \NORTON directory on the hard disk.

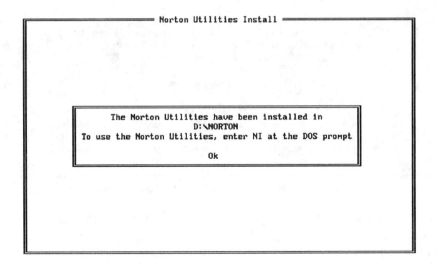

Figure 1-5 Final screen of installation program.

Opening a Search Path

There is one significant item not taken into account in the Installation program. That item is related to the DOS PATH command. The PATH command is used to create a list of directories in which DOS will look for a program if it cannot be found in the **active** directory. If you have used the Install program to place the Norton Utilities files, you will be able to execute any of the programs when you are logged into that directory.

But suppose you want to use one of the programs when another directory or drive is active? In order to use the programs when you are not logged into the **\NORTON** directory you must establish a **path** to that drive and directory using the PATH command. For example, the command below opens a search path to the **\NORTON** directory on drive **C**. The inclusion of the drive letter in the pathname enables DOS to search drives other than the active one for programs. In this example, using C:\NORTON instead of just \NORTON enables DOS to find the programs, even when you are logged onto another drive, such as drive A.

path c:\norton; ↵

With this path open you can execute any of the programs stored in **\NORTON**, from any directory or drive in the system.

If you are not sure what paths are currently open on your system, you can display the current path list by entering the command.

path ↵

In most cases, you will want to use the Norton Utilities programs from the directories in which you are working, not from the **\NORTON** directory. You can automatically establish this path each time the computer is turned on by adding a PATH command to the AUTOEXEC.BAT file.

If the file already contains a PATH command, add the **\NORTON** path to the path list. Suppose the current path command looks like this:

pathc:\dos;c:\lostus;c;\wordperf;

You can add the **\NORTON** to the list, as shown below. If you are not familiar with AUTOEXEC.BAT, see Section II, Batch Files.

path c:\dos;c:\lotus;c:\wordperf;c:\norton;

With the Norton Utilities programs installed and the path open to the directory in which they are stored, you are ready to begin. This book assumes that you will begin working from the root directory of the hard disk. To change to that directory, enter

cd\ ↵

Throughout this book the assumption is made that you have opened a path to the directory in which the Norton Utilities programs have been stored.

The next chapter deals with the writing of batch files and the use of the programs included in the Norton Utilities package to enhance your batch files.

2

A Hands-on Primer on Disk Organization

The Norton Utilities programs provide a unique method of inspecting and analyzing the operations of your computer, when it comes to storing information on the disk. This means you can actually see--not just read about--how a disk is organized.

Instead of discussing ideas of how a disk is used to store data, this section presents those ideas, using hands-on exploration.

You will begin by formatting a disk and performing simple operations, such as copying files, deleting files, and using directories. However, in order to obtain a more concrete understanding of how DOS performs its job, you will use the Norton Utilities programs at each stage in the process to examine in detail how the disk is changed.

Formatting a Disk

The first step is to create a blank, formatted disk. The examples in this book use IBM DOS Version 3.3 and a 360K (double-density) disk. If you have a different version of DOS or are using a different size disk (high-density or 3.5 inch), the information displayed on your screen will be different, but the principles remain the same. You should still be able to follow the steps if you make common sense adjustments, based on your system's configuration.

Place a disk to be formatted in drive A. Keep in mind that the DOS formatting process will erase any data on a disk, if it was previously used.

Here, use the Safe Format program instead of the DOS format program. Enter

sf ↵

The program loads and displays a screen consisting of several boxes. In the center of the screen is a box that lists the letters of the drives available for formattng (Figure 2-1). If you are working on a network, hard drives available to the network, even if they are physically located in your computer, will not be listed in the box.

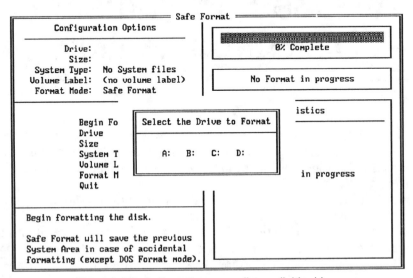

Figure 2-1 Safe Format program list available drives.

You can select the drive to format by using the → and ← keys to highlight the drive letter, or by simply typing the letter. Drive **A:** is highlighted by default. Select drive A for formatting by entering

↵

The box in the center of the screen is removed, revealing the main screen display for the program Figure 2-2. The display lists seven options:

1. **Begin Format.** Executes the formatting operation using the specified settings.

2. **Drive.** You can use this option to change the drive to be formatted. The list displayed will be the same as that which was automatically displayed when you loaded the program.

3. **Size.** This option displays a list of sizes to which the currently specified drive can be formatted. The list varies, depending upon the type of drive selected. For example, if the drive is a 1.2 megabyte, 5.25inch drive, you can choose from 160K, 180K, 320K, 360K, and 1.2M. Keep in mind that you must insert the correct disk media in the drive to match your selection. For example, selecting 1.2M requires that you place a high-density disk in the drive. If you place a double-density disk in the drive, the formatting will fail.

   This option has no effect if you are formatting a hard drive. The size of the hard disk format is set in the partition table and can only be changed by programs that effect the partition table, such as the DOS command FDISK, or special programs provided by the disk manufacturer.

4. **System Type.** This option deals with the system area of the disk to be formatted. The default is **No System files**, which means that the entire disk will be used for data. Such disks cannot be used to boot the computer. If you select **System files**, you can use the disk to boot the computer; however, you will have less space on the disk for data storage. Both of these options are available with the DOS FORMAT command. A third option, **Leave space**, is unique to the Safe Format program. This option leaves space for system files but does not actually copy them. System files can be added to this disk at a later time, in order to make it a bootable disk.

---

*The **Leave space** option typically would be used by a developer to distribute a program on a disk that could be made bootable by the buyer. In most cases, the developer does not have a license to sell MSDOS along with their program, but by leaving space, the buyer can simply copy the system files to the disk to make a bootable disk.*

---

5. **Volume Label.** This option allows you to write a volume label for the disk, of up to 11 characters.

6. **Format Mode.** The Safe Format program provides four different ways to format a disk. The **DOS Format** option duplicates the method used by DOS. When using a floppy disk, this erases all the data during formatting. The **Safe Format** option uses a different method. Unlike DOS, it does not erase all the data in the disk sectors. This means you can use Quick Unerase to recover files lost during formatting. Also, because Safe Format does not bother to erase the data, it will format the disk faster than the DOS format command.

While it is true that Safe Format formats the disk faster than the DOS format command, it also performs other operations, such as analyzing the disk, and saves recovery information for use with the Format Recover program. All this adds time to the formatting process.

The **Quick Format** option can be used to reformat an already formatted disk. When used, this option simply places a new system area on the disk. This is similar to what occurs when you erase all the files and remove all the directories from a disk. This option is a fast way to erase a disk, especially if the disk contains a complex directory tree.

The **Complete Format** option is used only with disks, not hard drives. It performs the same operation as the Safe Format option, but also takes time to reformat any *bad sectors*, in order to improve the reliability of the diskette.

7. **Quit.** Exit program and return to DOS. You can also exit by entering [Esc] or [F10].

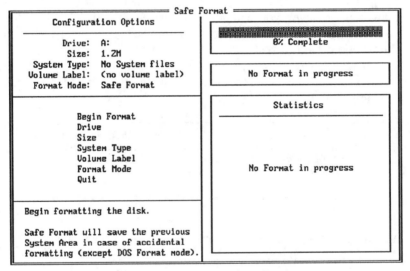

Figure 2-2 Full-screen display of Safe Format program.

Select a 360K size for formatting by entering

s

←

The ← key positions the highlight on 360K. Complete the selection by entering

⏎

Add a volume-label name to be placed on the newly formatted disk. Enter

v

You can enter an eleven-character label. Note that DOS does not permit the entry of a space in the volume label. You can use an underscore character to separate words. Enter

test_disk ⏎

Begin the formatting process by entering

b

If the disk in drive A is already formatted, the program displays a warning, as shown in Figure 2-3. If so, enter ⏎ to reformat the disk. If the disk is a new disk, the formatting takes place automatically.

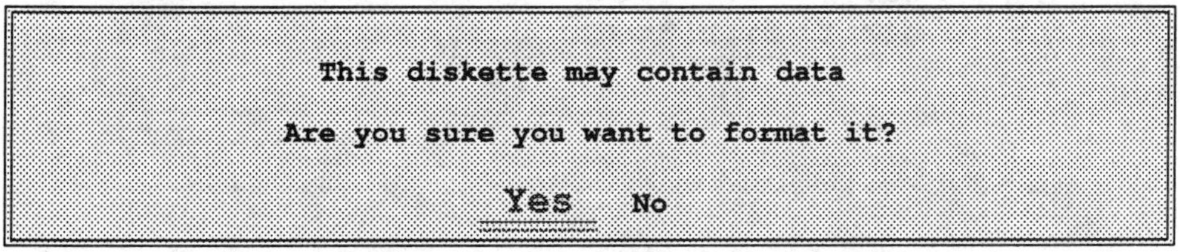

```
This diskette may contain data

Are you sure you want to format it?

        Yes    No
```

Figure 2-3 Safe Format warns you before overwriting data.

The right side of the display shows information about the formatting process, as shown in Figure 2-4. The box in the upper-right corner at the top of the screen shows a bar and value for the percentage of the formatting completed. Below that box is another box showing the action, if any, being performed. Typically, this box shows the drive head and cylinder number being formatted.

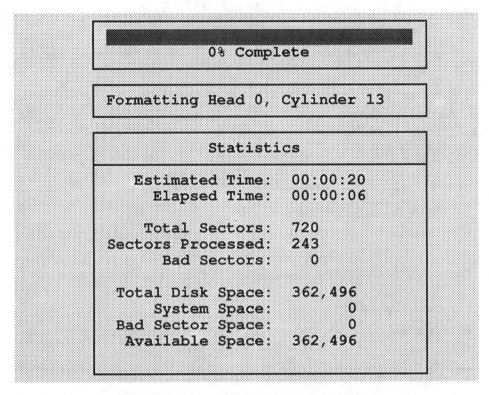

Figure 2-4 Safe Format displays information about the formatting process.

The box labeled "statistics" shows information about the formatting process. The estimated time shows how long the entire format will take to complete. Note that this time changes as the formatting process proceeds, adjusting to problems found during the formatting process. Below this is the actual elapsed time since the format began. The number of sectors on the disk, the number processed, and the number marked as bad sectors, is displayed. The last section shows the formatted and bad sector space, in terms of bytes (one sector = 512 bytes).

When the format is complete, a box appears in the center of the screen that reads **"Format Complete OK."** Enter

↵

Exit the program and return to DOS by entering

q

Examining Disk Structure

When you format a disk, you are performing an important task. You are creating an organizational structure on the disk that will enable DOS to store information. To understand that structure and how it works, you can use the main Norton Utilities to display information about the disk. (The main Norton Utilities uses the file name NU.EXE.) This is a complicated program with many sections and options. The main program always begins by reading the information from a disk. You can specify which disk to read by entering the drive designation, along with the command to run the program. If no drive is specified, the current active drive is used. You can also change drives from within the program. To activate the program and read the information from the newly formatted disk in drive A, enter

nu a: -"

The Norton Utilities main program menu appears, as shown in Figure 2-5.

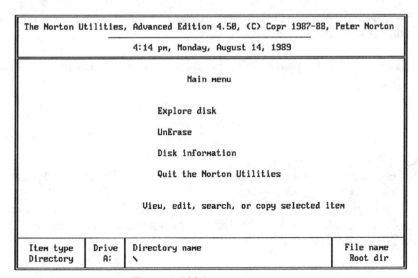

Figure 2-5 Main program menu.

The program's menu is divided into four options.

1. **Explore Disk.** This section allows you to explore, in detail, the exact information stored on the disk. You can also use these options to modify the information stored on the disk.

2. **Unerase.** This section contains a series of special commands and procedures that help you recover data from files that have been erased. Unerasing is covered in detail in Section IV of this book.

3. **Disk Information.** This is the simplest of the options. It displays summary information about the disk.

4. **Quit the Norton Utilities.**

Disk Information

Your exploration of the disk begins with the third option on the menu, Disk Information. Enter

d

The Disk Information menu consists of two parts.

1. **Map disk usage.** This option displays a visual representation of the disk and the data, if any, stored in it.

2. **Technical information.** This display lists the values for the current disk.

Enter

d

The program displays a map of the disk (Figure 2-6). The map is designed to show which parts of the disk are used and which are free for new data. Because you will have just formatted the disk, the map shows the data space as empty space. As you add information to the disk, the map will change to show where on this disk data has been stored.

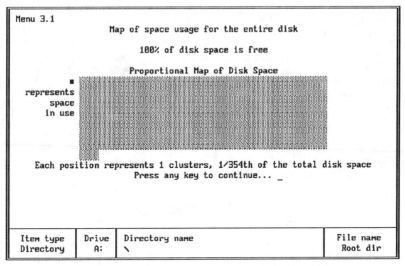

```
Menu 3.1
                    Map of space usage for the entire disk

                       100% of disk space is free

                     Proportional Map of Disk Space
               ■
   represents
        space
       in use

     Each position represents 1 clusters, 1/354th of the total disk space
                       Press any key to continue... _
```

Item type	Drive	Directory name	File name
Directory	A:	\	Root dir

Figure 2-6 Map of the disk.

Display the technical information by entering

The Technical Information screen lists three basic types of information about the disk (Figure 2-7).

1. **Type of Disk.** This section identifies the type of disk being analyzed.

2. **Storage Capacity.** This section tells you the total capacity of the disk in kilobytes, and what percentage of that space is currently free.

3. **Logical Dimensions.** This section contains the technical values associated with the disk's organization. The first item lists the number of bytes in each sector. That size is almost always 512 when working on an MS-DOS system.

The sector is the basic unit of storage on a disk. In MS-DOS, the size of the sector is determined when the disk is formatted. In almost all cases, that size is 512 bytes. The sector is the smallest unit of storage on the disk. DOS is capable of dealing with a variety of sector sizes. The 512K sector size is the most commonly used size. Because compatibility is so important to the average user, almost all hardware and software suppliers recognize 512 as the standard size for sectors. Only rarely will you encounter an exception.

The next item lists the number of sectors placed in each track, the number of surfaces (sides), and the number of tracks on each side. You can calculate the total number of sectors on the disk by multiplying these values.

$$9*2*40=720$$

By multiplying the value above by 512 bytes in each of the 720 sectors, you get the total formatted disk capacity.

$$720*512=368,640$$

Since 1K (kilobyte) = 1024 bytes you can divide the total number of bytes by 1,024.

$$368,640/1024 = 360L$$

The result shows that all the values displayed are consistent.

```
                        Technical information

    Drive A:

    Type of disk:
        Double-sided, double-density, 9-sector

    Basic storage capacity:
        360 thousand characters (kilobytes)
        100% of disk space is free

    Logical dimensions:
        Sectors are made up of 512 bytes
        Tracks are made up of 9 sectors per disk side
        There are 2 disk sides
        The disk is made up of 40 tracks
        Space for files is allocated in clusters of 2 sectors
        There are 354 clusters
        Each cluster is 1,024 bytes
        The disk's root directory can hold 112 files

                   Press any key to continue...
```

Figure 2-7 Technical disk Information.

The last three items under **Logical Dimensions** refer to the way in which the sectors are organized into data storage units. The sector is a physical unit; however, in using sectors, the operating system must organize the sectors into logical units for data storage. The basic logical unit is called a **cluster**. A cluster can consist of one or more sectors. Refer back to the disk used for Figure 2-2; each cluster consists of 1024 bytes, which is two 512 byte sectors. The entire disk contains 354 such clusters.

> *The size of the sector remains the same for almost all disks in an MS-DOS system. However, cluster size varies among the different floppy and hard disks. A cluster size of 1024 bytes is used on double density disks.*

This means that the cluster size determines the minimum amount of space used for a file. For example, suppose you had a file that contained only a single byte, e.g., the letter A. The file would be stored in a data cluster. All 1024 bytes would be reserved for use by the file, even though it only contains a single byte. The effect of cluster size is discussed in more detail in Chapter 7.

The final entry is the number of entries that can be made into the root directory of the disk. In this case, the maximum number is 112. This means you can store up to 112 files in the root directory. Because the disk contains 354 data clusters, you could in theory create 354 separate files. However, since the root directory is limited to 112 file name entries, you could not place all the files in the same directory.

> *You can get around the root directory limit by creating other directories on the disk.*
> *Note that each directory you create uses up one cluster of disk space.*

Return to the main menu by entering

[Esc] *(2 times)*

Organization

There are many numbers involved in the organization of a disk. In reading through the previous section you may have noticed that some of the figures don't seem to add up. It was calculated that there are some 720 sectors on a double sided double-density disk. If you use two sectors for each data cluster, there should be 360 clusters. But the Technical Information screen display shows there are only 354 data clusters. What happened to the other six clusters?

The answer is that in order to keep track of what data is stored on the disk, DOS must reserve some of the space for organization of the data. In this case, 6 of the 360 potential data clusters, 1.7 percent, of the total disk space are reserved.

The Norton Utilities program allows you to look at the way the disk is organized. You can use the **Explore Disk** option to reveal more details about how the disk space is used. **Explore Disk** acts like a computer microscope that allows you to peer into the actual structure of the disk. Enter

e

The **Choose Item** option on the **Explore Disk** menu allows you to select what part of the disk you want to explore. The upper-right corner of the screen display shows *Menu 1*. All the menus presented in the main Norton Utilities program are numbered, making it easier to refer to specific displays. Enter

c

The menu lists four different ways to examine the disk.

1. **File.** This option allows you to select an area of the disk to examine, based on the file name.

2. **Cluster.** This option allows you to select a specific data cluster to be examined. On the current disk, the clusters would be numbered 2-355.

3. **Sector.** This option allows you to select a sector or group of sectors by number. In this example, the sectors are numbered 0 through 719.

4. **Absolute Sector.** This option allows you to select a sector or group of sectors by their physical location. In this case, you must enter the side, cylinder, and sector number within the track of the sector you want to examine.

Select to display by **Sector** by entering

s

This displays the **Select Sector** menu. The menu allows you to enter a range of sectors for display, one sector at a time. You can enter a starting and ending sector to limit your display to a specific area of the disk.

At the bottom of the screen a chart is displayed that summarizes how the sectors on the disk are used, Figure 2-8.

```
          Outline of Sector Usage on This Disk

       0         Boot area        (used by DOS)
    1 - 4        FAT area         (used by DOS)
    5 - 11       Root Dir. area   (used by DOS)
   12 - 719      Data area        (where files are stored)
```

Figure 2-8 Outline of sector usage.

The sector usage is divided into four parts:

1. **Boot Area.** The boot area is always the first sector on the disk. It is in the boot area that DOS writes information describing how this disk is organized. This enables DOS to work with a variety of floppy and hard disks with different capacities. Because each disk carries with it a description of its organization, DOS can adjust to disks of different sizes. The boot area takes up only one sector.

2. **FAT Area.** FAT stands for File Allocation Table. This is an important table used by DOS to assign the disk sectors to various files. For each sector on the disk, there is an entry in the file allocation table that tells DOS if the sector is in use by a file, and if so, which one. The size of the file allocation table will vary with the size of the disk. The larger the capacity of the disk, the larger the file allocation table must be to keep track of all the sectors.

3. **Directory**. The directory is the area of the disk reserved for keeping information about the file stored on that disk. The directory stores the filenames, dates, size, and other necessary information. Combined with the information stored in the file allocation table, the directory enables DOS to store and retrieve data from the disk. Keep in mind that damage to the file directory will make it difficult or even impossible to locate files.

4. **Data Area**. All the space on the disk left over after the boot, FAT, and directory areas is data space. It is in these sectors that the actual information is stored.

Begin exploring the disk by looking at the boot sector. Enter

0 ↵ ↵

Once you have selected a sector or sectors to display, the program returns to the **Explore Disk** menu. Note that at the bottom of the screen the program displays the current exploration selection as shown in Figure 2-9. This makes it simple to keep track of what selection you are working with.

Item type	Drive	Sector number
Sector	A:	0

Figure 2-9 Current selection displayed.

You can use the **Edit/Display Item** option to display the contents of the specified items, in this case, the boot sector, on the screen. Enter

e

The Norton Utilities displays the information from the boot sector on the screen. Note that the display is broken into two parts.

1. **Left-side Hex Display.** The left side of the screen shows the hex values of each of the 512 bytes in the sector. Keep in mind that each hex number consists of two digits, so that values are read in pairs, e.g., EB, 28, 90, 49, etc.

2. **Right-side character display.** The right side of the display shows the character representation for each of the hex numbers on the left side.

There are 512 characters corresponding to each of the hex numbers on the left side of the screen.

```
┌ Sector 0 ══════════════════════════════════════ Hex format ═┐
│ Sector 0 in Boot Area                           Offset 0, hex 0│
│EBZ89049 424D2050 4E434900 02020100 027000D0 02FD0200 ╒KÉIBM PNCI.╝╕⌐.8p.ⁱ9²9.│
│09000200 00000000 00000000 00000000 0000FA33 C08ED0BC ∘.8.............3╚╙╙│
│F07BFBB8 C0078ED8 BE5B0090 FCAC0AC0 740B56B4 0EBB0700 ≡⌠╖ ᴸ∙ÄⅡ⌐.é╝¼▐⌠╔╛ ₧╥∙.│
│CD105EEB F03Z4ECD 16B40FCD 103Z4ECD 10CD190D 0A0D0A0D ⇒^δ≡ΣΣ=↓⦁⇒⇒Σ⦁Σ=↓♪▌╛⦁│
│0A0D0A0D 0A0D0A0D 0A0D0AZ0 Z0Z0Z054 68697320 6469736B ♪▌♪▌♪▌♪▌♪▌       This disk│
│Z0697320 6E6F7420 626F6F74 61626C65 0D0A0D0A 20496620  is not bootable♪▌♪▌ If│
│796F7520 77697368 Z0746F20 6D616B65 Z0697420 6Z6F6F74 you wish to make it boot│
│61626C65 Z0D0A7Z 756E2074 68652044 4F53Z070 72 6F6772 able,♪▌run the DOS progr│
│616D Z053 59532061 66746572 Z0746865 0D0AZ0Z0 Z0Z0Z073 am SYS after the♪▌     s│
│79737465 6D206861 73206265 656E206C 6F616465 640D0A0D ystem has been loaded♪▌♪│
│0A506C65 61736520 696E7365 72742061 20444F53 20646973 ⦁Please insert a DOS dis│
│6B657474 6520696E 746F0D0A Z0746865 Z0647269 76652061 kette into♪▌ the drive a│
│6E642073 7472696B 6520616E 79206B65 79ZEZEZE 00000000 nd strike any key.......│
│00000000 00000000 00000000 00000000 00000000 00000000 .......................│
│00000000 00000000 00000000 00000000 00000000 00000000 .......................│
│00000000 00000000 00000000 00000000 00000000 00000000 .......................│
│00000000 00000000 00000000 00000000 00000000 00000000 .......................│
│00000000 00000000 00000000 00000000 00000000 00000000 .......................│
│00000000 00000000 00000000 00000000 00000000 00000000 .......................│
│00000000 00000000 00000000 00000000 00000000 00000000 .......................│
│00000000 000055AA         Press Enter to continue    ......U┐│
│1Help  2Hex   3Text  4Dir   5FAT  6Partn  7       8Choose 9Undo  10QuitNU│
```

Figure 2-10 Contents of the boot sector displayed.

When you look at the character representations on the right side of the screen, some of the characters will be familiar alphanumeric characters, while others will be strange-looking symbols. This is a result of the characters built into the character set of the computer. On MS-DOS machines, this set consists of 255 characters. Each character is assigned a specific number value. Character 20 hex (32 decimal) is a blank space. This means that each time the hex value 20 appears on the left side of the screen, a corresponding blank space will appear on the right side of the screen.

Characters 20 hex (32 decimal) through 7E hex (126 decimal) are the familiar alphanumeric characters. Characters 1 through 1F hex (31 decimal) and 7F (127 decimal) through FF hex (255 decimal) appear as special characters and symbols. Keep in mind that the symbols are created by the display adaptor on your screen. The disk contains only binary numbers represented on the left side of the screen in hex notation, in order to compress the size of the numerical display.

Moving Around the Display

The current display shows that the 512 bytes of information stored in only a single disk sector can appear quite complicated. In order to work with and refer to individual parts of the data within a sector, programmers have evolved a system of numbering each byte, beginning with the first byte in the sector. The number is called the **offset.** For example, the first byte in the sector is **offset** 0. The second byte is offset 1, and so on. In the upper right corner of the screen, you will see an indicator that displays the offset of the currently highlighted byte in decimal values, 0 through 511, and hex values 0 through 1FF.

In the sector display you can change the position of the cursor highlight using the ←, →, ↑, and ↓ keys. The [Home] key moves the highlight to byte 0 and the [End] key moves the highlight to byte 511. Enter

$$\rightarrow$$

The highlight moves from the E to B. Notice that the offset indicator in the upper-right corner has not changed. That is because this digit is still part of the first byte. Enter

$$\rightarrow$$

This time the offset value does change to 1, because you are positioned on the first digit in the second byte.

You can switch between the hexadecimal and character displays by entering

[Tab]

The cursor jumps to the right side of the display. The offset indicator still shows byte 1. However, the highlight is now flashing on a character on the right side of the display. On the left side, the hex digit that corresponds to this character is highlighted. Enter

→ *(2 times)*

This places your cursor on byte 3. In the current example, this byte contains the hex value 49, which corresponds to the letter **I.**

Interpreting the Boot Sector

Part of the information displayed in the boot sector is quite clearly understandable by simply reading the characters. For example, beginning at byte 3, the familiar letters **IBM** can be read quite clearly. The **PNCI** stands for *Peter*

Norton Computing Inc., indicating that the disk was formatted with Safe Format, instead of the DOS FORMAT command.

Further down the right side of the display are short, legible phrases, such as *This disk is not bootable*. Between those items are symbols that appear to have no meaning at all.

The display is a mixture of two types of information. The readable parts are blocks of text stored on the disk for display. In this case, the phrases would be used to display a message, if the user attempted to boot a computer using this disk.

> *Recall that you did not format this disk as a bootable disk, but as a data-only disk. If you use the Norton Utilities Safe Format program to create a data disk, this message is placed into the boot sector. If you use the DOS FORMAT program to create a data disk, the message in the boot sector will read "Non-system disk or disk error."*

But what about the portion that appears as random symbols? This information appears random because it is not meant to be interpreted as text. Instead, it is information coded in binary values. The information contained in these values identifies the structure of the disk. Each of the values has a specific meaning, which is decoded by the computer when it reads the disk. This is a very important point because it explains how the operating system can work with a variety of different disk types.

In order to understand what the values say about the disk, you need to have a guide that tells you the significance of each value or group of values. Table 2-1 shows the meanings of bytes 13 through 21 of the boot sector. This is only a partial list, but it will serve to illustrate how the system works. You will notice that the information contained in the boot sector is similar to the data displayed on the Technical Information screen. Indeed, the Norton Utilities program is simply displaying the data stored in the boot sector, in a more readable form.

Table 2-1 Partial List of Boot Sector Values

Offset	Meaning
11-12	Number of **bytes** in each **sector**
13	Number of **sectors** in each data **cluster**
14-15	Number of reserved sectors
16	Number of FAT copies
17-18	Number of entries in root directory
19-20	Number of **sectors** on disk
21	Disk type code

To understand how to read boot sector values, begin with offsets 11 and 12. You can locate offset 11 by using the → key, until the value in the offset indicator, upper-right corner of the screen, reads 11. Enter

→ *(8 times)*

The values in offsets 11 and 12 are two digits, 00 and 02. The digits represent the number of bytes in each disk sector.

EB289049 424D2050 4E434900 02020100

The digits are interpreted as a single hex number. When this is done, the order of the digits is reversed so that the number of bytes in a sector is **0200** in hex.

> *You may wonder why it is that the number 0200 is used, and not 0002, since byte 11 was 00 and byte 12 was 02. The answer has to do with the way values are traditionally read from the disk. When a value is composed of 2 bytes, it is called a "word." The first byte is called the low-order byte, while the second is called the high-order byte. This is backward from the human point of view, since we tend to write numbers beginning with the highest place values on the left. However, computers cannot read with the same visual dexterity of humans. Humans learn to read text from left to right, but numbers from right to left. Computers read data sequentially in one direction only. By convention, the place value of the digits is stored left to right. When you interpret the data, you need to remember to reverse the order to the way humans are trained to read numbers.*

Translated to decimal value, 0200 is 2 times 256 or 512, which is exactly the value shown in the Technical Information display.

Place Value	4096	256	16	1
Hexadecimal	0	2	0	0
Decimal Value	0	512	0	0

The next byte, offset 13, is used by itself to indicate the sectors used to form a data cluster. In this case, the value is **02**. This tells you that 2 of the 512 byte sectors are used for the data cluster. Once again, this matches the information displayed previously by the program.

Move the highlight to offset 21 by entering

→ *(10 times)*

This byte identifies the type of disk. Table 2-2 shows the hex values used to indicate the disk type.

Table 2-2 Values Used for Disk Type

Hex Value	Type of Disk
FE	160K floppy disk
FC	180K floppy disk
FF	320K floppy disk
FD	360K floppy disk
F9	1.2M floppy disk
F9	720K floppy disk
F0	1.44M floppy disk
F8	Hard disk

Since the value in the boot sector is **FD**, you can conclude that the disk you are examining is a 360K floppy disk.

The boot sector reveals how the basic information about a disk's structure is stored on each disk. The data is stored as part of the formatting process and is used by DOS and other programs to determine what type of disk is being used.

Exit the program by entering

[F10]

How Files Are Stored

So far, you have looked at the structure of the boot sector of a newly formatted disk. What happens to the disk as files are added and deleted? You can use the main Norton Utilities program to examine the changes that take place when you add and remove files.

The first step is to add files to the disk. The fastest way to do this is to copy already existing files. In this case, you can copy some of the files supplied with the Norton Utilities package to the floppy disk. The following command copies all the files that begin with NU to the disk in drive A. Enter

copy \norton\nu.* a: ↵

The command causes two files, NU.EXE and NU.HLP to be copied to the floppy disk. What effect has this had on the floppy disk? You can explore the changes by loading the main Norton Utilities program, again. Enter

nu a: ↵

The first display you will look at is the map of disk usage. Since files have been added to the disk, you will expect that the map should reflect the additions. Enter

d
m

The map shown in Figure 2-11 shows the area on the disk that is now occupied by the files you copied to the disk. Fifty-eight percent of the disk is still free for the addition of more files.

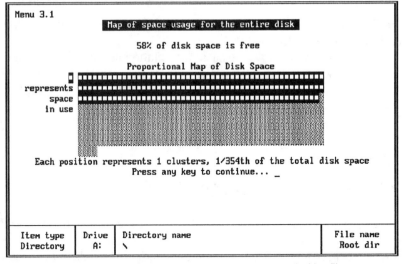

Figure 2-11 Disk usage map shows area occupied by files.

Return to the main menu by entering

↵
r

The Disk Directory

Disk directories are one of the first items any user learns to deal with. The Norton Utilities program provides you with a way to examine how the disk's directory is actually constructed and how it works. You can use the **Explore Disk** option to display the directory. Enter

e
c

This time, choose to select disk space according to **File** by entering

f

The program lists the names of the files, as well as the three reserved areas (boot, FAT, and root directory). You can select to examine any of the areas by highlighting the name and pressing ↵. By default, **Root dir** is highlighted. Display the directory by entering

↵
e

The directory display, as shown in Figure 2-12, shows how DOS records information about files stored on the disk.

> *The third entry on this list is actually the volume label you specified during the formatting process. In DOS 3.3, or earlier versions that support volume labels, the label is stored in the directory along with the file names. The **Vol** attribute is used to indicate that this is the volume label and not a file name. Note there is no cluster number associated with the volume label.*

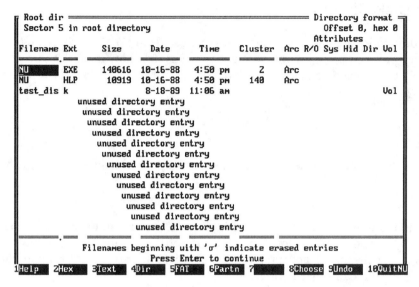

Figure 2-12 Disk directory displayed.

The directory displays a number of different items of information about each file.

1. **Filename.** This is the one-to eight-character name used for the file.

2. **Extension.** This is the optional one- to three-character file extension.

3. **Size in bytes.** This is the size, in bytes, of the file.

It is important to note that the value recorded for the size of the file is different than the total amount of space used by the file. Since DOS allocates space in terms of data clusters of a fixed size (e.g., 1024 bytes), it is unlikely that a file will end exactly at the end of a data cluster. More often than not, a file will end in the middle of the last data cluster, leaving some "slack" space at the end of the cluster that is not actually filled by the file. However, since the smallest unit DOS allocates to a file is a data cluster, no other file can use that "slack" space. The size noted by DOS does not include any "slack" space at the end of the last data cluster. The Norton Utilities program, FS (file size), does measure this space and the difference between the file size and the actual space used by the file on the disk.

---

4   **Date & Time.** Date and time are taken from the system's clock at the time a file is created or modified. Note that when a file is copied, DOS

writes the original date and time, not the date and time when the file was copied.

5. **Cluster**. This is the number of the starting cluster of the file. In this example, the NU.EXE file begins at data cluster 2. The next file, NU.HLP begins at cluster 140. Since most files contain more than one cluster, the location of the other clusters associated with a given file is stored in another area of the disk called the File Allocation Table (FAT).

6. **Attributes.** Each file can be assigned one or more attributes. The attributes are **arc**hive, **r**ead-only, **sys**tem, **hid**den, **dir**ectory, or **vol**ume label.

Archive. This attribute is designed to work with the BACKUP, RESTORE, and XCOPY commands. It helps these commands select files that have never been backed up.

Read-**O**nly. This attribute can be used to prevent changing or overwriting a file. Also used on networks to allow file sharing.

System. Used to designate a file as a system file.

Hidden. Used to suppress the display of a file in the DOS directory listing.

Directory. Indicates the entry is a directory not a data file.

Volume label. Indicates the entry is the disk volume label not a data file.

You will learn more about attributes in Chapter 8.

The program allows you to change any of the items of the directory items. For example, suppose that you wanted to change the date and time shown for the NU.EXE file. The [Tab] key will move the highlight to the next item. Move to the date by entering

[Tab] *(2 times)*

Change the date by entering

010189

Change the time by entering

0100

You can use the [space bar] to toggle the AM/PM value. Change the time to AM by entering

[space bar]

You can also change attributes in this display as well. Suppose you wanted to remove the **Arc** attribute from the file. Enter

[tab] *(2 times)*
[space bar]

The **Arc** is removed. You can add attributes in a similar way. If you wanted to make the NU.HLP file a **read-only** file you would activate that attribute. Enter

↓
[tab]
[space bar]

R/O appears in the **R/O** column, indicating that this file is now a read only file. Note that all the changes you made to the directory appear in bold video.

You can use the main Norton Utilities to change all the directory items, including Size, Cluster, Dir, and Vol. However, you should not make any changes in these values unless you have a very specific reason based on your analysis of a problem you are having with that disk. For example, many programs depend upon the value in the size column to determine where the end of the file is located. Changing the size can disrupt the use of that file. If you should make an accidental change to some part of the directory, you can restore the original value by pressing [F9], the Undo command.

Changing Views

You may have noticed that the program displays directory information in a format quite different from the one used to display the boot sector. In fact, the program has five different display modes which can be used when the information from a disk sector is displayed. The names of the modes appear at the bottom of the screen and are assigned to function keys [F2] through [F6].

F2 **Hex.** This mode displays the bytes stored on the disk in hex and character notation. This mode is the most literal display of information, since it displays exactly what is stored on the disk, byte for byte. The hex display was used when you examined the boot sector.

F3 **Text.** This mode attempts to display information in a text format similar to a word processor or editor. In this mode characters that are not normally included in text files are ignored. Also, hex number 1A, 26 in decimal, is treated as the <end of file> marker.

F4 **Dir.** This format is used to display directory information in an easy to read format.

F5 **FAT.** This format is designed to display the file allocation table in a format that makes it easy to read.

F6 **Partn.** This format is used to show the partition table stored in the boot sector, sector 0, of a disk. The partition table is used to divide a hard disk into several separate sections. Most DOS users place all of the hard disk space into a single DOS partition. If the hard drive is over 32 megabytes many users create extended DOS partitions to create several logical drive on the same disk.

The root directory was automatically displayed in the directory display mode. Formats Hex(F2) and Text(F3) can be applied to any part of the disk. The other formats are useful when you are looking at the specialized areas on a disk such as a directory, file allocation table, or hard disk partition table.

If you change the directory to the hex display you will see the directory information displayed as it actually is recorded on the disk. Enter

[F2]

The program switches to the hex display mode, (Figure 2-13). In this display mode the directory appears as simply a sequence of values.

In the upperleft corner, **Root dir** appears, indicating you are looking at the root directory of the disk. Below this, the program reveals that the root directory begins in sector 5 of the disk.

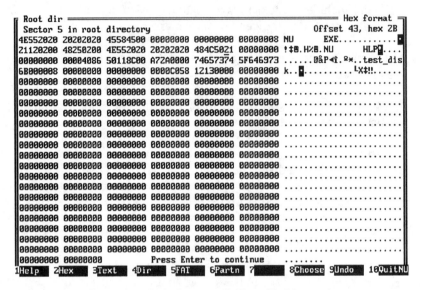

Figure 2-13 Disk directory displayed in hex mode.

Each directory entry consists of 32 bytes. The bytes are organized in the following manner:

Table 2-3 Directory Entry Byte Usage

Byte	Meaning
1-8	File name
9-11	File extension
12	File attributes
13-22	Reserved for DOS
23-24	Time
25-26	Date
27-28	Starting data cluster
29-32	File size

This 32 byte pattern repeats for each file in the directory. The total number of files stored in the root directory is limited by the number of sectors on the disk allocated for the root directory. On a 360K disk there are seven sectors allocated for the root directory. Since each sector is 512 bytes and each entry takes up 32 bytes you can calculate the total number of entries.

512 bytes per sector/32 bytes per file = 16

16 files * 7 sectors = 112 files

The calculation reveals that you can store up to 112 files in the root directory. Note that the volume label takes up one position in the directory leaving 111 slots for file names.

Saving Changes

The hex display shows the hex values in bold video that correspond to the changes you made in the directory mode display. These changes are still in bold because they are only temporary changes. The Norton Utilities program will not write the changes into the actual disk sector until specifically instructed to do so. This is done to reduce the possibility of accidental changes in the disk's information.

If you have made changes to a sector, you will be prompted when you attempt to leave that sector's display. Enter

[Esc]

The program displays a box which prompts you to either save or discard the changes made to the sector, as shown in Figure 2-14. Keep in mind that if you save the changes to the disk, you cannot recall the original disk data, since it is being overwritten.

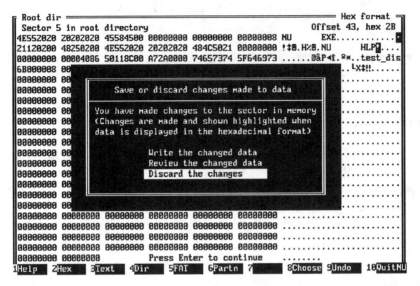

Figure 2-14 Prompts for saving or discarding changes made to disk sector.

In this case, write the changes to the disk by entering

w

The changes have been saved to the disk.

File Allocation Table

So far, you have looked at two of the three areas on the disk that are reserved for system information: the boot sector and the root directory. The third area is located between those two and is called the *File Allocation Table* or FAT. The *File Allocation Table* is used to keep track of which data clusters belong to which files. You will recall that the directory had room to record the number of only the **first** data cluster used by a file. Any additional data stored for that file is recorded in the FAT.

The FAT is an interesting solution to a complicated problem. When a file is stored on a disk it can use one or more data clusters. In order to retrieve the file, you need to know two things: (1) Which clusters contain the data you want and (2) In what order should the clusters be read?

As a disk has files of varying sizes added, removed, shortened, or lengthened, the job of keeping track of what sequence of clusters contain the data from each file gets more complex. The problem is solved in the FAT by using a system of *pointers*. A *pointer* is a value that indicates the location of another value. The pointer system works like a cross-reference in a book in which you are referred to a different page for more information on the same subject. Each FAT value tells DOS which data cluster contains the next section of file.

The main Norton Utilities program provides a special mode that displays the information in the FAT, in a way that is easy to understand. Display the FAT by entering

The screen shows a new form of data display, as seen in Figure 2-15. In the upper-left corner of the display, the message **Sector 1 in 1st copy of FAT** tells you that you are at the beginning of the FAT. Recall that the outline of disk structure shown on page 2 shows that sectors 1 through 4 are used for the FAT.

> *The FAT space actually contains two copies of the FAT in the FAT area of the disk. DOS uses only the first copy of the FAT to locate data. In general, DOS utilities do not make use of this second copy, but some of the Norton Utilities programs do. The main Norton Utilitie program allows you to display and edit both copies of the FAT. In some cases, you can recover files by copying data from the second copy into the first copy.*

This display is used to show the data stored in the FAT of the disk. The meaning of the FAT is not as simple to pick up as the directory. In order to make sense out of the FAT display you need to understand how it works.

```
┌ FAT area ═══════════════════════════════════════════════════ FAT format ┐
│ Sector 1 in 1st copy of FAT                                 Cluster 2, hex 2 │
│                                                                              │
│   3▐███▌  4     5     6     7     8     9    10    11    12    13    14        │
│   15    16    17    18    19    20    21    22    23    24    25    26        │
│   27    28    29    30    31    32    33    34    35    36    37    38        │
│   39    40    41    42    43    44    45    46    47    48    49    50        │
│   51    52    53    54    55    56    57    58    59    60    61    62        │
│   63    64    65    66    67    68    69    70    71    72    73    74        │
│   75    76    77    78    79    80    81    82    83    84    85    86        │
│   87    88    89    90    91    92    93    94    95    96    97    98        │
│   99   100   101   102   103   104   105   106   107   108   109   110        │
│  111   112   113   114   115   116   117   118   119   120   121   122        │
│  123   124   125   126   127   128   129   130   131   132   133   134        │
│  135   136   137   138   139 <EOF>  141   142   143   144   145   146        │
│  147   148   149   150 <EOF>    0     0     0     0     0     0     0        │
│    0     0     0     0     0     0     0     0     0     0     0     0        │
│    0     0     0     0     0     0     0     0     0     0     0     0        │
│    0     0     0     0     0     0     0     0     0     0     0     0        │
│    0     0     0     0     0     0     0     0     0     0     0     0        │
│    0     0     0     0     0     0     0     0     0     0     0     0        │
│    0     0     0     0     0     0     0     0     0     0     0     0        │
│                                                                              │
│                       Press Enter to continue                                │
└──────────────────────────────────────────────────────────────────────────┘
 1Help  2Hex   3Text  4Dir   5FAT   6Partn 7      8Choose 9Undo  10QuitNU
```

Figure 2-15 FAT table displayed.

The FAT consists of a series of values. The program displays these values in rows. In the FAT there is **one value** for each of the **data clusters** on the disk. The values in the FAT can be one of three types.

1. **Zero.** If the FAT shows a zero it indicates that the data cluster is not in use by the file. This indicates the locations on the disk where new data can be added.

2. **Value.** If the FAT entry contains a value, it indicates two things. First, the value tells DOS that this cluster is in use by a file. Second it points out the next data cluster that belongs to the same file.

3. **EOF.** EOF stands for end of file. This marker indicates that this cluster is used by a file and that it is the last cluster in the file. The <EOF> symbol stands for *end of file*.

It is possible for the FAT to contain a value indicating that the cluster is "bad." A "bad" cluster is one that is marked because of an error. It is not unusual to have some of these clusters on a hard or floppy disk. The marks are used to tell DOS not to attempt to use this area of the disk for data storage because that area of the disk appears to unreliable. "Bad" clusters will cause you no problem and can be ignored. If you are using a floppy disk you may want to copy the files to another floppy as a precaution. Chapter 11 details how the Norton Utilities can be used to handle problems that occur on disks.

To understand the FAT you need to understand how the *pointer* system works. The significance of each value in the table depends upon its position in the table.

As an example, look at the first value that appears in the FAT display. The first value is **3**. If you look at the upper-right corner of the display it shows **Cluster 2, hex 2.** The display indicates that the currently highlighted value represents the usage of data cluster **2**. Because the entry for cluster **2** is a value greater than zero, you can conclude that cluster 2 is in use by one of the files on the disk.

The exact value contained in position 2 in the table is 3. This value indicates the location of the next data cluster for the same file. The 3 stipulates that the next cluster in the file is data cluster 3.

The 3 also has a second meaning. It specifies where in the table you need to look to find what cluster comes after 3.

When DOS reads the data starting in position 2 in the table, it interprets the information in the following way:

1. Read the data in cluster 2.

2. Look at the value in the current position in the FAT. In this case, that value is 3.

3. Read the information stored in the cluster that corresponds to the value in the FAT. In this example the value is 3, so that DOS reads disk cluster 3.

4. Move to the position in the table that corresponds to the cluster number. In this example the value is 3, so that DOS moves to position 3 in the FAT.

The steps repeat until DOS reaches a FAT entry with an **<EOF>**, end of file, symbol. This means all the clusters belonging to the file have been read. The end of file is clearly marked in the FAT, but how does DOS know where to find the beginning of a file in the table? Recall that the beginning cluster for each file is specified in the directory display, as shown earlier in Figure 2-13.

The current FAT is organized sequentially. Each position points to the next position in the table. But this does not have to be the case. The advantage of the FAT scheme is that it can be used to connect any of the disk clusters in any order. This makes it possible to store files in fragmented sections scattered throughout the disk. The FAT makes it possible to add, remove, expand, and contract files, while still making use of all of clusters on the disk.

> *The Norton Utilities program allows you to edit the values in the FAT table. This ability should be used only when you are sure that the file allocation table is in error and you know the modifications needed to correct the error. The implication is that only advanced users will want to make changes in the FAT table. If you should accidentally make a change, you can restore the original FAT by pressing [F9].*

How FAT Information Is Stored

The FAT display mode makes it easy to read and understand the FAT table. However, like all disk data, the FAT is really a collection of binary values. You can display the actual values in hex format, by using the [F2] key to activate the hex display mode. Enter

[F2]

The Norton Utilities program displays the FAT in hex view, showing the values as they are actually stored on the disk, (Figure 2-16).

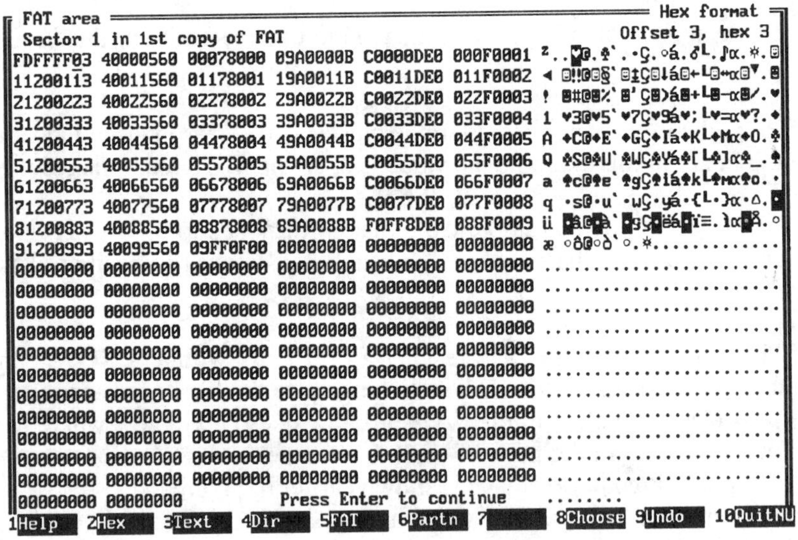

Figure 2-16 FAT displayed in hex view.

The meaning of values shown in the hex mode is much harder to grasp than the values displayed in the FAT mode display. The hex view of the FAT is much more complicated to read than the directory, because the table is organized in groups of bits rather than bytes. DOS uses two types of FAT structures: 12 and 16 bit. Since 8 bits make up 1 byte, the 16 bit structure falls neatly into two byte pairs. But the 16-bit tables are used on high-capacity hard disks. Most floppy disks, like the one in the example, have a 12 bit structure. The Norton Utilities make it unnecessary to decode the complicated 12 bit structure, however it might be interesting to try to decode a little bit of the FAT displayed on the screen.

Unlike the directory, the FAT begins with a value that acts as identification of the disk format. In this example the first byte is **FD**, indicating that this is a 360K disk.

The first part of the actual file allocation table begins at offset 3. The 12 bit, FAT table is not easy to decode because it is meant to be read by the computers microprocessor, which stores data in special areas called registers. The format that is most efficient for the microprocessor is not necessarily the easiest for a human to decode. As an example, take the first three bytes of the FAT as shown in Figure 2-17. DOS uses a special pattern to derive the value of the first FAT entry by using the first byte and half of the second.

```
┌ FAT area ════════════════════════════════════════════ Hex format ═┐
│ Sector 1 in 1st copy of FAT                         Offset 3, hex 3 │
│FDFFFF03 40000560 00078000 09A0000B C0000DE0 000F0001 ².. 0.♠`.·Ç.°å.δL.♪α.*.0│
│11200113 40011560 01178001 19A0011B C0011DE0 011F0002 ◄ 0!!00§`01Ç01á0+L0→α0▼.0│
│21200223 40022560 02278002 29A0022B C0022DE0 022F0003 ! 0#00%`0'Ç0)á0+L0→α0/.♥│
│31200333 40033560 03378003 39A0033B C0033DE0 033F0004 1 ♥30♥5`♥7Ç♥9á♥;L♥=α♥?.♦│
│41200443 40044560 04478004 49A0044B C0044DE0 044F0005 A ♦C0♦E`♦GÇ♦Iá♦KL♦Mα♦0.♣│
│51200553 40055560 05578005 59A0055B C0055DE0 055F0006 Q ♦S0♦U`♦WÇ♦Yá♦[L♦]α♣_.♠│
│61200663 40066560 06678006 69A0066B C0066DE0 066F0007 a ♦c0♦e`♦gÇ♦iá♦kL♦mα♦o.·│
│71200773 40077560 07778007 79A0077B C0077DE0 077F0008 q ·s0·u`·wÇ·yá·{L·}α·.0│
│81200883 40088560 08878008 89A0088B F0FF8DE0 088F0009 ü 0á0©0`0gÇ0éá0©0¶≡.)α0%.°│
│91200993 40099560 09FF0F00 00000000 00000000 00000000 æ °å00ò`°.◊..........│
│00000000 00000000 00000000 00000000 00000000 00000000 .....................│
│00000000 00000000 00000000 00000000 00000000 00000000 .....................│
│00000000 00000000 00000000 00000000 00000000 00000000 .....................│
│00000000 00000000 00000000 00000000 00000000 00000000 .....................│
│00000000 00000000 00000000 00000000 00000000 00000000 .....................│
│00000000 00000000 00000000 00000000 00000000 00000000 .....................│
│00000000 00000000 00000000 00000000 00000000 00000000 .....................│
│00000000 00000000 00000000 00000000 00000000 00000000 .....................│
│00000000 00000000 00000000 00000000 00000000 00000000 .....................│
│00000000 00000000 00000000 00000000 00000000 00000000 .....................│
│00000000 00000000       Press Enter to continue      .......│
│1Help   2Hex    3Text   4Dir   5FAT   6Partn  7       8Choose 9Undo  10QuitNU│
```

Figure 2-17 Pattern used to derive the first FAT value.

Figure 2-18 shows the pattern used to calculate the second FAT value. The first byte is followed by the fourth digit and the last byte is followed by the third digit. This complicated system works quite well on the microprocessor level and maximizes the amount of information that can be placed into the file allocation table area. This is important because the file allocation table determines the number of data clusters that you can have on a disk. A 12 bit table will limit the largest cluster number to FFF hex, 4095 decimal. In a 16 bit FAT, that value rises to FFFF hex, 65,535 decimal. Currently, DOS supports a maximum of 65,535 data clusters on a hard disk.

> *Versions of DOS that support larger hard drives require extended FAT to keep track of all the clusters on larger disks.*

```
┌ FAT area ══════════════════════════════════════════════ Hex format ═┐
│ Sector 1 in 1st copy of FAT                            Offset 3, hex 3 │
│FDFFFF03 40000560 00078000 89A0000B C0000DE0 000F0001 ²..▓0.♠`.-Ç.○á.δᴸ.ʃ∝.◆.0│
│11200113 40011560 01178001 19A0011B C0011DE0 011F0002 ◄ 0!!008' 0‡Ç0↓á0←ᴸ0→∝0▼.0│
│21200223 40022560 02278002 29A0022B C0022DE0 022F0003 ! 0#08Z'0'Ç0)á0+ᴸ0-∝0/.♥│
│31200333 40033560 03378003 39A0033B C0033DE0 033F0004 1 ♥30♥5' ♥7Ç♥9á♥; ᴸ♥=∝♥?.◆│
│41200443 40044560 04478004 49A0044B C0044DE0 044F0005 A ◆C0◆E' ◆G Ç◆Iá◆Kᴸ◆M∝◆0.♠│
│51200553 40055560 05578005 59A0055B C0055DE0 055F0006 Q ♠S0♣U' ♠UÇ♣Vá♣[ ᴸ♣]∝♣_.♠│
│61200663 40066560 06678006 69A0066B C0066DE0 066F0007 a ↑c0↑e' ↑gÇ↑iá↑kᴸ↑m∝↑o. ·│
│71200773 40077560 07778007 79A0077B C0077DE0 077F0008 q ·s0·u' ·uÇ·yá·{ᴸ·}∝·△.█│
│81200883 40088560 08878008 89A0088B F0FF8DE0 088F0009 ü ▒A0A▒' ▒gÇ▒6á▒Y=.1∝▒ℝ.○│
│91200993 40099560 09FF0F00 00000000 00000000 00000000 æ ○δ0○δ'○.◆............│
│00000000 00000000 00000000 00000000 00000000 00000000 ......................│
│00000000 00000000 00000000 00000000 00000000 00000000 ......................│
│00000000 00000000 00000000 00000000 00000000 00000000 ......................│
│00000000 00000000 00000000 00000000 00000000 00000000 ......................│
│00000000 00000000 00000000 00000000 00000000 00000000 ......................│
│00000000 00000000 00000000 00000000 00000000 00000000 ......................│
│00000000 00000000 00000000 00000000 00000000 00000000 ......................│
│00000000 00000000 00000000 00000000 00000000 00000000 ......................│
│00000000 00000000 00000000 00000000 00000000 00000000 ......................│
│00000000 00000000 00000000 00000000 00000000 00000000 ......................│
│00000000 00000000         Press Enter to continue       ........           │
│1Help  2Hex  3Text  4Dir  5FAT  6Partn 7     8Choose 9Undo 10QuitNU│
```

Figure 2-18 Pattern used to derive the second FAT value.

As mentioned earlier, disk manufacturers provide special software with high-capacity hard disks (40 megabytes or more) that allow DOS to access drives with more than 32 megabytes.

FAT Problems

Unlike the directory, the FAT cannot be quickly or visually understood or analyzed. The only way to evaluate the information in the FAT is to follow the chain of values that link the data clusters together in files.

DOS provides the CHKDSK command to analyze the FAT. The Norton Disk Doctor (NDD) program included in Version 4.5 of the Utilities also finds and corrects problems in the FAT. When you run CHKDSK or NDD, the programs do more than check the disk space or read the directory. In order to analyze the disk, the programs put together the information in the directory with the information in the FAT to make sure that they match up. In checking the FAT against the directory, two types of problems commonly occur: lost clusters and cross-linked clusters.

Lost clusters are very much what their name suggests. These clusters have a value entered in their position in the file allocation table. However, none of the active files in the directory use this cluster. A lost cluster creates no active danger to existing data files. It does mean that DOS will not allocate this cluster to any new files because the value in the FAT is greater than zero.

A cross-linked cluster is a more serious matter. In this case, the FAT indicates the use of a data cluster by two or more different files. This situation is difficult because the data in the cluster should belong to one or the other of the cross-linked files. In the case of cross-linked data, it is highly probable that one, or all the cross-linked files, have suffered damage.

You might wonder how lost clusters or cross-linked clusters occur. In general, these problems are the result of an interruption taking place while DOS is attempting to write information to the disk. The interruption can be the result of a hardware, software, or user error. For example, entering a [Ctrl/Alt][Del] reboot instruction while the computer is writing data to the disk can cause such problems. This has the same effect as a power failure. Errors can be caused if a program hangs up while writing data to the disk. Other errors are caused by problems with the hard disk itself.

The DOS program CHKDSK accepts a switch /F(fix) that causes the program to modify the FAT and directory in order to deal with lost clusters. Suppose that your computer lost power as it was writing a file from drive C to drive A.

> *You can create just such an interruption as an experiment. The goal is to interrupt DOS while it is writing information to the disk. Timing is crucial in this experiment. The first step is to enter a COPY command, for example, copying a file from drive C to drive A. While the red light on drive A is lit, reboot the computer with [Ctrl/Alt][Del]. The effect will be to interrupt the normal DOS operation. If your timing is right, you will create lost clusters on the disk in drive A. The example illustrated below was created by entering COPY COMMAND.COM A:TESTING.COM and rebooting while the red light on A was lit.*
>
> *Getting lost clusters in this manner is a matter of luck, so be aware that the experiment might not succeed the first time.*
>
> *Also keep in mind that if you reboot your computer you will need to remove the disk from drive A and reset any paths necessary to gain access to the Norton Utilities programs.*
>
> *You will also have to delete the filename TESTING.COM from the disk in drive A. Why is that? The answer indicates how DOS actually goes about writing a file. When you copy a file, DOS first enters the filename into the directory. It then examines the FAT to determine what clusters are free for its use. DOS then writes the data into the clusters. When the writing is done, it returns to the directory and completes the entry for that file by writing the location of the first cluster for that file and its size.*
>
> *This means that if DOS is interrupted while writing a file, you will often see the name of the file in the directory with a size of 0 bytes. This is usually an indication of an interrupted file-writing process. It is possible that some or all of that file was actually written to the disk before the error occurred. Using the Unerase feature of the Norton Utilities program you might be able to recover part, or all, of this data. Section IV on Survival Skills details these operations.*

The CHKDSK command, when used with the /F(fix) switch, will perform one of two operations on the lost clusters. For example, CHKDSK/F will display a message indicating the number of lost clusters and asking how you want to deal with them. The following command would check the integrity of the FAT in drive A.

chkdsk a:/f ↵

If lost clusters are encountered, the program displays a message like this:

```
[C:\DOS]chkdsk a:/f

24 lost clusters found in 1 chains.
Convert lost chains to files  (Y/N)?
```

If you enter Y you are telling the program that you want to correct the problem by creating a filename in the directory that will correspond to the lost clusters. In that case the FAT table is left pretty much intact and the directory is modified by having a new filename or names added to it. The term "chain" refers to group of clusters that are numbered consecutively in the FAT. The assumption is made that all consecutively numbered clusters should be placed into a single file. If DOS finds clusters that are not consecutive it counts each group as a separate chain and assigns a separate filename for each chain.

The file naming convention is to use the name FILE0000.CHK for the first chain of clusters, FILE0001.CHK for the second chain, and so on. Keep in mind that collecting the lost clusters into files does not free up any disk space. The purpose of the collected files is to allow you to examine the contents of the clusters to determine if you really want to preserve this data. If you don't intend to go through this trouble, it is better to select N.

If you enter N to the prompt, the program leaves the directory as it is and alters the FAT by setting all lost clusters back to a value of zero. This also resolves the problem of the lost clusters and in so doing releases all the data clusters to be used with other files.

> *The Norton Disk Doctor performs the same correction tasks as CHKDSK along with other procedures. See Chapter 11.*

Cross-linked clusters present a more difficult problem. When a disk contains cross-linked clusters the CHKDSK command will display a list of the cross-links and the files that they relate to. Example:

```
B:\COMMAND.COM
    Is cross linked on cluster 4
B:\SAMPLE.COM
    Is cross linked on cluster 4
```

The list will always contain pairs of entries, one for each file cross-linked to the same cluster. CHKDSK, even with the /F parameter, will not affect cross-linked clusters. The reason is that the disk directory or FAT provides no clues as to which file the cluster should belong.

How can you solve this problem? The simplest way to eliminate the cross-links is to delete the files.

If the files contain valuable data, another solution is to copy both files to another name on the same disk, or preferably to another disk. Then, delete the cross-linked files and copy them back to their original disk or filenames. Keep in mind that while this will eliminate the cross-link, because DOS copies the cross-linked sector into both files, it does not mean that the files are undamaged. You will have to test the files to see which one, if either, still functions correctly.

One further note about CHKDSK and FAT problems. The CHKDSK program does not actually check the integrity of the clusters--it merely analyzes the FAT table. Exit the Norton Utilities program by entering

[F10]

Erasing a File

What happens to the disk when you erase a file? The question is important because it reveals something about how the operation works, which enables you to recover part or all of a file once it has been erased. (This process is discussed in detail in Chapter 10.) In this chapter you will take a brief look at the changes that occur when a file is erased.

In this example, erase the NU.EXE file form the floppy disk. Enter

del a:nu.exe ↵

Return to the main Norton Utilities program by entering

nu a: ↵

Display the disk directory by entering

↵ (4 times)
e

The program displays the directory as shown in Figure 2-18. The interesting thing about the directory display is that most of the directory information about the file is intact. The only change in the directory is that the first character of the file name has been replaced with a symbol that is used to indicate an erased file.

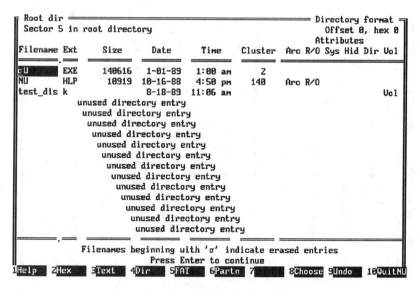

Figure 2-19 Directory after file has been erased.

What changes have taken place in the FAT? Change the display to show the contents of the FAT. You can change your selection directly from the current display by using the [F8] key. Enter

[F8] ↵

Select the FAT area by entering

↑ ↵

The FAT display, as shown in Figure 2-20, reveals a much greater degree of change than did the directory. Here, all the values in the FAT that were related to the erased file have been set to zero. This is necessary in order to show DOS that the clusters used for the erased file can be overwritten with new information.

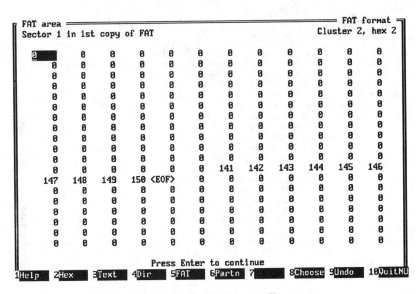

Figure 2-20 FAT changed due to file erasure.

What about the data areas themselves? Has the information been erased in the clusters? Use the program to display the contents of cluster 2 which was the beginning of the NU.EXE program. Enter

[F8] L

2 ↵ ↵

The program displays the contents of the data cluster as shown in Figure 2-21. The information is the cluster is not readable text but it does contain the binary values that belonged to the NU.EXE file that had been stored there.

```
┌ Cluster 2 ══════════════════════════════════════════════ Hex format ═┐
│ Cluster 2, Sectors 12-13                                Offset 0, hex 0 │
4D5A4801 13014907 E0012F03 FFFFA922 A00FE50E 47000000 MZH0!!0I·α0⁄♥..┌"á✳σ♫G...
1E000000 01005F00 7F1B4800 000000A1 00009600 A2006F00 ▲...0._.∆+H...█0..û.6.o.
A2004D00 A2003500 A2001A00 A2009203 AC007A03 AC006D03 6.M.6.5.6.→.6.╔♥¼.z♥¼.м♥
AC00BC00 AC006700 AC00C606 AC00B606 AC00AA06 AC009A06 ¼.".¼.g.¼.╞↑¼.║↑¼.¬↑¼.ü↑
AC008106 AC005F06 AC004C06 AC001F06 AC00F605 AC00EE05 ¼.ü↕¼._↕¼.L↕¼.▼↕¼.÷↕¼.€↕
AC00DC05 AC00C605 AC009705 AC003A05 AC001605 AC00D004 ¼.▬♠¼.╞♠¼.ù♠¼.:♠¼.▬♠¼.╨♠
AC00C304 AC003604 AC001D04 AC000204 AC008E02 19016802 ¼.╞♦¼.6♦¼.↔♦¼.Ä█↓☺h█
1901B401 19017F01 19016A01 19010701 1901EF00 1901DB00 ↓█·↓█∆↓█j↓█·↓█π.↓█.
1901C900 19017300 19016100 19011405 19010C05 1901F704 ↓█╔.↓█s.↓█a.↓█╥↕↓█♀↕↓█≈♦
1901AD04 1901A104 19017004 19012204 19010104 1901CB03 ↓█↓↕█i↕█p↕█"↕█↓↕█┬↕
1901BB03 19012803 19010503 1901E202 1901B502 1901A102 ↓█╥♥↓█(♥↓█♣♥↓█Γ☻↓█B☻↓█i☻
19019008 19018808 19016708 19016008 19013408 1901E607 ↓█É↓█Ê↓█g↓█`↓█4↓█μ·
19017D07 1901D706 19010C06 1901E605 1901B005 19019705 ↓█}·↓█╫▲↓█♀▲↓█μ♠↓█░♠↓█ù♠
19018805 19013E05 1901470C 1901340C 1901D00B 1901BF0B ↓█Ê♠↓█>♠↓█G◊↓█4◊↓█╨♂↓█┐♂
1901AC0B 1901680B 1901CC0A 1901B10A 1901740A 1901590A ↓█¼♂↓█h♂↓█╠◙↓█▒◙↓█t◙↓█Y◙
1901B309 19019809 19015609 19014509 19013009 1901B108 ↓█│○↓█Ø○↓█V○↓█E○↓█0○↓█▒
1901C50F 1901B10F 1901A90F 1901A10F 19013F0F 1901470E ↓█╞*↓█▒*↓█é*↓█i*↓█?*↓█G∂
19013F0E 1901310E 1901FC0D 1901A70D 1901790D 1901790D ↓█?♫↓█1♫↓█n♪↓█�º♪↓█ƒ♪↓█y♪
1901720D 19011F0D 1901830C 1901E511 1901D911 1901CD11 ↓█r♪↓█▼♪↓█â♀↓█σ◄↓█┘◄↓█╠◄
1901BF11 1901B111 1901A311 19010211 1901FD10 1901F510 ↓█┐◄↓█▒◄↓█ú◄↓█☻◄↓█²◄↓█►
1901DD10 1901AA10 19012210 1901CF0F 1901FB15 1901D315 ↓█▬►↓█ª►↓█"►↓█╧*↓█√§↓█╙§
1901CD14 19018F14         Press Enter to continue       ↓█╠♀↓█Å♀
1Help  2Hex  3Text  4Dir  5FAT  6Partn  7       8Choose 9Undo  10QuitNU
```

Figure 2-21 FAT changed due to file erasure.

Erasing a file from the disk changes some things, but not others.

1. **Directory.** The directory entry for the erased file remains intact with the exception of the first character in the filename which is used to mark the file as erased.

2. **FAT.** Each entry in the FAT that was used for that file is removed and replaced with a zero, indicating that the corresponding cluster is open for new data.

3. **Data Clusters.** The data stored in the clusters remains intact. This data will only be changed if a new file with new information is written into this clusters.

You will see in Chapter 10 that this system allows the Norton Utilities programs to recover part or all of a file after it has been deleted from the disk directory. Exit the program by entering

[F10]

Directories

The previous exploration of the directory and file allocation table pointed out a limitation in the directory structure. Because the directory is fixed in size when the disk is formatted it limits the number of files you can place on a disk. The 112 file limit on a floppy disk is rarely a problem. But it is not unusual to want to store a thousand files on a hard disk. If the root directory were the only directory on the disk you would be limited to 512 files on a hard disk. But with the release of DOS 2.0 and all subsequent versions, DOS can create additional directories on the disk. This structure has several benefits besides allowing more than 512 files on a disk. The system of directories helps to organize files into logical groups so that operations can be performed more efficiently, as discussed in the beginning of Section I.

It might be interesting to look at exactly how the new directories are handled by DOS in terms of data clusters and the FAT.

While directories are usually associated with hard disk drives, DOS will create them on any disk that has data clusters available. In this example, create a directory on drive A called **SUBDIR**. Enter

md a:\subdir ↵

Display a directory of the disk in drive A by entering

dir a: ↵

The directory shows SUBDIR with the **<DIR>** symbol in the listing.

```
Volume in drive A is test_disk
Directory of  A:\

SUBDIR        <DIR>        8-21-89      1:35p
NU        HLP      10919   10-16-88     4:50p
        2 File(s)       350208 bytes free
```

Copy a file into the new directory. Enter

copy \norton\nu.exe a:\subdir ↵

What types of changes occur on the disk when a new directory is added? Once again the main Norton Utilities program provides a means of examining the changes made to the disk. Enter

nu a: ↵

Display the root directory once again by entering

↵ *(4 times)*
e

The root directory is displayed as shown in Figure 2-22. The new directory appears in this display as if it were a file name. Note that the directory entry has been written in the slot formerly occupied by the NU.EXE file. The entry has the **Dir** attribute active to indicate that this entry is not a file but a directory.

```
 Root dir                                              Directory format
  Sector 5 in root directory                               Offset 0, hex 0
                                                            Attributes
 Filename Ext     Size      Date      Time     Cluster  Arc R/O Sys Hid Dir Uol
        .
 SUBDIR                    8-21-89    1:35 pm      2                       Dir
 NU       HLP    10919   10-16-88    4:50 pm    140     Arc R/O
 test_dis k                8-18-89   11:06 am                                  Uol
                 unused directory entry
                 unused directory entry
                 unused directory entry
                  unused directory entry
                  unused directory entry
                  unused directory entry
                   unused directory entry
                    unused directory entry
                    unused directory entry
                     unused directory entry
                      unused directory entry
                       unused directory entry
                       unused directory entry
        .
         Filenames beginning with 'σ' indicate erased entries
                     Press Enter to continue
 1Help  2Hex   3Text  4Dir   5FAT   6Partn  7       8Choose 9Undo  10QuitNU
```

Figure 2-22 New directory appears in the root directory listing.

There are several points worth noting.

1. The directory is listed just like a file with a few minor exceptions. The directory entry has no extension and no file size. Also the attribute display shows Dir in the directory column. The directory is allocated a starting cluster number, 2, just like a file. When you create a directory you use up one data cluster, even if you never put any files in that directory.

2. Remember that you made three additions to disk A, two directories and a file, but the root directory shows only one change, the addition of the SUBDIR directory. This is an indication that adding a directory expands the total amount of files you can have on the disk.

To get a more detailed look at the structure of a directory, display the contents of the SUBDIR directory. Enter

[F8] ↵

↓ ↵

The program displays the contents of the new directory which is stored in cluster 2 as shown in Figure 2-23. DOS automatically places two entries at the beginning of each data cluster, which will function as a directory. The names of the files are . (period) and .. (double period). The period entry is assigned to cluster 2 and represents the SUBDIR directory. The double period file indicates the location of the parent directory. In this case there is no value entered for the starting cluster indicating that the parent of this directory is the root directory. The third entry in the directory is a normal file entry, the file that you copied into the directory from the hard disk drive.

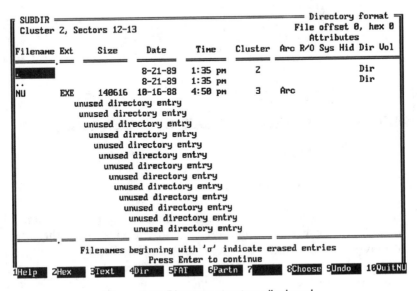

Figure 2-23 Directory structure displayed.

The two files period and double period make it possible to have the DOS tree-structured directory system since each directory could be linked to its parent directories.

It is important to keep in mind that even though you can have many directories, there is only one FAT table. Directories allow you to increase the total number of files stored on a disk by adding more slots for directory entries but they do not increase the amount of space you have to store them in or the size of the FAT. In fact, since each directory takes up a cluster that otherwise would be used for data storage, the directories decrease the total amount of data stored on the disk.

If you erase all the files in a directory, you will probably want to remove the directory as well using the RD command. If you don't remove the directory the data cluster used for the directory will still occupy a cluster even though you have removed all the files.

Exit the Norton Utilities program by entering

[F10]

Summary

This section was designed to provide a primer on the fundamental concepts employed by MS DOS computers to store information on disks, both hard and floppy. It also demonstrated how the main Norton Utilities program allows you to peer beneath the surface and see exactly how a disk is organized. Below is a brief summary of the major ideas presented in this section.

- **Role of DOS.** DOS is a master program used to oversee all of the operations on your computer.

- **Disk Organization.** One of the primary roles of DOS is to organize and maintain data and program files on disk storage. DOS creates physical unit--tracks and sectors-, -and logical units--directories, file allocation tables, and data clusters.

- **The Main Norton Utilities**. The Norton Utilities main program enables you to examine each of these structures directly. By using this program you can display disk information in a way that DOS normally will not permit.

This ability is the basis for the Norton Utility programs discussed in this book. These programs allow you to manipulate the disk structures in ways that are easier and more powerful than the tools provided by DOS.

Section II

Batch Files

Batch files, one of the most powerful features of MS-DOS, allow you to create simple programs from text files containing DOS commands. With batch files you can automate a wide variety of operations that would otherwise require manual entry of a series of DOS commands.

In addition, as with most programming situations, the effect of a batch file often appears to be more than the sum of its individual commands. For example, one of the most important uses of a batch file is to build a menu that can help organize your computer. No single DOS command can create a menu but by using a series of commands organized in a batch file you can create the effect.

When batch files are combined with some of the programs supplied in Norton Utilities you will find that you can create a variety of useful tools that help make operation of your computer system easier for you or for others using your computer.

The first objective of this chapter is to show you how to create a number of useful batch file programs. The second objective is to teach you the basic principles behind DOS batch file creation so that you can develop your own ideas beyond the examples given in this chapter.

Getting Ready To Work

In order to perform the operations discussed in this section you will need access to the following files:

DOS Programs:
EDLIN.EXE(DOS 3) or EDLIN.COM(DOS 2) FORMAT.EXE(DOS 3) or FORMAT.COM(DOS 2)

Norton Utility Programs:

NU (Norton Utilities Main Program) BE.EXE (Batch Enhancer program) TM.EXE (Time Mark program) LP.EXE (Line Printing program) NI.EXE (Norton Integrator program)

If you followed the instructions in Chapter 1 you should have all these files copied to a directory called \NORTON on your hard disk. In order to get access to these files you must make sure that a PATH has been opened to this directory. You will also need access to DOS programs such as EDLIN. If they are stored in a directory different from your Norton Utilities programs you must open a path to both directories. Example:

PATH c:\dos;c:\norton; ↵

Access to these programs will enable you to carry out the procedures outlined in this chapter.

For information about path and installing the Norton Utility programs, see Chapter 1.

Floppy Disk

The chapters in this section make use of the floppy disk described in Section 1. The disk is assumed to be a 360K floppy with a directory called SUBDIR on it. There are also two files on the disk: NU.HLP in the root directory and NU.EXE in the \SUBDIR directory.

Safety Storage

The procedures used in Chapters 3 through 5 require you to create a new **AUTOEXEC.BAT** file. If you already have an **AUTOEXEC.BAT** in the root directory of your hard drive, make a copy of it so you can restore the original after you have worked through this chapter. You can create a copy of the file by entering

COPY autoexec.bat saveexec.bat ↵

Should you later desire to restore this file to its original name, simply reverse the process by entering

COPY saveexec.bat autoexec.bat ↵

3

Batch File Basics

Batch files are a means by which you can create your own custom-designed DOS routines. Batch files use the commands available in DOS to create *batches* of commands that execute when you enter the name of the batch file. Batch files allow you to create a customized environment from the DOS commands, that would ordinarily be entered one at a time. In addition to the basic set of DOS commands, batch files can contain some specialized DOS batch subcommands that operate **only** in batch files.

The purpose of this chapter is to provide the reader with a basic understanding of how DOS batch files work and what the basic batch subcommands are. In Chapter 4 you will use the Norton Utilities Batch Enhancer and Time Mark programs to create sophisticated batch file programs. If you are already familiar with writing batch files you may want to skip this chapter.

Creating Batch Files

A common misconception is the belief that in order to create DOS batch files you **must** use the EDLIN program. EDLIN is a *line editor* program supplied with DOS. Most books covering batch files use EDLIN for the creation of batch files, since every person who has DOS also has EDLIN. However, a DOS batch file can be created by any program that creates ASCII-compatible text files. The list of programs that can create ASCII files involves almost every major computer application, including most word processors. For example, you could create an ASCII text file with Lotus 1-2-3 by using the / Print File command. While this is not the best way to create batch files, it certainly can be done.

> *When you create a text file with 1-2-3, you can suppress page formatting, such as page breaks and margins, by using the / Print File Options Other Unformatted command. This will produce an ASCII file without extra blank lines or spaces used for page formatting.*

The most common ways to create text files such as batch files are listed below:

- **COPY CON:** *filename*. This method requires no special programs and can be implemented whenever you have a DOS prompt. This approach uses the DOS COPY command to transfer text directly from the keyboard to a text file. Example:

    copy con: autoexec.bat ↵

    lotus ↵

    [F6] ↵

    The first line of this sequence tells DOS to copy the keystrokes entered from the keyboard into a file called AUTOEXEC.BAT. The second line enters the keystrokes l-o-t-u-s-↵ as the text of the file. The [F6] key is used to insert a [Ctrl/z] character into the file. In an ASCII text file, the [Ctrl/z] character marks the end of the file. In this technique, [F6] serves a dual purpose: it inserts the [Ctrl/z] at the end of the file and it signals DOS that you have completed the entry and wish to return to the systems level.

    The advantage of this method of creating text files is that the DOS command COPY is memory resident and can be executed at any time. On the other hand, there is no way to edit text, that is, to make changes or corrections. In practice this method is used only to create the simplest files that consist of one or two modest commands.

- **EDLIN.** The EDLIN (line editor) program is supplied with DOS. It is a popular way to create batch files because everyone who has DOS has it available. Keep in mind that EDLIN is a program, EDLIN.EXE (DOS 3 or higher) or EDLIN.COM (DOS 1 and 2). This means that the file must be available when you try to edit. Available means that the file is located in the disk directory you are working in or is located in a disk and directory to which you have a path to DOS open. (For a discussion of DOS paths, see Chapter 1.)

    EDLIN is superior to COPY CON: because you can enter, revise, copy, even search and replace information. Another important capability of EDLIN is that you can insert special characters, such as Control characters, into your files. As you will see, these control characters enable your batch files to use special attributes of your screen display (brightness or colors) and your printer (font and point size.)

Word Processing

Batch files can be created with word processing programs such as WordStar, WordPerfect, Microsoft Word, and PFS Write. Word processing programs offer many editing advantages over EDLIN and are generally easier to use. Of course, since they are more complex programs they require more disk space and take longer to load than a simple editor like EDLIN. A word processor makes sense when you already have the program installed on your hard disk and are familiar with its use.

While all of these programs use slightly different file structures to store word processing documents, they also have commands that store the text as an ASCII text file.

- **WordStar.** Create text files by using the **N**(on-document) command from the main menu. If you are using WordStar 2000 you must select the UNFORM format file when you create the document.

- **Word.** To create a text file use the Transfer Save command. This command displays a menu with an option called Formatted, in Version 4.0 and earlier. When Formatted is On, the text is saved as a Word Document. Change the setting to Off and Word saves the file in ASCII text format. In Version 5.0 the option is called Format and the item to select is called **Text-only.**

- **WordPerfect.** The [Ctrl/F5] command displays a menu that lists the WordPerfect options for saving text in ASCII format. Option 1 will create a text file. You can also create a text file using option 6. The two options differ with respect to the way that paragraph text is treated. In option 1, a paragraph is saved as a series of individual lines of text, each one ending with a ↵ character. In option 6, WordPerfect saves all the text of a single paragraph as one long line of text and places only a single ↵ at the end of the paragraph. This file format is identical to the ASCII format created by Word. Note that the distinction affects text typed in paragraph form. Since batch files are always composed of single lines, this difference is irrelevant to batch file creation.

- **PFS Write.** The [Ctrl/s] command allows you to specify ASCII as the file type. Enter [Tab] twice, then A. The file will be saved as an ASCII text file.

- **The Norton Editor.** The Norton Editor, discussed in Chapter 13 of this book, is specifically designed for creating programs and batch files on the IBM PC. It combines a word processor-like interface with the speed and compactness of a line editor.

In this book the assumption is made that you will be creating your batch files with EDLIN. If you are more comfortable using a word processing program, you should have no problem creating the same batch files. If you are using a word processing program, keep in mind that EDLIN-specific editing instructions shown in this text will not apply.

Using EDLIN to Create a Batch File

The simplest form of batch file is one that consists of a list of DOS commands. For example, suppose you wanted to list the files stored on the floppy disk in drive A. You would need to enter two separate DIR commands because each DIR command will list files from only one directory. Since there are two directories on the disk in drive A, you need to enter two commands:

DIR a:\ ↵
DIR a:\subdir ↵

In order to make the relationship between command words and user-defined terms clearer, all command words used in batch commands will appear in upper-case characters. You have the option of entering the characters as lower-case since DOS will not distinguish between upper- and lower- case characters, unless they are part of a text string. These exceptions will be noted.

You could save some time by creating a batch file that would perform both commands. The EDLIN program can be used to create batch files. Suppose you want to name the batch you are about to create, FILELIST. The batch file must have a BAT extension making the full batch file name FILELIST.BAT. To create that file with EDLIN, enter

EDLIN filelist.bat ↵

EDLIN displays the words **New file** and a * prompt. The * means that EDLIN is ready to accept a command as shown in Figure 3-0.

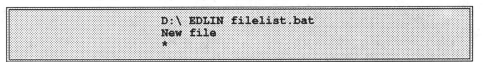

Figure 3-1 EDLIN displays * prompt.

A full discussion of the command in the EDLIN program is beyond the scope of this book. Below are a list of the most important commands in EDLIN. Note that EDLIN commands consist of single-letter commands.

i   **Insert.** Add new lines to the file. Once initiated, a new line is added each time a ↵ is entered. To stop inserting lines, enter [Ctrl/c].

l   **List.** This command lists the lines in the current file.

d   **Delete.** This command deletes the specified line or lines from the file.

e   **Exit.** This command saves the current file and exits the EDLIN program.

Begin inserting lines into the file by entering

i ↵

The program responds by listing the number of the new line, in this case 1, with an * next to it as shown in Figure 3-2.

```
D:\ EDLIN filelist.bat
New file
*i
        1:*
```

Figure 3-2 EDLIN Insert mode active.

Enter the two DIR commands.

DIR a: ↵
DIR a:\subdir ↵

To exit the insertion mode, enter

[Ctrl/c]

Save the file by entering

e ↵

You can use the DOS command TYPE to display the contents of the file you have just created as shown in Figure 3-3.

TYPE filelist.bat ↵

```
D:\ type filelist.bat
DIR a:\
DIR a:\subdir
```

Figure 3-3 Contents of batch file displayed on screen.

Execute the batch file by entering

filelist ↵

The batch file executes both commands and displays the listings generated by the DIR commands, as shown in Figure 3-4.

```
D:\ filelist

D:\ DIR a:\

 Volume in drive A is test_disk
 Directory of  A:\

SUBDIR        <DIR>        8-21-89    1:35p
NU      HLP     10919  10-16-88    4:50p
        2 File(s)     208896 bytes free

D:\ DIR a:\subdir

 Volume in drive A is test_disk
 Directory of  A:\SUBDIR

.             <DIR>        8-21-89    1:35p
..            <DIR>        8-21-89    1:35p
NU      EXE    140616  10-16-88    4:50p
        3 File(s)     208896 bytes free
```

Figure 3-4 Output of batch file.

Using ECHO OFF

When you look at the results of the FILELIST batch, you will notice that the commands in the batch file appear with the results. In most cases there is no need to clutter the display with the commands. It would be better to output only the results of the commands. You can control the display with the DOS command,

ECHO. When the command ECHO OFF is issued in a batch file, none of the commands that follow are displayed, only their results.

Since ECHO OFF counts as a command, it would normally appear because the effect of ECHO OFF would follow, not precede, the ECHO OFF command. In order to get around this problem, DOS allows you to precede the ECHO OFF command with an @ character. This causes DOS to suppress the display of the ECHO OFF command, making the batch run without the display of commands.

The CLS command will clear the screen so that any information currently on the screen will be erased before the batch file displays its output.

Add the @ECHO OFF and CLS commands to the FILELIST batch file.

EDLIN filelist.bat ↵

The prompt this time reads **End of input file**, indicating that you are revising an existing file, not creating a new file. Insert two lines at the beginning of the file. Enter

i ↵
@ECHO OFF ↵
CLS ↵
[Ctrl/c]

The batch file now has four commands, as shown in Figure 3-5. List the batch file by entering

l ↵

```
*1
        1: @ECHO OFF
        2: CLS
        3:*DIR a:\
        4: DIR a:\subdir

    *
```

Figure 3-5 Modified batch file.

Save and execute the batch file by entering

e ↵
filelist ↵

The results of the batch file, shown in Figure 3-6, no longer contain the DIR commands. This makes for a cleaner, more readable display.

```
        Volume in drive A is test_disk
        Directory of  A:\

SUBDIR          <DIR>        8-21-89    1:35p
NU         HLP      10919  10-16-88    4:50p
        2 File(s)      208896 bytes free

        Volume in drive A is test_disk
        Directory of  A:\SUBDIR

   .            <DIR>        8-21-89    1:35p
   ..           <DIR>        8-21-89    1:35p
NU         EXE     140616  10-16-88    4:50p
        3 File(s)      208896 bytes free
```

Figure 3-6 ECHO OFF suppresses display of commands in batch file.

Batch Files with Variables

You can create batch files that accept variables. For example, suppose you want to copy individual Norton Utilities programs to the \SUBDIR directory of the floppy disk. If you wanted to copy the Safe Format program, you would use a command that reads:

COPY\norton\sf.exe a:\subdir

If you wanted to copy the File Attribute program. you would use a command like the following:

COPY\norton\fa.exe a:\subdir

If you examine the two commands, you will notice that they are the same, except for the filename portion of the command. A general form of the command would read as follows, where ???????? stands for the filename.

COPY\norton???????.exe a:\subdir

The ???????? is a type of fill-in blank into which you substitute various file names. This can be done in batch files by placing a variable into the batch file command at the point where the substitution takes place. Batch file variables begin with % symbols and are followed by a single digit, 1-9. This allows you to use up to nine different variables in the same batch file.

In this example, the batch file will be a very simple one. Create the batch file by entering

EDLIN move.bat ↵

Activate the insert mode by entering

i ↵

The first command will be the @ECHO OFF to suppress the echo of the commands to the screen.

@ECHO OFF ↵

The next command is the one that actually copies the file. Note that a variable symbol, %1, is inserted into the command where the name of the file would ordinarily be placed. No extra space is needed between the other characters and the variable.

COPY \norton\%1.exe a:\subdir ↵

The last command in the batch file is an ECHO command used to display a message on the screen. The message simply comfirms that the batch file has completed the task. The variable name is used again to insert the variable text into the message. Enter

ECHO %1.EXE copied to drive A ↵

Save and exit by entering

[Ctrl/c] e ↵

Executing a Program with a Variable

You may be wondering how the variable symbol used in the batch file is assigned a specific value. DOS allows you to assign the variable a specific value by using an *argument* with the name of the batch file. An *argument* is a word that follows the batch file. DOS automatically assigns the first word following the name of the batch file to the variable %1. For example, the command below will execute the MOVE batch file and assign the name SF to the variable %1.

MOVE sf

If the batch file name is followed by more than one word, they are, in turn, assigned to the variables %2, %3, %4, etc. up to %9.

> *The variable %0 can also be used in a batch file. %0 refers to the first item in the batch command line, which will always be the name of the batch file itself.*

Use the MOVE batch file to copy the SF.EXE file to the disk in drive A. Enter

MOVE sf ↵

The batch copies the file and displays a message that confirms its action, as shown in Figure 3-7. The batch file used the argument SF as the value for the %1 variable.

```
                      1 File(s) copied
              sf.EXE copied to drive A
```

Figure 3-7 Message displayed by MOVE batch file.

You can copy a different file with MOVE by changing the argument. Enter

MOVE ff ↵

The batch file uses the new argument to copy a different file. Using variables is important in batch files because doing so allows you to create more generalized batch programs, which can be used in a variety of circumstances.

Suppressing Program Output

Batch files often make use of DOS utility or other programs, to carry out operations during the batch processing. In the MOVE batch, the actual copying is carried out by the DOS Copy command. These commands often have standard output sent that they send to the screen automatically. In the MOVE batch, the message **"1 File(s) copied**" is automatically generated by the COPY command. In many cases, you may find that the standard screen output of these commands, or programs, places text on the screen that might be confusing to a user.

DOS provides a technique that can be used to suppress the display of this information. This allows you to control exactly what messages are placed on the screen. If the command in the batch file is followed by **>NUL**, DOS will not display the messages generated by that command or DOS utility program.

The **>NUL** is a special form of the DOS redirection command. It literally tells the command to redirect its output to a *null device*. The term null device refers to a nonexistent hardware item. The practical effect is that instead of placing the output on the screen, it does not appear at all.

Adding this option to the COPY command in the MOVE batch file will suppress the **1 File(s) copied** message. You might want to use ECHO to add a message of your own.

Load the MOVE.BAT file into the EDLIN edit program by entering

EDLIN move.bat ↵

List the lines in the batch file.

L ↵

Line 2 is the one you want to modify. In EDLIN, you can gain access to an existing line by entering the line number. Enter

2 ↵

The [F1] and [F3] keys operate just as they do when entering commands directly in DOS. The [F1] key displays the next character and [F3] displays the rest of the characters. In this case, repeat the entire line and add the redirection to the end. Enter

[F3]
>NUL ↵

Because you are suppressing the message, you might want to add a message of your own design in its place. In this case, it will be a message that tells the user what file is being copied. To insert a new line at a specific location in the file, enter the line number along with the **i** command. Enter

2i ↵
ECHO Copying File %1.EXE ... ↵

Save and exit the batch file by entering

[Ctrl/c] e ↵

Use the MOVE.BAT file to copy the FA.EXE (File Attribute program) to drive A.

MOVE fa ↵

The output of the program consists of the two messages you issued with ECHO commands, as shown in Figure 3-8.

```
          Copying File fa.EXE ...
          fa.EXE copied to drive A
```

Figure 3-8 ECHO commands display message for MOVE batch file.

The MOVE batch file now displays only the information you specifically designed it to display.

Conditional Structures

Suppressing the standard message with the >NUL option has one disadvantage. The messages displayed by the program will be the same, whether or not a file has actually been copied. For example, suppose the argument you enter for the MOVE batch file is XXX. This means that the batch would attempt to copy the file XXX.EXE. Since there is probably no file in the \NORTON directory with that name, the COPY command will not copy any files.

The standard message used by the copy command would be **XXX.EXE not found** and **0 File(s) copied**. However, because you have suppressed this output, no warning would appear. As an example, enter

MOVE xxx ↵

The program displays a message indicating that it **did** copy the file, when in fact it did **not**. One solution is to remove the >NUL and let the standard message appear.

A second solution is to create a more complex batch file that takes into account the possibility that a file matching the variable name might not exist. In order to create such a batch file, you have to add a *conditional* structure to it. A conditional structure uses several commands to set up a batch file that reacts to specific conditions. In this case, you want the batch file to determine if the file exists, before it tries to copy the file.

Building conditional structures in batch files requires the use of the following:

- **IF.** The IF command allows you to perform a test inside of a batch file. For example, the command **"IF EXISTS autoexec.bat"** tests for the existance of the AUTOEXEC.BAT file. The IF command can be used to activate a specific GOTO command so that the batch will jump to a specific part of the batch file. Example:

IF EXISTS autoexec.bat GOTO make copy

- **GOTO.** The GOTO command can be used by itself or in conjunction with an IF command. GOTO allows you to skip to a specific section of the batch file. Example:1

GOTO end

- **Labels.** A **label** is used to mark a specific location in the batch file. Labels begin with a colon character. Labels work in conjunction with GOTO commands. When a GOTO command is issued, the batch file is searched for a label that matches the name used in the GOTO command. The batch resumes execution with the command following the label. Example:

:end

Create a new batch file called MOVEIT.BAT by entering

EDLIN moveit.bat ↵

Begin the batch file with the @ECHO OFF command.

i ↵
@ECHO OFF ↵

The next command is an IF command that tests if the file that is designated as the file to be copied actually exists. The IF command will use a GOTO command to skip to the label MOVEFILE, if the file exists. Note that the label MOVEFILE does not exist as yet. You will create it later in the batch. Enter

IF EXIST %1.EXE GOTO movefile ↵

The previous command jumps to the MOVEFILE label if the file exists. What will happen if the file does not exist? The answer is that instead of going to MOVEFILE, the batch will continue with the next command. This means that if the file does **not** exist, the next command is the one that will be executed. In this case that command should inform the user that the file he wanted to copy does not exist. Enter

ECHO File %1.EXE Not Found. Copy not make. ↵

The next command is a GOTO command. It will jump to a label called **end**. This ensures that the batch file will not attempt to copy a nonexistent file. Enter

GOTO end ↵
↵

This ends the first section of the program. The next line, line 6, is a label that identifies the next section of the batch file. In this case, that section will be labeled MOVEFILE. Enter

:movefile

Note that the colon preceding MOVEFILE identifies this as a label. The MOVEFILE section contains the commands you used in the MOVE.BAT file. Enter

ECHO Copying File %1.EXE ... ↵
COPY \norton\%1.exe a:\subdir>NUL ↵
ECHO %1.EXE copied to drive A ↵
↵

You have now completed the MOVEFILE section of the batch file. The last entry is another label called END. The END label will not have any commands. It is placed in the batch file so that the MOVEFILE section can be skipped when the file does not exist. It matches up with the **GOTO end** command used in the beginning of the program. Exit the Insert mode and list the batch file by entering

[Ctrl/c] L ↵

Below is the listing of the batch file. The lines are added to show how the GOTO command controls the flow of the commands, allowing the batch file to display different messages, depending upon the existence of the specified file.

```
 1: @ECHO OFF
 2: IF EXIST \norton\%1.exe GOTO movefile
 3: ECHO File %1.EXE Not Found. Copy not make.
 4: GOTO end
 5:
 6: :movefile
 7: ECHO Copying File %1.EXE ...
 8: COPY \norton\%1.exe a:\subdir>NUL
 9: ECHO %1.EXE copied to drive A
10:
11:*:end
```

Save the batch file by entering

e ↵

Use the new program to copy a file that does exist. Enter

MOVEIT si ↵

The program copies the file to drive A and displays the same set of messages as the MOVE batch file. Now try the same process using a non existent file name.

MOVEIT xxx ↵

This time the program reacts to the fact that no file with the name XXX.EXE exists in the \NORTON directory. It displays the message **"File xxx.EXE Not Found. Copy not made."**

Conditional structures make batch files much more flexible, and therefore more useful to you and other users.

The Autoexec Batch File

The AUTOEXEC.BAT file is special because of its relationship to DOS. When the computer boots, DOS automatically looks for a batch file called

AUTOEXEC.BAT in the root directory of the disk from which it is booting. If a batch file with exactly that name exists, the commands in the file are automatically executed.

> *The instruction to look for a file with exactly the name of AUTOEXEC.BAT is actually contained in the COMMAND.COM file. You can test this idea by using TS (Text Search), a program used to locate a specific group of characters on your disk. The program tells you what files contain that string of characters. (You will find more details about Text Search in Section 3.)*

The AUTOEXEC.BAT is important because it allows you to create a *turnkey* system, based on one or more batch files. A *turnkey* system is one that automatically executes each time the computer is turned on. Creation of batch files can be used to created a *shell* around DOS so that someone using the computer can perform tasks and run programs without having to deal directly with DOS.

Config.sys and the Ansi.sys Driver

Certain of the features discussed in this next section depend upon the use of the ANSI device driver. This driver is supplied with MS-DOS in a file called ANSI.SYS. The reason for discussing this file now is that you will need to have the ANSI driver loaded, in order for the utilities to operate properly.

One way to tell if the ANSI system is loaded is to execute the Batch Enhancer program. Enter

be sa normal ↵

If the ANSI driver is not installed, the program will display the following message:

Setting the Screen Attributes requires the ANSI.SYS element of DOS Color may change

Another way to determine if the ANSI driver is loaded is to list the contents of CONFIG.SYS file which should be located in the root directory of the disk from which the computer boots. Enter

type \config.sys ↵

This command lists the contents of the CONFIG.SYS file that are on your hard disk. The CONFIG.SYS file is the one that loads the ANSI.SYS driver into memory when the system boots. Remember that just having the file ANSI.SYS on your hard disk is not enough. The CONFIG.SYS file, if any, must contain an instruction to load that driver into memory, or it will have no effect. If you get the message "File not found," you will need to create a CONFIG.SYS file. If you have a CONFIG.SYS it should contain a line that loads the ANSI.SYS driver. Examples:

DEVICE=ANSI.SYS
or
DEVICE=C:\DOS\ANSI.SYS

The ANSI driver allows you to use batch file commands to control various aspects of the screen display, including the colors used if you are working with a color monitor.

> *The ANSI driver can be used with batch commands that issue special [Esc] code sequences. The Batch Enhancer program included with the Norton Utilities package allows you to access the ANSI features without having to create the [Esc] sequences. The Norton Control Center program also makes use of the ANSI driver.*

The ANSI.SYS driver is needed by some options in the Batch Enhancer program which will be used in the next chapter. If you do not load the ANSI driver the Batch Enhancer program will not operate properly.

Summary

This chapter introduced the basic concepts involved in DOS batch files.

- **Batch Files.** Batch files are text files that contain DOS commands. These files can be stored on the disk and directly executed by DOS. They allow you to record and execute lists of DOS commands by simply entering the name of the batch file. All batch files **must** have a BAT file extension.

- **EDLIN.** DOS batch files are standard ASCII text files. The EDLIN program is provided with DOS to enable you to create ASCII text files. You can also create ASCII text files, including batch files, with popular word processing programs such as Word, WordPerfect, and WordStar.

- **ECHO.** The ECHO command can be used in two ways: (1) It turns ON or OFF the display of the commands in the batch file as they are executed. When ECHO is OFF the commands do not appear. (2) It can be used to display a text string on the screen from a batch file. ECHO enables you to display messages during a batch file. The command

@ECHO OFF will also suppress itself. It is used to create a batch file where none of the commands, including ECHO OFF, are displayed.

- **NUL.** The name NUL is used to represent a nonexistent device. The NUL device is used with a DOS redirection command to suppress output from a command or program. This technique is used in batch files to suppress the usual screen output of DOS commands that are executing as part of the batch file.

- **Variables.** DOS allows you to define up to nine variables for use in a batch file. The variables are %1 through %9. The variables are assigned values when you execute the batch file by using arguments following the batch file name. The symbol %0 will always be a variable equal to the name of the batch file.

- **IF.** The IF command can be used to test for conditions during the execution of a batch file. The EXISTS clause tests for the existence of a specific file. The IF command is usually combined with a GOTO command which will cause execution to jump to a new location inside the batch file.

- **GOTO.** The GOTO command causes the execution within a batch file to continue at a specific location. The locations are determined by the entry of labels into the batch file. GOTO can be used by itself, or in conjunction with an IF command.

- **Labels.** A label is used to mark a specific location within a batch file. The location is referenced in GOTO commands. When a GOTO command is issued, the execution in the batch file stops until the specified label is located. Execution resumes with the first command in the batch file following the label. Labels always begin with a colon.

- **ANSI driver.** The ANSI driver is a device driver supplied with DOS. When installed, it enables you to control various aspects of the screen display from DOS batch files using special [Esc] commands. The Batch Enhancer and Norton Control Center programs make use of ANSI commands and require that the ANSI.SYS driver be loaded into memory if these programs are to operate properly. The ANSI.SYS driver is loaded using the CONFIG.SYS file.

Batch Files Listings

The batch files created in this chapter were:

FILELIST.BAT

```
@ECHO OFF
CLS
DIR a:\
DIR a:\subdir
```

MOVE.BAT

```
@ECHO OFF
ECHO Copying File %1.EXE ...
COPY \norton\%1.exe a:\subdir>NUL
ECHO %1.EXE copied to drive A
```

MOVEIT.BAT

```
@ECHO OFF
IF EXIST \norton\%1.exe GOTO movefile
ECHO File %1.EXE Not Found. Copy not make.
GOTO end

:movefile
ECHO Copying File %1.EXE ...
COPY \norton\%1.exe a:\subdir>NUL
ECHO %1.EXE copied to drive A

:end
```

4

Enhanced Batch Files

In the previous chapter you learned the basic operations of DOS batch files. DOS batch files represent powerful tools that can be used to organize and systematize your computer. On many systems, batch files are used to present arrangements of menus that allow the user to run programs and carry out tasks-such as backing up files or formatting disks-without ever having to enter a DOS command. Such systems are easier and faster to use than are direct entries of DOS commands. These systems also eliminate potential loss of data, which may occur when entering DOS commands. In addition, a system organized with batch files can be used by people with little or no experience with MS-DOS.

While useful, DOS batch files have a number of limitations.

- **Interactive Commands.** If you want to create and use menus, a method is necessary by which you can display a question on the screen and have the user enter a response. With menus, the response is usually a single character. DOS does not have any built-in facility for this type of interactive dialog. Typically, a menu created with DOS commands displays any number of options, labeled 1, 2, 3, etc. The batch file then ends. The user responds by typing a number. The number has no meaning to DOS but you can create an illusion of meaning by creating batch files with names, like 1.BAT, 2.BAT, 3.BAT, etc. When the user types 1 ↵, he executes the 1.BAT batch file. Though workable, this method is rather clumsy to program and to use.

- **Colors.** The ANSI driver enables you to change the screen colors; however, to do so in DOS requires the creation and output of special [Esc] strings. For example, to change the screen colors to white letters on a blue background, you would have to use a command like this:

PROMPT $e[37;44m

In the previous command, 37 is the code for a white foreground color, and 44 is the code for a blue background color. The strings are difficult to create and the code numbers are hard to remember.

- **Location of Text.** The ANSI driver also provides [Esc] commands that place text at certain locations on the screen. Like the [Esc] commands used for colors, these require you to remember or look up special codes that control the horizontal and vertical location of the text.

The Batch Enhancer program solves these problems and also offers other useful options that can greatly improve the appearance and utility of your batch files. In this chapter you learn how to use the features of the Batch Enhancer program and how to develop batch files that combine DOS batch file commands with the Batch Enhancer program.

The Batch Enhancer Program

The previous chapter demonstrated some of the basic tools provided by DOS, with which batch files can be created. However, in many respects, those basic batch file tools are incomplete. The Batch Enhancer was created to augment the DOS batch file commands with the additional tools needed to facilitate batch file programming.

> *If you have used previous versions of the Norton Utilities, you will find that the Batch Enhancer program combines the features found in several individual programs from earlier versions with some new features. The functions of the ASK.EXE, SA.EXE, and BEEP.EXE programs can now be executed as options within the Batch Enhancer program.*

The Batch Enhancer program consists of nine subcommands that can be used to extend the types of programs you can create with DOS batch files.

- **ASK.** The ASK subcommand is one of the most important parts of the Batch Enhancer program because it provides a method by which menu selections can be made within batch files. ASK allows you to display a message and receive a single character response from the user. This response can be used with the DOS batch file command IF to branch the batch file execution to a specific label within the batch file, similar to the structure used in the MOVEIT.BAT. (See Chapter 3.)

- **BEEP.** The BEEP command provides control over the speaker so you can create audio prompts as part of your batch files. The BEEP commands allow you to select the frequency, duration, and repetitions of the tones that sound during your batch file execution.

- **BOX.** The BOX subcommand is used to draw single- or double-lined boxes at specific screen locations.

- **CLS.** Clears the screen and returns the cursor to its home position in the upper-left corner of the screen. Note that this subcommand functions slightly differently from the DOS CLS command, in terms of how it treats colors. The DOS CLS command repaints the entire screen in the current colors set for DOS. These colors can be assigned using the SA subcommand. The Batch Enhancer CLS subcommand always paints the screen black when used.

- **DELAY.** This subcommand causes a pause in the execution of the batch file for a specified amount of time. The time is specified in terms of *ticks*, which are equal to 1/18 of a second. When the time is elapsed the batch file continues with the next command, if any.

- **PRINTCHAR.** This subcommand displays a specified number of repetitions of a single character.

- **ROWCOL.** This subcommand is used to position the cursor at specific locations on the screen display. This enables you to display information on any part of the screen during batch file processing.

- **SA.** The subcommand is the equivalent of the System Attributes program provided with earlier version of the Norton Utilities. It allows you to select screen colors and attributes, such as blinking.

- **WINDOW.** This subcommand is similar to BOX, in that it draws a double-lined box at the specified screen position. Windows differ from boxes in that they are always double-lined and they can have special visual effects called exploding or shadows.

The CLS and DELAY subcommands do not appear in the Norton Utilities manuals because they were added to the program after the manuals were printed.

You can use the Batch Enhancer program to execute some or all of the subcommands as part of a batch file.

> *When used at the DOS prompt, you can obtain help for any of the subcommands by entering a ? following the subcommand. Example: BE WINDOW ? ↲.*

Enhancing the Screen Display

One of the areas addressed by the Batch Enhancer subcommands is control of the screen display. The basic tool provided by DOS for displaying messages and other information during the execution of a batch file is the ECHO command.

The Batch Enhancer subcommands-OX, PRINTCHAR, ROWCOL, and WINDOW-provide you with a set of tools that allow you to place text, boxes, or groups of characters at any location on the screen display.

The BOX, ROWCOL, and WINDOW place information at specific locations on the screen. These commands view the screen as a grid of rows (horizontal) and columns (vertical). The standard screen display is divided into 25 rows and 80 columns. It may seem unusual but the first row and column are assigned the number zero, not 1. This means that the bottom row on the screen is row 24 and the column on the right edge is column 79. Table 4-1 shows a sample of the row-column address used by these commands.

Table 4-1 Screen Locations

Row-Column	Address
0,0	Upper-left corner
0,79	Upper-right corner
24,0	Lower-left corner
24,79	Lower-right corner
11,39	Center of screen

The box and window commands require two addresses. They draw the box or window between the upper-left and lower-right addresses.

The ROWCOL Subcommand

The ROWCOL subcommand performs the same basic function as the ECHO command in that it places text on the screen display. Unlike ECHO, ROWCOL allows you to specify the exact location on the screen where the text should appear. To see the effect of ROWCOL on even the simplest batch file, create a new batch file called **MOVE1.BAT**. This file will perform the same operation as the MOVE.BAT created in Chapter 3. The only difference is that you will use the Batch Enhancer ROWCOL subcommand to handle the screen display. Begin by entering

EDLIN move1.bat ↵
i ↵

The first command is the ECHO OFF command.

@ECHO OFF ↵

You can use the CLS subcommand to clear the screen. This is done to remove any text, including the DOS prompt, from the screen display.

BE CLS ↵

The next command is used to display the name of the file you are copying. Instead of using ECHO, you will use the ROWCOL Batch Enhancer subcommand. The command has the following general form:

BE ROWCOL row_number,column_number,"text"

Note that the text to be displayed **must** be enclosed in quotation marks.

> *If the text that you want to display is a single word, you do not have to enclose the text in quotations, e.g., BE ROWCOL 1,1,Hello.*

In this case the text will be placed on line 11, the middle row on the screen. Recall that if you used ECHO the text would be automatically placed on the next available row of the screen display.

BE ROWCOL 11,20,"Copying File %1.exe ..." ↵

Note that the variable %1 is simply included inside the quotation marks with the rest of the text. DOS will make the substitution in the BE command just as if BE were a DOS command. When batch files are executed, DOS treats all references to variables the same, even when they appear in command lines that refer to commands other than those provided with DOS. Complete the batch file by entering

COPY \norton\%1.exe a:\subdir>NUL ↵
BE ROWCOL 12,20,"File %1.EXE copied to drive A" ↵

The batch file reads as shown in Figure 4-1.

```
1:*@ECHO OFF
2:*BE CLS
3:*BE ROWCOL 11,20,"Copying File %1.exe ..."
4:*COPY \norton\%1.exe a:\subdir>NUL
5:*BE ROWCOL 12,20,"File %1.EXE copied to drive A"
6:*
```

Figure 4-1 ROWCOL subcommand used in batch file.

Save the batch file by entering

[Ctrl/c] e ↵

Execute the batch file by entering

move1 ff ↵

When the batch file executes, the text appears at the specified locations on the screen instead of at the top of the screen where it would have appeared if ECHO commands had been used, as shown in Figure 4-2.

```
              Copying File ff.exe ...
              File ff.exe copied to drive AC:\>
```

Figure 4-2 ROWCOL commands display text at specific locations.

If you look carefully at the display, you will notice that the DOS prompt is placed immediately following the text, rather than at the left edge of the screen where you would usually find it. This is caused by the ROWCOL subcommand. When the ROWCOL command finishes displaying text, the cursor is left next to the last position. In this case the batch file ended with the cursor being positioned following ... *drive A*. DOS displayed the system prompt following the termination of the batch file.

The DOS prompt will function normally but it presents an odd appearance. You can avoid this by ending the batch file with a command that places the DOS prompt at a more conventional location. For example, you might want to place the systems prompt in the lower-left corner of the screen when the batch file has terminated.

Load the MOVE1.BAT file into the EDLIN editor by entering

EDLIN move1.bat ↵

Add a new line to the end of the batch file by entering

6i ↵

The ROWCOL subcommand that follows uses only a row and column number with no text specified. This use of the ROWCOL subcommand simply positions the screen cursor at a location. The next text item is displayed at the specified location. In this case, the next item is the system prompt displayed by DOS. Enter

BE ROWCOL 24,0 ↵

Save and execute the batch file by entering

[Ctrl/c] r ↵
move1 ff ↵

This time the system prompt appears in the bottom left corner of the screen following the end of the batch file.

The ROWCOL commands used in this simple batch file illustrate how you can control the placement of information on the screen, during the execution of a batch file. Even in a simple program like MOVE1.BAT you can see that placing information in the center of the screen makes the program more comfortable to work with and to read. Since the data displayed on the screen is the only information a user will have about what is going on in a batch file, it is important to be able to present that information in the most understandable fashion.

Overwriting Screen Data

Because each ROWCOL subcommand contains a specific address, the information can be placed on the screen in any order you desire. When you use the ECHO command, the text is placed on the screen consecutively. Also, the screen display scrolls up one line each time an ECHO command is given. This tends to make reading the information generated by the batch file uncomfortable.

The ROWCOL command is not restricted to placing information on the screen in a top-to-bottom order. The command permits you to place information on the screen in any order. You can even overwrite information with new information.

For example, the two messages displayed in the MOVE1.BAT batch file don't need to be displayed at the same time. It would make more sense to have the second message overwrite the first message, reinforcing the idea that the file has been copied.

You can make this change by simply writing both ROWCOL messages to the same row, row 11. Load the MOVE1.BAT file into Edlin.

EDLIN move1.bat ↵

The line that needs to be changed is Line 5. This command currently displays the text on Line 12. Change the 12 to 11 so that it will overwrite the previous message. Enter

5 ↵
BE ROWCOL 11
[F3] ↵

Save and execute the batch file by entering

e ↵
move1 ff ↵

This time the second message, **File ff.exe copied to drive A**, overwrites the first message. The effect is that the screen appears to update as soon as the file copy is complete. Making this small change in the way that the information is displayed gives the program a more intuitive look because only information that is currently relevant is displayed.

Using Boxes and Windows

Another way that you can improve the appearance of the screens during a batch file is to use windows and/or boxes as part of the screen display. Boxes and windows create rectangular areas on the screen. These areas are useful in emphasizing definite areas of interest. The simplest form is the placement of a box or a window around the message. If you have more than one type of message generated by the batch file, you can display information of specific types in individual boxes or windows.

Both commands draw rectangles on the screen. However, there are some subtle but significant differences between the two commands.

- **Lines.** The Box subcommand allows you to draw either single- or double-lined boxes. Windows always have double-line borders.

- **Transparent Boxes.** Boxes are transparent in the sense that any information already on the screen that falls within the interior of the box being drawn, remains on the screen. A box will overwrite a character only if the box border is drawn directly over that character. This means that boxes can be drawn around information that has been placed on the screen before the box is drawn.

- **Opaque Windows.** Windows overwrite all information that is currently written to the area that will be covered by the window. A window always begins as a blank box, regardless of what has been written to the screen previously.

- **Special Effects.** Windows have two built-in, special visual effects: (1) EXPLODE or ZOOM affects the way the window is drawn. When selected, the window is drawn smaller than specified. The program then redraws the box one or more times until it reaches the specified size. The effect is to create the appearance of a window which is growing in size. (2) SHADOW creates a *drop shadow* effect so that the window is given a 3-D look. The shadow itself is transparent so that text covered by the shadow shows through.

    You can use either or both options when you draw a window.

The shadow effect uses a black shadow to outline the right and bottom sides of the window. On screens where the background color is black the effect of the SHADOW option will be to blank out an area to the right and bottom of the window.

Begin by adding a window to the MOVE1.BAT file. Load the file into the EDLIN editor.

EDLIN move1.bat ↵

List the lines of the batch file by entering

L ↵

You can place the messages inside a window by placing a WINDOW subcommand between Lines 2 and 3. Enter

3i ↵
BE WINDOW 7,15,15,64 ZOOM ↵

Save and execute the modified batch file.

[Ctrl/c] e ↵
move1 ff ↵

The batch file draws the window and then displays the messages within that window. The window serves to frame the information within the screen, which enhances its appearance.

Using DOS Messages

The batch files that have been run used the NUL redirection option to suppress the messages generated by the DOS commands. The messages were suppressed because the placement of the DOS messages could not be controlled. However, the ROWCOL subcommand can be used to help integrate messages automatically generated from DOS commands, into your own screen design.

For example, the COPY command generates a message that tells you the number of files copied. Up to this point you have suppressed that message. But suppose you wanted to place that message inside the window you have drawn.

This can be accomplished by using the ROWCOL subcommand. Recall what happened when you first used the ROWCOL subcommand in a batch file. The DOS prompt, which is displayed when the batch file terminates, was placed directly after the last ROWCOL text. In that instance, that was not the desired effect. But that effect can be used to your advantage. If you use a ROWCOL subcommand to position the screen cursor **before** you execute the COPY command, the message generated by the copy command will appear at the row and column location specified in the previous ROWCOL subcommand. This means you can place the message inside the window so it appears as if it were part of your screen display design.

Load the MOVE1.BAT file into the batch file EDLIN editor and list the batch file.

EDLIN move1.bat ↵
L ↵

Remove the >NUL redirection option from the COPY command in Line 5 of the batch file. Enter

5 ↵
[F3]
[backspace] *(4 times)*
↵

The standard message will now be generated when the COPY command is executed from within the batch file. In order to place that message within the window you need to execute a ROWCOL subcommand **before** the COPY command. Insert the ROWCOL subcommand by entering

5i ↵

Position the message at row 13 column 20. Enter

BE ROWCOL 13,20 ↵

In addition, use the box command to draw a box around the message. Recall that a box will not overwrite data contained within that box. Note that you need to draw the box **after** the message is generated by the COPY command.

Enter

[Ctrl/c]
7i ↵
BE BOX 12,19,14,45 ↵

Save and execute the modified batch file by entering

[Ctrl/c] e ↵
move1 ff ↵

The batch file is able to display the message, **1 File(s) copied** generated by the COPY command within the windows, with a box drawn around it as shown in Figure 4-3.

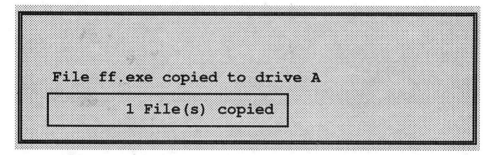

File ff.exe copied to drive A

1 File(s) copied

Figure 4-3 DOS message integrated into output window.

The ROWCOL subcommand is useful in integrating the standard messages generated by DOS commands or programs, as well as directly placing text on the screen.

Adding Special Characters

You can combine boxes and windows with other screen characters to create fully formatted screen displays. As an example you will create a new version of the MOVEIT.BAT file created in Chapter 3 that uses the Batch Enhancer subcommands to control the screen display.

Begin by creating a new batch file called MOVE2.BAT.

EDLIN move2.bat ⏎
i ⏎

Begin with the ECHO OFF command.

@ECHO OFF ⏎
BE CLS ⏎

Draw a window with the WINDOW subcommand.

BE WINDOW 8,15,16,64 ZOOM ⏎

Use ROWCOL to place a title at the top of the window. Enter

BE ROWCOL 8,27,"Move Norton Utilities Files" ⏎

Drawing Lines Within Boxes

Suppose you wanted to draw a line across the window frame under the text you just placed inside the box. The line would separate the title from the rest of the information in the box.

To create lines on the screen display you need to place characters from the IBM extended character set onto the screen with the Batch Enhancer subcommands. MS-DOS computers use a system of 254 different characters that can be displayed on the screen. Part of that set are the characters that appear on your keyboard. The other part of that set are the special characters that appear on your screen but are not found on your keyboard. The box and window borders are composed of some of these characters.

But how can you enter characters that do not appear on the keyboard? The answer is that each character has a numeric value from 1 to 254 assigned to it. Using the [Alt] key in combination with the numeric keypad allows you to enter the code number of the character you want to display. This allows you to add these characters to your text even though there are no keys on the keyboard that directly type those characters.

This method requires you to type the number that corresponds to the character you want to display. Tables 4-2 and 4-3 show the characters and the matching numeric values used to create double lines and boxes. You can see that if you wanted to draw a single line across the screen you would use character 196. A double line would use character 205.

Table 4-2 Line Characters

Single-Line Characters

179	|
180	┤
191	┐
192	└
193	┴
194	┬
195	├
196	─
217	┘
218	┌

Table 4-3 Line Characters

Double-Line Characters

185	╣
186	║
187	╗
188	╝
200	╚
201	╔
202	╩
203	╦
204	╠
205	═
206	╬

The tricky part is not the straight line, but where that line meets the frame of the window or box. In order to account for cases where single and double lines meet, the characters in Table 4-4 can be used.

Suppose you wanted to draw a single line across the window. Character 196 would be used to draw the line. The left end of the line would intersect the double line frame of the window. Character 199 could be used for the left end of the line. The right end would require character 182.

To begin drawing the line, use a ROWCOL command to position the cursor at the left border of the window, the row below the text. Display character 199 at that position.

Table 4-4 Single Line Characters

Mixed Single- and Double-Line Characters

181	╡
182	╢
183	╖
184	╕
189	╜
190	╛
198	╞
199	╟
207	╧
208	╨
209	╤
210	╥
211	╙
212	╘
213	╒
214	╓
215	╫
216	╪

> *When you want to enter a special character you begin by holding down the [Alt] key. While the [Alt] key is depressed you must type the number of the character, e.g. 199, on the numeric keypad. Note that you cannot use the numbers on the top row of the keyboard for this purpose. When you have completed typing the number, release the [Alt] key and the character will appear on the screen.*

Enter

BE ROWCOL 10,15,
[Alt/199]
↵

The ╟ character appears in the command when you use the [Alt/199] combination. Following that character you want to draw a horizontal line across the window. The window is 48 characters wide. You can use the PRINTCHAR command to display a series of repetitions of the same character. In this case that character is also a special character, 196. Enter

BE PRINTCHAR
[spacebar]
[Alt/196]
,48 ↵

The last character on the line is character 182. Because that character should be printed at the next position, you can use the PRINTCHAR subcommand to place the final character in the horizontal line. Enter

BE PRINTCHAR
[spacebar]
[Alt/182]
,1 ↵

The batch file now contains seven commands, six of which are Batch Enhancer commands used to create a window with a title.

```
1: @ECHO OFF
2: BE CLS
3: BE WINDOW 8,15,16,64 ZOOM
4: BE ROWCOL 9,27,"Move Norton Utilities Files"
5: BE ROWCOL 10,15, ╟
6: BE PRINTCHAR -,48
7: BE PRINTCHAR ╢,1
```

To see what you have accomplished so far, save and execute the batch file.

[Ctrl/c] e ↵
move2 ↵

The batch file draws the window and then draws a line across the window below the title. The special characters used at the end of the line create smooth blending of the window and the additional line as shown in Figure 4-4.

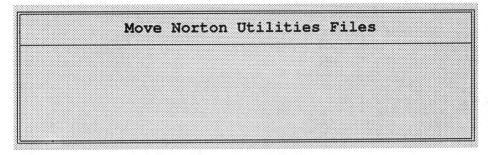

Figure 4-4 Window combined with line characters.

It took quite a few commands to create this simple display, but it is an example of how much control the Batch Enhancer program provides over the screen layout of batch files. The only major drawback to the Batch Enhancer program is that since it must be loaded and executed each time a Batch Enhancer subcommand is used, the Batch Enhancer subcommands execute slowly.

Load the MOVE2.BAT file into the EDLIN editor so that you can complete the batch file.

EDLIN move2.bat ↵

List the commands entered so far.

L ↵

The next step is to place the name of the file inside of the window. Enter

8i ↵

BE ROWCOL 12,33,"Coping File" ↵

Using Colors

The next item that needs to be placed on the screen is the name of the file that the program is copying. In order to make the name of the file stand out, you might want to change the color of the video in which the name is displayed. The BOX, PRINTCHAR, ROWCOL, and WINDOW commands provide the option of specifying the colors. The color option can apply to monochrome screens as well, allowing you to select single color attributes, such as bold or underlined text.

Color settings used with the BOX, PRINTCHAR, ROWCOL, and WINDOW commands are entered as color phrases that specify a foreground and an optional background color. There are eight colors that can be used for either foreground or background: WHITE, BLACK, RED, MAGENTA, BLUE, CYAN, YELLOW, GREEN.

> *When used with the BRIGHT attribute, the 8 colors provide 16 different colors that can be used for the foreground color. If you are using EGA or VGA display adapters the actual colors displayed for the 16 named colors can be changed to one of 64 possible colors by using the Palette option in the Norton Control Center program. Note that when you select a color from the 64 color palette it replaces one of the existing 16 colors, meaning that you are still limited to 16 colors at one time.*

The command below will display in red letters the text *Hello* using the ROWCOL subcommand.

BE ROWCOL 10,10,"Hello" RED

> *If desired, you can abbreviate the names of the colors by entering the first 3 letters of the color name: BLA, WHI, RED, GRE, YEL, BLU, CYA and MAG.*

If you want to specify a background color you would add an *on color* phrase. The command below displays the text in red letters on a blue background.

BE ROWCOL 10,10,"Hello" RED ON BLUE

In addition to colors, you can specify an attribute, either BOLD or BLINKING, for the foreground color. The command below will display the *Warning!* in blinking red letters on a white background.

BE ROWCOL 10,10,"Hello" BLINKING RED ON WHITE

> *If you want to use the BLINKING option you must specify a foreground and a background color. Using BLINKING RED without a background color will only display red letters. If you don't want to change the background color, simply specify the color currently used for the background, e.g., BLINKING RED ON BLACK. You can use the words BOLD and BRIGHT interchangeably in color specifications to produce a bright color.*

If you are using a monochrome type screen display, all colors produce white, with the exception of black which produces black, and blue which displays the character with an underline.

In this example the colors used will be BLACK and WHITE so that the batch will run the same on any type of monitor. If you are using a color display you may feel free to substitute colors of your on preference since they will not have a substantial effect on the operation of the Batch Enhancer commands. Use a ROWCOL command to display the name of the file in reverse video (black on white). Enter

BE ROWCOL 14,35,"%1.exe" BLACK ON WHITE ↵

The batch file that you have created so far simply creates a screen display. You have not placed within the batch file any commands that actually perform operations. The operations used in the MOVEIT.BAT file created in Chapter 3 involved the use of an IF command to determine if the specified file actually existed. This allowed the batch to display a warning if the file did not exist, or to display a confirmation if the file was found and copied.

The Batch Enhancer screen display option allows you to create conditional window displays that dramatically bring problems to the attention of the user. In this example batch file you would want to perform a similar test to that used in MOVEIT.BAT to determine if the file name actually matches an existing file. The command below uses a variation on the EXIST option. The test uses NOT EXIST. This option will be true if the file **does not exist**. The logic in this program is to use IF commands to test for exceptional conditions. If nothing exceptional occurs, the file is copied normally.

The command below will jump to the label NOFILE if the specified file does not exist. Enter

IF NOT EXIST \norton\%1.exe GOTO nofile ↵

Another useful test not performed in the MOVEIT.BAT program would be to check the destination disk to see if a copy of the specified file already exists. If you have already copied it, you can avoid making another copy and wasting time. Enter

IF EXIST a:\subdir\%1.exe GOTO duplicate ↵

If neither of the previous conditions is true you can assume that it is safe to make the copy. Since you will want to place the message generated by the COPY command within the window, you will first issue a ROWCOL subcommand to place the cursor at the proper position. In this case the command will position the message on the row below the file name.

BE ROWCOL 15,23 ↵

You can now use the COPY command to actually transfer the file. Enter

COPY \norton\%1.exe a:\subdir\ ↵

The final command in this section is a GOTO command that jumps to the END label. This enables the batch to skip over all the other commands in the batch that are used to handle exceptional circumstances.

GOTO end ↵
↵

Using Windows with Conditions

The next sections in the batch file will be used to present messages that warn the user if the source file does not exist, or if the destination file already exists. The message can be dramatically displayed using windows. The first window will be created under the NOFILE label and will tell the user that the specified file does not exist. To make the window more noticeable, the WINDOW subcommand uses the color option to print black on white. Enter

:nofile ↵
BE WINDOW 13,20,17,59 BLACK ON WHITE ZOOM ↵
BE ROWCOL 14,22,"The file %1.exe does not exist."
BE ROWCOL 16,22,"Program terminated without copying."
GOTO end ↵
↵

The next section, under the label DUPLICATE, will display a window with a message that warns that the file already exists. The commands are very similar to the previous section. Enter

:duplicate ↵
BE WINDOW 13,20,17,59 BLACK ON WHITE ZOOM ↵
BE ROWCOL 14,22,"The file %1.exe already exists on drive A."
BE ROWCOL 16,22,"Program terminated without copying."
GOTO end ↵
↵

The final section is the END label, which ends the program by using a ROWCOL command to place the screen cursor in the bottom left corner of the screen.

:end ↵
BE ROWCOL 24,0 ↵

Listing Long Files

The batch file you have created consists of 29 lines. Before you save the file you may want to review what you have entered. Enter

[Ctrl/c] L ↵

The EDLIN program lists Lines 19 through 29. In order to list the batch file from the beginning, you need to specify the starting line number as Line 1. Enter

1L ↵

The program lists Lines 1 through 23. To continue with the next group of lines, enter

L ↵

The batch file should contain the following commands:

```
1: @ECHO OFF
2: BE CLS
3: BE WINDOW 8,15,16,64 ZOOM
4: BE ROWCOL 9,27,"Move Norton Utilities Files"
5: BE ROWCOL 10,15, ⊬
6: BE PRINTCHAR -,48
7: BE PRINTCHAR ⊦,1
8: BE ROWCOL 12,33,"Copying File"
9: BE ROWCOL 14,35,"%1.exe" BLACK ON WHITE
10: IF NOT EXIST \norton\%1.exe GOTO nofile
11: IF EXIST a:\subdir\%1.exe GOTO duplicate
12: BE ROWCOL 15,23
13: COPY \norton\%1.exe a:\subdir
14: GOTO end
15:
16: :nofile
17: BE WINDOW 13,20,17,59 BLACK ON WHITE ZOOM
18: BE ROWCOL 14,22,"The file %1.exe does not exist."
19: BE ROWCOL 16,22,"Program terminated without copying."
20: GOTO end
21:
22: :duplicate
23: BE WINDOW 13,20,17,59 BLACK ON WHITE ZOOM
24: BE ROWCOL 14,22,"The file already exists on drive A."
25: BE ROWCOL 16,22,"Program terminated without copying."
26: GOTO end
27:
28: :end
29: BE ROWCOL 24,0
```

Save the file by entering

e ↵

Since the batch file has three possible ways of operating you will need to enter three different commands to test its operation. Begin by using the batch file to copy the SI.EXE program to drive A. Enter

move2 si ↵

The batch file displays the window with the file name in reverse video. When the file has been copied, the message is displayed within the box as shown in Figure 4-5.

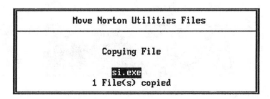

E: ↳_

Figure 4-5 Window displays message when file copied.

This time repeat the same command. Keep in mind that the SI.EXE file already exists on drive A. The program should display a message indicating that the copy will not be made because the destination file already exists. Enter

move2 si ↵

The program displays a second window with the message indicating that the specified file already exists, Figure 4-6. The IF command correctly analyzes the situation and executes the Batch Enhancer commands, that display the reverse video warning box.

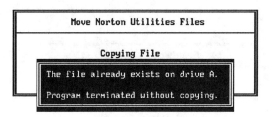

E: ↘_

Figure 4-6 Additional window display about duplicate file.

Finally, execute the batch file using the name of a nonexistent file, so you can test the display of the other warning boxes programmed into the batch. Enter

move2 xx ↵

The batch file displays the warning box, shown in Figure 4-7, which tells you no file with that name exists.

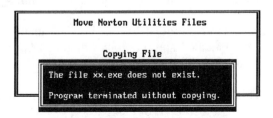

E: ↲_

Figure 4-7 Window displayed when file cannot be located.

The Batch Enhancer subcommands combined with a conditional structure of batch files enables the batch file to display information in a sophisticated manner. The appearance of the batch files more closely resembles an application, than it does the crude output usually associated with batch file operations.

Adding Sound to Batch Files

The BOX, WINDOW, ROWCOL, and PRINTCHAR subcommands provide tools for the enhancement of the screen display. The Batch Enhancer also contains a subcommand called BEEP that allows you to add sound to your batch files. Typically, sound is used to get the user's attention when an error or problem arises.

DOS has a built-in sound called the *bell*. The bell tone is inherited from the ASCII coding system used originally for Teletype machines. The [Ctrl/g] character was used to ring the bell on the Teletype machine. In the newspaper business the number of bells, i.e., the number of [Ctrl/g] characters, used to precede a story on the Teletype machine, indicated the importance of the story being sent.

You can still access the bell by using the ECHO command to send [Ctrl/g] characters. Enter

ECHO
[Ctrl/g] *(5 times)*
↵

When you enter the command, DOS responds by issuing one tone for each [Ctrl/g].

The BEEP subcommand provided by the Batch Enhancer program allows you to create more sophisticated audio output which can be integrated with the operations of a batch file. BEEP subcommand uses four switches to create a tone.

/D **Duration.** This option allows you to specify the length in clock ticks (1 clock tick = 1/18 of a second) of the tone.

/F **Frequency.** Frequency is a value in cycles per second. The greater the value the higher the pitch of the tone. For example, 262 Hz (cycles per second) is approximately the same tone as middle C. 523 Hz is close to high C.

/R **Repetitions.** This value is used to repeat a tone a specific number of times.

/W **Wait.** This switch allows you to specify in clock ticks (1/18 of a second) how much time should pass between repetitions of the tone.

As an example of the type of tones you can sound, enter the following command.

BE BEEP /F880 /D4 /R10 /W2 ↵

Sounds composed of multiple tones can be created with the BEEP subcommand by using a *tone file*. A tone file is a text file that contains the switch value for one or more tones. Instead of specifying the tone values in the BEEP subcommand, you would enter the name of the tone file. There are several advantages to using tone files.

• **Speed.** If you want to create a sound that combines several tones, a tone file will execute the series of tones faster than individual Batch Enhancer BEEP commands.

• **Easy to recall.** If you have worked out a tone that you wish to use, you can simply access the tone file instead of having to write the switch details each time.

- **Words and sound.** By adding comments to a tone file you can display characters or phrases as the tones are sounded.

Suppose you wanted to use a multiple tone sound that would flash the word **Warning!** as it sounded. You could create a tone file using the EDLIN program. Enter

EDLIN buzzer.snd ↵
i ↵

Enter the tones for the buzzer sound. The file will consist of three tones. The second and third tones will display *Warning* and *!*, respectively. The ; separates the tone information from the text comment. Enter

/F10 /D3 ↵
/F30 /D6 ; "Warning" ↵
/F20 /D9 ; "!" ↵

Save the file by entering

[Ctrl/c] e ↵

Sound the buzzer by entering

BE BEEP buzzer.snd ↵

The buzzer tone is played based on the values in the tone file. To display the words along with the sound, use the /E switch. Enter

BE BEEP buzzer.snd/E ↵

The word **Warning!** is displayed as the tone is sounded.

The BEEP subcommand can be used to play long sequences of tones by storing the tone values in a separate text file. Such a file can be used to play melodies since tone values in Hz correspond to musical notes. The Norton Utilities programs are supplied with a file called MARY which contains tones that play Mary Had a Little Lamb. To play this file, enter the command:

BE BEEP \norton\mary ↵. If you use the /E switch with this command the program will display the words to the melody as the tones are played. The words are stored as comments in the MARY tone file.

You can integrate tones, such as the buzzer sound, into batch files so your visual prompts are accompanied by audio prompts as well. For example, you might want to sound a tone when the specified file is not found. Load the MOVE2.BAT file into the EDLIN editor.

EDLIN move2.bat ↵

Insert the BEEP subcommand between lines 17 and 18 by entering

18i ↵
BE BEEP buzzer.snd ↵

Save and execute the batch file by entering

[Ctrl/c] e ↵
move2 xx ↵

This time the buzzer sound accompanies the display of the warning window.

Interactive Batch Files

So far in this chapter you have overcome the screen formatting limitation usually associated with batch files. However, there is one more major Batch Enhancer subcommand to discuss. The subcommand is the ASK subcommand. ASK provides a means by which the batch file can carry on a dialog with the user. The term dialog refers to the process by which the user can enter responses into a program while it is running.

For example, in the MOVE2.BAT program it might make sense to allow the user to decide if they want to overwrite a file if the file name already exists on the destination disk. In the current version of MOVE2.BAT, the batch file is designed to terminate whenever a duplicate file is found. The ASK subcommand allows you to create batch files in which the user can make a choice about how the batch should proceed.

The ASK Subcommand

The ASK subcommand allows the batch file to receive a single keystroke input from the user. This means that ASK allows users to answer yes or no questions, or select options from a list or menu. It does not allow the user to enter strings of characters.

The ASK subcommand will typically have two parts.

BE ASK "prompt text",key_list

- **Prompt Text.** The prompt text is simply a phrase or question you want to display so that the user will have an opportunity to enter a response. The ASK subcommand displays the prompt and then waits for the user to press a key.

- **Key List.** The key list is a list of the keys that the user might enter in response to the prompt. The key list serves two functions. First, it limits the entry made by the user to the keys in the list. If the key pressed is one of the keys in the key list, the ASK command terminates and allows the batch file to continue. If the key pressed is not part of the key list, a beep is sounded and the prompt remains active until a key list key is pressed.

    The second function of the key list is to pass a specific value to the DOS batch file option, ERRORLEVEL. The ERRORLEVEL option is used with the batch command IF. ERRORLEVEL will always have a numeric value from 0 to 255. By default the value is set at 0. The option was built into DOS to work with commands such as FORMAT, BACKUP, and RESTORE. If an error occurred during the execution of a batch file, DOS would place a value into the ERRORLEVEL that could be used to evaluate the error. The ASK subcommand takes advantage of the existence of the ERRORLEVEL option by assigning the option a value based on the user's input. The value corresponds to the position in the key list of the key that was pressed by the user.

    For example, if the key list contains the characters **abcde** and the user presses c, then ERRORLEVEL is set equal to 3. Following an ASK subcommand, a series of IF commands with ERRORLEVEL tests can be used to determine which key was pressed by the user and what actions should be taken based on that selection.

> *If you do not specify a key list with the ASK subcommand, ASK will accept any key that is pressed. The ERRORLEVEL value is set to zero. Using ASK in this manner creates a pause in the execution of the batch file which will terminate when any key is pressed.*

The ASK subcommand also accepts the following optional specifications.

- **Default.** This option sets a character which will automatically be entered if the user presses ↵ when the ASK prompt is displayed. The character set as the default does not have to be one of the characters in the key list.

The default key is also related to the use of the Timeout option. The default will be automatically entered if the user fails to make a selection during the timeout.

- **Timeout.** The Timeout option places a limit on the time the user has to respond to the ASK subcommand prompt. If the user does not enter a response with the specified number of seconds the default key is automatically entered. When Timeout is not used, the ASK subcommand will wait forever for the user to make a selection.

- **Adjust.** This option is used to add a fixed value to the ERRORLEVEL code. For example, the option ADJUST=10 would add 10 to the value of the key pressed, e.g., 3 + 10 = 13. This option would be used when the user is asked to make a selection from a series of layered menus and still have each selection create a unique ERRORLEVEL value.

- **Color.** You can use color phrases such as those used with WINDOW or ROWCOL, to set the color of the prompt text.

The ASK subcommand could be used within the MOVE2.BAT file to allow the user to decide if he wants to overwrite an existing file or not. Load the file into the EDLIN editor.

EDLIN move2.bat ↵

The changes you need to make begin on Line 26 of the batch file. Line 26 currently contains the command **BE ROWCOL 16,22,"Program terminated without copying."** Before that command executes, use the ASK subcommand to display a question that asks the user if he wants to overwrite the existing file. The user enters Y to overwrite or N to terminate the batch file. Enter

26i ↵

Since you want to display the ASK prompt inside the current window, you first have to use a ROWCOL subcommand to position the screen cursor, before issuing the ASK subcommand. Enter

BE ROWCOL 15\,22 ↵

Next, use an ASK subcommand to display the question. The ASK command allows only a Y or N answer. It also sets N as the default, so that entering ↵ will be the same as entering N.

BE ASK "Overwrite the existing file? (Y/N)",ny,DEFAULT=n ↵

Using ERRORLEVEL with ASK

If you look carefully at the ASK subcommand you will notice that the key list is sequenced differently, **ny**, than the prompt which reads (**Y/N**). The sequence used in the key list is significant because it controls the ERRORLEVEL value assigned to the user's entry. In this arrangement of the key list, an entry of N or ↵ sets the ERRORLEVEL at 1. Entering a Y sets the ERRORLEVEL at 2. In order to understand why this key sequence is so significant, it is necessary to think ahead to see how the rest of the batch file will be organized.

The commands currently used in the DUPLICATE section of the batch represent what should happen if the user does not want to overwrite the file. There is no need to jump to another section of the batch file if the user enters N or ↵. However, should the user select to overwrite the file, it would be necessary to avoid executing the existing commands, and jump to a label that would contain instructions that overwrite the file.

For example, an IF command could be used to jump to a label called OVERWRITE if the user entered Y.

IF ERRORLEVEL 2 GOTO overwrite

In using the ERRORLEVEL option you must take into consideration the arrangement of the key list. This is due to the way ERRORLEVEL determines whether the IF command is true or false. The ERRORLEVEL option does not test for **equality**, i.e., IF ERRORLEVEL does **not** mean *Is Errorlevel equal to 2*. The option actually tests the ERRORLEVEL to determine if the ERRORLEVEL is **less than or equal to** the ERRORLEVEL value. This means if the ERRORLEVEL is 2, the commands IF ERRORLEVEL **2**, IF ERRORLEVEL 1 and IF ERRORLEVEL 0 would **all** be true. Only commands that test for an

ERRORLEVEL greater than 2, e.g., IF ERRORLEVEL 3 or IF ERRORLEVEL 4, would be treated as false.

This means you should arrange the key list so that the option with the highest ERRORLEVEL value is tested first. If you have a number of options to test, the IF ERRORLEVEL commands should be arranged in descending order. That is why it is significant in this example to arrange the key list as **ny**, so that a Y response will be assigned the high ERRORLEVEL value.

Enter the IF command that evaluates the user's response.

IF ERRORLEVEL 2 GOTO overwrite ↵

The next task is to create the OVERWRITE section. Cancel the current insert mode and begin a new label at what is now Line 32.

[Ctrl/c] 32i ↵

Create the OVERWRITE label.

:overwrite ↵

The commands in this section should display messages that indicate what is going on, and also include the same copy command used earlier in the batch to COPY the specified file.

The first step is to remove the prompt on row 15 and replace it with a new message. Since the new message is a different length than the existing message, you should erase the prompt before displaying the new message. To do this, use the PRINTCHAR subcommand to display blank spaces. Note that " " is used to specify a blank space as the character. Enter

BE ROWCOL 15,22 ↵
BE PRINTCHAR " ",35
↵

Next, display the message confirming the overwrite.

BE ROWCOL 15,29,"File being Overwritten" ↵

The next command actually overwrites the file. The >NUL command is used to suppress the message usually generated by the COPY command.

COPY \norton\%1.exe a:\subdir > NUL ↵
GOTO end ↵
↵

Note that the GOTO end command is not strictly necessary. This is because the END label is the next one in the batch file and would automatically execute anyway. However, it is good form when writing a procedure to explicitly state what you want to happen. This makes it easier to understand and revise a batch file.

Using a Delay

The last modification you will make is the addition of a timed delay to the end of the batch file. When the current version of the batch file ends, the windows displayed during the program remain on the screen. It might be useful to clear the screen at the end of the program. This would help confirm in the mind of the user that the program has terminated. Leaving the windows on the screen is a bit messy and potentially confusing.

However, inserting a clear the screen command at the end of the batch file would remove the windows before the user had time to read all of the messages. The solution is to use a timed delay. The DELAY subcommand allows you to pause execution of the batch file for a specified number of clock ticks (1/18 of a second). When the time has elapsed the batch file resumes execution.

In the current batch file you can use the DELAY subcommand to pause a few seconds before the screen is cleared. The commands to create this pause should be placed in the END section of the batch file. Enter

[Ctrl/c] 40i ↵

Create a 2 second (36 ticks) delay before the screen is cleared. Enter

BE DELAY 36 ↵
CLS ↵

> *Note that the DOS CLS command is used in this case rather than the Batch Enhancer CLS subcommand. This is done in order to restore the screen to its assigned colors if they were other than white on black. The BE CLS subcommand would have left the screen painted black regardless of the colors assigned for DOS using the SA subcommand.*

Save and execute the batch file specifying the SI.EXE file which had already been copied to the floppy disk. This will cause the modified DUPLICATE section of the batch file to execute. Enter

[Ctrl/c] e ↵
move2 si ↵

When the batch file executes DUPLICATE section the ASK subcommand displays the prompt (Figure 4-8) and uses the batch file to allow the user to enter a response. Enter

x

The computer issues a beep. This is because the ASK subcommand has limited the entry to Y, N, or ↵. All other keys are rejected.

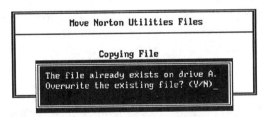

Figure 4-8 ASK pauses batch for user to enter a response.

Enter a valid response this time.

↵

Figure 4-9 shows that the batch file response to the entry by confirming the user's decision not to overwrite the file. After a 2 second pause the screen is cleared and the batch file terminates.

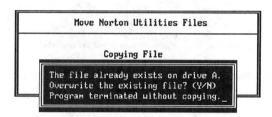

Figure 4-9 Message confirms decision not to overwrite file.

Execute the batch file again but this time select to overwrite the conflicting file.

move2 si ↵

Overwrite the file by entering

y

The message displayed this time, Figure 4-10, indicates that the file is being overwritten.

The program terminates. The ASK subcommand had created a batch file that allows the user to make selections about operating options while it is executing. The tools provided by the Batch Enhancer program allows batch files to present a sophisticated display along with an interactive dialog. Enhanced with these features, batch files can be used to create a custom designed shell in which DOS operations can be tailored to individual needs.

In Chapter 5, the concepts developed in the creation of the MOVE2.BAT file will be applied to the creation of a hard disk management system that will change the DOS interface to a menu driven shell.

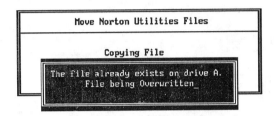

Figure 4-10 Message confirms the batch is overwriting the existing file.

Summary

This chapter discussed the use of the Batch Enhancer program to create sophisticated batch files.

- **The Batch Enhancer.** The Batch Enhancer program provides features that extend and enhance the utility of DOS batch files.

- **ROWCOL.** This subcommand allows you to position the screen cursor at a specific row and column location on the screen. The command can place text at that locations or cause the next command that output, text to the screen to begin at that location. You can also set the color of the text displayed.

- **BOX.** This subcommand draws a box specified by the upper left and lower right corner locations supplied in the command. The box can have a single- or double-line border and you can select colors for the border. Boxes are hollow, meaning that screen data already present within the parameters of the box is unchanged.

- **WINDOW.** A window is similar to a box with the exception that it clears the interior of the window when it is drawn. Windows always have a double-line border. The background color selected for the window fills the interior of the window. The subcommand also has special effects options ZOOM (or EXPLODE) and SHADOW.

- **PRINTCHAR.** This subcommand is used to print a specified number of repetitions of the same character. You can use the command to erase portions of the screen display by printing repetitions of a blank space.

- **Colors.** You can specify the foreground and background colors to be used with the ROWCOL, BOX, WINDOW, PRINTCHAR, and ASK commands. You can use the colors BLACK, WHITE, RED, GREEN, YELLOW, BLUE, CYAN, and MAGENTA. Foreground colors can also be set as BRIGHT or BLINKING.

- **BEEP.** This subcommand allows you to sound tones to create audio prompts in your batch files. You can specify the frequency, duration, repetitions, and wait between tones for each sound generated. Optional comments allow text to be displayed as each tone is sounded.

- **DELAY.** This subcommand allows you to insert timed delays into batch files. Time is specified in click ticks which are equal to 1/18 of a second.

- **CLS.** This subcommand clears the screen to black.

- **ERRORLEVEL.** This command is an option that can be used with the DOS IF command. The ASK subcommand can be used to set the ERRORLEVEL value according to user input from 0 to 255.

- **ASK.** This subcommand allows the user to make responses that can be evaluated by the batch file while it is running. The ASK command can accept a key list that specifies which keys the user can enter. The sequence of the key list determines the value assigned to the ERRORLEVEL option. A default key can be specified so that the user can enter ↵. A timeout option allows you to limit the amount of time the user has to enter a response. If no response is made during the allotted time the default key is selected.

Batch Files Listings

MOVE2.BAT (Final form)

```
@ECHO OFF
BE CLS
BE WINDOW 8,15,16,64 ZOOM
BE ROWCOL 9,27,"Move Norton Utilities Files"
BE ROWCOL 10,15,õ
BE PRINTCHAR -,48
BE PRINTCHAR È,1
BE ROWCOL 12,33,"Copying File"
BE ROWCOL 14,35,"%1.exe" BLACK ON WHITE
IF NOT EXIST \norton\%1.exe GOTO nofile
IF EXIST a:\subdir\%1.exe GOTO duplicate
BE ROWCOL 15,23
COPY \norton\%1.exe a:\subdir
GOTO end

:nofile
BE WINDOW 13,20,17,59 BLACK ON WHITE ZOOM
BE BEEP buzzer.snd
BE ROWCOL 14,22,"The file %1.exe does not exist."
BE ROWCOL 16,22,"Program terminated without copying."
GOTO end

:duplicate
BE WINDOW 13,20,17,59 BLACK ON WHITE ZOOM
BE ROWCOL 14,22,"The file already exists on drive A."
BE ROWCOL 15,22
BE ASK "Overwrite the existing file? (Y/N)",ny,DEFAULT=n
IF ERRORLEVEL 2 GOTO overwrite
BE ROWCOL 16,22,"Program terminated without copying."
GOTO end

:overwrite
BE ROWCOL 15,22
BE PRINTCHAR " ",35
BE ROWCOL 15,29,"File being Overwritten"
COPY \norton\%1.exe a:\subdir >NUL
GOTO end

:end
BE DELAY 36
CLS
BE ROWCOL 24,0
```

5

Hard Disk Menus

The previous chapter used a simple batch file to demonstrate how the Batch Enhancer subcommands can be used to create a sophisticated user interface, using Batch Enhancer and DOS batch file commands. In this chapter the ideas presented in Chapters 3 and 4 will be put to use in designing a hard disk menu system that can serve as a custom-designed shell. This shell can be used to insulate users from directly dealing with DOS. The goal is to create a *turnkey* system of menus that load when the computer is booted. The term *shell* refers to a program that stands between the user and the DOS operations being performed. The goal of a hard disk menu system is to present the user with lists of choices, instead of simply a DOS prompt.

In this chapter you will learn how the Batch Enhancer commands can be used to create menus and systems of menus that help organize hard disk operations.

Creating a Menu

The basic tool of any hard disk organizing system is the *menu*. A menu is simply a screen display listing a series of options that can be selected by entering a number or a letter. The menu options may execute DOS commands, run applications, or lead to other submenus. The Batch Enhancer program provides the tools needed to create menus or systems of menus.

In the MOVE2.BAT file, screen displays were constructed using the ROWCOL, BOX, WINDOW, and PRINTCHAR subcommands. A menu can be created in the same way by using individual commands to place the menu options on the screen. However, when individual Batch Enhancer commands are used to create a screen display there can be an awkward delay as each Batch Enhancer is executed.

The delay is due to the time it takes to load the Batch Enhancer program in order to execute the subcommand. For example, if four ROWCOL commands are needed to write the text on the screen, the Batch Enhancer program is loaded four consecutive times, slowing down the process of placing the text on the screen.

Since each item on the menu would require a ROWCOL subcommand, the longer the menu the more time it will take to appear on the screen.

If this were the only way to use the Batch Enhancer subcommands it would not be practical to use Batch Enhancer subcommands to display menus. However, there is an alternative method of using the Batch Enhancer program. This method allows you to execute a sequence of Batch Enhancer subcommands while loading the Batch Enhancer program only once. The method involves the creation of a *subcommand file*. A subcommand file is a text file that contains a list of ROWCOL, WINDOW, BOX, or PRINTCHAR commands. The advantage of the subcommand file is that all the commands in the file are executed without having to reload the BE.EXE program for each subcommand. The result is that you can fill the screen display with information in a fraction of the time it would take with individual Batch Enhancer commands.

Suppose you want to create a hard disk organizer menu that allows you to select among four applications: Lotus 1-2-3, dBASE IV, Microsoft Word, and Ventura desktop publisher. The first step is to create a menu that displays these options for the user.

> *If you do not have all or some of these applications you can substitute programs that you do have.*

Instead of beginning with a batch file you will begin with a subcommand file. The subcommand file will contain only the commands needed to create the menu display. That file, in turn, will be used by the actual batch file as a subroutine.

The Batch Enhancer subcommand files are not required to have any special file extension. In this case, you will use the file extension MNU to indicate that this file contains menu subcommands. Enter

EDLIN main.mnu ↵
i ↵

When you enter commands into a subcommand file it is not necessary to use the BE command each time. Instead, each command begins with the subcommand name.

The first command in the file is a CLS subcommand. Enter

CLS ↵

Next, create a window inside of which the menu will be placed. Enter

WINDOW 5,15,20,64 ZOOM ↵

The next two commands place a title at the top of the window. This time a box is drawn around the title. Enter

BOX 6,20,8,59 ↵
ROWCOL 7,25,"Hard Disk Organizer - Main Menu" ↵

The remainder of the menu consists of the items from which the user can select. In this menu structure there will be three ROWCOL subcommands for each item. The first prints the name of the item. This will be displayed in bright white characters. The second command displays a comment or remark about the option. This is displayed in normal white characters. The third ROWCOL is used to redisplay the first letter of the item name in black on white. This is done to indicate that the item can be selected by entering the first letter of the item. In this type of menu, take care to ensure that no two options use the same first letter.

The first item on the menu will be Lotus 1-2-3. The first subcommand displays the name of the item in bright white. Enter

ROWCOL 10,25,"Lotus 1-2-3" BRIGHT WHITE ↵

Next, on the same row but at column 45, a comment about the item is displayed. Enter

ROWCOL 10,45,Spreadsheet ↵

The last ROWCOL subcommand for this line will redisplay the first character of the item in reverse color, black on white. Enter

ROWCOL 10,25,L BLACK ON WHITE ↵

The next set of commands creates a menu entry for Word.

ROWCOL 11,25,"Word" BRIGHT WHITE ↵
ROWCOL 11,45,"Word Processing" ↵
ROWCOL 11,25,W BLACK ON WHITE ↵

The pattern repeats, this time creating a dBASE IV item on the menu.

ROWCOL 12,25,"dBASE IV" BRIGHT WHITE ↵
ROWCOL 12,45,Database ↵
ROWCOL 12,25,d BLACK ON WHITE ↵

The last item on the menu will be Ventura. Enter

ROWCOL 13,25,"Ventura" BRIGHT WHITE ↵
ROWCOL 13,45,"Desktop Publisher" ↵
ROWCOL 13,25,V BLACK ON WHITE ↵

In addition to the menu items, the menu subcommand file will contain an option for exiting the menu system and returning to the DOS command level. Enter

ROWCOL 17,25,"Exit to DOS" BRIGHT WHITE ↵
ROWCOL 17,45,"Terminate Menus" ↵
ROWCOL 17,25,E BLACK ON WHITE ↵

Save the subcommand file by entering

[Ctrl/c] e ↵

Executing a Subcommand File

Once you have created a subcommand file you can execute all the commands in the subcommand file with a single Batch Enhancer command. When you enter the BE command, instead of entering a subcommand you will use the name of the subcommand file. The Batch Enhancer will load and execute all the subcommands in the specified file. The primary advantage is the speed at which the items are displayed. On most computers, all the BOX, WINDOW, ROWCOL, and PRINTCHAR items will display in the same instant with little or no perceptible delay between items. Execute the subcommand file directly from DOS by entering

BE main.mnu ↵

The subcommand file produces the menu, shown in Figure 5-1, by executing all of the subcommands in the file.

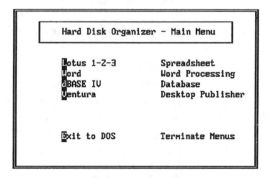

Figure 5-1 Menu created with subcommand file.

Batch Files with Menus

The subcommand file is an efficient way to display a menu. This technique can be used as part of a menu processing batch file. Create a batch file called MAIN.BAT by entering

EDLIN main.bat ⏎

i ⏎

The first command in the this batch file is the ECHO OFF command.

@ECHO OFF ⏎

The next item is not a command, but a label. The reason for this label is that unlike the previous batch files, the menu will contain a loop. Loop is used to describe a program whose flow of execution moves in a circular fashion. This means a command later in the batch refers to a label which was passed earlier. If a GOTO command refers to that label, then the execution in the batch file will move backward to that label and repeat the commands listed in that section.

In a menu type batch file such as the one you are creating, the section of the batch file that actually displays the menu will be repeated after each selection.

Creating a label at the beginning of the program will enable you to loop back to that point later in the program. Enter

:main_menu ↵

The next step is to display the menu using the subcommand file. Enter

BE main.mnu ↵

Once the menu has been displayed, you need to have the user enter his selection. This requires the use of an ASK subcommand. First, use a ROWCOL subcommand to position the cursor at the correct location within the window for the ASK prompt.

BE ROWCOL 19,25 ↵

With the screen cursor position you can use the ASK subcommand to obtain the user's selection. The DEFAULT option is used to allow the entry of ↵ as a selection to exit the menu. Enter

BE ASK "Enter your choice:",lwdve,default=e ↵

> *You may wonder why the ASK subcommand was not included with the subcommand file. This would make the display of the ASK prompt instantaneous with the display of the rest of the menu. The reason is that if the ASK command is included in the subcommand file, the command fails to set the ERRORLEVEL to the value indicated by the user's selection. In order to operate properly, the ASK subcommand must be in the batch file, not the subcommand file.*

Creating a Looping Menu

Before you go on to create the full working menu program, you must work out how a menu program can be made to return to the menu after a selection has been made. You can work out this technique by making an abbreviated version of the program. In this version you will set up only one of the four options on the menu, that for Lotus 1-2-3.

Following the displays of the ASK prompt you need to enter a series of IF ERRORLEVEL commands. The commands are listed in descending order beginning with the highest value you expect to use for an ERRORLEVEL. Recall that the descending order is required because ERRORLEVEL tests for equal to or less than the specified value. In this case, the key list of the ASK subcommand contains five keys; the IF commands should cover ERRORLEVEL 5 through 1. Each command will specify a different label. The first IF command, the one for ERRORLEVEL 5, will specify a label called EXIT. All of the others will use labels that are program4, program3, and so on. Enter

IF ERRORLEVEL 5 GOTO exit ↵
IF ERRORLEVEL 4 GOTO program4 ↵
IF ERRORLEVEL 3 GOTO program3 ↵
IF ERRORLEVEL 2 GOTO program2 ↵
IF ERRORLEVEL 1 GOTO program13 ↵
↵

The next section of the batch file contains the labels and commands related to executing each of the items. For the most part, these commands are the same for each program you want to run from the menu. The only difference is the name of the program and the name of the file that is executed to start the program. For example, with Lotus 1-2-3, the name of the file that is executed to start the program is 123.EXE. A second way to start 1-2-3 is to use the file LOTUS.COM, which loads the Lotus Access menu from which you can run 1-2-3 or 1-2-3 related utilities.

Begin by entering the label that identifies this section of the batch file. Since the letter to select Lotus is L and L is the first key in the ASK key list, Lotus will be loaded under the PROGRAM1 label. Enter

:program1 ↵

In order to confirm that the user has selected to load Lotus 1-2-3, you can display a message to this effect in a window superimposed on the menu. Enter

BE WINDOW 8,10,12,70 ZOOM ↵
BE ROWCOL 10,22 "Loading Lotus 1-2-3 ..." BRIGHT WHITE ↵

The next commands in the batch are those you would use to actually load the program if you were manually loading it from DOS. Typically, this consists of a directory change to enter the directory in which the program files are stored and a command to load the program. For example, suppose the Lotus 1-2-3 program is stored in a directory called \LOTUS. You would enter **cd\lotus**, then **123**, in order to start the program. Enter these commands.

CD\lotus ↵

123 ↵

At this point, 1-2-3 loads and takes over the operation of the computer. The next series of commands entered into the batch file will be executed **after** the user has exited from the application. The purpose of these commands is to return the user to the original menu, so he can make another selection. The batch file will display a window that tells the user he or she is returning to the main menu. Enter

BE WINDOW 8,10,12,70 ZOOM ↵

BE ROWCOL 10,22 "Returning to Main menu ..." BRIGHT WHITE ↵

Change back to the directory in which the menu batch file is stored. The assumption is that this is the root directory of the hard disk. Enter

CD ↵

If you are using a system that has multiple physical or logical drives, you need to include commands to switch to the appropriate drives, e.g., d:, e:, etc.

The final command in this section is a GOTO command. The GOTO command directs the batch file to jump to the **main_menu** label. This creates a loop because the processing returns to the section of the batch where it began. This means that this menu batch file can remain active for an entire session. So long as the user can find the options he or she needs on the menus, the batch can continue running all the time the computer is in use. This is in contrast to the single-purpose batch file created in Chapters 3 and 4. Enter

GOTO main_menu ↵

Exiting the Loop

When you create a loop within a batch file, or for that matter any type of program, it is necessary to create an exit option. The exit option is essential because without such an option a batch file or computer program would run forever. The only way to stop it would be to turn off the computer. Every loop must have at least one exit.

In the current example, the exit is assigned to the Exit option on the menu which is activated by entering the letter E. The DEFAULT option used with the ASK subcommand allows you to select E by entering ↵ as well.

In this batch file you need to create a label called EXIT which will be used as the exit from the menu loop. The simplest way to use this LABEL is to place it at the end of the batch file. When a GOTO command is used to jump to an exit, the batch file will end because there are no more commands to process. Create the exit label by entering

↵

:exit ↵

CLS ↵

Below is a listing of the MAIN.BAT file:

```
@ECHO OFF
:main_menu
BE main.mnu
BE ROWCOL 19,25
BE ASK "Enter your choice:",lwdve,DEFAULT=e
IF ERRORLEVEL 5 GOTO exit
IF ERRORLEVEL 4 GOTO program4
IF ERRORLEVEL 3 GOTO program3
IF ERRORLEVEL 2 GOTO program2
IF ERRORLEVEL 1 GOTO program1

:program1
BE WINDOW 8,10,12,70 ZOOM
BE ROWCOL 10,22,"Loading Lotus 1-2-3 ..." BRIGHT WHITE
CD\lotus
123
BE WINDOW 8,10,12,70 ZOOM
BE ROWCOL 10,22,"Returning to Main menu ..." BRIGHT WHITE
CD\
GOTO main_menu

:exit
CLS
```

Running the Menu

The batch file now contains sufficient commands to enable you to test the menu structure. Save and execute this batch file by entering

[Ctrl/c] e ↵
main ↵

The batch file begins with the display of the menu as shown in Figure 5-2. The ASK subcommand causes the prompt to appear inside the menu window, waiting for the user to make a selection.

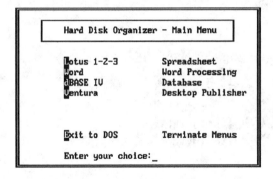

Figure 5-2 Menu paused for user entry.

The batch file is capable of running the Lotus 1-2-3. Enter

L

When the selection is made, a window is displayed with the name of the program that has been selected, as shown in Figure 5-3.

The window is erased when the application begins to control the screen display. The final result is that the application, in this example Lotus 1-2-3, is loaded.

When you exit the application (in Lotus 1-2-3 the command is /QY) the batch file resumes execution. Note that when a program like 1-2-3 is executed from the batch file it is treated as a single command, even though you may work with the program for several hours. When you exit, DOS continues by executing the next command in the batch file. In this case, the batch displays another window informing the user that the batch is returning to the main menu, as shown in Figure 5-4.

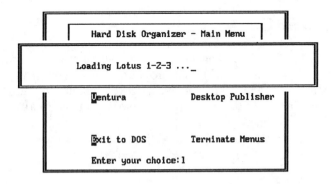

Figure 5-3 Window confirms user's selection.

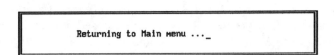

Figure 5-4 Message displayed after application is terminated.

Once you have returned to the main menu you can make another selection. You can select the same program or a different program. By always returning to the main menu after each application, the menu program will function as a continuously running hard disk organizer. Exit the menu by entering

↵

The batch file terminates and you are returned to the DOS command mode.

Timing Usage

In addition to the Batch Enhancer program, another useful Norton Utility program is the Time Mark (TM.EXE) program. This program uses the system clock to create *stopwatches* that can be used to time the duration of various activities. To time an event you need to issue two TM (Time Mark) commands.

- **TM START.** This command initializes the TM stopwatch to zero. It also displays on the screen the current time and date.

- **TM STOP.** This option is a bit misleading. When used, it causes the program to display the current time and date, as well as the elapsed time since the TM START command was used. It does **not** stop the timing. The stopwatch continues to accumulate time. This means you can issue several TM STOP commands and see the accumulated elapsed time since the stopwatch was started. To restart a stopwatch, you must issue a TM START command.

If you want to keep times for several events concurrently you can specify up to four different stopwatches using the /C options. For example, the commands TM START /C1 and TM START /C2 will start two clocks, C1 and C2, that will run independently. When you want to obtain the elapsed time for a specific clock you would use its clock number in the command, e.g., TM STOP /C2. Note that if you do not specify a clock number, the default, clock 1, is assumed. This means that TM START and TM START /C1 have the same effect.

You can start a clock timer by entering the command

TM START ↵

The program displays the current date and time, including the day of the week on the right side of the screen. To display the elapsed time, enter

TM STOP ↵

The program displays the date and time again. Below the current time appears the time since the elapsed timer was started. Note the elapsed time is written in hours, minutes, and seconds, e.g. *1 minute, 30 seconds*.

When using the TM program from a batch file, you may need to employ some available options.

- **/L.** This option places the output of the Time Mark program on the left edge of the screen instead of the right. This option is useful because it allows you to place the TM output at a specific screen location by preceding it with a Batch Enhancer ROWCOL subcommand.

- **/N.** This option suppresses the display of the current time and date. When used with a TM STOP command, it limits the display to the elapsed time only.

- **Comment.** You can add a text string that will be displayed preceding TM output. This allows you to create a message that includes the Time Mark information.

For example, to display the elapsed time alone on the left side of the screen, enter

TM STOP /L/N ↵

The TM program can be used to calculate the elapsed time for a specific menu option. For example, you could display the elapsed time after the user exits an application before returning to the main menu.

Load the MAIN.BAT file into the EDLIN editor by entering

EDLIN main.bat ↵

List the section of the batch that executes program 1.

12L ↵

In order to calculate the elapsed time you need to enter a TM START command before the application is loaded. Insert this command between Lines 14 and 15. Note that the /N switch is used to suppress the display of the time and date. The purpose of the command is merely to start the timer at zero. Enter

15i ↵
TM START /N↵
[Ctrl/c]

In order to display the time and date, you need to insert a TM STOP command before the user is returned to the main menu. Here, insert the commands needed after Line 17. Because a window has just been displayed, you will want to place the TM output inside the window. Begin with a ROWCOL command to place the screen cursor inside the window.

19i ↵

BE ROWCOL 10,22 ↵

You can use a text string to add a comment to the elapsed time display. The text you specify will precede the elapsed time. For example, the command **TM STOP "In use"/N/L** will display something like *In use 5 minutes 10 seconds*.

> The TM program automatically inserts a space following the comment text, in order to separate the comment from the elapsed time. It is not necessary to include a trailing space in the comment string.

Enter

TM STOP "Lotus in use for"/N/L ↵

Optional Delays

In order to give the user a chance to read the elapsed time information you might want to include a pause. There are two ways to do this:

1. **Delay.** Use a DELAY subcommand to pause the batch file for a specified period of time.

2. **Ask.** Use an ASK subcommand with the TIMEOUT option. The ASK method has the advantage of allowing the user to terminate the pause pressing a key. To use the ASK subcommand to make such a pause, you would not use a key list with the command. You would use the TIMEOUT option to create a timed pause. If the user does not enter a key by the specified time limit, the command automatically terminates.

In this instance, you might want to display a message such as *Press* ↵ and pause the batch for 5 seconds. If the user does not want to wait for the pause to complete, he or she can press ↵. Enter

**BE ASK "Press
[space bar]**

Entering Control Character Symbols with EDLIN

In the command you are entering, it is necessary to use a special method to create a screen display that looks like the ↵ symbol.

There are about 27 characters in the IBM character set that cannot be inserted with the [Alt/keypad] method discussed in Chapter 4. These are the characters that match up to the [Ctrl-letter] combinations, such as [Ctrl/r], [Ctrl/o], and [Ctrl/z]. You cannot make a direct entry of these keys in DOS because DOS accepts their entry as direct commands.

The method is to use the [Ctrl/v] EDLIN command. You can signify that you want to enter a control character symbol by entering [Ctrl/v] followed by the uppercase control letter. The entry produces ^V followed by the letter. However, when the file is stored, the symbol appears correctly. Complete the command by entering

**[Ctrl/v]O
[Alt/196]
[Alt/217]
",TIMEOUT=5 ↵**

Use a PRINTCHAR subcommand to erase the prompt before the next message appears.

**BE ROWCOL 10,22 ↵
BE PRINTCHAR " ",40 ↵**

The modified section of the batch file looks like this:

```
:program1
BE WINDOW 8,10,12,70 ZOOM
BE ROWCOL 10,22,"Loading Lotus 1-2-3 ..." BRIGHT WHITE
TM START /N
CD\lotus
123
BE WINDOW 8,10,12,70 ZOOM
BE ROWCOL 10,22
TM STOP "Lotus in use for"/N/L
BE ASK "- Press ^QO-"",TIMEOUT=5
BE ROWCOL 10,22
BE PRINTCHAR " ",40
BE ROWCOL 10,22,"Returning to Main menu ..." BRIGHT WHITE
CD\
GOTO main_menu
```

Save the modified batch file by entering

[Ctrl/c] e ⏎

Execute the batch file by entering

main ⏎

Run Lotus 1-2-3 by entering

L

Although you did not see it, the TM command has started a timer for this application. Exit the program by entering

/qy

After the application has terminated, the batch resumes by displaying the time elapsed since the application was loaded. The message, as shown in Figure 5-5, will be displayed for 5 seconds. You can terminate the pause earlier by entering ⏎. Note how the ^VO is displayed as a left pointing arrow.

```
┌─────────────────────────────────────────────────────┐
│ ┌─────────────────────────────────────────────────┐ │
│ │      Lotus in use for 36 seconds - Press ↵_      │ │
│ └─────────────────────────────────────────────────┘ │
└─────────────────────────────────────────────────────┘
```

Figure 5-5 Elapsed time displayed after exiting the application..

When the delay is over (or you press ↵) the batch file returns to the main menu. Exit the batch file by entering

↵

Logging Usage

In the previous version of the MAIN.BAT program, the TM information is displayed for 5 seconds following the termination of the application. The information is not preserved or stored. However, storing the information may be useful because it represents a log of all the applications used and the amount of time each application was run.

How could the Time Mark data be used to create a log? The answer involves the use of another DOS redirection option. In Chapter 3 the >NUL redirection option was used to suppress the output from a command. Redirection can also be employed to send the output to disk file. The > followed by the name of a file tells DOS to store the output of the command in the specified text file. If you use >>, the output is appended onto the text file if it already exists. If no file exists one will be created.

The command below stores the current time and date as output from the TM program into a text file called CLOCK.DAT. Enter

TM /L >> clock.dat ↵

Wait about a minute and repeat the command.

TM /L >> clock.dat ↵

The effect of the two commands was to write two consecutive time and date entries into the CLOCK.DAT file. Display the contents of the CLOCK.DAT file by entering

TYPE clock.dat ↵

The file displays information similar to that shown below in Figure 5-6.

```
2:25 pm, Tuesday, September 5, 1989 2:26 pm, Tuesday, September 5, 1989
```

Figure 5-6 Redirection stores output in text file.

The information stored in the file would read more easily if each item was on a separate line. The TM program has a switch, /LOG, that is used to format the output so it will read properly in a text file. Erase the existing CLOCK.DAT file and create a new one with redirected TM command. Enter

DEL clock.dat ↵
TM /L/LOG >> clock.dat ↵
TM /L/LOG >> clock.dat ↵
TYPE clock.dat ↵

This time the dates are on separate lines. You can use this principle to create a log automatically, as choices are made from the batch file menu. Load the MAIN.BAT file into the EDLIN editor by entering

EDLIN main.bat ↵

Each menu selection will make two log entries: one for login (loading the application) and one for logout (exiting the application). Place the login TM command on Line 16. Note that this is not a TM START command but simply a TM. There is no need to restart the timer since the commands will execute one after the other. Enter

16i ⏎
TM "Login: Lotus 1-2-3"/L/LOG >> userlog.dat ⏎
[Ctrl/c]

The TM STOP command is on Line 21. Following that command, enter a second TM STOP which will use redirection options to store the logout data. Enter

22i ⏎
TM "Logout:"/L/LOG >> userlog.dat ⏎
[Ctrl/c]

Save the batch file by entering

e ⏎

Each time you run the batch file and select Lotus 1-2-3, the batch file makes an automatic entry into the log. Below is a sample of what the log contents would look like:

Login: Lotus 1-2-3 3:16 pm, Tuesday, September 5, 1989

Logout: 3:16 pm, Tuesday, September 5, 1989
7 seconds

Login: Lotus 1-2-3 3:24 pm, Tuesday, September 5, 1989

Logout: 3:24 pm, Tuesday, September 5, 1989
6 seconds

Keep in mind that the log file will continue to expand every time you make a selection from the menu. In order to control the file's size you may want to backup or erase the USERLOG.DAT from time to time.

Submenus

When creating menu choices you will find that often there is more than one way to operate the selected item. For example, Microsoft Word can be loaded in one of two ways: with a blank document (normal) or with the last document used.

In such cases, you might want to display a *submenu* when the Word option is selected from the main menu.

To create a submenu begin by creating a menu subcommand file that will display the submenu. Call the file WORD.MNU. Enter

EDLIN word.mnu ↵

i ↵

Create a menu that has two options corresponding to the two ways in which word can be loaded. Enter

WINDOW 15,40,22,79 ZOOM ↵

ROWCOL 16,50,"Microsoft Word" BRIGHT WHITE ↵

ROWCOL 18,50,"Normal (blank document)" ↵

ROWCOL 18,50,N BLACK ON WHITE ↵

ROWCOL 19,50,"Last Document" ↵

ROWCOL 19,50,L BLACK ON WHITE ↵

ROWCOL 21,50 ↵

Save the submenu subcommand file by entering

[Ctrl/c] e ↵

The next step is to modify the MAIN.BAT file to utilize the submenu. Enter

EDLIN main.bat ↵

The commands that control the loading of the Word program will fall under the label PROGRAM2. Insert this new section following PROGRAM1 but preceding EXIT, Line 30.

30i ↵

:program2 ↵

The first command in this section is a Batch Enhancer command that uses subcommand file WORD.MNU.

BE word.mnu ↵

Use the ASK subcommand to pause the batch for the user's selection.

BE ASK "Enter your choice:",nl,DEFAULT=n ↵

Passing Strings Within a Batch File

For the most part, this section of the batch file will use the same commands as were used with the section that ran Lotus 1-2-3. The only part that is different is that in this case there are two alternative ways to load the program: WORD to load the program with a blank document or WORD/L to load the program and also load the last document that was being edited the last time the application was used.

The general approach is to use ERRORLEVEL, GOTO and labels to select the loading instruction. However, you are not at the point in the batch file where you actually want to execute the loading instruction. That comes after you have displayed the window with the confirming message.

DOS provides the SET command which allows you to define variable names within a program that can be used to pass a text string to another part of the batch file. For example, the command below defines a variable called LOAD as the character string *word*.

SET load=word

Once this command has been issued, you can use the variable name to insert the text strings of other commands within the batch file. Variable names are written with % sign before and after the name: e.g., %load%. The command below shows how the variable name could be used to insert the text string into a ROWCOL subcommand.

BE ROWCOL 10,10,"Loading %load%"

When DOS encounters a variable symbol in a command it substitutes the current value of the variable and then executes the command. In this case the characters *word* are substituted for the **%load%** symbol.

In the current program the variable symbol, %load%, will be set to the text of the loading instruction that matches the menu selection. If the user selects N from the menu, %load% will be simply *word*. If the user selects L then the variable will be assigned *word/l*. This will be done by using ERRORLEVEL options to GOTO different labels, based on the user's entry.

As with the main menu, the first ERRORLEVEL option will evaluate the highest ERRORLEVEL value. In this instance, this is 2 because there are two characters in the ASK subcommand key list. The command will jump to the label P2_LAST if the user has selected L from the menu. Enter

IF ERRORLEVEL 2 GOTO p2_last ↵

The next command represents what ought to happen if the user did not select the second menu item. In this program that means the user wants to load WORD normally. The SET command assigns the normal loading instruction to the variable LOAD.

SET load=word ↵

Once the loading instruction has been set the batch should jump to a label, in this case P2_CONT, where the batch can continue with the loading process. Enter

GOTO p2_cont ↵
↵

The next section of the batch file is P2_LAST. This section assigns the loading instruction to be used if the user has selected L from the menu. Enter

:p2_last ↵
SET load=word/l ↵
↵

You have now completed the section of the batch file that responds to the entry made by the user from the submenu. The rest of this section will be the same, regardless of which submenu option the user selects. The technique used will be to place the variable %load% into the batch file at the point where the loading instruction (either word or word/l) would be entered. DOS will insert the text assigned by the SET command into the batch file at that point, loading the program according to the user's preference.

The commands entered in the remainder of this section, with the exception of the loading instruction, follow the pattern established in PROGRAM1.

Menu batch files contain a large degree of repetition of commands, with only small changes. The cut, paste, copy, and edit features found in most word processing programs can speed up the process of creating this type of batch file.

Enter the following section into the batch file.

:p2_cont ↵
BE WINDOW 8,10,12,70 ZOOM ↵
BE ROWCOL 10,22,"Loading Word ..." BRIGHT WHITE ↵

```
                TM START /N ↵
      TM "Login: Word"/L/LOG >> \userlog.dat ↵
                  CD\word5 ↵
                  %load% ↵
        BE WINDOW 8,10,12,70 ZOOM ↵
            BE ROWCOL 10,22 ↵
        TM STOP "Word in use for"/N/L ↵
   TM STOP "Logout:"/L/LOG >> \userlog.dat ↵
              BE ASK "- Press
                 [Ctrl/v]O
                 [Alt/196]
                 [Alt/217]
            ",TIMEOUT=5 ↵
            BE ROWCOL 10,22 ↵
          BE PRINTCHAR " ",40 ↵
BE ROWCOL 10,22,"Returning to Main menu ..." ↵ BRIGHT WHITE
                  CD\ ↵
             GOTO main_menu ↵
                    ↵
```

The new section of the batch file under PROGRAM2 will read as follows:

```
:program2
BE word.mnu
BE ASK "Enter your choice:",nl,DEFAULT=n
IF ERRORLEVEL 2 GOTO p2_last
SET load=word
GOTO p2_cont

:p2_last
SET load=word/l

:p2_cont
BE WINDOW 8,10,12,70 ZOOM
BE ROWCOL 10,22,"Loading Word ..." BRIGHT WHITE
TM START /N
TM "Login: Word"/L/LOG >> \userlog.dat
CD\word5
%load%
BE WINDOW 8,10,12,70 ZOOM
BE ROWCOL 10,22
TM STOP "Word in use for"/N/L
TM STOP "Logout:"/L/LOG >> \userlog.dat
BE ASK "- Press -"",TIMEOUT=5
BE ROWCOL 10,22
BE PRINTCHAR " ",40
BE ROWCOL 10,22,"Returning to Main menu ..." BRIGHT WHITE
CD\
GOTO main_menu
```

Save and execute the modified batch file by entering

[Ctrl/c] e ↵
main ↵

Select Word from the menu by entering

w

The batch file reacts to the entry by displaying the submenu in a window position in the lower right portion of the screen. The placement of the windows allows you to read both the main and submenu, as shown in Figure 5-7.

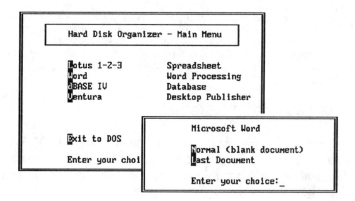

Figure 5-7 Menu paused for user entry.

Select to load the program normally by entering

↵

The program is loaded according to the selection made on the submenu. Exit the program by entering

[Esc] q

The Time Mark commands display the elapsed time for the application and then return to the main menu. Exit the batch file by entering

e

Submenus are useful because they allow you to organize options more logically than can be done on a single menu display. Submenus reduce the size of the main menu by allowing you distribute items to smaller submenus. They also allow you to organize options into a tree-type structure. The submenus display only options related to the initial selection.

The example in this chapter showed only a single level of submenus. However, the same approach can be used to create as many levels of submenus as you desire.

If you are using Microsoft Windows applications you can use the technique shown in this section to load those applications from a batch file menu. Normally, a Windows application such as Windows Write is loaded by selecting the program name from the DOS executive display. However, you can load Windows and execute a Windows application directly from DOS by using the name of the application as an argument when loading windows. For example, entering WIN WRITE will cause Windows to automatically load and run the WRITE program. If you are creating a submenu for Windows applications you can run individual Windows applications by using loading instructions such as WIN WRITE, WIN EXCEL, WIN PM as part of your batch file.

Batch Files Within Batch Files

While it is true that popular applications such as dBASE IV, Word, WordPerfect, and Lotus 1-2-3 are loaded directly from DOS, there are some applications that are designed to be loaded indirectly through the use of batch files created specifically for that program.

For example, Ventura Desktop Publisher creates a batch file called VP.BAT (or VPPROF.BAT for the Professional Extension Edition) which is used to load the program. The batch file is created as part of the installation process. It contains a number of options that relate to the type of hardware on which the application is being run.

A Ventura user would load the program by entering VP ↵ to execute the batch file, which in turn loads the program. To the user, loading from a batch file or directly from a program file (COM or EXE extension) makes very little difference.

However, when you want to load a program from a batch file, there is a significant difference. When you execute a command in one batch file to run another batch file, DOS transfers control to the specified batch file. The first batch file is the *primary* batch file. It contains the instruction that starts the *secondary* batch file.

Under normal circumstances when the secondary batch file completes its operation DOS will not automatically return to the primary batch file. Instead, it will simply exit to DOS when the secondary batch file has terminated.

In such a case, you would need to add a command to the end of the secondary batch file that executes the main batch file again. For example, in the case of the VP.BAT file used by Ventura you would have to add a command to the end of the file that runs the MAIN menu batch file. This completes a loop that will create the appearance of a continuously running menu.

If you are using DOS 3.3 or higher you can avoid the need to modify the application batch files, such as the VP.BAT used by Ventura. DOS 3.3 includes a command called CALL, which will cause DOS to automatically return to the primary batch file after the secondary file terminates. When CALL returns to the primary batch file it continues executing batch file instructions immediately following the CALL command.

The CALL command has two advantages. First, it simplifies the process of running batch files from within batch files because it eliminates the need to modify the batch files called from the primary program. Second, CALL allows the primary batch file to continue in sequence instead of having to start over again, which is what happens when you reexecute the batch file.

In the sample batch file in this chapter, Ventura is the fourth option on the main menu. Below is a listing of a section of this batch file, PROGRAM4, that uses the CALL command to execute the VP.BAT file. The position of the CALL command is indicated by the arrow.

```
:program4
BE WINDOW 8,10,12,70 ZOOM
BE ROWCOL 10,22,"Loading Ventura ..." BRIGHT WHITE
TM START /N
TM "Login: Ventura"/L/LOG >> \userlog.dat
CALL vp  ←
BE WINDOW 8,10,12,70 ZOOM
BE ROWCOL 10,22
TM STOP "Ventura in use for"/N/L
TM STOP "Logout:"/L/LOG >> \userlog.dat
BE ASK "- Press -",TIMEOUT=5
BE ROWCOL 10,22
BE PRINTCHAR " ",40
BE ROWCOL 10,22,"Returning to Main menu ..." BRIGHT WHITE
CD\
GOTO main_menu
```

Making the Menu Automatic

Once you have created a batch menu file that suits your needs you may want to take the final step and make that menu execute automatically when you turn on the computer.

All that is needed to accomplish this is to insert a line into the AUTOEXEC.BAT file in the root directory of the hard disk which executes the MAIN.BAT file. In most cases this will be the last command in the AUTOEXEC.BAT.

Note that the AUTOEXEC.BAT file that actually executes when you turn on or boot your computer is the one stored in the root directory of the drive from which the computer boots. It is often the case that there are several AUTOEXEC.BAT files stored on a hard disk in various directories. They are often created by installation programs for applications or copied from floppy disks. These files do not do any harm but are often the cause of some confusion since modifications made to these files will have no effect on the computer when it boots.

Summary

This chapter explored how the Batch Enhancer program can be used to create batch file menus that help you organize the applications stored on a hard disk.

- **Subcommand Files.** In addition to executing individual subcommands, the Batch Enhancer program can read text files that contain two or more subcommand specifications, using ROWCOL, WINDOW, BOX, and PRINTCHAR subcommands. The subcommand file greatly improves the speed of execution of subcommands that place text on the screen. An entire screen display can be placed on the screen instantaneously, avoiding the delays that occur when individual Batch Enhancer commands are used.

- **Menu Structure.** A menu batch file will typically contain the following elements: (1) A Batch Enhancer subcommand file to display the menu, (2) a ASK subcommand to obtain the user selection, (3) a series of IF ERRORLEVEL commands arranged in descending order to evaluate the user entry, (4) individual batch file sections marked by labels to execute the functions selected from the menu, and (5) a GOTO command that loops the batch file back to the main menu after each individual operation has been completed.

- **Submenus.** Submenus allows you to create a tree-like structure, in which additional options are displayed on menus when a specific item is selected. Submenus use the same basic structure as the main menu to display the items, and to allow user entry and execution of the selected option.

- **CALL.** This DOS batch file command is used when you want to execute a batch file from within a batch file. CALL causes DOS to resume execution of the primary batch file with the command immediately following the CALL command.

- **SET.** This DOS command allows you to define text strings that can be inserted into other batch commands. The SET command assigns the specified text to a variable name. The name can be inserted into a batch command. Variable names are surrounded with % signs.

- **Time Mark.** The Time Mark program is primarily used to calculate the elapsed time between two events. TM START initializes a new timer clock. TM STOP displays the elapsed time without resetting the timer. You can time up to four different events simultaneously. Timer clocks will continue to accumulate time until they are specifically reset.

Section III

Everyday Tasks

This section discusses typical computer tasks that are performed everyday. It also describes how the Norton Utilities program can be used to execute those tasks faster, in a better way, and with more assurance. The Norton Utilities complements and enhances DOS operations in some cases, and in other cases provides a means of bypassing DOS procedures.

The programs and procedures in this section cover the most common uses of the small utilities packages supplied with the Norton Utilities programs. The exception to this involves the commands used to recover files or entire disks. These operations are discussed in detail in Section IV.

If you are looking for information about a specific Norton Utilities program, the lists below show what programs are discussed in which chapters.

Programs in Chapter 6 -- System Tasks

Norton Control Center, NCC.EXE
System Information, SI.EXE
Speed Disk, SD.EXE
Batch Enhancer, BE.EXE(screen attributes subcommand)

Programs in Chapter 7 -- Hard Disk Organizing Tasks

File Find, FF.EXE
Text Search, TS.EXE
Main Norton Utilities, NU.EXE (text search options)
List Directories, LD.EXE

Norton Change Directory, NCD.EXE
Directory Sort, DS.EXE

Programs in Chapter 8 -- File Organizing Tasks

File Date, FD.EXE
Volume Label, VL.EXE
File Size, FS.EXE
File Attributes, FA.EXE
File Information, FI.EXE
Line Print, LP.EXE
Norton Integrator, NI.EXE

The assumption is made that you are working on a hard disk and that you have a path open to the directory, e.g., \NORTON, that contains the Norton Utilities programs.

> *If you find that when executing any of the commands in this chapter, you see the message **Bad command or filename**, see Chapter 1 for how to setup the Norton Utilities programs.*

6

System Tasks

In this chapter you will look at the Norton Utilities programs that can be used on a regular basis to control or obtain information about your computer system. This includes one of the most interesting and powerful new commands added to version 4.5, the Norton Control Center program.

The Norton Utilities Screen Interface

Each of the Norton Utilities programs is designed as a tool that is focused on a specific aspect of computer use. However, in order to simplify the use of these varied programs, certain commands and techniques can be generally applied to all or most of the programs. Before you begin to learn about the purpose and function of individual programs, this section will outline the common elements in the Norton Utilities user interface.

Full Screen Versus Command Line Operation

The Norton Utilities package consists of a number of individual programs. The programs can be divided into two types, based on their mode of operation.

- **Full-Screen Operation.** A full-screen operation program is one that presents a full-screen user interface when loaded. These programs will present menu and dialog boxes from which the user can make selections. The program will stay active until the user selects to exit the program and return to DOS. The primary advantage of full-screen programs is that their menus and dialog boxes can guide you through complicated operations.

- **Command Line Operation.** Command line operation refers to programs that are executed by entering a full command line at DOS. These programs will not present full-screen menus and dialog boxes, although

they will occasionally prompt the user for an entry. The information
output by the command line programs will be fed to the screen display
through DOS. This means that the information will appear line-by-line,
scrolling up the screen similar to the way a directory listing scrolls. The
primary advantages of command line operations are the speed at which
commands can be entered and executed, and that these commands can be
used in DOS batch files (see Section II for information about batch files).

The programs that can operate in the full screen mode are:

DS.EXE	Directory Sort
FI.EXE	File Information
FR.EXE	Format Recover
NCC.EXE	Norton Control Center
NCD.EXE	Norton Change Directory
NDD.EXE	Norton Disk Doctor
NI.EXE	Norton Integrator
NU.EXE	Main Norton Utilities
SD.EXE	Speed Disk
SF.EXE	Safe Format

The programs that operate in the command line mode are:

BE.EXE	Batch Enhancer
DS.EXE	Directory Sort
DI.EXE	Disk Information
DT.EXE	Disk Test
FA.EXE	File Attributes
FD.EXE	File Date
FF.EXE	File Find
FI.EXE	File Information
FR.EXE	Format Recover
FS.EXE	File Size
LD.EXE	List Directories
LP.EXE	Line Print
NCC.EXE	Norton Control Center
NCD.EXE	Norton Change Directory
NDD.EXE	Norton Disk Doctor
QU.EXE	Quick Unerase
SD.EXE	Speed Disk
SF.EXE	Safe Format

SI.EXE	System Information
TM.EXE	Time Mark
TS.EXE	Test Search
UD.EXE	Undelete Directory
VL.EXE	Volume Label
WIPEDISK.EXE	Wipeout Disk
WIPEFILE.EXE	Wipeout File

You may have noticed that some of the programs appear on both lists. This means they can be operated in either the full-screen or command line modes. The reason for this dual character is to allow you to use features of a program which would normally be operated from a full-screen display as part of a batch file operation.

Full-Screen Operation

When you are working in a program that displays a full-screen type interface, you will find two ways to make selections: menus and dialog boxes.

A menu is a list of items listed vertically on the screen, as shown in Figure 6-1. You can make a selection from a menu in two ways. First, you can position the highlight, using the ↑ and ↓ keys, to the item you want to select and press ↵. An alternative is to type the first letter of the option. For example, in Figure 6-1 you could select UnErase by entering **u**.

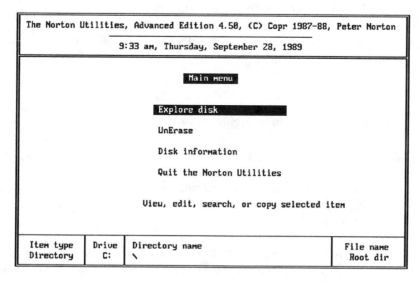

Figure 6-1 Typical menu display.

A dialog box is a window that is displayed over the current screen display. Figure 6-2 shows a dialog box labeled **Select the Drive to Format**. You can select an option from the dialog box display in the same manner as you do from a menu. Note that dialog box options can be displayed horizontally, in which case the ← and → keys would be used to move the highlight. Also keep in mind that you can exit a dialog box without making a selection by pressing [Esc].

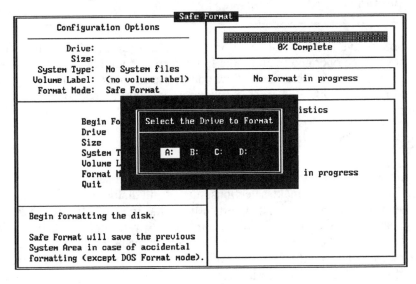

Figure 6-2 Typical dialog box display.

In most cases the following function keys can be used during full-screen operations.

- **[F1].** Display help screens.

- **[F10].** Exit the program and return to DOS.

Command Line Operation

Command line operations mean that all the options or specifications are entered as part of a single command line entered at DOS. Some of the items commonly used in command lines are:

- **File Spec.** A file spec is used to indicate a group of files. The file specs follow the same format used by DOS, including directory names and wildcards.

- **Switches.** Switches are used to select options for the program you are executing. A switch is usually a single letter preceded by a /, e.g., /R. Some switches use more than one character, e.g., /LOG. Switches can be entered as a group when more than one is needed, e.g., /L/N/LOG. Note that each switch is the group is preceded by a /.

Editing Keys

The majority of entries made in the full-screen displays of the Norton Utilities programs are made by selecting options and choices from menus and windows. However, some of the programs permit some text entry. This is usually in the form of a filename. The File Info program allows the entry of text comments about files.

In cases where editing is performed, you will note that the editing keys are WordStar compatible.

[Del]	
[Ctrl/g]	Delete one character
[Ctrl/t]	Delete next word
[Ctrl/y]	Delete entire line

Scrolling Output

Command line programs frequently output lists of files or directories that can exceed the length of the screen. These programs are:

FA.EXE	File Attributes
FD.EXE	File Date
FI.EXE	File Find
FS.EXE	File Size
LD.EXE	List Directories
SD.EXE	Speed Disk

Since these log screen displays will continue to scroll until they have reached the end, you may want to pause the display to give you time to read the information. You can pause a display by **pressing any key** while the list is scrolling. Note there are four exceptions to this rule: [Esc], [F10], [Ctrl/break], or [Ctrl/c]. These keys will terminate the program.

Once you have paused the program you have the following options.

- ↵. Advances the display one line each time.

- **[Esc] or [F10].** Quits the program. No more data displayed.

- **[space bar].** Displays the next screenful.

- **Any Other Key.** Resumes scrolling.

Note that using the /P switch with any of these programs will cause the program to automatically pause as soon as one screen is filled.

Using DOS Redirection

The programs that operate in command line mode are subject to redirection by using the standard DOS redirection options. Redirection refers to the ability of DOS to send the output to a different device than would normally be used by the program.

Usually with the Norton Utilities programs the output is sent to the screen. You can use DOS to redirect that output to the printer, to a text file, or to suppress the display.

- **Printing.** You can use DOS redirection to send the output of a program to the printer. The redirection option > PRN can be placed at the end of any command line. Example:

SI > PRN

Note that output redirected to the printer in this manner is not formatted into pages. This means the output will not break for pages or issue a form feed at the end of the printing.

Also note that the screen output of some of the programs does not contain the line feed/carriage return characters. This means that information appearing on separate lines on the screen display may not appear this way when redirected to the printer. Programs that have this problem allow you to use a switch, /LOG, which will add these characters to the output, making it more appropriate for printing. Example:

TM /L/LOG > PRN

Keep in mind that by itself /LOG does not redirect the output to the printer. You must remember to use the > PRN or else the output will appear on the screen.

If you are working with DOS you can use the ECHO command to issue a form feed command to your printer. This is useful following a redirected printing in order to move the paper to the top of the next form. The trick is to send a [Ctrl/L] character to the printer. You would enter: ECHO [Ctrl/L] > PRN. Note that [Ctrl/L] refers to holding down the [Ctrl] key while hitting L. When you enter this keystroke DOS displays ^L which is the DOS symbol for that key combination.

- **Text File.** You can use redirection to place the output into a text file on the disk. The file can then be edited, printed, copied or erased, just as any text file created with a word processing program. For example, the command below would capture in a text file called STATS.DAT the output of the SI(system information) program.

SI > stats.dat

The use of the /LOG option to improve the readability of the output also applies to storing data in a text file. Example:

TM/L/LOG > stats.dat

You can append the output onto a file using >> as the redirection option. This allows you to create a text file that is updated with new data each time the command is run. Example:

TM/L/LOG >> stats.dat

If STATS.DAT did not exist it would be created.

- **Suppress Display.** In some circumstances, usually in batch files, you may want to prevent the program from displaying information on the screen. This can be done by redirecting the output to a NUL device. NUL refers to a nonexistent device. The command below executes the Format Recover SAVE option but suppresses the message usually generated by this command.

FR/SAVE > NUL

Redirection can also be used to input information into a program from a source other than the keyboard typically, a text file. For example, the command FORMAT < KEYS tells DOS to input the text found in the KEYS file once the FORMAT program loads. Since the Norton Utilities programs generally have switches that cover the program's option, this technique is not needed.

Getting Help

You can display help information about command line programs by executing the program, followed by a ?. The command below display help for the Safe Format program.

SF ?

Special Screen Display Settings

One of the differences between the full-screen programs and the command line programs is that the command line programs rely on DOS to handle the screen display. The full-screen programs use more sophisticated screen display techniques which may require the use of special screen options to adjust the display to your system if it is not 100% compatible with IBM screen standards.

- **Driver.** If your computer has problems running the full screen programs, you should activate the BIOS compatible driver using the /D1 switch. Example:

NI/D1

- **Black and White Display.** If you are using a (CGA) Color Graphics Adapter you may want to suppress the display of colors in full-screen mode and have the program run in black and white. This option is usually associated with CGA adapters running single-color monitors. Example:

NI/BW

- **Snow.** Another problem associated with some CGA adapters is a pattern of interference called snow. You can adjust the full-screen programs to run in a display mode that minimizes this problem.

NI/NOSNOW

Batch File Analysis

If you are using the Norton Utilities programs as part of batch file programs, such as those discussed in Section II, you can use the ERRORLEVEL option of the IF command to test for successful completion of a Norton Utility program. If the program fails or encounters an error the ERRORLEVEL will be 1. Otherwise the ERRORLEVEL will be set at 0.

> *If the Disk Text command encounters bad clusters the ERRORLEVEL will be set at 1, even though the program runs successfully.*

Screen Color

The ANSI.SYS driver, discussed in Chapter 1, makes it possible to vary the screen colors, or in monochrome, the video attributes, of the screen while DOS is active. The screen colors can be set or changed using the SA (System Attributes) subcommand of the Batch Enhancer program.

> *The SA program included in version 4.0 of the Utilities has been incorporated into the Batch Enhancer program as the SA subcommand.*

The SA subcommand allows you to control the following qualities of the screen displays:

- **Intensity.** Intensity refers to how the characters are displayed. You can select BRIGHT, BOLD, or BLINKING. The BOLD and BRIGHT options are synonymous.

- **Main Setting.** There are three options, Normal, Reverse, or Underline. The Normal option will always produce white on black, even on color screens.

- **Foreground/background.** These options allow you to set *color* on *color* display. There are eight colors that can be used with this command: white, black, red, yellow, green, blue, magenta, and cyan. When specifying a foreground color you can use BRIGHT to produce a different shade or color. This means you can combine 16 different foreground colors with 8 background colors.

Note that the names do not always indicate what the color will look like. For example, YELLOW will generally produce a shade that most people would call *brown*. BRIGHT YELLOW will produce a color that is closer to yellow.

> *If you are using a display set up such as VGA (Video Graphics Adapter), your adapter may be able to produce more than 16 colors. The Norton Control Center program discussed later in this chapter provides access to a larger color palette.*

Suppose you want to reverse the video. You would do so by entering

BE SA REVERSE ↵

The video is changed to black on white. To return to the normal colors, enter

BE SA NORMAL ↵

Note that NORMAL and REVERSE always assume that the colors are black and white. Color screens can set combinations of white, black, red, yellow, magenta, blue, cyan, or green. If you have a color display, enter

BE SA BOLD RED ON WHITE ↵

Notice that the bold (or bright) attribute can be used only with the foreground color. Return the display to normal by entering

SA NOR ↵

Note that you only need to enter the first three letters, for example, YEL for yellow, BLI for blinking. If you want to use the system attributes to set the colors for DOS each time you turn on the computer, the best way is to add an SA subcommand to the AUTOEXEC file. Below is an example of such a command. This command sets the background color to blue and the foreground color to bright yellow. Note that the /CLS option is used to clear the screen after the colors have been set.

BE SA BRIGHT YELLOW ON BLUE/CLS

The SA subcommand also recognizes a /N switch. This switch will restrict the background color to the text area of the screen. This will leave a small border around the screen that retains its previous color. The pair of commands below illustrate how a border can be set to a different color than the rest of the screen. In this example, the first command sets the background to white. The second sets the background to blue but the /N switch preserves the white color in the border area.

BE SA RED ON WHITE
BE SA BRIGHT YELLOW ON BLUE/N

The colors assigned to DOS are recorded in the system's memory for the duration of the session or until you issue another SA subcommand. However, not all programs reset the screen properly after they terminate. In some cases a CLS (Clear Screen) command will restore the colors. In other cases, you will need to issue the SA subcommand again.

The Norton Control Center

The Norton Control Center appears in Version 4.5 only. This program combines some features found in separate Norton Utilities programs with some new features that can found only in the Control Center programs. The Norton Control Center program is oriented toward control of non-disk-related aspects of your system. The program provides you with eight areas of control.

- **Cursor Size.** This option allows you to change the size of the cursor that appears when working with DOS. Many applications will use the DOS cursor so that changes made in the Control Center will affect the size of the cursor within applications as well. Note that some applications are designed to alter the shape of the cursor. For example, Microsoft Word will automatically enlarge the cursor when it runs and reset the cursor to a thin line when it completes running, overruling the Control Center cursor setting.

- **DOS Colors.** This option is used to set the colors in DOS. It performs the same function as the SA Batch Enhancer subcommand. However, the Control Center display allows you to pick from a palette of colors instead of using the names of the colors.

- **Palette Colors.** This option is available on EGA and VGA monitors only. It provides a palette of 64 colors from which you can choose 16 as the active DOS color palette.

- **Video Mode.** Available on systems that have multiple mode adapters, e.g., CGA, EGA, VGA. The options list the display mode available on your adapter and allows you to select a new mode if desired. On EGA and VGA monitors you can have modes that display more than 25 lines on the screen at one time. Note that software programs are often written with the assumption that all screens are 25 lines in length. Running these programs in a 40 or more line mode can cause unpredictable results.

- **Keyboard Rate.** This option works on 80286 and 80386 computers. You can set two rates related to keyboard operation: (1) the rate at which repeating characters are entered when you press and hold down a key, and (2) the amount of time you need to hold down a key before the automatic repetition begins.

- **Serial Ports.** This option provides you with information about and direct control of the serial interface ports in your computer. Unlike parallel interface ports, serial ports can be programmed to transfer data at different rates using different formats. The Control Center displays show you the current values for each serial port and allow you to change the Baud rate, parity, databits, and stopbits values. This option provides a simple, easy to understand, and easy to use alternative to the DOS mode command to set serial port values. It also provides a quick way to determine what serial ports are installed in a given computer.

- **Watches.** This option allows you to use the computer's memory to time up to four different events simultaneously. The display performs the same function as the (TM) Time Mark program discussed in Chapter 5. Clocks started with the TM program will appear running with the correct elapsed time in the Watches display. Conversely, clocks started with the Watches display can also be controlled by TM commands. One feature available in the Watches display that is not available with TM is the ability to pause a clock and restart it.

- **Time and Date.** This option allows you to set the system time and date. It performs the same function as the DOS TIME and DATE commands.

Changing the Cursor Size

When you load the Norton Control Center program, the first option on the menu is the cursor size option. Enter

ncc ↵

The Control Center display is divided into two parts. The column on the left will always show the Control Center menu. The column on the right will show the display for the option currently highlighted in the menu, as shown in Figure 6-3.

The center of the right side of the display is a box that shows an enlarged version of the current system cursor. The cursor is composed of a line beginning with 0. In Figure 6-3 the cursor consists of the last two lines in the box, lines 6 and 7. Note that the total number of lines in the cursor box will vary with each display type. For example, most color screens will show 8 lines (0-7) while monochrome screens will show 14 lines (0-13).

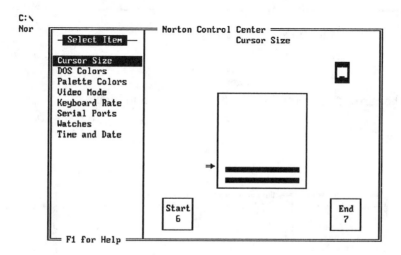

Figure 6-3 Cursor Size display.

You can change the cursor by activating the Cursor Size option. This is done by pressing ↵ while the option is highlighted, or pressing the first letter of the option, in this case C. Enter

↵

When you activate the Cursor Size option the highlight moves from the menu on the left side of the display, to the right side, highlighting the title **Cursor Size**. The boxes at the bottom of the display show the starting and ending line numbers. The small box in the upper right shows how the cursor will appear when you return to DOS.

The following keys can be used in Cursor Size.

↑ ↓	Toggle on/off lines
← →	
[tab]	Change between start and end
↵	Save cursor and return to menu
[Home]	
[Pg Up]	Move to top line
[End]	
[Pg Dn]	Move to last line
[Esc]	Return to menu -- no save
*	Set cursor to default size

Set the cursor to full size by entering

[Home] ↵

The cursor is now a full-height block as shown in Figure 6-4.

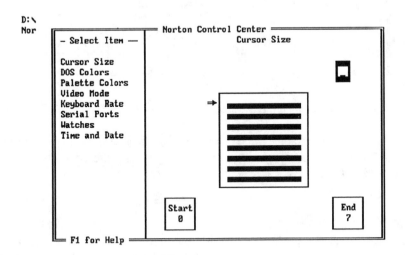

Figure 6-4 Cursor size altered.

Return to the menu by entering

↵

Colors

There are two settings on the Control Center menu that affect the colors used on the screen display. The first is the **DOS Colors** setting. This applies to monochrome, CGA, EGA, and VGA color adapters. This option allows you to select a color for the foreground, background, and border area. These colors will be active when DOS is active. Most applications will reset the screen colors while they are running. These colors may differ from those used by DOS.

The second setting, **Palette Colors,** applies only to EGA and VGA displays. This palette contains 64 colors. Although DOS will work with only 16 colors at one time, the palette allows you to select your own set of 16 out of the 64 possible colors.

Activate the **DOS Colors** option by entering

d

When activated, the DOS Colors options displays three blocks that show the 16 colors available. If you are working with a monochrome screen you will see only white, black, and bold white, shade (Figure 6-5). On color screens you will see 16 different colors: black, blue, green, cyan, red, magenta, yellow, and white, plus a bold of each color.

Although DOS has 16 colors there are some limitations in the way that they actually appear. The 16 standard colors contain black twice, once for black and once for bold black. A color defined as bold black doesn't make much sense. You will find that on most monitors bold black is a charcoal gray shade, just a bit lighter than actual black. Also note that if you attempt to select a bold color as a background color the effect will be to use the normal color but set the foreground color to blinking.

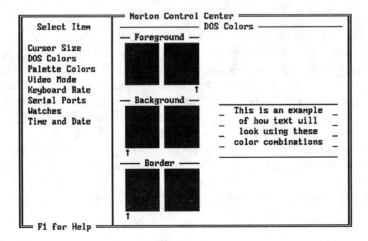

Figure 6-5 DOS Colors selection.

In this display you can use the following keys.

↑↓	
[tab]	Select foreground, background, border
←→	Select 1 of 16 colors
↵	Save colors and return to menu
[Esc]	Return to menu-no save
*	Return to default colors

Note that the default colors refer to those colors that were in effect when the option was activated, not to the default colors for DOS which are always black and white when the system is first booted.

Return to the menu by entering

↵

The EGA/VGA Palette

If you are using EGA or VGA displays you can use the Palette Colors function to select 16 colors from among 64 possible colors for use with DOS.

To understand what you can do with the Palette, it might be useful to think of the 16 DOS colors not as actual fixed colors, such as green or red, but as spaces or slots that can be filled with a single color. DOS has only 16 slots for colors. But EGA and VGA displays can display a much wider array of colors. The Palette Colors option provides access to 64 colors although some VGA displays are capable of many times that number of color combinations.

The Palette can be used to fill any one of the 16 DOS slots with any one of the 64 colors. The Control Center numbers these colors 0 through 63. It is interesting to note that you are not restricted in your selection to colors that match the names usually associated with particular color slots or numbers. For example, color 1 is usually blue. However, you can select any one of the 64 colors for that slot, even if it is in a shade of a different color, such as green, red or grey.

Activate the Palette by entering

p

The right side of the display shows a list of 16 colors. The list has four columns. The first column is numbered from 0 to 15. The second column lists the names of the colors. The third column shows a sample of the color. The final column shows the number of that color.

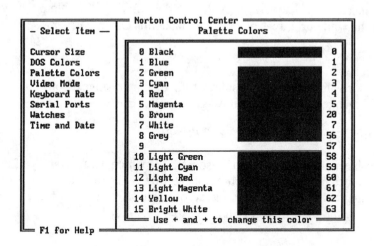

Figure 6-6 Color Palette display (color not reproduced).

In this display you can use the following keys.

+	Changes to the next color value
-	Changes to the previous color value

*	Restores original color
→ ←	Displays color menu-selects next color
[tab]	Moves down the menu to next color slot
↑ ↓	Moves to the next or previous color slot
↵	Save colors and return to menu
[Esc]	Return to menu-no save

Suppose you want to change some of colors currently used in the 16 color slots. First, select the color slot you want to change, probably a color you do not like or use very much. In this example, change color 6. This is the color labeled Brown. Enter

↓ (6 times)

> *The color labeled as brown in the Control Center display is the same color that is used for yellow in the Batch Enhancer SA subcommand.*

There are two ways to select a color for the current slot. The + and - minus keys will increase or decrease the value of the color by one. Note that you can use either the white or gray + or - keys to make this change. Enter

-

The color value on the right sides of the display changes from 20 to 19. The color itself changes to a bright yellow-green color. Enter

+ (3 times)

The value of the color is increased to 22, which is a bright yellow-green color. The other method by which colors can be changed is to use the ← or → keys. Pressing either one displays the color menu. Note that both the ← and → keys will have the same effect. Enter

→

The Control Center displays a window showing the colors available in the 64 color palette, as shown in Figure 6-7. The advantage of the color menu display is that the colors are arranged according to shade rather than color number.

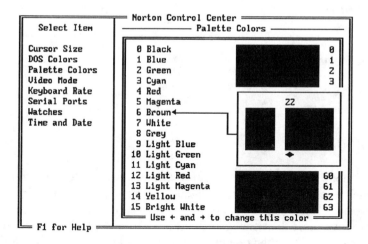

Figure 6-7 Color choice menu displayed.

You can select a color from the color menu by using the ← and → keys to scroll horizontally within the menu. Enter

← (5 times)

The display scrolls to the left, moving through various shades of green. The number that appears at the top of the menu shows the color number of the selected color. Note that because the colors are grouped by shade the values that appear as you move are not in numeric order. For example, the shades of green through which you have just scrolled were numbered 58, 50, 18, 26, and 2. When you find a color you like, save it by entering ↵. Select a color by entering

← (6 times)
↵

You have selected color 55 as the color to use as **brown.** This means any time the color brown (called yellow in the Batch Enhancer and other programs) is used, color 55, a pale yellow or cream color, will appear.

Keep in mind that alterations made to the color palette will effect only the current session. In order to return to activate a different set of colors you will need to use the Control Center program each time the computer is booted. Later in this chapter you will learn how palette colors and other Control Center settings can be saved to files and reloaded using batch file commands.

> *The colors used in the palette can also be affected by applications that reset the palette.*

Exit the Palette by entering

↵

Video Mode

The video mode option on the Control Center menu allows you to switch between the various display modes available on your display adapter. MS-DOS computers can be used with a variety of display adapters and monitors. Many of the adapters have more than one display mode. You can use this option to change the display mode if more than one mode is available on your display set-up.

> *Display modes refer to text display modes that can be selected from EGA and VGA displays. Graphics modes available on CGA, EGA, and VGA adapters cannot be accessed through the Control Center.*

On EGA screens you can select a 43 line display mode. On VGA displays you can select 40 or 50 lines displays, shown in Figure 6-8.

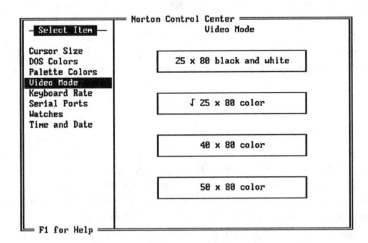

Figure 6-8 Screen display of video mode options.

For example, suppose you want to change your VGA screen display to a 50 line mode. Activate the video mode display by entering

v

Use the ↑ or ↓ to highlight the display mode you want. In this case you would want to jump to the last option on the display. Enter

[Pg Dn] ↵

When you select a video mode the screen will immediately change to reflect the new selection. In this example the screen shows the Control Center display in 50 line mode. If you were to exit the Control Center program at this point, all DOS operations would display information in the 50 line mode.

> *While it is true that the information generated by DOS commands will appear in the 50 line mode, this is not to say that DOS Version 3.x will take advantage of the 50 line display to show more information. For example, the DIR command will still display only 25 lines at a time in the top half of the screen. In order to take advantage of the compressed text modes, the application needs to support more than a 25 line display. For example, the Norton Commander will recognize the compressed line mode and lengthen its display accordingly.*

Switch back to the original 25 line mode by entering

↑ *(2 times)*
↵

Note that to exit the Videomode display you need to enter a ← key, not the ↵ used in previous options. Enter

←

Keyboard Rate

If you are using an 80286 (AT) or 80386 based computer you can use the Keyboard Rate option to alter sensitivity of the keyboard when a key is held down, in order to repeat the character automatically. You can control the rate at which characters are repeated and the length of time a key must be held down before the repetitions begin.

To activate the Keyboard Rate option, enter

k

The display on the right side of the screen is divided into two parts, as shown in Figure 6-9. The top part of the screen shows the number of characters per second that will be typed if a key is held down long enough to activate repetition. The default rate is ten characters per second. The bottom part of the display controls the length of time a key must be held down before automatic repetitions begin. The default is a delay of .5 seconds.

> *The keyboard rate changes affect all the keyboard keys, including the cursor arrow keys which are usually the keys most often used with automatic repetition. For example, if you feel that the response of the arrows is sluggish when cursoring through word processing text, you can use the Control Center keyboard rates to increase the response sensitivity of the keyboard. Keep in mind that the change affects all the other keys, as well as the arrow keys.*

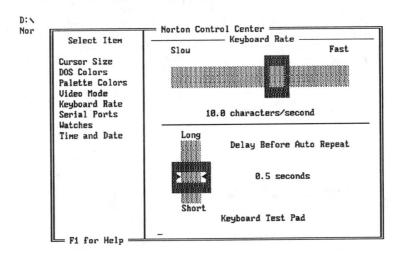

Figure 6-9 Keyboard rate display.

Suppose you want to make your keyboard less sensitive to repetitions. The ← and → keys will decrease or increase the rate of the number of characters per second. The ↑ and ↓ keys will change the delay time before the auto repeat kicks in.

If you want to set the keyboard to its maximum sensitivity, enter

[End]
[Pg Dn]

This sets the repetition rate at 30 characters per second and the delay factor at .25 seconds. Pressing ↵ will set the keyboard to these rates. [Esc] exits the option ignoring the changes. You can press * to restore the original values. You can also test the response of the keyboard by pressing any character. The character will display in the highlighted area at the bottom of the display. Exit without saving the changes by entering

[Esc]

Note DOS 4.0 allows you to set the keyboard rates with the MODE command. Not available in earlier versions of DOS.

Serial Ports

MS-DOS computers use two types of communications ports: parallel and serial. Parallel ports are most commonly used for sending data to printers. Serial ports can be used for printers, modems, mice, or forms of network communications.

The essential difference between parallel and serial communications can be inferred from their names. One byte of data is actually composed of 8 data bits. When you want to send a byte of information from your computer to another device such as a printer or modem, there are two basic approaches. The parallel approach uses a multi-wire cable to send all the bits across at the same time. This is a simple, fast approach, but is reliable only over short distances. Serial communication sends data as a series of bits, one after the other. While ostensibly slower than sending 8 bits all at one time, serial communication has significant advantages. Serial communications can be a variety of methods to ensure that the information has been received correctly. Serial interfaces are generally used when the communication is two-way, such as telecommunications using modems.

The Control Center Serial Ports option has two functions: (1) it provides information about the serial ports in your system and (2) it allows you to change the parameters used by the individual serial ports. To activate the Serial Ports option, enter

s

The Serial Ports display is divided into two parts, as shown in Figure 6-10. The upper portion of the display lists the serial ports and their settings options. A check mark appears beside the current value. The bottom of the display is a summary of the current settings of the serial ports.

```
 ══════════════════ Norton Control Center ══════════════
┌─────────────────┬──────────────── Serial Ports ──────────────┐
│   Select Item   │                                            │
│                 │  Port   Baud    Parity Databits  Stopbits   │
│  Cursor Size    │                                            │
│  DOS Colors     │                                            │
│  Palette Colors │ √ COM1   110      None     7         1      │
│  Video Mode     │   COM2   150    √ Odd   √ 8       √ 2      │
│  Keyboard Rate  │          300      Even                      │
│  Serial Ports   │          600                               │
│  Watches        │         1200                               │
│  Time and Date  │       √ 2400                               │
│                 │         4800                               │
│                 │         9600                               │
│                 │                                            │
│                 │                 ── Summary ──               │
│                 │   COM1   2400     Odd      8         2      │
│                 │   COM2   2400     None     8         1      │
│                 │   COM3          Not available               │
│                 │   COM4          Not available               │
└─────────────────┤                                            │
 ══ F1 for Help ══└────────────────────────────────────────────┘
```

Figure 6-10 Serial Ports option display.

Each serial port has a special name that DOS will recognize, and four settings that control the way it functions.

- **Port Names.** DOS uses the names COM1, COM2, COM3, and COM4 to refer to the serial ports, if any, used in the system.

- **Baud.** The baud rate is the number of bits per second that the serial port will send. Values for this can be 100, 150, 300, 600, 1200, 2400, 4800, or 9600. Printers typically run at 9600 baud, while modems range from 300 to 2400 baud. The higher the baud rate the faster the communications.

- **Parity.** Parity refers to a method by which the number of binary 1 values sent with each data sequence can be checked to prevent transmission errors. Parity checking can be set for even, odd, or none.

- **Databits.** This value indicates the number of bits in each data sequence that are actual data. The values can be 7 or 8. When data is set for 7, only standard ASCII characters can be sent.

- **Stopbits.** This value indicates the number of extra bits that are sent to mark the end of a data transmission sequence. The value can be either 1 or 2.

The settings indicate that serial ports can be programmed to send data in different ways, including additional bits that can aid in communication and error checking.

The reason for setting these various options is to make sure that the data you are sending matches up with the data format the receiving device or computer expects. The default values are usually 2400 baud, odd parity, 8 databits, and 2 stopbits.

In this display the ↑ and ↓ keys are used to select a different value in the current column. The ← and → keys move the highlight from column to column. The ↵ key saves the current settings and programs the serial ports accordingly. [Esc] cancels any changes, while the * key resets the values to the original settings.

Suppose you want to set up the serial port COM2 to communicate with a printer that has a serial interface. You need to check the printer documentation to find what values the printer uses for baud rate, parity, data, and stopbits. Typically, these would be 9600 baud, parity None, 8 databits, and 1 stopbit. You can use the Control Center to set the values of the COM2 port to match the printer's serial interface. First select COM2 by entering

↓

To set the baud rate move the highlight into the baud column and select 9600 by entering

→
↓ *(2 times)*

Change the parity to none by entering

→ ↓

Save the changes by entering

↵

COM2 is now set to communicate within the correct format for the printer. Note that not all programs select the communications port to use for printing. Word processing programs such as Microsoft Word have options by which you can designate that you want to print through a particular port. Once you have programmed the port with the Control Center you can use it with Word by selecting the port name from the Printer Options menu. WordPerfect also programs the serial port options so that the Control Center Serial Port options are not needed by WordPerfect users.

Other applications such as Lotus 1-2-3 Release 2, or dBASE III Plus simply use the DOS PRN device for printed output. With these programs it is necessary to use the DOS MODE command to assign the communications port to the PRN name. Example:

MODE LPT1:=COM2

Watches

The Watches options provide you with the ability to create stopwatch timers using the computer's system clock and memory to calculate the elapsed time between two events. This is the same function performed by the Time Mark (TM.EXE) program discussed in Chapter 5. Clocks started by the TM program appear on and can be controlled by the Watches option. Conversely, watch timers started in the Control Center can be accessed by the TM command. Both programs use the same methods and memory areas. The Watches display has one command not found in the TM program. In the Watches display you can pause and then restart a watch timer without resetting it.

Activate the watch timer display by entering

W

The display shows four timers. The timers correspond to the /C1, /C2, /C3, and /C4 timers that can be set with the TM program.

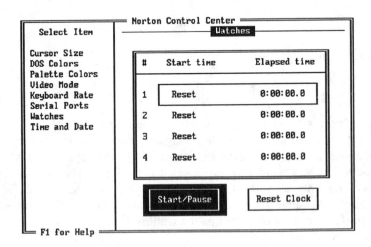

Figure 6-11 Watch timer display.

The following keys can be used in this option window:

↑ ↓	Select timers 1-4
← →	Select Start/Pause or Reset Clock
↵	Activate option start, pause or reset
r	Reset highlighted clock
s	Start or pause highlighted clock
[Esc]	Return to menu-timers continue

Return to the menu by entering

[Esc]

Time and Date

The last item in the Control Center display is the Time and Date setting option. This option is similar to the DOS DATE and TIME commands in that it allows you to set the system date and time.

In addition to setting the DOS date and time, if the program is run on an 80286 (AT) or 80386 machine the date and time is permanently changed. This avoids the need to run a special diagnostics program in order to reset the system clock for daylight savings or time zone changes. Note that the DOS commands DATE and TIME do not reset the internal clock, only the DOS clock, which remains active until you reboot the computer.

To activate the Date and Time option, enter

t

Figure 6-12 shows the display window that appears when the Date and Time option is selected.

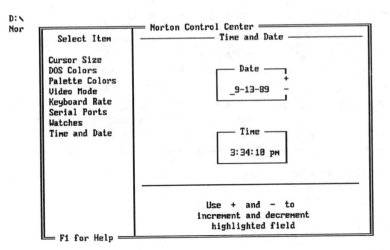

Figure 6-12 Date and time setting window.

While in this window, the following keys can be used.

↑ ↓	
[Tab]	Select date or time to change
→ ←	Highlight value within date or time
+	Increase highlighted value
-	Decrease highlighted value
↵	Set system clock and return to menu
[Esc]	Ignore changes and return to menu

Return to the menu by entering

↵

> *The ability of the Date and Time option to permanently reset the system clock is related to the BIOS used in the computer. Some BIOS chips do not allow the program to operate properly, requiring you to run the diagnostic program to set the clock.*

Saving Control Center Settings

So far the discussion has centered around the manual use of the Control Center. There are two other ways in which the Norton Control Center program can be used.

- **Options Switches.** You can set the video mode and keyboard rate to its most sensitive by executing the Control Center from DOS using switches. Note that the DOS Colors options can be executed using the Batch Enhancer SA subcommand, and that the Watches options can be controlled with the TM program. Thus four of the eight Control Center options can be included in batch files.

- **Stored Settings.** With the exception of the Date and Time option, you can store the current set of Control Center specifications in a file that can be used to restore those settings in part or in whole at some later time. You can create as many different specification files as you desire. This makes it easy to access Control Center options from within batch files.

A specification file is created by pressing [F2] while the Control Center menu is active. Enter

[F2]

The program displays a window in the center of the screen as shown in Figure 6-13. Enter a filename to be used to store the specifications. The filename can be any valid DOS filename. Keep in mind that despite the size of the entry area you are restricted to DOS filename sizes, i.e. eight character names and optional three-character extensions.

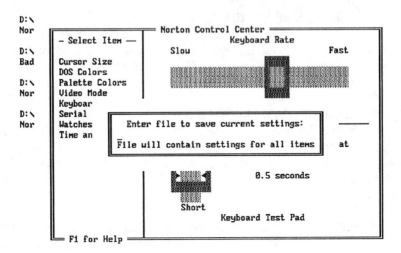

Figure 6-13 Set name for specification file.

Enter

sample.spc ↵

When you enter the filename the Control Center does not actually save the file settings. Instead, the filename is stored in memory. You can make additional changes to settings using the Control Center commands. When you exit the Control Center program using [Esc] or [F10], a window will be displayed asking you if you want to save the current setting under the selected filename. Enter

[Esc]

The program displays a window like the one in Figure 6-14 asking you to confirm the creation of the specification file. Note that the settings saved are those that are currently in force in the Control Center.

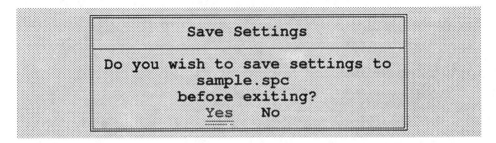

Figure 6-14 Window asks you to confirm saving of specifications.

Enter

y

Using Control Center Options Switches

The Control Center can be used as a command line in order to set the video mode from DOS or a DOS batch file. The switches are:

/BW80	25 x 80 black and white
/CO80	
/25	25 x 80 in color
/35	35 lines (EGA adapter)
/43	43 lines (EGA adapter)
/40	40 lines (VGA adapter)
/50	50 lines (VGA adapter)

For example, to set the video mode on a VGA monitor to 50 lines, enter

NCC/50 ↵

The program displays a message **Display changed to 50 rows.** The video display changes to the compressed line height needed to display 50 lines of text on the screen. To return to the default video mode, CO80 on a VGA monitor, enter

NCC/25 ↵

In addition to the video mode options, you can also set the keyboard to maximum sensitivity using the **/FASTKEY.** You can use **/FASTKEY** alone or in combination with a video switch. The command below sets the VGA video to 40 lines and maximizes the keyboard sensitivity.

NCC/40/FASTKEY ↵

This time the message confirms that the keyboard rates are set to 30 character per second and a delay of .25 seconds.

> *There is no switch command that resets the keyboard rates to any other values except maximum sensitivity. If you wish to reduce the sensitivity of the keyboard following the use of /FASTKEY you must do so using the Control Center manually or by accessing a Control Center specification file.*

You can suppress the display of the messages by using the >NUL redirection command. Enter

NCC/25>NUL ↵

The display changes but no message is displayed. Using the Control Center in this way allows it to operate in the background while running a batch file.

Using a Specification File

Once you have created a specification file there are two ways that it can be used.

- **Restore Control Center.** You can use the specification file to load the Control Center with the same settings as were saved when you exited it previously. You can then use the Control Center menu to make alterations to the setting, or exit the program.

- **Set attributes from DOS.** Use special switches to set some or all of the specifications from DOS. Note that when these settings switches are used a filename of a specification file is required. The Control Center program performs the settings changes but does not enter its full screen mode. Instead it operates like a command line program which can be executed from DOS or a DOS batch file.

Once you have created a Control Center specification file you can activate the Control Center with the settings stored in the specification by following the NCC command with the name of the file. The command below loads the Control Center program and uses the SAMPLE.SPC file to set the options to the way they were when the SAMPLE.SPC file was created.

NCC sample.spc ↵

The Control Center loads using the specifications from the SAMPLE.SPC as the default settings. The use of a specification file also automatically designates that file as the current specification file. This means that if you make any changes to the settings, when you exit the program you will be asked if you want to save the current settings in the SAMPLE.SPC file. If you want to save the modified settings in a different filename you will need to use [F2] to change the name of the specification file.

Exit the program by entering

[Esc]

The second way in which a specification file can be used is to use a set of switches that activate attributes without loading the full-screen version of the Control Center program. This method can be used at the DOS prompt and is particularly useful in batch files. The special switches are:

/SETALL	Sets all stored specifications
/CURSOR	Sets the cursor size
/DOSCOLOR	Sets the DOS colors
/PALETTE	Sets the color palette
/DISPLAY	Sets the display mode
/KEYRATE	Sets the keyboard rates
/COM#	Programs the serial ports

These switch commands are a bit different than the usual switch commands, in that they do not specifically designate what settings to activate. The switches correspond to the option on the Control Center menu. Each one activates the settings for that menu option stored in the specification file. For example, suppose you want to use the Control Center program to set the COM ports for printing. The correct specifications are stored in the SAMPLE.SPC file. Enter

NCC sample.spc/COM2 ↵

The program executes as a command line application. The communications port specified, COM2, is programmed to the values stored in the SAMPLE.SPC file. The Control Center confirms the result by displaying the name of the program and **COM2: 9600,None,8,1.**

You can load all the settings from a specification file using the /SETALL switch. Enter

NCC sample.spc/SETALL ↵

Use the >NUL redirection option to suppress the display. This is useful in batch files where you want the Control Center to operate in the background. The previous command can be executed with no screen output by entering

NCC sample.spc/SET ALL > NUL ↵

The Norton Control Center represents a powerful new addition to the Norton Utilities package. The Control Center can be used manually to select system options in a full-screen mode. By saving specifications in a file you can also execute stored settings using the Control Center as a command line program. Note that you can set watch timers using the TM program since the Control Center does not support switches for watch settings.

Speed Disk

In Part I of this book the system used by MS-DOS to allocate space for files has been described in some detail. The key element to this system is the use of the directory and file allocation table to assign data clusters to specific filenames. The major advantage of this system is its ability to use all available disk space for files currently in use. When a file is erased, the clusters that were occupied by that file are now free to be used for other files. These can be existing files that are expanded or entirely new files.

One result of this type of system is that the clusters allocated to a given file are not necessarily consecutive in order. In fact, the allocation chain of clusters may jump back and forth between lower and higher cluster numbers. Remember that DOS seeks to use up all the unallocated clusters on the disk to maximize your storage space. When files consist of scattered groups of clusters they are called "fragmented" files. Fragmented files generally take longer to read and write because the disk drive must move back and forth around the disk to locate the clusters.

Fragmentation of directories is another aspect of organization that can affect hard disk performance. One of the primary functions of DOS directories is to group together related files. However, the files that are listed in a single directory are not necessarily stored as a physical group. They may be scattered throughout the disk. When you add a file to a directory DOS stores the file in the first available space. This space may be quite some distance from the other files listed in the directory.

Depending upon the amount of deleting and adding of files that has been performed on a disk, a certain degree of file and directory fragmentation will exist. A high degree of fragmentation will serve to decrease the overall speed of your hard disk. If your hard disk is very full and you delete old files to make room for new ones, you probably have noticed a decrease in performance since you first started using it.

The solution to this problem is to give DOS an opportunity to rearrange the clusters so that the logical groupings, the files and directories, match up with the physical groups, the list of clusters allocated to that file.

Fragmentation can occur on disks of any type, hard or floppy. While the concern for performance is usually related to hard disks only, you can unfragment floppy disks.

One way to do this is to backup your entire hard disk, reformat the disk, then restore the files. The Norton Utilities programs provides a much simpler and safer method of eliminating the fragmentation from a disk. The SD (Speed Disk) program can both analyze and correct fragmentation on a hard or floppy disk. SD works by analyzing the fragmentation on the disk as reflected in the file allocation table. It can then correct the fragmentation by reading cluster data into the memory and rewriting it into contiguous clusters. In addition, the SD performs other organizational operations such as placing all the directory information at the beginning of the disk. Remember that directories, other than the root, are stored in data clusters like files and are therefore subject to problems with fragmentation also.

SD also collects all the empty clusters on the disk and places them into a single block at the end of the existing files. This helps new files to be written in contiguous blocks and so cuts down on fragmenting of new files and increasing the time period before another SD is necessary.

The SD program will take some time to run because it will need to read and rewrite the information on the entire disk. It is important to remember that programs like SD can be potentially dangerous because they are changing the data on the hard disk. If the SD program is interrupted by a reboot, disk error, power failure, and so on, permanent loss of information is possible. Before you perform an SD it is probably a good idea to run the Norton Disk Doctor or use CHKDSK/F and DT (Disk Test) to eliminate any existing problems on the disk.

Caution! Because SD actually rewrites the data on the disk into new locations, it will probably make unerasing of files impossible. If you need to recover data in the unused areas of the disk, do not perform a SD until you have completed your unerase operations.

You can interrupt the SD program once it has begun by pressing [Esc]. Remember that when you enter [Esc], the Speed Disk program will not stop immediately. Instead it completes the operation it was performing when you entered [Esc] and stops at the next safe point.

Analyzing the Disk

How do you know the degree of fragmentation that exists on your hard disk? The Speed Disk program has a **REPORT** option that summarizes the current state of fragmentation on the disk. The simplest type of report is one that summarizes the total amount of fragmentation on the disk. Enter

SD/REPORT ↵

The program reads the data from the disk and returns a percentage of the disk that is unfragmented.

```
         Total of the entire disk: 75% unfragmented
```

You can get a file-by-file listing showing the degree of fragmentation of individual files by specifying a DOS path name with the command. The command below generates a detailed report about the files in the \NORTON directory as shown in Figure 6-15. Enter

SD \norton/REPORT ↵

```
D:\NORTON
read.me        100%   fr.exe        45%   ndd.exe       86%   nu.exe         82%
nu.hlp         100%   ds.exe        88%   dt.exe        83%   ff.exe        100%
ncc.exe        100%   ncd.exe      100%   ni.exe       100%   qu.exe        100%
sd.exe         100%   sf.exe       100%   ud.exe       100%   be.exe        100%
di.exe         100%   fa.exe       100%   fd.exe       100%   fi.exe        100%
fs.exe         100%   ld.exe       100%   lp.exe       100%   tm.exe        100%
si.exe         100%   ts.exe       100%   vl.exe       100%   wipedisk.exe  100%
wipefile.exe   100%   fileinfo.fi  100%   mary.~       100%   bedemo.bat    100%
bedemo.dat     100%   menu.dat     100%   make-tut.bin  74%   make-tut.bat  100%
tut-read.me    100%   format.exe   100%   test.~ba     100%   test.bat      100%
buzzer.snd     100%   mary         100%   buzzer.~sn   100%

Directory Total: 95% unfragmented
```

Figure 6-15 Fragmentation reports with individual files.

If you wanted to list all the files on a hard disk as part of a fragmentation report you would select the root directory, \, and use the /S option to include all subdirectories on the disk. In most cases you would want to also include a pause option, /P, so that the report stops after each screen of information is displayed. Enter

SD \REPORT/S/P ↵

The report fills the screen with the data about the file on the disk, listing each directory as a group. Pressing [space bar] displays the next screen. Enter

[space bar]

To stop the report, enter

[F10]

You can produce a directory-by-directory summary of the fragmentation by using the /T option. Enter

SD \REPORT/S/T ↵

The report lists unfragmentation for each of the directories on the disk.

If you want to print the report you can use the DOS redirection option >PRN to send the output to the printer. The command below will print the directory by directory report.

SD \REPORT/S/T >PRN ↵

Unfragmenting a Disk

If your report indicates that there is significant fragmentation, e.g., less than 75 percent, of the disk is unfragmented, your next step is to run the SD program and reorganize the data on the disk. Usually this is done by running SD in the full-screen display mode. Enter

SD ↵

The program displays a window in the center of the screen asking you to select the drive that you want to work with, as shown below.

```
┌──────────────────────────────┐
│   Select drive to optimize   │
├──────────────────────────────┤
│     A:     C:     D:         │
├──────────────────────────────┤
│   Current drive: D:          │
└──────────────────────────────┘
```

Note that if you want to skip this window you can start SD with a drive designation, e.g., **SD d:**. The program will load and automatically read the specified disk by passing the disk selection window. Enter

↵

The program then displays a map of the current state of space usage on the disk, as shown in Figure 6-16. The map displays special symbols to indicate the status of the disk space. There are four different types of symbols used on the map.

- **Used Block**. This is space that used by normal files. Data in areas marked with this symbol can be relocated by SD to reduce the disk fragmentation. (Note that because the data in these blocks is overwritten as part of the condensing operation, unerasing of files is probably not possible following SD condensing.)

- **Unused Block**. These are clusters not currently allocated to a file. Ideally, all unused blocks should be positioned as a single block following the data on the disk. When these blocks appear interspersed between used blocks they are referred to as *holes*.

- **Unmovable Block.** Certain files on the disk may be position-sensitive. This means that the exact locations of these files may be significant to certain programs. The most common example of this type of file includes the DOS system files IO.SYS (IBMBIO.COM) and MSDOS.SYS (IBMDOS.COM). Other position-sensitive files are placed on the disk as part of copy protection schemes implemented by some programs. The SD program will treat as position sensitive any files with a **hidden** or **system** attribute. If you have used the File Attribute or DOS Attrib command to mark files as hidden, they will not be unfragmented.

- **Bad Block**. These are areas marked by DOS at the time of formatting as unusable. They can also include clusters marked as bad by the Disk Test or Norton Disk Doctor program.

- **Block Size.** The last value in the map legend tells you the number of clusters represented by each block. Note that a block will be marked as used, bad, or unmovable, if only part of the data represented by block falls into that category. For this reason the map may appear to indicate that there are more unmovable or bad blocks than there really are.

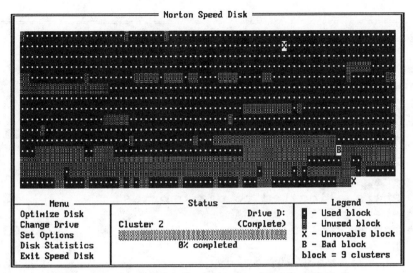

Figure 6-16 Speed Disk displays map of disk fragmentation.

In addition to the map, the SD program provides a statistical summary of the analysis. This summary can be displayed by using the **Disk Statistics** option found on the menu in the lower left corner of the display. Enter

d

The program displays a window, shown in Figure 6-17, showing information about disk usage. The display shows the actual number of clusters that are used, unused, unmovable, and bad on the current disk. The summary is a more accurate representation of the actual disk usage than is the disk map.

```
┌──────────────────────────────────────────────┐
│            Disk Statistics for Drive D:        │
├──────────────────────────────────────────────┤
│ Disk Size:                              41M    │
│ Percentage of disk used:                80%    │
│ Percentage of unfragmented files:       90%    │
│ Number of directories on drive:         24     │
│ Number of files on drive:             1,214    │
│                                                │
│ Clusters allocated to movable files:    8,123  │
│ Clusters allocated to unmovable files: +    2  │
│ Clusters allocated to directories:     +   26  │
│ Clusters marked as bad:                +    3  │
│ Unused (free) clusters:                + 2,031 │
│                                        ──────── │
│ Total clusters on drive:               10,185  │
│                                                │
│                      Ok                        │
└──────────────────────────────────────────────┘
```

Figure 6-17 Statistical summary of disk fragmentation.

Return to the disk map display by entering

↵

Speed Disk Option

The SD has several ways in which it can attempt to improve disk performance by rearranging the data on the disk. You can select the method that you want to use by picking **Set Options** from the menu. Enter

s

The program displays a window, as shown in Figure 6-18, that lists the option you can select.

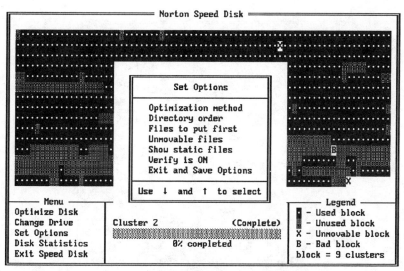

Figure 6-18 Speed Disk options window.

- **Optimization Method.** This is the most important option because it controls what actual techniques are used in the optimization process.

- **Directory Order.** As part of the optimization process, the Speed Disk program will make changes in the order in which the directories on the disk are stored. You can use this option to display information about the directories that SD will place at the beginning of the disk. You can also use the option to modify or extend the directory order.

- **Files to Put First.** You can specify files that you want to place at the beginning of the disk (Figure 6-19). The default is to place all files with COM or EXE extensions at the front of the disk because the files are often read but rarely rewritten.

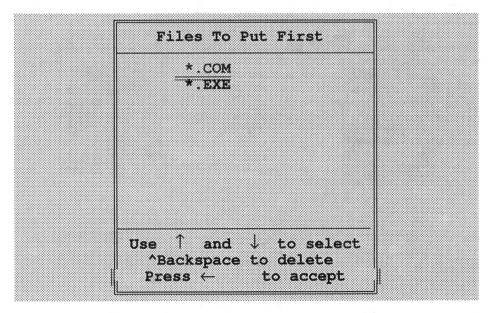

Figure 6-19 Files listed are placed at the beginning of the disk.

- **Unmovable Files.** This option presents a list of the unmovable files located during the disk analysis. In addition to displaying the unmovable files you can use this option to add files to the list by entering their names.

- **Show Static Files.** This option lists files that are considered static files, as shown in Figure 6-20. Files with a *system* attribute are considered static. The Format Recover program creates a static files called FRECOVER.IDX. These files are treated like unmovable files when the disk is reorganized.

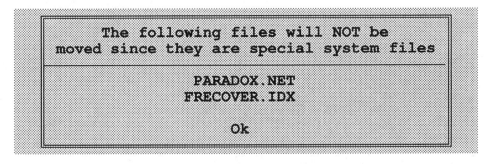

Figure 6-20 Files listed are placed at the beginning of the disk.

- **Verify is ON/OFF.** This option selects whether or not the program should verify each data cluster after it is rewritten. The default is OFF. When verify is on, the program immediately rereads each cluster after it is written, as an extra measure to ensure accuracy. Verification lengthens the time required to reorganize a disk.

Turn on the verify option by entering

v ↵

Optimization Methods

The SD program allows you to select the method to be used to reorganize the disk. The primary issue involved is the amount of time required to perform the optimization. The more thorough the reorganization the more time is required for the processing. Enter

o

The program displays a window with four options, as shown in Figure 6-21. The √ indicates the current method. By default, Complete Optimization is selected.

- **Complete Optimization.** This method performs the most complete reorganization of the disk data, resulting in the largest improvement in disk performance. This method uses your list of directories and files to place those items at the beginning of the disk. By default this would place all the program files, EXE and COM, at the beginning of the disk. The remainder of the files are unfragmented and moved forward to fill any *holes* on the disk. This method requires the most amount of time to complete.

- **File Unfragment.** This option reorganizes the most fragmented files on the disk. It does not move files or directories, nor will it fill all the holes on the disk. This method eliminates significant file fragmentation in less time than the **Complete Optimization** method.

- **Quick Compress.** This method of disk reorganization is concerned chiefly with filling holes left on the disk. It does not unfragment existing files. This method may not improve performance on a significantly fragmented disk. However, by filling the holes and placing all free space at the end of the disk, any new file added to the disk will be unfragmented. Typically, you would use this option on a disk that has recently undergone a **Complete Optimization**, following which you would delete a large amount of data. The existing files would still be unfragmented but there would be gaps in the data spacing needing to be filled.

- **Only Optimize Directories.** This is the fastest method of organization. It affects only the directories on the disk. This method does not unfragment files or fill holes in the disk data. While this method moves a minimum amount of data, it can have a significant effect on disk performance. Keep in mind that directories are stored in disk clusters just like files are. When you create a directory, the directory is stored at the next available cluster. If the disk already contains a large amount of data, the new directory can be placed quite far from other directories-in particular, those that were first created when the disk was new. This option moves all directory data to the front of the disk. This means that directory searches used to locate files are carried out with maximum efficiency.

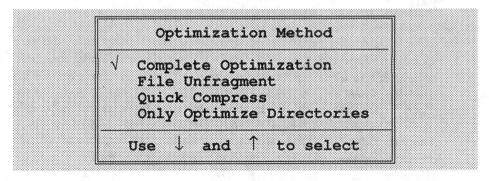

Figure 6-21 Files listed are placed at the beginning of the disk.

In this example, select complete optimization by entering

c

The **Directory Order** option displays information about the disk's directories. Enter

d

The **Directory Order** display is divided into two vertical windows, as shown in Figure 6-22. The left window shows the directory tree for the entire disk. If the tree is large, the remainder of the tree can be displayed by scrolling through the window.

The window on the right side contains a list of the directories that are specified for moving to the front of the disk, if the Complete Optimization or Only Optimize Directories methods are used. The reason for the selection of these directories may not be obvious. It is because they are located in data clusters that are far from the beginning of the disk. If you were to use the Main Norton Utilities program to display the disk clusters for those directories you would find the cluster numbers of the directories that would indicate that they are not near the front of the disk. The SD program performs this analysis automatically.

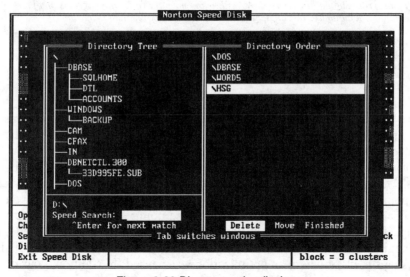

Figure 6-22 Directory order display.

The SD program allows you to alter the list of directories by changing their order, adding or deleting names. To add a directory name you would use the [tab] key to place the highlight in the left window. The ↑ and ↓ keys are used to select the directory that you want to add to the list. Pressing ↵ adds the name of the directory list in the right window. Note that changing the order of the list or adding more directories will not improve the performance of the disk. The option is provided to help you rearrange the order in which the directories are listed when the DOS DIR command is used. The Directory Sort program can also be used to rearrange directories but it does not optimize the performance of the disk.

Exit the display and return to the main Speed Disk screen by entering

[Esc] e

When you have set the options to the desired setting, begin the optimization by entering

o

The program displays a window with information about rebooting following the optimization.

> *Rebooting the computer is suggested because of DOS commands added to DOS 3.3 and higher, that function as memory resident programs, e.g., FASTOPEN, which copies the information from the most recently opened directories into a memory buffer. Since some of the optimization methods can change the location of directories, this program should be reloaded. As with many memory resident programs you must reboot the computer to terminate and reload the memory resident program.*

To begin, enter

o

The Status display in the bottom center of the screen shows the progress of the optimization, showing the cluster numbers being read and written, and the percentage of the optimization that has been completed.

You can stop the condensing by pressing [Esc] and waiting for the program to finish. Keep in mind that it may take a minute or two for the program to reach a safe point at which it can stop condensing. If you stop the condensing, you can return to the condensing procedure at the same point at which you ended it by entering SD again. For example, if you stop at 50 percent and restart Speed Disk, it will begin at 50 percent, not the beginning of the disk. SD writes a file SD.INI, which keeps track of where an optimization was paused. In addition, your option selections are also stored so that they will be the default values the next time you use SD. If you write or update files after you halt condensing, SD may need to begin its condensing from the beginning of the disk over again.

When the condensing is complete the screen will display a graphic map that looks like Figure 6-23. Note that the map no longer shows data holes.

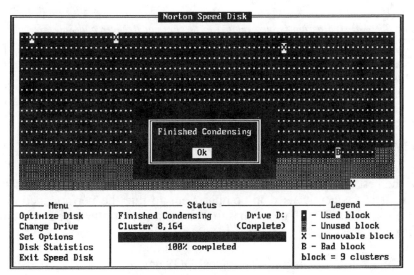

Figure 6-23 Optimization completed.

Exit the SD program by entering

↵ **e**

A window appears asking if you want to reboot the system in order to update memory resident functions such as the FASTOPEN DOS command. Enter

↵

SD is a program that should be run on a regular basis. Most users will run the program every month or so. If you load and unload large numbers of files (such as I do when I am working on various book and programming projects) you may want to perform SD weekly.

Also remember that while copy protected programs are becoming more rare, it is impossible to know if SD is 100 percent compatible with the myriad of copy protection schemes that were developed during the heyday of protection in the mid-1980s. If you are using a major product from Lotus or Ashton-Tate you are safe. If you are using a less well-known program, usually vertical market software, consult the manufacturer before running SD.

> *The Speed Disk program is also related to the Format Recover and Safe Format programs because it creates format recovery files, FRECOVER.DAT and FRECOVER.IDX. These files can be used to recover a hard disk after it has been formatted with either the DOS Format command or the Norton Utilities Safe Format program. Floppy disks formatted with Safe Format can also be recovered. See Chapter 9.*

Performance Information

One of the best known Norton Utilities programs is the SI (System Information) program. It is frequently used in computer ads to rate the performance of the advertised system. The SI program supplies information about your system in three different areas.

1. **Environment.** Displays the logical DOS environment. This refers to the settings that DOS reads from your hardware, such as the number and type of disks, the amount and type of memory, and the input/output ports installed in the computer.

2. **Memory Map.** This map details the installed memory in the computer, including its type and the hex locations used for that memory.

3. **Performance Tests.** System Information tests your computer's CPU (Central Processing Unit) and hard disk performance against the performance of a standard IBM XT.

> *The IBM XT refers to a 8088 based computer running at 4.77 Mhz, which is what was used in the IBM XT. IBM no longer sells XT computers. Most XT compatible computers being sold today use 8088 processors running at higher speeds, typically 10 Mhz. These computers will usually perform at about twice the speed of the IBM XT.*

The SI program can run in two ways.

1. **System Information Only**. This option returns system information based on the internal memory only. The system is tested for CPU performance only, skipping the hard disk test. Since testing the hard disk requires more time than the internal memory test, skipping the hard disk test saves time when you only need to see internal memory information. To perform the internal test only, execute the SI program without any drive argument. Example:

SD

2. **System and Disk Test.** You can include a hard disk performance test as part of the SI program's output by specifying the drive you want to test as part of the command. Example:

SD c:

Including a hard disk test lengthens the time required for the SI program. For example, on a typical AT-type computer, the SI program will complete its internal test in about 4 seconds. When the hard disk test is included, the time will lengthen to 18-25 seconds depending on the speed of the hard drive being tested.

Figure 6-24 shows the output from a typical AT compatible computer.

```
SI-System Information, Advanced Edition 4.50, (C) Copr 1987-88, Peter Norton


        Computer Name: IBM AT
     Operating System: DOS 3.30
   Built-in BIOS dated: Wednesday, January 13, 1988
        Main Processor: Intel 80286          Serial Ports: 2
          Co-Processor: None               Parallel Ports: 1
 Video Display Adapter: Color/Graphics (CGA)
    Current Video Mode: Text, 80 x 25 Color
 Available Disk Drives: 4, A: - D:


DOS reports 640 K-bytes of memory:
   158 K-bytes used by DOS and resident programs
   482 K-bytes available for application programs
A search for active memory finds:
   640 K-bytes main memory      (at hex 00000-0A000)
    16 K-bytes display memory   (at hex 0A800-0AC00)
    48 K-bytes display memory   (at hex 0B000-0BC00)
   384 K-bytes extended memory  (at hex 10000-16000)
 1,024 K-bytes expanded memory
ROM-BIOS Extensions are found at hex paragraphs: E000 F000


  Computing Index (CI), relative to IBM/XT: 13.1
      Disk Index (DI), relative to IBM/XT: 2.6


Performance Index (PI), relative to IBM/XT: 9.6
```

Figure 6-24 System Information output.

You can use the DOS redirection commands to print the output of the SI command or store that output in a text file. The /LOG options should be used when the output is redirected to ensure that the captured data is in standard ASCII output suitable for editing or printing. The command below prints the SI output.

SI d:/LOG >PRN

The command below creates a text file, SYSINFO.DOC, out of the SI output.

SI d:/LOG > sysinfo.doc

The SI program is particularly useful in helping you manage your system's memory. The only standard DOS utility that displays memory information is the CHKDSK program. The SI program is superior to CHKDSK in several regards. CHKDSK displays only the total amount of conventional memory and the amount that is currently free. It does not report expanded or extended memory, nor does it detail the addresses used for that memory. Another important consideration is that because CHKDSK always executes a disk operation along with the memory check it cannot be used on networks. Since the disk portion of the SI program is optional, SI will return memory information on networks, as well as stand-alone computers.

The SI program is also very helpful when you are installing adapters such as memory boards, input/output ports, or video adapters. Running SI will quickly tell you if you have installed the boards correctly so that DOS recognizes the hardware. If you are working with an unknown computer, SI quickly summarizes the configuration of the system.

Special Considerations

Some computer systems will have problems with certain aspects of the SI programs operations. The program contains two switches that can be used separately or together to eliminate problems that certain systems have with SI.

/N   **Skip Memory Probe.** This option should be used if the computer system *freezes up* when SI is run. This is caused by SI attempting to search memory that does not exist. If you encounter this problem, reboot the system and run SI with the /N switch. The SI display will not include the section entitled **A search for active memory finds:**.

/A   **Skip BIOS specific features.** If the message *invalid error* appears when SI is run, the /A switch will eliminate the portion of the display, the video information, that causes this problem.

System Information Details

The following sections contain a detailed breakdown of the information contained in the SI display as illustrated in Figure 6-24.

- **Computer Name.** This is the name of the computer stored in the system's ROM memory. Some systems will not show a name, while others will show a copyright. It is the case that many compatible computers will show names such as IBM AT because that is the name used in the BIOS chip of that computer.

```
                     Computer Name:   IBM AT
```

- **Operating System.** The line displays the version of DOS running in the computer at the tim the SI test is performed.

```
                   Operating System:   DOS 3.30
```

- **BIOS Date.** The BIOS is a ROM chip that contains the hardware portion of the operating system. BIOS stands for **Basic Input Output System.** The BIOS is a very important part of the computer because it is the link between software, including DOS, and the basic hardware. The BIOS contains a date to identify when it was manufactured.

```
              Built-in BIOS dated:   Thursday, April 30, 1987
```

Since the MS-DOS program is available from IBM and other manufacturers, it is the BIOS built into the computer that determines how compatible one PC is with another. It also determines the limitations of the hardware. For example, old IBM PC computers with BIOS dates earlier than 10/27/82 will not accept a hard disk drive. Since the BIOS is a ROM (Read-Only-Memory) chip it cannot be altered. It can be replaced in some case, with an updated ROM, that will increase the capabilities.

Obtaining the BIOS date is often important if you suspect that your computer may be incompatible with a specific device or software application.

- **Main Processor.** The main processor refers to the microprocessor in your computer. The microprocessor is the *brain* of the computer that decodes the instructions stored in program files and turns them into actual computer operations. The most common microprocessor in PC/XT and compatible machines is the Intel 8088 chip. It still comes as a bit of a surprise to some people that IBM or Compaq don't make the main component of the computer. For example, the 8088 processor found in the IBM PC and XT has a set of about 150 instruction codes that it will recognize. All of the programs that run on that computer are constructed, at base, of these 150 basic instructions.

The PC AT and compatible machines use the Intel 80286 microprocessor. The 80286 can translate all the codes used for the 8088 but contains additional features. Because the 80286 is compatible with the instruction set of the 8088 processor, PC programs can run on AT machines. The AT class machines will run the program faster than the 8088 machine. 80286 computers also have the potential to run some programs that cannot operate on 8088 computers, such as Excel from Microsoft. The 80386 is the newest processor from Intel with the 80486 expected to be available in computers by the end of 1989.

```
                    Main Processor:  Intel 80286
```

- **Coprocessor.** The PC/XT- AT, and 80386 type machines are based on the general purpose computing power of the Intel CPU series. Computers designed for these chips usually include room on their circuit boards for additional processors called *coprocessors*. The *coprocessor* is usually used to help speed up programs by performing specialized tasks such as intensive mathematical calculations. Engineering and spreadsheet programs will often benefit from a math coprocessor. Word processing programs that don't do a lot of math calculations would not benefit particularly from the installation of a math coprocessor. Keep in mind that programs **must** be specifically designed to take advantage of the coprocessor. Just inserting a coprocessor into the computer will have no effect. The software programs must be specifically designed to use the co-processor. For example, Lotus 1-2-3 Version 1A does not support a co-processor, while 1-2-3 Release 2.01, 2.2, and 3.0 do support math co-processors.

  The coprocessor used with the Intel 8088 is the Intel 8087, which costs about $200. Intel makes coprocessors for the 80286 and 80386 microprocessor as well. The Weitek 1167 is also popular with 80386 systems.

```
                    Co-Processor:  None
```

- **Parallel and Serial Ports.** These items report the number of parallel and serial interfaces installed in the computer. Parallel interfaces are usually used for printers. Serial interfaces are used for printers, modems, mice, and some types of networks. The difference between parallel and serial interfaces is the sequence in which they transmit data. Each character set to a printer usually requires 1 byte of information. The byte is composed of 8 individual signals called bits. (For an in-depth explanation see Chapter 1.) A parallel interface sends all 8 signals over a multi-wire at one time. A serial interface sends 1 bit at a time until all 8 bits have been transmitted. The parallel interface is generally faster than the serial. But traditionally, the reliability of parallel transmission declines the longer the transmission distance. The longest parallel cables are between 6 and 12 feet long. Serial transmission of data is the preferred means of transmission over longer distances. This includes printers in remote locations, other computers on a network, or telecommunications via modem.

Another advantage of serial communication is that serial interfaces can be programmed to transmit at different rates of speed and can add special error checking information to the transmitted data. Error checking can be accomplished by adding extra databits to the transmitted information. For example, the sending computer might add an extra bit with a value of 1 following each character. If the receiving computer encountered a 0 in the position where the 1 should be, it would assume that some error has taken place during transmission and inform the user.

Current versions of DOS are limited in the number of interfaces that can be used. DOS 2.1 and 3.2 support only two serial interfaces. DOS 3.3 and 4.0 support four serial ports.

```
                    Serial Ports: 2
                    Parallel Ports: 1
```

- **Video Display Adapter.** This information describes the type of display monitor attached to the computer and what video mode is active. For example, the CGA can run in 80 x 25 or 40 x 25 modes. This information can also be obtained from the Norton Control Center program.

```
        Video Display Adapter: Color/Graphics (CGA)
           Current Video Mode: Text, 80 x 25 Color
```

- **Available Disk Drives.** This line tells you the number of logical disks available in the system. Note that a logical drive can be a RAM disk, which is really part of the computer's memory emulating a disk or network disk that is located in a remote computer, not a physical disk drive.

```
            Available Disk Drives:  4, A: - D:
```

- **DOS Memory Report.** These lines display a summary of the same information displayed at the bottom of the DOS CHKDSK display. It tells you the total amount of memory available to DOS, the amount already in use by resident programs, which include DOS and TSR (Terminate and Stay Resident) programs like Sidekick, and the amount available for programs to use. The amount Available for applications is called the *transient program area (TPA)*. Note that DOS still does not directly support additional memory installed in the computer for program usage. Below you will see how that memory is reported.

```
DOS reports 640 K-bytes of memory:
    158 K-bytes used by DOS and resident programs
    482 K-bytes available for application programs
```

- **Active Memory.** This section of the output describes the memory in the computer based on a live search of the computer's memory. This information is different from the previous display which reports what DOS sees as the memory capacity of the computer. Note that because DOS has a fixed limit on memory, 640K, which it can use, it does not report on additional types of memory that might be installed in the computer. The display reports on the amount of main memory (usually called conventional memory) which stops at 640K, video memory used by display adapters, and extended and expanded memory.

    The memory items are listed with the size of the blocks they occupy and the starting and ending addresses. The term "address" refers to the scheme by which the computer organizes memory. The scheme assigns each byte of memory a specific address. The address numbers in the PC can vary from 0-1,048,575 (FFFFF in hex notation). This is referred to as *conventional* memory. Not all 1,048,576 bytes of *conventional* memory are available for user programs. The conventional memory is divided into blocks, and each block assigned a specific purpose. For the average user, the most significant block is the one numbered from 0 to 655,360 (A0000 in hex format). It is this block of memory that is used for user programs. When people rate computers by the amount of "memory" they contain, it is this specific block of memory they are usually referring to. The 640K limit refers to the largest possible block of conventional memory used for programs in today's MS-DOS computers. In the illustration, the first block of memory is shown as a block of 640K from 00000 to 0A000, expressed in hex notation. This means that this PC contains the maximum amount of conventional memory.

    The actual address of memory locations in the IBM PC and compatibles is a complicated method in which each address is composed of two segments. The addresses here have an assumed segment of F000 hex.

The display also shows the locations used for display memory. For example, a CGA will use a block of 16K located at B800. A monochrome adapter uses a 4K block located at B000. Note that this scheme allows you to have both a monochrome and a CGA. EGA use a block of memory, usually 64K, located at A800. Not reported in the SI is the memory at C800 used for hard disks. The locating of display memory is usually not very important. It is useful to know when you are installing new hardware expansion such as extended boards.

When you install an extended memory board, the software requests the type of monitor you are using, for example, Monochrome, CGA, or EGA. This may seem an odd question to ask when you are adding memory, but the reason for the request is that the software used with the memory card is attempting to avoid a conflict in addressing between the display adapter and the extended memory card.

The install software will create a special device driver command based on your monitor type. The AST Rampage board uses a driver called REMM.SYS. For example, the AST Rampage Board software will automatically exclude the block of memory from B800 to BFFF if you select color graphics, or B000 to BFFF for a Hercules graphics card. The /X stands for EXCLUDE. Note that the Hercules card requires more memory than the CGA.

DEVICE=REMM.SYS /X=B800-BFFF (color/graphics)
DEVICE=REMM.SYS /X=B000-BFFF (Hercules)

The next two values will be displayed if your computer has additional user memory installed beyond the 640K limit. Although DOS cannot use this memory directly for applications, it can be used in one of two special ways.

1. **Extended Memory**. Extended memory refers to memory added on following the first 1,048,576 bytes of memory address in the standard PC. The extended memory is addressed consecutively starting with the ending address of conventional memory, 10000 hex. While this memory cannot be used by applications like spreadsheets, it can be used for creating performance enhancements such as RAM drives, disk caching or print buffers.

2. **Expanded Memory**. Expanded memory refers to blocks of memory, 16K each, that are not allocated as part of the DOS memory scheme. Rather, these blocks are addressed by a special programming technique called LIM (Lotus-Intel-Microsoft) expanded memory specification. This programming technique requires that special boards,

designed for LIM compatibility, be used in conjunction with programs that are specifically programmed to use LIM memory. Examples of such programs are Lotus 1-2-3 Release 2, Microsoft Excel, and Ashton-Tate's Framework. Note that many memory boards can be configured as either expanded or extended.

If you are working with a 80286 or 80386 system with 1 megabyte of memory you will notice that SI reports 384K of extended memory. This memory is the memory area above 640K up to 1 megabyte. However, for the most part this memory is useless. DOS does not recognize it and when extended or expanded memory boards are added they also ignore this memory. This 384K is referred to as shadow memory. Shadow memory is a potential resource that some hardware and software products are now seeking to exploit. Some computers use shadow memory to hold a copy of the ROM BIOS program. Since RAM memory is generally faster to access than the BIOS ROM this can improve computer performance. Some software products such as Lotus 1-2-3 Release 3.0 use DOS extenders which exploit the shadow memory to permit the loading of larger programs than DOS would otherwise allow. However, the attempt to exploit shadow memory is so new that conflicts can occur. For example, running 1-2-3 3.0 on a system that is using shadow memory for the BIOS will cause a conflict. As standards emerge for shadow memory use, these conflicts should be resolved.

```
A search for active memory finds:
   640 K-bytes main memory      (at hex 00000-0A000)
    16 K-bytes display memory   (at hex 0A800-0AC00)
    48 K-bytes display memory   (at hex 0B000-0BC00)
   384 K-bytes extended memory  (at hex 10000-16000)
 1,024 K-bytes expanded memory
```

- **ROM-BIOS Extensions.** Boards, typically hard disk controllers or video adapters, will contain ROMs that are mapped into the ROM BIOS of the computer. These on-board ROMs appear as ROM BIOS extensions. For example, the controller boards used with PC and XT hard disks report a ROM extension at address C800. These extensions are of interest to advanced users only.

```
ROM-BIOS Extensions are found at hex paragraphs: E000 F000
```

- **Performance Index.** The final section of the SI display shows the results of the three performance index texts. The CI (Computing Index) tests the speed of the processor and memory. The DI (Disk Index) tests the speed of hard disks. The PI (Performance Index) is a combined score reflecting the results of the CI and DI.

The index uses the speed of the IBM XT as 1.0 for both the CI and DI. In this example, the CI is 13.1 which means that the processor is more than 13 times faster than the processing speed of the original 4.77 MHz 8088 processor used on the IBM XT. The DI test shows that the hard disk is running 2.6 times faster than the 10 megabyte disk on the IBM XT. The combined PI is 9.6.

The performance tests are very handy for evaluating the speed of various computers and configurations. It is important to understand that no one number can be reified into a total evaluation of the worth of a given computer. The way the hardware is used by specific software programs will affect the final performance. The SI is a quick way to get a detailed description of the internal set up of a computer. If you are working on an unfamiliar machine, the SI will provide a fast summary of the hardware.

```
       Computing Index (CI), relative to IBM/XT: 13.1
             Disk Index (DI), relative to IBM/XT: 2.6

       Performance Index (PI), relative to IBM/XT: 9.6
```

Summary

This chapter discussed the programs and features provided by the Norton Utilities that help you get information about, and select options that affect, the overall operation of your computer system.

- **System Attributes.** In Version 4.5 of the Norton Utilities the Screen Attributes program has been converted to operate as a subcommand of the Batch Enhancer program. The SA subcommand can be used to set the colors, or the video attributes on monochrome monitors, used by DOS. SA can be executed from the DOS prompt or from DOS batch files.

- **Norton Control Center.** The Control Center program provides the user the ability to select system attributes such as the size of the DOS screen cursor, the colors used by DOS, the palette of colors available to DOS on EGA and VGA display adapters, the sensitivity of the keyboard on AT and 80386 computers, and the attributes of the serial communications ports. The Control Center also allows you to work with watch times that can also be controlled by the TM program. The Control Center can also be used to reset the internal clock on AT and 80386 systems avoiding the necessity of running the diagnostic program.

- **Speed Disk.** The SD program is designed to optimize hard disk performance by arranging the files and the directories stored on the disk. The SD program will unfragment files, place the directory and specified files at the front of the disk, and remove *holes* in the data storage area of the disk.

- **System Information.** This program displays detailed information about the computer's memory. It will also perform microprocessor and hard disk performance tests.

7

Hard Disk Organization Tasks

Locating Files and Information

One of the most difficult problems to solve on a hard disk system is how to locate a file when you don't know what directory you stored it in. A few years ago this was particularly difficult because many of the popular applications, WordStar, dBASE II, and so on, did not take advantage of the DOS directory system. However, today, that situation has been resolved. Almost without exception, most programs allow you to enter a pathname, not just a filename, as a file specification. This advantage can become a nightmare, however, if you can't remember where in the system you stored a particular file.

Why is this such a problem? The answer goes back to the way DOS commands are structured. The DIR (directory command), will list files from only one directory at a time. If you are not sure what directory a file has been stored in, the only solution is to change directories and enter DIR to get a listing. This tedious process usually nets poor results because when you're forced to do tedious work your attention level declines. After listing a few directories you may not catch the file, even if you are lucky enough to stumble on it.

The idea is, wherever possible, to get the computer to do the tedious work. Your job is to enter the correct command that will skillfully locate the information you require.

The key is to find a command that will search not just a specific directory but the entire disk. Both DOS and the Norton Utilities programs supply such a command. Before looking at the Norton Utilities program you might find it instructive to look at the DOS command first.

The command that searches the entire disk, or at least all the directories, is CHKDSK (Check Disk). The main purpose of CHKDSK is to check the file allocation table and the disk directories for consistency. In order to perform this function CHKDSK must look at the names of all of the files on the disk; thus

235

CHKDSK has the power to view all the filenames. The CHKDSK command accepts a switch **/V**, which stands for **Verbose**. The **/V** switch is a prompt to the CHKDSK command to display a list of the files it is examining. To see how this works, enter

CHKDSK/V ↵

The program displays a long list of files on the screen. The list will greatly exceed the length of the screen so that the names of the files will scroll by too quickly for you to read. The end of the display will look like Figure 7-1.

```
                    D:\DBASE\TEST.QBE
                    D:\DBASE\TEST.FRM
                    D:\DBASE\TEST.FRG
                    D:\DBASE\TEST.FRO
                    D:\DBASE\STUDENT.CAT
                    D:\DBASE\BUYERS.DBF
                    D:\DBASE\BUYERS.MDX
                    D:\DBASE\84562310
                    D:\DBASE\80762310
                    D:\DBASE\PP.DBF
                    D:\DBASE\BUYERS.LBO
                    D:\DBASE\XXX.SCR
                    D:\DBASE\XXX.FMT
                    D:\DBASE\XXX.FMO
                    D:\MENU1.BAT

      41717760 bytes total disk space
             0 bytes in 1 hidden files
        122880 bytes in 26 directories
      32665600 bytes in 1350 user files
       8912896 bytes available on disk
        655360 bytes total memory
        569072 bytes free
```

Figure 7-1 CHKDSK used to display files.

The filenames listed with this command display the directory name as a prefix to the filename. You can create a printed copy of this list by entering

CHKDSK/V>PRN ↵

So far, you have only created a list of all the files. In theory this solves your problem, but in practice it is still difficult to find a file from these lists.

One possible solution is to employ another DOS command called FIND. FIND, a program supplied with MS DOS as FIND.EXE or FIND.COM, was first introduced in Version 2.0 of DOS and is not a program that can be used alone, like CHKDSK. It is called a "filter" because it is used to control the output of other programs. In theory, the FIND command can be used to filter the output of any command to include or exclude specific characters.

For example, suppose that you want to list all the files on the hard disk that contain the characters **DISK**. The FIND filter is attached to a command by using the | (vertical line) character. FIND is then followed by the text string you want to locate. The command below combines CHKDSK/V with FIND to create a command that produces a list of items containing the letters DISK. Note that the text string, DISK, is entered in uppercase characters because DOS is sensitive to the case of the text string. Since DOS always prints filenames in uppercase your search string must also be entered in uppercase. Enter

CHKDSK/V|FIND "DISK" ↵

The screen displays the lines from the CHKDSK/V output that contain the word **DISK**, as shown Figure 7-2.

```
        Volume DISK1_VOL2  created Mar 15, 1989 10:43p
               D:\DISK1_VO.L2
               D:\DOS\DISKCOMP.COM
               D:\DOS\DISKCOPY.COM
               D:\DOS\FDISK.COM
               D:\DOS\WIPEDISK.EXE
               D:\OWP\DISKCOPY.COM
```

Figure 7-2 CHKDSK searches for files.

You may have noticed that for a long time the disk was being accessed but nothing was displayed on the screen. Why? The reason has to do with the way a filter command like FIND operates.

The FIND command cannot interfere or change the normal operation of the CHKDSK command. Rather, it is meant to filter its output. The FIND command is used to select only those lines of output that contain the specified characters, **DISK**. But if Find cannot interfere with CHKDSK, how can the results of the command be altered?

The answer is that FIND allows CHKDSK to output its usual list of filenames. But instead of allowing the lines to appear on the screen they are captured in files called pipe files. In the DOS 2 level the filenames for the piping files are always %PIPE1.$$$ and %PIPE2.$$$. In DOS 3 level the names of the piping files are determined by the values in the date and time area of the memory. The filenames will vary each time you run a DOS filter program. The filenames created by piping in DOS 3 are eight-character names that usually contain numbers and letters. Examples: 001e2c22 or 001e2c01.

The command then displays the contents of these files, selecting lines that contain the search string. You might ask why you have never seen these filenames on any directory. The answer is that FIND erases the files as soon as the command is completed.

Using CHKDSK to locate files has a number of drawbacks. First a filtering command like **CHKDSK** is a very slow process because: (1) the **CHKDSK** command must complete its usual operation and, then, (2) have its output written to a file which is then, (3) filtered for a match of a specified string. Also, it does not allow you to match the text string against any specific part of text. For example, suppose that you had a directory on your disk called **DISKUTILS**. The FIND command would select the line c:**DISK**UTILS\\QU.EXE because the directory name contained the letters **DISK**, even though the filename did not.

Also note that if you are working on a network CHKDSK will not run because it could potentially damage the disk if it was accessed by other users on the network.

The Norton Utilities programs offer a better and faster solution to problems related to file and directory organization. Also these programs will operate on networks as well as single user computers.

Finding Files

The way to use FF is to search for a specific file. Suppose that you want to know if the file WIPEDISK.EXE is located on your hard disk. Enter

FF wipedisk.exe ↵

The program displays the file you are searching for. This program operates much more quickly than CHKDSK because it is concerned only with reading the names of the files and reporting the information back to you. CHKDSK needs to analyze the file allocation table for errors which slows down its performance.

```
FF-File Find, Advanced Edition 4.50, (C) Copr 1987-88, Peter Norton
D:\DOS
        wipefile.exe    13,176 bytes   4:50 pm  Sun Oct 16 88


D:\NORTON
        wipefile.exe    13,176 bytes   4:50 pm  Sun Oct 16 88


2 files found
```

Figure 7-3 File Find program locates files.

Notice that FF displays the full directory entry for the file, including time and date of creation and size of the file, as well as the name of the directory in which it is contained.

Search For Groups Of Files

Another advantage that FF has over CHKDSK is that you can enter a DOS wildcard as a file specification. In that way you can locate files that have similar but not identical names. The README or READ files commonly waste space on hard disks. README or READ are text files usually placed onto a program disk by the manufacturer and contain information garnered too late to be printed in the program's documentation. In many cases these files are copied onto the hard disk along with a new program. After a while you find that these files begin to accumulate on the disk. To find out if you have any such files, enter

FF read*.* ⏎

The program displays all the files on your hard disk that begin with **READ**, as shown in Figure 7-4.

```
D:\DOS
        read.me             366 bytes     2:00 pm   Mon Jul 25 88
        read.me!          2,275 bytes     2:48 pm   Tue Oct 30 84
        readme.bat           59 bytes     2:10 pm   Mon Feb 29 88
        readme.now       12,733 bytes    12:00 am   Fri Jul  1 88
        readme.txt        4,539 bytes     9:27 am   Tue Sep 27 88
D:\TNE
        readme.doc          553 bytes     4:28 pm   Sat Apr  1 89
D:\NORTON
        read.me           3,864 bytes     4:50 pm   Sun Oct 16 88
D:\FW
        read_me.fw2         288 bytes    12:00 pm   Tue Oct 22 85
D:\QP\HLP
        readme.doc        2,405 bytes    10:14 am   Fri May  5 89
D:\WORD5
        readme.doc       18,520 bytes    10:01 am   Tue Apr 25 89
11 files found
```

Figure 7-4 File Find selects files using wildcard.

You can compress the display style used by the FF program so that it lists the filenames across the display by using the **/W** switch. This type of display takes up less vertical space but it does not include the size and creation time and date of each file. The following command displays the files that begin with READ, in a wide format. Enter

FF read*.*/W ↵

The wide display is shown in Figure 7-5.

```
D:\IN
    readme.com
D:\DOS
    read.me          read.me!         readme.bat      readme.now
D:\TNE
    readme.doc
D:\NORTON
    read.me
D:\FW
    read_me.fw2
D:\QP\HLP
    readme.doc
D:\WORD5
    readme.doc
11 files found
```

Figure 7-5 File Find wide display format.

Using the **/P** switch causes the program to automatically pause after each full screen of files are listed. This is useful when the command generates long lists of files.

Search All Drives

The FF program also contains an option that enables you to search all drives in the system with a single command. This is very valuable if you are running more than one hard disk, or you have a large-capacity drive, greater than 32 megabytes, which is partitioned in several logical drives. The switch, /A, causes the FF command to begin its search on the first drive in the system and continue the search through all the drives. Keep in mind that the program reads the drive table in the memory of the computer so that logical drives such as RAM drives will be included in the search.

Also note that in the case of floppy drives, the FF program is prepared to handle empty drives. Unlike a DOS command that will display the Abort, Retry,

Ignore message, File Find will simply proceed to the next available drive if there is no disk in the floppy drive.

To see how this works, leave your A drive empty and enter

FF read*.*/A -"

The red light on the A drive is lit indicating that FF is searching for a disk. After a few moments (1.2 megabyte drives take longer than 360K drives) the program will display the message:

```
                    Unable to read from drive A
```

The program will then proceed to search the next drive in the system and so on until all the drives have been searched. The program produces a list of the SYS files on all of the disks in the system.

File Catalogs

The FF command is capable of providing a detailed summary of all the files stored on a hard disk, or with the /A parameter, all the files stored in a multi-drive system. Entering FF with no file specifications will cause the program to list all of the files on the disk. Keep in mind that hidden files are included in this list along with the files that normally appear in the directory listing.

There are two ways to produce a printed catalog of files: unformatted and formatted. The catalog can be useful in maintaining a computer system and for recovering erased files. A list of filenames is useful, but not absolutely necessary, in trying to reconstruct the erased information.

Unformatted File Lists

An unformatted list is one in which no accommodation is made for page breaks, page numbers, margins, or other formatting niceties. To produce an unformatted list, simply take advantage of the DOS redirection options and send the output of the FF program to the printer. Since this printing can take some time, you may want to skip this command until you are ready to print the long list. The command is:

FF >PRN ↵

As an example, you can produce a shorter list by selecting files. Enter

FF read*.* >PRN ↵

Notice that unformatted printing does not advance the paper to the end of the page. It simply stops when there is no more data to print.

Formatted Output

If you intend to keep a catalog of disk files, it might be preferable to have a formatted printout with page numbers, page breaks, margins, and so on. This can be done by combining the operations of two Norton Utilities programs. The FF command is used to generate the file information. Instead of putting the information on the screen or sending it to the printer, you can use the DOS redirection commands to create a text file. The LP (Line Print) program can then print the contents of the text file created by FF and insert the desired formatting.

The first step is to create the text file that contains the list of files you want to catalog. This is done by adding a redirection command, >, to the FF command and following it with the name of the text file you want to create. You can catalog all of the files on the hard disk by using FF with no wildcard. In this case you will want to limit the number of files by using a wildcard, *.SYS, to catalog only those files with a SYS extension. Enter

FF *.sys > catalog ↵

The program begins but no files appear on the screen. Instead, the data is being captured in a file on the disk called CATALOG. When the file is complete, the DOS prompt returns.

The file created by the command contains the same information that would normally appear on the screen or printer. If you are listing all of the files on a hard disk the text file might be fairly large, e.g., a listing of 800 files might take up 55K.

You can now use the LP command to print out the contents of the CATALOG file with page formatting. (Skip this command at this time if you wish.) You can stop the printing at any time by entering [Esc]. Enter

LP catalog ↵

> *There is one file listed in the catalog whose information will be inaccurate, the CATALOG text file. It appears in the list but its file size will show 0 because DOS creates the filename in the directory before the FF program sends its information to the file. In that way FF includes the CATALOG entry in its list. But because the file is still open while the writing is taking place, DOS has not yet written the file size into the directory. Of course, this minor defect won't have a practical consequence.*

The LP command will automatically number lines. This might be a convenient feature when you are printing out file lists. You can add line numbers with the /N switch. Example:

LP catalog/N ↵

The logic of redirection allows you to take advantage of the DOS Print command. PRINT.COM is a program provided with DOS that allows you to print a text file in the background while you proceed to other tasks. This means that you do not have to wait for the printing to complete before you can enter commands.

To take advantage of the PRINT command, you will create a second text file which is the output of the LP command. This produces a text file that contains the data produced by FF. The formatting added by LP. PRINT can then finally send the formatted text file to the printer in the background as you go on to other tasks.

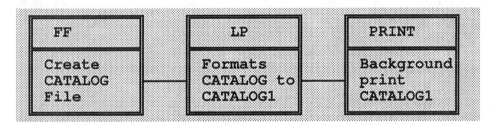

To create the formatted text file, **CATALOG1**, you need to run the LP command and specify a text file as the output, rather than the printer. This is easy to do. If you follow the LP command with a name, the program will create a text file with that name instead of sending the data to the printer. Remember that the filenames must be different. Enter

LP catalog catalog1 ↵

The LP program creates a file with the formatted contents of the CATALOG file, and displays the number of pages that the new file contains. The LP program will print 53 lines of data on each page. Remember that the File Find listing includes directories as well as files.

The final step is to use the DOS PRINT program to print this file in the background. Enter

PRINT catalog1 ↵

The DOS program will display a prompt:

> **Name of list device [PRN]:**

This allows you to enter the name of an alternate print device. The default is
PRN, the normal DOS print device. To begin the printing, enter

↵

The printing begins. You can now enter commands while the printing is
taking place. Enter

DIR/W ↵

You may notice that while the disk is being read for the directory, the
printing pauses. This is because DOS does not support true multitasking. As soon
as the disk read operation is performed the print continues.

Cancelling a background print started with the DOS PRINT program is not
quite as easy as stopping a foreground printing operation. Enter PRINT with a /T
(terminate) switch that will stop the printing and clear the print queue. Enter

PRINT/T ↵

The queue refers to the ability of the PRINT program to create a queue of
files to print. You can cancel the printing of a specific file in the queue by using
the /. Example:

PRINT catalog1/C

This would cancel only the printing of CATALOG1 and leave any other files
in the queue alone.

To simplify the process you can place all the necessary commands into a
batch file. Below is a sample of what that batch file might contain.

Listing of File CATALOG.BAT

```
FF > catalog
LP catalog catalog1
PRINT catalog1
DEL catalog
```

When the printing is complete, you might want to delete the CATALOG1 file. Note that the command to delete the text file CATALOG is included in the batch, but the command to delete CATALOG1 is not. This is because the PRINT command will go back to the CATALOG1 file from time to time to get more text to print. Because the printing is taking place in the background, DOS will execute a command in the batch that follows the print command before the printing is complete. This means that when PRINT looks for the rest of the text file it will fail to find it because it is now erased. For that reason you must wait until the background printing is complete to delete the CATALOG1 file (For more information about batch files see Section II.)

Building Selected Lists

The previous procedure for creating a catalog of all the disk files can be modified to create a more selective list of files. Suppose you want to create a catalog of only the EXE and COM files on the disk. This could be done by using the FF command twice. The tactic is to combine the output of both commands into a single file and print it out as a single catalog. This can be done by using a slightly modified redirection command. DOS recognizes >> as the command to append text onto an existing text file.

> *If >> is used and the specified file does not already exist, DOS will simply create the file. Subsequent >> commands will append text to that file.*

Begin by creating a text file with the file of all COM files. Enter

FF *.com > programs ↵

Next, append onto the PROGRAMS file the list of EXE files. The key to this command is >> redirection command. Enter

FF *.exe >> programs ↵

You can now use LP to print the combined lists.

LP catalog ↵

> *Keep in mind that programs often require other files to support their operations, such as configuration and overlay files. The COM and EXE programs listed probably do not represent a complete list of all the files needed to run all the programs on your hard disk.*

You can see that having a distinctive file extension makes it easy to locate and catalog files. For example, Lotus 1-2-3 produces files that are automatically assigned file extensions beginning with WK to all the Lotus files on a hard disk. Enter

FF *.wk* ↵

The same is true of dBASE III Plus. The database and memo files have extensions that begin with DB. To list all the dBASE III files, enter

FF *.db* ↵

---

dBASE III files keep data in DBF files with the exception of data entered into memo fields, which are stored in DBT files. If you copy a DBF file without the DBT that goes with it, dBASE will refuse to open the file.

Most word processing programs do not impose a file extension automatically. Microsoft Word and Multimate are exceptions to that rule because they add DOC extensions to their document files. WordPerfect and WordStar do not add extensions. If you use such programs you might want to adapt the habit of adding an extension that would identify the files as word processing files, e.g., WP.

Text Search

The File Find command locates files based on their filenames. But the Norton Utilities programs provide a way to locate files based on the information they contain. The TS (Text Search) program performs this operation and it is one of the most helpful of all the very useful programs included with the Norton Utilities package.

While DOS has similar commands to FF, there is no method by which DOS can help you locate text stored within a file. The ability to search the contents of a file for specific information is important because you are more likely to remember the content of a file than you are the filename.

The Text Search program is designed to search the disk to find any instances of a specific group of characters. Text Search can operate from a command line or interactive mode. To see how TS works in an interactive mode, assume that you want to locate a file or files that contain a key word, **FATAL.** Start the TS program by entering

ts ↵

The first option that you need to select concerns the part of the disk you want to search, as shown in Figure 7-6.

```
[C:\]ts
 TS-Text Search, Advanced Edition 4.50, (C) Copr 1987-88, Peter Norton


Select search within FILES, all of DISK, or ERASED file space
Press F, D, or E ...
```

Figure 7-6 Text Search program prompts user.

The TS program has three options.

F   **Files.** This option limits the search to data clusters currently marked as **in use** by active files. This is the most common way to search. The program will specify the file that contains the text you are looking for.

D   **Disk.** This option searches all of the disk sectors. Included in this search are the boot sector, FAT and directory areas, file areas, and data areas not currently in use by any data files. Note that if the text is found the program tells you its location in terms of disk sector rather than filename.

E   **Erased.** This limits the search to space not in use by active files. This space may contain information that belongs to files that have been erased. Note that DOS does not remove data when a file is erased. If a match is found the program tells you the sector and cluster numbers.

In this case choose the file area. Keep in mind that the TS program will tell you the name of the file in which the text is found only if you select the File option. Selecting **D**isk or **E**rase will prove the text's location on the disk in terms of disk sector or cluster numbers. Enter

f

The next prompt asks you to enter a wildcard or filename, as shown in Figure 7-7.

```
[C:\]ts
 TS-Text Search, Advanced Edition 4.50, (C) Copr 1987-88, Peter Norton


Select search within FILES, all of DISK, or ERASED file space
Press F, D, or E ... F


Searching contents of files


Enter the file specification for the files to search
  File:
```

Figure 7-7 Enter file specification for text search.

The purpose of this option is to limit the search to a file or group of files. For example, if you were searching for a 1-2-3 worksheet you would enter ***.wk*** to limit the search to worksheet files. Entering ↵ automatically selects ***.***, i.e., all the files in the active directory. In this case select the files in the \NORTON directory. Enter

\norton*.* ↵

The next prompt asks you to enter the text you want to search for (Figure 7-8).

```
 TS-Text Search, Advanced Edition 4.50, (C) Copr 1987-88, Peter Norton

 Select search within FILES, all of DISK, or ERASED file space
 Press F, D, or E ... F


 Searching contents of files


 Enter the file specification for the files to search
   File: \norton\*.*


 Enter specific text to search for
 Or press enter for any text
   Text:
```

Figure 7-8 Enter search text.

You are also presented with the option to enter ↵ to search for any text. If you enter ↵ the TS program scans the selected area and files for any block of text. Remember that the program cannot use the same logical criterion used by a person to detect *text*. Instead, the program looks for a block of information that contains text characters. Data that contain control characters are automatically excluded.

In this case you will enter a word that you want to find. The TS program does not take into consideration differences in case when matching characters. Entering **U** or **u** will match **U** or **u**. In this example, you are looking for the word **unerase.** Enter

unerase ↵

The program displays the names of the files it is searching. When the program locates a match, the screen displays the name of the file, the location within the file where the match was found, and the matched text along with its context. In this example the text was found in the file NU.EXE, shown in Figure 7-9. Keep in mind that even though text is found in a file it does not mean that the file is a *text* file. In this example, the file NU.EXE is a program file that also includes text. The text is used by the program in menu and message displays. The location of the text is shown in terms of lines and byte offset. The line number is useful if the file is a pure text file that can be edited with a text editor or word processing program. If not, the byte offset can be used to locate the text using the main Norton Utilities program.

> *Files are searched in the order in which they are written into the directory. You can change the order of the file names in a directory by using the Directory Sort program discussed later in this chapter.*

One important aspect of this display is that it shows the text context, if any, in which the matching text was found. In the example shown in Figure 7-9 the absence of any text context indicates that the text is surrounded by non-text information. This is typical of text located in program files.

```
Searching D:\NORTON\nu.exe

Found at line 1,116, file offset 124,682

UnErase

Search for more (Y/N) ?
```

Figure 7-9 Text located in NU.EXE file.

At the bottom of the display you can select Y to continue the search. Entering N will terminate the program. Enter

y

The program will continue reading the current file for more occurrences of the search text. Figure 7-10 shows the next occurrence of *unerase*. It is found in the same file, NU.EXE. This time the text is part of a larger phrase.

```
Searching D:\NORTON\nu.exe

Found at line 1,116, file offset 124,775

UnErase a deleted or erased file

Search for more (Y/N) ?
```

Figure 7-10 Another occurrence of the search text located.

You can terminate the program by entering N or [F10] when asked if you want to continue the search. Enter

n

Command Line Entry

The TS program can also be executed as a command line program. For example, suppose you were searching for **Mary** within one of the files in the \NORTON directory. You can specify the file specification and the text search as arguments on the command line. For example the command that performs the proposed search would look like this:

TS \norton mary

The command has three parts:

TS	\norton	mary
Program name	Directory or files to search	Text to search for

Enter

TS \norton mary ↵

The program searches the files and stops when it finds a match. In Figure 7-11 you can see that the command will match the text in the word Summary because the last four letters are **mary.**

```
Searching D:\NORTON\ncc.exe

Found at line 306, file offset 47,420

 Summary

Search for more (Y/N) ?
```

Figure 7-11 Partial match for "mary".

If you want to search for whole words only you have to include space characters before and after the search letters. Exit the current search by entering

n

The command below uses **" mary "** as the search text. Note that there is a space following the first quotation mark, and one before the second. The quotation marks are needed when the search text includes more than a single word. Enter

TS \norton " mary " ↵

This time the program fails to match any of the text in any of the specified files, since **mary** does not appear within the context as a individual word.

> *Keep in mind that this search would miss instances that a human reader would clearly identify as the word **Mary**. For example, if the word was at the beginning of a line the search would fail to match the text because it would be preceded by a CR/LF character not a space. If Mary was stored in a file surrounded by quotations within the text, e.g., "Mary", the search would also miss the word. You may need to try a variety of searches to locate data when you are unsure of the context in which it is stored.*

You can locate a phrase with several words by enclosing the phrase in quotation marks. For example, suppose you wanted to locate files that contained the message "Abort, Retry, Ignore" which is frequently displayed when an error occurs. In this case, designate the search to the directory that contains the DOS files. The assumption is made that you have these files stored in a directory called \DOS. Enter

TS \dos "abort, retry, ignore" ↵

The program will locate the message within one of the DOS programs, e.g., CHKDSK.COM or RECOVER.EXE, if those files occur in your \DOS directory. Exit the search by entering

n

Broad or Narrow Searches

The TS program can be used to perform broad or narrow searches. The /S switch will cause the program to search the files stored in all the subdirectories that branch from the current directory. If the current directory is the root directory, then the program will search all the files on the hard disk. Suppose you want to see if any of the files on the hard disk contain the date **March 1, 1989**. If you are not sure what file or what directory the file might be stored in, you can use the Text Search command in its broadest application. This means that you will start the search at the root directory (\) of the drive and search all the subdirectories.

To perform a search for the text use the /S switch. Enter

TS \ "march 1, 1989"/S ↵

The TS program displays the names of the files as it searches. The time it takes to perform this search will vary with the number of files stored on the hard disk, their arrangement of the directories, and the speed of your computer system.

Since this search may take some time to complete, you can stop the TS program at any time by entering the *break* combination, [Ctrl/Scroll Lock]. Enter

[Ctrl/Scroll Lock]

Logging the Results

So far, the TS command has been used in an interactive mode to locate specific text items within files. This means that the program performs assuming that someone is watching the progress of the search on the screen. The program displays the names of the files that are being searched, to inform the observer about the progress being made. When a match is found, the program comes to a halt, displays the information about the matched text, and awaits the entry of a Y or N before continuing the search.

The TS program has two switches that alter or suppress the interactive nature of the program. By combining these switches in different ways and using the DOS redirection commands, you can obtain text files or printed reports about the text search, in contrast to simply reading the information as it comes up on the screen. The two switches are:

- T **Total.** This switch changes the goal of the Text Search program. With /T active the program does not attempt to show you where or how many times the text occurs in a given file. Instead, it produces a list of the filenames that contain a match for the search text. No interaction on the part of the user is needed.

- Log **Log Data.** With this mode active the program outputs information in a form suitable for printing or storing in a disk file. The parts of the normal display that would make sense only when someone is monitoring the screen are suppressed.

For example, suppose you want to know which files in the DOS directory contain the phrase "Incorrect DOS version". Because you were interested only in filenames, not the location of the phrase Incorrect DOS version within them, you would use the /T option. Enter

TS \dos "incorrect dos version"/T ⏎

In this case, the Text Search program produces a list of filenames that contain the selected phrase. There should be quite a few of these names since most DOS programs contain this message. Notice that the program does not stop for user input while it is working, and that entering the directory name, /**DOS**, was sufficient to search all the files in that directory. At the bottom of the list a summary of the results is displayed, Figure 7-12.

```
        select.com
        speed.com
        sys.com
        tree.com
        append.exe
        ask.exe
        attrib.exe
        fastopen.exe
        fc.exe
        find.exe
        join.exe
        link.exe
        nlsfunc.exe
        replace.exe
        sa.exe
        share.exe
        sort.exe
        subst.exe
        sys.exe
        xcopy.exe
        ramdrive.sys

38 files found containing the text "incorrect dos version"
```

Figure 7-12 Text Search totals the number of matches.

Suppose you want to print out this long list, instead of scrolling the screen. You would have to enter the same command, but add two items.

1. A DOS redirection command to send the output to the printer.

2. The /LOG option. Remember that TS displays the names of all the files that it searches as it is running. This output is designed for the screen where text can be printed over in the same position. Such output would not print correctly. The /LOG option suppresses this output and replaces it with a format appropriate for a printer. Enter

TS \dos "incorrect dos version"/T/LOG > PRN ↵

The /LOG command can be used without the /T. If it is, the output lists both the files and the occurrences of the search text. As an example, search the DOS directory for the word COMSPEC in any of the files. Enter

TS \dos comspec/LOG ↵

> *Comspec is a DOS term that refers to the drive and directory location of the COMMAND.COM. file. Some programs, like the Norton Command program and Lotus 1-2-3, prompt DOS to reload the COMMAND.COM files after they have been terminated. The COMSPEC value stored in memory tells DOS where to look for the COMMAND.COM file. Usually, the COMSPEC is the drive and directory from which the computer booted, C:\. In some cases, usually when running programs with multiple disks on a floppy disk system, the COMSPEC is changed to a different drive other than the boot drive. Borland's Quattro running on a floppy drive system does this.*

The program displays the data about each occurrence of *Comspec*. The /LOG also suppresses the pauses in the program because they would be inappropriate for a printed output. A summary appears at the bottom of the display. This summary lists the number of files and total number of occurrences of the search text.

Using the DOS redirection command you can obtain a printed copy of this information. Enter

TS \dos comspec/LOG > PRN -"

Notice that output from the TS program is not page formatted. To get a page-formatted listing you can use the same method applied to the FF program. The first step is to capture the output into a text file. Then use LP to print the text with page formatting. Example:

TS \dos comspec/LOG > search.txt
LP search.txt

Another purpose in directing the output of the TS program to a text file is so that you can load that text file into a word processor or text editor. This enables you to examine at your own pace the information returned by the TS program. Because a word processor allows you to move forward and backward in the text you can compare the items found by TS by skipping around in the file. When you run the TS program the information is displayed as it is found and you cannot go back to previous displays.

About Searching Files

The TS program is one of the most valuable of the utilities provided in the Norton Utilities package. The most common usage is to search word processor files for phrases or keywords. The TS program can quickly locate all the files that contain references to specific topics. Because TS displays the context in which the search text is found, you can quickly decide if this match is relevant to your needs. The filenames provided with the match make it simple to know which files to load and examine.

When searching for text, it is important to understand that the contents of the files created by various applications do not correspond directly to the data you see displayed on your screen. Most programs store additional information, usually in a nontext format, along with the data you enter.

For example, most word processing programs insert special characters or codes into the text you type, to indicate formatting attributes. The most common attribute to enter is a line ending code. This code indicates where the word processor should wrap text to the next line. This code or character is significant when you search for a phrase. For example, if you look for the phrase **vagaries and vicissitudes**, TS would fail to make a match if the phrase was broken by a line wrap code. The illustration below shows the phrase in a WordPerfect document format. Notice that the phrase contains a character that did not appear on the WordPerfect display, a soft return (Figure 7-13).

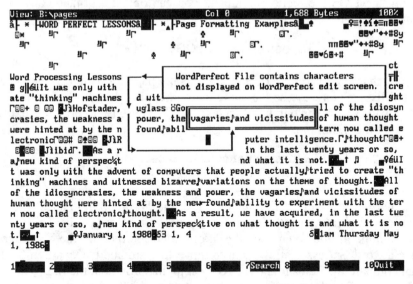

Figure 7-13 Nontext codes used in word processor files.

Text Search would fail to find this phrase because your search text would contain a space, not a [Ctrl/m] character (represented by the musical note symbol). For this reason it is better to search for individual words rather than phrases when searching through some file formats.

Text Search also tells you what line the text appears on. Most word processing programs do not count lines consecutively but restart the line counting on each page. The Norton Editor program is not page oriented and can locate text by line number. If you use WordStar, the nondocument mode counts both consecutive lines and characters. For example, suppose you load a WordStar document with the D command and want to locate the seventy-fifth line in the file. The status line normally displays page, line, and character. Entering the command **[Ctrl/o]p** will turn off the page break display. WordStar will display FL for File Line and FC for File Character, which count those values consecutively from the beginning of the file.

While on the subject of WordStar, it is important to mention that WordStar document files use a special system of coding that should be taken into consideration if you are searching these files with TS. When WordStar implements wraparound typing, it changes some of the normal text characters by adding 128 to their ASCII character value. This technique is called changing the "high-order bit," referring to the change made in the binary number that represents the character.

The diagram belows shows how the a character is changed when its "high-order bit" is manipulated.

		ASCII value
Character	a	97
Plus	+	128
Equals	ß	225

The text of a WordStar file will have many such changes. When you use WordStar, the text appears as normal because WordStar subtracts the high order bit when it displays the text. However, to programs like TS the document appears with the high order bit in place, as shown in Figure 7-14.

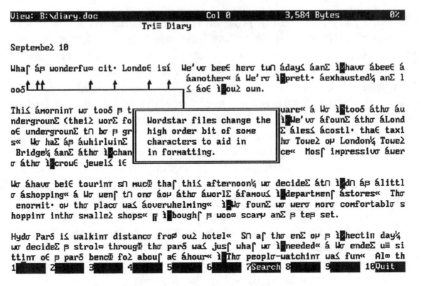

Figure 7-14 Document files with high-order bits manipulated.

The TS program has a special option that should be used when searching WordStar or WordStar compatible files (e.g., NewWord files). The switch /WS will tell TS to ignore the high-order bits (Figure 7-15). For example, suppose you want to search WordStar files for the word **London**, you would enter a command that looks like this:

TS *.* london/WS

```
Searching B:\diary.doc

Found at line 5, file offset 80

                        Trip Diary

September 10

What a wonderful city London is! We've been here two days and
have been literally running from one tour to another.  We're
pretty exhausted, and look ferward to exploring a few sights  on
our own.

This morning we took a tour that began at Trafalgar Square.    We


Search for more (Y/N) ? _
```

Figure 7-15 WordStar switch ignores high-order bits.

Note that this applies to WordStar Versions 3 and 4. It does not apply to WordStar 2000 files, which do not use the high-order bit technique.

Also keep in mind that using the /WS on non-WordStar files will cause the TS program to match characters based on only the first 7 bits, which is misleading. Limit /WS to WordStar or compatible document files.

Microsoft Word files are the closest to pure text files, since most of the formatting codes are stored at the bottom of the file. This means phrases occurring within paragraphs will not contain line ending codes. These files can be searched for phrases much more reliably than can WordPerfect, Multimate, or WordStar.

dBASE III Plus files are executed in a way that work well with TS. dBASE DBF files begin with a file structure header that is not text. But the rest of the file, which contains the actual data, is a pure ASCII text file. dBASE does not insert any special codes to mark field or record endings, which might interfere with matching. An exception to this rule are dBASE date and logical fields. dBASE stores dates in a different format than they appear on the screen. For example, the date 01/05/87 would appear as 19870105 in the actual DBF file. Logical fields are **T** or **F**, even if they appear on the screen as **Y** or **N**.

dBASE DBT files, used to hold memos, are also text files. Note that the dBASE word processor will insert line ending character, ASCII 141 (the same as WordStar) into the text of memos.

PFS Files, on the other hand, store data in a binary format that bears no resemblance to the text you type in.

Spreadsheet files also contain a great deal of binary coding. Numeric values and formulas are not stored as text and cannot be searched for. However, labels are stored as text and can be searched for.

EBCDIC Option

The Text Search program, along with the main Norton Utilities program and the LP program, provide an option for using the EBCDIC coding system.

EBCDIC stands for Extended Binary Coded Decimal Interchange Code. The coding system is commonly used on IBM and other mainframe computers. The system serves the same purpose as the ASCII coding system but assigns characters to different values than does ASCII.

The name EBCDIC implies that it is an enhanced coding system. The ASCII coding system was originally developed as a 7-bit system with a total of 128 (2 to the seventh power = 128) characters. The eighth bit was not used for characters and was reserved for parity checking, a technique commonly used in telecommunications to trap errors in long distance communications. EBCDIC code was considered extended because it used all 8 bits for characters, doubling the total number of characters in the coding (2 to the eighth power = 256).

Today, most MS-DOS computers treat ASCII as an extended character set with 256 characters. The additional character usually conforms to the extended set supplied on the original IBM PC. Before that time, computer manufacturers chose to provide or not to provide characters for the extended codes. The Osborne I computer supplied a set of graphics characters for the extended code values that were quite different from the one used by most MS-DOS computers.

> While most MS-DOS computers display the extended character set on the screen, the same cannot be said of most printers. Daisy wheel printers use 96-character wheels which do not support the extended characters. Even most dot matrix printers do not support the full character set. The term "IBM graphics compatible" is often used to express the fact that this printer will print the extended character set. The fonts used on most laser printers are usually limited to the standard 128 character ASCII set. To produce the full character set you will have to look for fonts that specifically support the full extended character set.

If you have text files, usually downloaded from a mainframe computer, that are stored in EBCDIC code, use the /EBCDIC switch with the TS, LP, and NU (Norton Utilities) programs so that the text will be interpreted correctly.

In the main Norton Utilities program, [Alt/F5] will toggle the character display from ASCII to EBCDIC, and then from EBCDIC to ASCII. You might try this just to see what happens when you change coding systems. Note that if you enter [Alt/F5] the program will not automatically redraw the screen in EBCDIC. If you enter [Pg Dn], causing the program to redraw the screen, the EBCDIC coding will be used for that and all subsequent screens. The word EBCDIC will appear at the top of the display to remind you that you have activated EBCDIC coding.

Searching for Nontext Characters

The Text Search program is primarily designed to search for text files. This means that the characters you search for are the normal keyboard characters.

However, it is possible to search for characters in the extended character set. For example, one of the batch files supplied with the Norton Utilities programs uses some of the nonkeyboard characters to create graphics. One of the characters is character #219. Suppose you want to use TS to determine which file contains this character. Begin by entering a normal TS command. Note you need to type a space after **dat.** Enter

**TS \dos*.dat
[space bar]**

You have now reached the part of the command where you enter the text to search for. To enter an extended character as the search text you can use the [Alt/keypad] method. Note that you should hold the [Alt] key down while you are typing each of the digits, and that you must type the digits on the numeric keypad. The numbers on the top row of the keyboard will not work. Enter

[Alt/219] ⏎

If you have the BEDEMO.DAT file in the DOS directory the program will stop at Line 288, offset 6256. The character is part of a ROWCOL Batch Enhancer subcommand. However, you cannot see the character on the screen. What does this mean? The answer is that the character at offset 6256 matches the [Alt/219] character. But the TS program is designed to display in reverse video the character located by the search. However, since character 219 is a solid white block, when it is shown in reverse it appears as a blank space. If you don't take this quirk into account you would think that the program is displaying a blank rather than the character you were searching for. Exit the search by entering

n

Searching with the Main Norton Utilities Program

The previous example raises a point about the Norton Utilities programs. The TS program is not the only means by which you can search the disk. The main Norton Utilities program also contains a search facility. To clarify the differences between the two search facilities, load the main Norton Utilities program by entering

nu ↵

Choose the Explore Disk option by entering

e

The next menu lists the options for locating data on the disk. The fourth item on the list is a search option. Enter

s

Menu 1.4 is the as search menu, as shown in Figure 7-16.

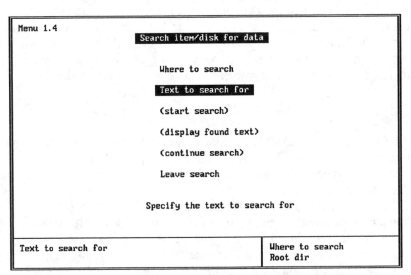

Figure 7-16 Search menu of main Norton Utilities program.

The first task is to select the area to search by using the **Where to search** option. Enter

w

This displays menu 1.4.1, as shown in Figure 7-17.

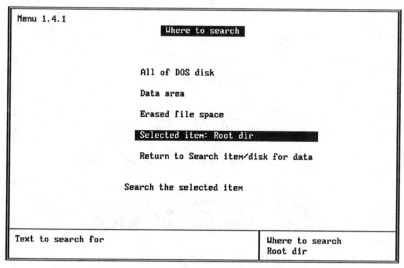

Figure 7-17 Search menu of main Norton Utilities program.

The menu offers options that are similar to TS.

- **All.** This option searches the entire disk, sector by sector.

- **Data.** This option searches all data clusters on the disk. This area includes areas in use by files, and data clusters not currently in use by files.

- **Erased.** This limits the search to data areas not in use by active files. This may include areas used by erased files or areas never used by any files.

- **Select.** This option allows you to select an item such as a directory, FAT, or file to search. The program automatically displays the root directory as the selected item. If you select another item anywhere else in the program, that will appear as the selected item.

In this case choose the data area. Enter

d

You return to the search menu. The next step is to select the text to search for. Enter

t

The text entry menu appears as shown in Figure 7-18.

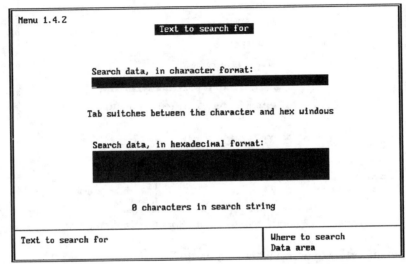

Figure 7-18 Search text can be entered as text or hex values.

The text entry screen is divided into two windows. The top area allows you to enter text characters, while the bottom window allows you to enter hexadecimal values. You can move between the two windows with the [Tab] key. Whatever you enter in one window is automatically echoed in the other.

This display points up the major difference between the TS program and the text search facility of the main Norton Utilities program. The main Norton Utilities program allows you to search for nontext characters as well as text items.

In order to take advantage of this ability you need to have in mind some non-text items to search for. For example, Lotus 1-2-3, Version 2.01 worksheet files always begin with a specific sequence of hex values. Lotus File beginning:

00	00	02	00	06	04	06	00

You can enter those hex values as the search key. Switch to the hex window. Enter

[Tab]

Enter the hex values. Note that you do not have to enter a space between the numbers, the program will automatically separate the hex values for you.

00 00 02 00 06 04 06 00

The other window displays the character symbol, if any, for the hex values as you enter them.

When you have completed the search key, enter

↵

The menu now shows the search key and the selected area at the bottom of the screen, as shown in Figure 7-19.

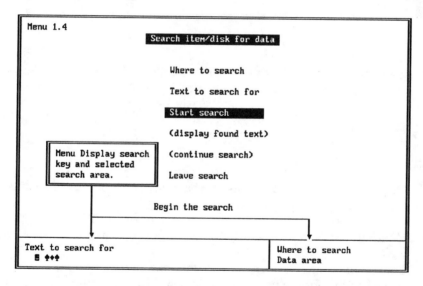

Figure 7-19 Selected characters at bottom of display.

To start the actual search, enter

s

The program displays the cluster numbers as it searches. If it encounters a match, it stops the search and displays the cluster number, as shown in Figure 7-20.

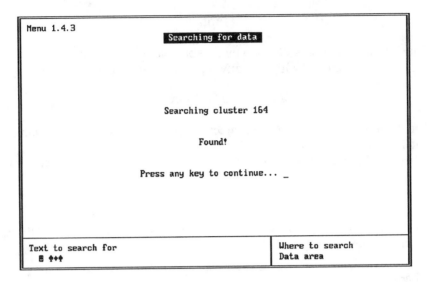

Figure 7-20 Selected characters at bottom of display.

If you use 1-2-3 Release 2.01 the program should find a worksheet file. Once the search has located a match you can return to the search menu by entering

↵

The program now offers you two additional options.

- **Display.** Displays the data cluster where the match was found, using the Edit disk cluster display discussed in Chapter 2.

- **Continue.** Activates the search to find the next match, if any.

- **Leave.** Exits search menu. Note that the search specifications will remain in memory until you quit the main Norton Utilities program or start another search. This means that you can return and continue the same search later without having to re-enter all of the information.

In this case, display the data. Enter

d

Since 1-2-3 worksheets are not stored as text files, the program displays the contents of the sector in hex format. There is one problem. The program tells you what data cluster you are looking at but not what file, if any, this cluster belongs to. This is another difference between the TS program and the text search in the main program.

One possible solution is to look at the information in the cluster and try to find text that you might use with Text Search. For example, the words **@isapp** and **@isaaf**, and the cell range **A11.A12** are also part of this cluster, as shown in Figure 7-21.

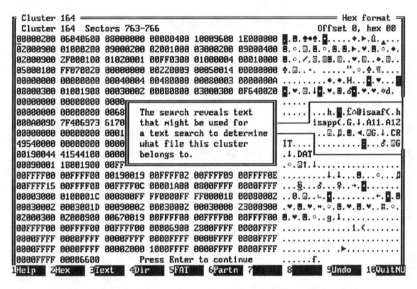

Figure 7-21 Function names appear as text in worksheet file.

> The **@isapp** function indicates that this file was created using a Lotus add-in program. You can use the text to search worksheet files to find the ones that have information related to add-in products, as opposed to files that contain only normal 1-2-3 information. This is important if you want to share files with other users who may not have the same add-ins.

But there is a simpler method. Return to the search menu. Enter

↵

Leave the search menu by entering

I

You are now at menu 1, Explore Disk. You know that the search key is found in cluster 164. But what file, if any, is that? To find out, select I for information. Enter

i

The program analyzes the directory and FAT information and displays the file and directory related to that cluster, as shown in Figure 7-22.

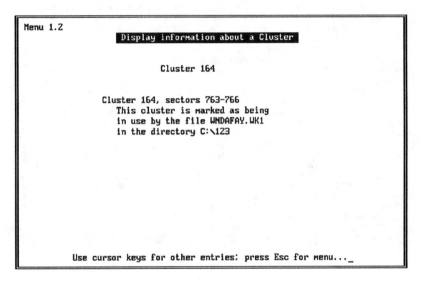

Figure 7-22 File related to selected cluster identified.

In this example the file is called WNDAFAY.WK1 in the \123 directory. Return to the explore disk menu by entering

[F10]

You can return to the search menu, exactly where you left it, by entering

s

The program has maintained the search options that you had selected earlier. You can continue the search or change some or all of the options. Suppose you want to see if there were erased worksheet files on the disk. You could change your selection for where to search. Enter

w
e
s

The program would search for the search key in all of the unused sectors. What good does it do to search erased areas? Because the Norton Utilities programs provide a means by which files can be recovered, in some cases, after they have been erased. A full discussion of erased files and recovered files can be found in Section IV.

The program may encounter the data in an erased area, or simply go until it has reached the end of disk. Exit the main program by entering

[F10]

The search facility of the main Norton Utilities program approaches the task of locating disk information in a slightly different way than the TS program.

1. The TS program is oriented toward text search, while the main program can search for text and nontext sequences.

2. The TS program allows you to select groups of files to search using DOS wildcards. The main program searches one file at a time, or the entire disk.

3. The Text Search program takes a complete search command and carries it out. The main program allows you to go back and forth, change text or location selection, continue, suspend, or restart a selected search.

Depending upon your needs you may find that one or both programs are necessary. The major factor in determining which program you use is the type of files you are searching. Files that contain non text information, like worksheet files, will often require you to use the main program's search facility since you can include hex values as well as text.

The TS program's major advantage is that it can be aimed at a specific group of files, instead of checking all the disk clusters like the main program does. In either case, the search abilities form an invaluable aid in locating information. They also play a key role in recovering erased data, as discussed in Section IV.

Searching in Nonfile Areas

The TS program can also duplicate the sector-by-sector or erased cluster searches performed by the main Norton Utilities program. Text Search will accept two switches that change its orientation from files to clusters and sectors.

D This option places TS into a full-disk scan. When this switch is used, any file wildcards included in the command line are ignored. Text Search searches the disk, beginning with sector 0. You are prompted to enter the letter of the disk you want to search.

E This option places TS into a mode in which all data clusters not assigned to a file in the FAT are searched for the specified text. When this switch is used, any file specifications are ignored by TS. The search begins with the first unused cluster on the disk.

C# The /C switch is followed by a decimal number corresponding to the cluster number where you want the search to begin. Note that /C can only be used if /D or /E are also used. If you enter /C# without /E or /D on the command line, the /C# is ignored.

Using the TS program with the /E or /D options allows you to take advantage of a special option that will copy the data from any located data clusters to a new file. As you locate the clusters, TS will paste them together into a new file by copying clusters. This technique is usually related to recovering erased data but can be used with any disk cluster if desired.

> *The copying feature of the Text Search program requires that the data to be copied should be stored on a different disk than the one being searched. This is done to avoid overwriting any data that is currently stored in unused clusters. As discussed in Chapter 4, data from erased files remains in the disk clusters until that cluster is used by another file to hold new data. By copying the cluster to a different disk, TS makes sure that you are not destroying any of the information you might be searching for.*

For example, suppose you want to see if the name Peter Norton was stored in any of the clusters on the disk. Enter

TS "peter norton"/D ↵

> *This option of the Text Search program will not run on network drives.*

The program prompts you to enter the name of the disk to search. Enter

c

You are prompted for the name of a file into which you can copy the data in the located clusters. You must copy the data to a different disk than you are searching. Text Search will reject any entry that uses the search disk. You do not have to use this option. Entering ↵ will skip this option. Enter

↵

The program should find a match in one of the Norton Utilities programs. The ASK.EXE file is probably the first Norton Utilities program copied to the hard disk and chances are that the program will stop at that file. To stop the search, enter

[Ctrl/Scroll Lock]

To search only the unused clusters, you would substitute a /E for the /D switch. Example:

TS "peter norton"/E ↵

The /C option allows you to begin the search at a specific cluster number. Suppose that in a previous search you found a match in cluster 500. The next search should begin in the unused portions of the disk, starting at cluster 501. The following command would be used:

TS "peter norton"/E/C501

Directories

In Section I the DOS concept of directories was discussed. Directories are essential to efficient use of hard disks. But the DOS commands supplied to deal with directories are difficult and obtuse. Even if you understand the commands well, they are not easy to use because they require you to remember the organization of the disk's directories. The commands themselves provide no information about what directories are on the disk.

To simplify life with hard disks, the Norton Utilities provide two programs that address directory problems. The first program, LD (List Directories), is carried over from earlier versions of the Norton Utilities. The second, NCD (Norton Change Directory), is a new program supplied with Version 4.0. The NCD program is a visual, interactive program that combines the functions of all the DOS directory commands into an easy to operate format.

To learn more about these programs, place a blank, formatted disk in drive A of your computer. This disk will allow you to experiment with directories without affecting your current hard disk. In Chapter 2 the Safe Format program was used to format a floppy disk. In that case the program was used in a full-screen interactive mode. However, the Safe Format command can also be used as a command line program. It accepts all the switches that are used with the DOS format command and has some special options that work only with Safe Format. The switches available are:

Table 7-2 Safe Format Switches

/A	Automatic operation, no full dialog
/S	Transfer DOS system files
/B	Leave space for DOS system files
/V:label	Write volume label
/1	Single-sided format
/4	360K format
/8	Eight sectors per track, 320K
/N:#	Format # sectors per track
/T:#	Format # tracks
/###	Disk # K, e.g., 360, 720
/Q	Quick format method
/D	DOS format method
/C	Complete format method

Format the disk without using the full-screen menus, using the following command.

SF a:/A ↵

When the format is complete, change the active drive to A by entering

a: ↵

Start by making some directories on the floppy disk use the standard DOS commands. Begin with three directories for the three most popular applications. Enter

MD\dbase ↵
MD\wp ↵
MD lotus↵

Notice that the backslash (\) was left out of the last command. With the backslash inserted, DOS creates a new directory with the root directory as the parent. If a blank space is used instead of a backslash, DOS assumes that the parent of the new directory is the active directory. Since the root was the active directory, the command MD\LOTUS and MD LOTUS would have the same result. But if the active directory was something other than the root, then the two commands would have a different result. For example, suppose you want to make two directories under Lotus, one for 1-2-3 and one for Symphony. One way to accomplish this is to use the explicit name for that directory, i.e., using the parent directory's name. Enter

MD\lotus\123 ↵

The other method would be to change to the parent directory and let DOS fill in the default directory in the MD (Make Directory) command. Enter

CD lotus ↵
MD symphony ↵

The new directory is \LOTUS\SYMPHONY because DOS automatically filled in the parent directory with the directory selected with the previous CD command.

The explicit form of the command has the advantage of not depending on any previous commands. For example, even though the active directory is **\lotus**, you can create subdirectories for **\wp**. Enter

MD\wp\letters ↵
MD\wp\memos ↵

For good measure, create a MEMOS directory under letters called PLANS. Enter

MD\wp\memos\plans ↵

You now have plenty of directories to work with. Return to the root directory by entering

cd ↵

List Directories

The LD (List Directories) program is a much simpler program than NCD. The purpose of this program is to provide a list of the directories on the disk. The program will display the list on the screen but it is probably more useful to use the command to print the list, or save the list in a text file for later use.

The LD command can display directory information in two formats.

- **DOS Style.** This is the default style for the LD command. DOS style refers to a linear list of the directories. Subdirectories are listed after their parent directories showing their full path name. The relationship between directories is implied by the names of the directories. Example:

    C:\LOTUS
    C:\LOTUS\123
    C:\LOTUS\SYMPHONY

- **Graphics.** The graphics style is selected by using the /G switch with the LD program. In this mode the relationship between directories is shown visually. Subdirectories are indented and lines are drawn between related items. Example:

To see the difference between the two styles, enter

ld ↵

ld/g ↵

The command produces two styles of directory displays generated by the LD command shown in Figure 7-23. Each ends with a count of the number of directories at the bottom of the listing.

```
A:\ (root)
A:\DBASE
A:\WP
A:\WP\LETTERS
A:\WP\MEMOS
A:\WP\MEMOS\PLANS
A:\LOTUS
A:\LOTUS\123
A:\LOTUS\SYMPHONY

9 directories

A:\>LD/G
LD-List Directories, Advanced Edition 4.50, (C) Copr 1987-88, Peter Norton

A:\┬─DBASE
    ├WP─────────┬─LETTERS
    │           └─MEMOS────────PLANS
    └LOTUS──────┬─123
                └─SYMPHONY

9 directories

A:\>_
```

Figure 7-23 Two styles of List Directory output.

The main purpose of the LD command is to print the directory list. This is done by taking advantage of DOS redirection. Enter

LD >PRN ↵

Printing the graphics display poses a question about the capabilities of your printer. As mentioned in the previous section on EBCDIC coding, not all printers are capable of supporting the full extended character set that is used to display such graphics items as lines and boxes on the screen. In order to print the graphic display on printers that do not support the full IBM character set, the /N switch is provided. Used with /G, it tells LD to substitute normal characters in place of the graphic lines. Enter

LD/G/N ↵

The nongraphics tree-type display is shown in Figure 7-24.

```
LD-List Directories, Advanced Edition 4.50, (C) Copr 1987-88, Peter Norton

A:\-+-DBASE

    +-WP----------+-LETTERS
    |             +-MEMOS---------PLANS
    +-LOTUS-------+-123
                  +-SYMPHONY


9 directories
```

Figure 7-24 Nongraphics directory tree display.

To send that display to print, enter

LD/G/N >PRN ↵

List Directory also recognizes a /A switch that will list the directories on all the drives. Enter

LD/G/A ↵

Finally, the LD command accepts /T. /T enhances the list of directories by counting the number of files and the amount of disk space for each directory with a summary for the entire disk. The /T switch can help you get an idea of how much room a given directory is taking up. How much room does the DOS directory on drive C take up? Answer that question by entering

LD c:\dos/T ↵

The DOS pathname **c:\dos** was used to narrow the scope of the LD command. You can get a listing of the size of all the directories on a disk by entering

LD/T ↵

Figure 7-25 shows the file totals added to the directory list. In this example the totals are all zero because you have not added files to any of the directories yet. If the directories did contain files the listing would show the number of files in each directory and the total amount of space occupied by those files. You can use the DOS redirection commands to store the results of a LD command, usually with the /T switch on, to a text file.

```
LD-List Directories, Advanced Edition 4.50, (C) Copr 1987-88, Peter Norton
  A:\ (root)
        0 files
  A:\DBASE
        0 files
  A:\WP
        0 files
  A:\WP\LETTERS
        0 files
  A:\WP\MEMOS
        0 files
  A:\WP\MEMOS\PLANS
        0 files
  A:\LOTUS
        0 files
  A:\LOTUS\123
        0 files
  A:\LOTUS\SYMPHONY
        0 files

9 directories        0 files
```

Figure 7-25 File number and space totaled.

You can then get an idea of which directories are growing. If a directory gets too large you might want to divide its files into smaller directories. Some of the LD switches are mutually exclusive. For example, /T will not operate if /G is used.

Norton Change Directories

The second program provided with the Norton Utilities to help with directory operations is the NCD (Norton Change Directory) program. This program is similar to the main Norton Utilities program in that it is a full-screen, interactive program. To see how it works, enter

NCD ↵

When the program loads for the first time, it creates a special file called TREEINFO.NCD, which contains a list of the directories on the disk. With this file in place, the NCD program can quickly display diagram of the directories without having to read the entire disk, each time it is loaded. The program now displays a graphics diagram of the directories on the disk, as shown in Figure 7-26.

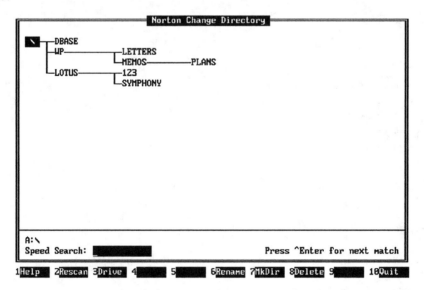

Figure 7-26 Norton Change Directory display.

The directory tree displayed by this program is not simply a display such as the one produced by the LD command, but an interactive tree in which you can change the active DOS directory by moving the highlight to the directory name and pressing ↵. The ↓, →, ↑, and ↓ keys will move the highlight around the displays. In addition, you can use the following keys (Table 7-2).

Table 7-2 Norton Change Directory Keys

[Home]	Highlights the first directory on the list
[End]	Highlights the last directory on the list
[Pg Dn]	Displays the next screen, if any
[Pg Up]	Displays the previous screen, if any

At the bottom of the screen a bar listing the function keys that can be used in this display.

F1 **Help.** Display the Help screen.

F2 **Rescan.** This option causes the program to create a new copy of the TREEINFO.NCD file. This option is used when the current

TREEINFO.NCD file needs to be updated to match the current state of the drive.

F3 **Change Drive.** Use this option to change the active drive. When the drive is changed the program will look for the TREEINFO.NCD file. If it is not found, the disk is scanned and a new TREEINFO.NCD file is created for that drive.

F6 **Rename.** This option allows you to change the name of the highlighted directory.

F7 **Make Directory.** Creates a new directory in the segment of the tree currently highlighted.

F8 **Delete.** Removes the directory from the disk. Note that you can only delete a directory if it does not contain any files. Attempts to delete a directory that is not empty will result in the message **"Error removing the directory** *dir_name*, **Directory is not empty."**

F9 **Display.** This key is active on EGA and VGA displays. You can select the number of lines to display on the screen. This is useful for looking at large directory trees.

The [F10] will exit the program but will not change the directory.

To change to a directory, all you need do is use the arrow keys to move the highlight to the part of the tree that represents the directory you want to activate. For example, suppose you want to change to the PLANS directory. Enter

$$\rightarrow \textit{(5 times)}$$

When a directory name is highlighted you can return to DOS with that directory active by entering ↵. Enter

↵

The program terminates. You are returned to DOS with the active directory \WP\MEMOS\PLANS. To change to a different directory, enter

NCD↵

Note that the highlight is on the current directory PLANS.

Speed Search

In addition to the use of the arrow keys to select a directory from the display, the Norton Change Directory program has a feature called *speed search*. A speed search is initiated any time you enter any alphanumeric characters. The character or characters are displayed in the lower-left corner of the screen, in a box labeled **Speed Search.** As you enter each character the program searches the directory tree to locate a directory with a matching name.

> *If the character you enter does not appear in the directory tree, it is ignored. For example, if you enter Z and there are no directories that begin with that letter the character is ignored.*

Suppose you want to move to the LETTERS directory. Enter

l *(the letter L)*

The program automatically moves the highlight to the next directory in the tree that matches that letter; here, the LOTUS directory. Note that the letter l appears in the Speed Search box in the lower left corner of the screen. Also note that PLANS appears in bold to indicate that it is the active DOS directory.

Since there are two directories (LOTUS and LETTERS) that begin with the letter L, you can continue the search in two different ways:

- **More Characters.** You can add more characters to the speed search criterion. As each new character is added, the program extends the search to find a match for the new criterion.

- **Continue Search.** Pressing the [Ctrl ↵] combination causes the program to move to the next match, if any, for the speed search criterion.

Continue the search by entering

[Ctrl ↵]

The highlight is now on LETTERS. To start a new search you can remove the current criterion by entering [Backspace] to remove one character at a time, or [Ctrl/Backspace] to clear the entire Speed Search box. Also keep in mind that the Speed Search box is automatically cleared when you move the highlight with any of the arrow keys.

Move the highlight to **SYMPHONY** by entering

[backspace]
s

SYMPHONY is now highlighted.

Adding, Deleting, and Renaming Directories

In addition to the ability to change the active directory, the NCD program can add, delete, or rename directories. The program duplicates the function of the DOS commands MD (Make Directory) and RD (Remove Directory). DOS does not have a command that enables you to rename an existing directory.

> *Deleting a directory requires that the directory be empty. This means that you must erase all the files in that directory before attempting to delete it. Keep in mind that a subdirectory represents an entry in a directory similar to a file. Thus even if you have deleted all the files from a directory, it is not empty if it serves as the parent directory for one or more directories. In this example, you could not remove LOTUS, even though it has no file, unless you first removed both of the subdirectories, 123 and SYMPHONY.*

Suppose you want to create a directory of **123** called **BUDGETS**. Highlight 123 by entering

1

To create a new directory, enter

[F7]

When you press [F7] the program inserts a blank directory under the previously highlighted directory. In this instance the blank directory is positioned as a subdirectory of 123. You can now fill in the name for that directory. Enter

budgets ↵

The directory is now added to the tree, as shown in Figure 7-27. The directory is added to the disk drive at the same time it is displayed on the NCD tree display. If you were to quit the program [F10], the new directory would have already been added to the disk.

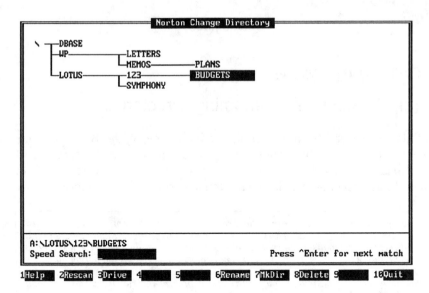

Figure 7-27 Directory added.

Add a second subdirectory to 123. You must remember to move the highlight back to the 123 directory **before** you enter [F7] to make the new directory because the highlight is now on the BUDGETS directory. Enter

← **[F7]**
finance ↵

The [F8] key can be used to remove a directory. First highlight the directory you want to remove. In this example, highlight PLANS. Enter

p

Remove the directory by entering

[F8]

The program responds with a message window informing you that you cannot delete the directory that is the currently active DOS directory (Figure 7-28).

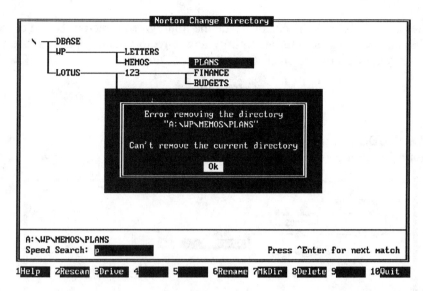

Figure 7-28 Warning that active directory cannot be removed.

In order to remove this directory you must first activate a different directory-that means selecting a directory and exiting and reentering the program. Enter

↵

[Home} ↵

NCD ↵

The root directory is now the active directory which means PLANS can be removed. Enter

p
[F8]

Note that the single keystroke [F8] removes the directory--no ↵ is necessary.

You can change the name of a directory using the NCD program, which is something that cannot be done with DOS commands. The name can be changed when there are files in the directory. In this example, change the BUDGETS directory to ACCOUNTS. Enter

b
[F6]

Pressing [F6] places the cursor inside the highlighted directory box. You can edit the current name or enter an entirely new directory name. You can use the [Ctrl/y] key combination to create the input area. Enter

[Ctrl/y]
accounts ↵

The BUDGETS directory has now been changed to the ACCOUNTS directory (Figure 7-29).

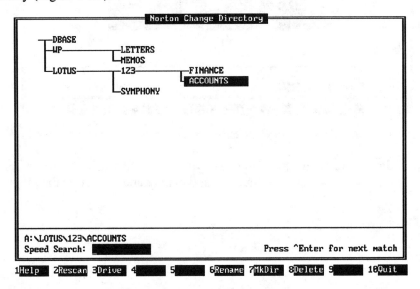

Figure 7-29 Directory name changed.

Select the ACCOUNTS directory by entering

↵

When you exit the program it automatically updates the TREEINFO.NCD files to reflect the alterations made to the directory tree.

Change Directories Command Line Operation

In addition to the full screen operations previously discussed, the NCD program can be operated as a line command program. Its primary advantage over the DOS CD (change directory) command is that the NCD program allows you to perform a type of *speed search* directly from DOS. Unlike the DOS CD command, the NCD command does not require that you enter the full pathname of the directory in order to activate that directory. For example, suppose you wanted to change to the \WP\MEMO directory. In DOS you would need to specify the exact directory path name, e.g., \WP\MEMO. With the NCD program you need enter only one or more characters. The program will search the directory tree information stored in the TREEINFO.NCD file and locate the matching directory for you. Enter

NCD memo ↵

The program displays the message **"Changing to A:\WP\MEMOS"**. Note that the program found the correct directory even through you left off the **S** and did not specify that it was a subdirectory of WP.

If two directories match the name you have entered, you can repeat the NCD command in order to locate the next matching directory. Enter

NCD L ↵

The program selects the \WP\LETTERS directory. To activate the next match, repeat the command. You can use the DOS shortcut, [F3], to repeat the command. Enter

[F3] ↵

The LOTUS directory is selected. The NCD directory command makes it much simpler to change directories from DOS in either full-screen or command line modes. Its search ability makes it easy to locate a directory without having to remember and enter the full pathname of each directory.

Updating the Directory Tree

The operation of the NCD program depends on the information in the TREEINFO.NCD file stored on each disk you work with. When the program is run, it automatically creates this file on each disk it operates on. When you make changes in the full screen mode using the [F6] (rename), [F7] (make directory), or [F8] (delete) commands, those changes are automatically written into the TREEINFO.NCD file.

However, this system cannot guarantee that the directory tree is always accurate. Changes made to the disk directory using DOS commands or other applications such as WordPerfect that allow you to add, delete, or rename directories, will not be reflected in the NCD directory tree.

For example, if you were to create a new directory with the DOS MD command the tree stored by NCD would not contain that new directory. Enter

MD\dbase\clients ↵

Enter

NCD clients ↵

The program returns the message **"Can't find directory A:CLIENTS"**. This is because the new directory is not included in the TREEINFO.NCD file. You can update the file in two ways:

- **Full Screen.** The [F2] command in the full-screen display will update the directory information on the screen and in the TREEINFO.NCD file.

- **/R switch.** The /R switch can be used to update the TREEINFO.NCD file before the program is loaded. This ensures that the tree display is accurate. Example:

NCD/R

Load the program in full screen mode. Enter

NCD ↵

The CLIENTS directory does not appear on the display. Enter

[F2] ↵

The program scans the disk and displays the updated tree. Exit by entering

↵

Now activate the directory by entering

NCD clients ↵

This time the program finds the directory correctly. You can update the TREEINFO.NCD file each time you add or delete a directory by using the NCD program to perform the operation. Instead of MD or RD, use NCD MD or NCD RD. For example, suppose you want to add a directory under DBASE called SALES. Enter

NCD MD sales ⏎

In addition to creating the directory, you have also updated the TREEINFO.NCD file. You can now use NCD to find the directory. Enter

NCD sal ⏎

The program locates the \DBASE\SALES directory correctly. The NCD program makes it easier to operate a hard disk system that uses a complex tree structure. It also makes it easy for someone who is not familiar with the structure of a particular disk to quickly navigate around the disk. Change back to the root directory. Since this directory does not have a name, use the \ symbol to indicate the root. Enter

NCD \ ⏎

Since the NCD program generates the TREEINFO.NCD file if none exists, you will encounter an error if you attempt to use the NCD program on a write-protect or read-only disk. Programs such as the Norton Utilities are usually supplied on write-protected disks, i.e., disks without a notch. Network file servers often have read-only drives to prevent user files from being placed on these drives. You can prevent the error by using a /N switch, which stops the program from writing the TREEINFO.NCD file. The /N requires that the program scan the disk each time it is executed, causing it to operate more slowly.

Sorting Directories

When working with DOS, one is constantly reminded that it was originally designed for a "personal" computer. The power of "personal" computers is far beyond what was expected in 1981. But DOS still retains many of the limited structures that would not have been much of a problem on a 64K floppy.

You may have noticed that the order in which the files appear in directory listings seems to vary as files are added and deleted. The reason is that DOS attempts to reuse empty spaces in the directory in order to save space. For example, if you copy four files, A, B, C, and D onto a blank disk, DOS logically places them into the directory in the order in which they are copied.

1	FileA
2	FileB
3	FileC
4	FileD

But suppose you erase file B and copy a new file, E, to the disk. The new file will appear in the place in the directory left vacant by the erased file.

1	FileA
2	FileE
3	FileC
4	FileD

The directory now reads A, E, C, D. As you add new files and directories to the disk, the order in which they appear will vary depending upon the open spaces created in the directory by deletions. Reusing the directory entries is efficient in terms of space but perplexing to read. New filenames pop up all over the directory.

The same is true of the names of directories. When you add a directory, it is placed into the first available location within the parent directory. Like filenames, the order of the directory names is not organized in a logical order.

The DS (Directory Sort) program provides a means by which you can order the files and directories on your hard disk into a logical sequence, such as alphabetical order.

> DOS offers a filter program called SORT. Although it does not solve the problem of directory order, it does sort the output of the DIR command. It does not affect the actual information written in the disk directory. The Norton Utilities program DS (Directory Sort) will rewrite the directory information on the disk itself. Note that because DS rearranges disk data it will not run while a drive is accessible by a network.

To experiment with DS, place some files onto the floppy disk you have been working with in drive A. You can use the Norton Utilities files stored in the \NORTON directory of the hard disk. Put the files in the root directory.

> *The assumption is made that you are working with a 1.2 megabyte floppy drive. If you are working with a 360K or 720K disk drive you will not have room for all the files in the \NORTON directory, which adds up to about 1000K, or 1 megabyte of information. If that is the case, copy only selected files to the floppy disk. Example COPY c:\norton\f*.*. This will copy eight files that use about 160K of space.*

COPY c:\norton ↵

The DS program can operate in two different modes.

- **Full Screen**. In this mode the directory sort program works the main Norton Utilities and NCD programs. The directory is displayed on the screen along with special commands that change the sequence of the filenames. You can select to sort the file's name, extension, time, date, or size. In addition, you can manually rearrange the directory, file by file, to create a custom-designed order. The full screen mode also permits you to view the file arrangement before it is actually written to the disk.

- **Command Line**. The DS program can be operated in a command line mode from DOS or a DOS batch file. You can create sorting orders based on filename, extension, time, date, or size. The cursor sort order option is not available in the command line mode. However, the /S switch allows you to sort more than one directory at time.

Begin exploring the DS program by loading the program in the full-screen interactive mode. Enter

DS ↵

The full-screen display shows a list of the first 17 items in the current directory, in a window on the left side of the screen as shown in Figure 7-30. Note that the directory items, <DIR>, are listed at the top of the file list.

> *When a directory is created, the name of the directory is entered into the current directory in a manner similar to a filename. The directory is distinguished by the DIR attribute, which is activated by that directory's entries. See pages 78-81.*

Below the window the four commands used for manipulating the files are listed. The right side of the screen shows the status of any manipulations made to the directory listing. The interactive program has two functions. You can use the program in two basic ways.

- **Sort Files**. This function uses a logical criterion to rearrange all the filenames in a directory. The program can sort files according to one or more factors. They are name, extension, date, time, and size. The criterion can be used to sort files in ascending or descending order. You can specify keys in a priority list so that the program knows how to subsort files that have the same value for the primary key. You can perform the same function using DS in the command line mode.

- **Move Individual Files**. Directory Sort allows you to manually rearrange the order of files and directories by moving one or more files at a time to a specific location in the file directory list. You can combine individual file placement with a sort order. For example, you might sort all files by date and time. Then use the individual file options to move certain files to the top or bottom of the list. This function can only be carried out in the interactive mode.

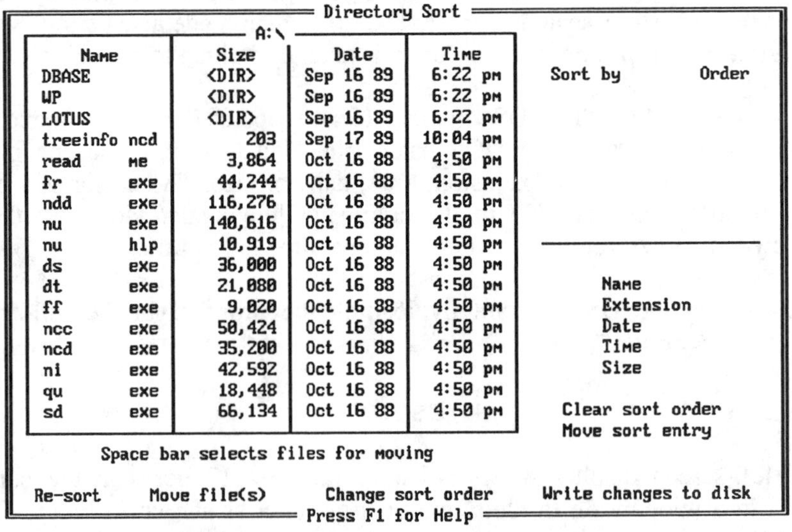

```
═══════════════════════ Directory Sort ═══════════════════════
                        ═══ A:\ ═══
    ┌──────────────────┬─────────┬───────────┬──────────┐
    │      Name        │  Size   │   Date    │   Time   │    Sort by        Order
    │ DBASE            │ <DIR>   │ Sep 16 89 │ 6:22 pm  │
    │ WP               │ <DIR>   │ Sep 16 89 │ 6:22 pm  │
    │ LOTUS            │ <DIR>   │ Sep 16 89 │ 6:22 pm  │
    │ treeinfo  ncd    │   203   │ Sep 17 89 │ 10:04 pm │
    │ read      me     │  3,864  │ Oct 16 88 │ 4:50 pm  │
    │ fr        exe    │ 44,244  │ Oct 16 88 │ 4:50 pm  │
    │ ndd       exe    │116,276  │ Oct 16 88 │ 4:50 pm  │
    │ nu        exe    │140,616  │ Oct 16 88 │ 4:50 pm  │
    │ nu        hlp    │ 10,919  │ Oct 16 88 │ 4:50 pm  │  ─────────────────────
    │ ds        exe    │ 36,000  │ Oct 16 88 │ 4:50 pm  │
    │ dt        exe    │ 21,080  │ Oct 16 88 │ 4:50 pm  │    Name
    │ ff        exe    │  9,020  │ Oct 16 88 │ 4:50 pm  │    Extension
    │ ncc       exe    │ 50,424  │ Oct 16 88 │ 4:50 pm  │    Date
    │ ncd       exe    │ 35,200  │ Oct 16 88 │ 4:50 pm  │    Time
    │ ni        exe    │ 42,592  │ Oct 16 88 │ 4:50 pm  │    Size
    │ qu        exe    │ 18,448  │ Oct 16 88 │ 4:50 pm  │
    │ sd        exe    │ 66,134  │ Oct 16 88 │ 4:50 pm  │    Clear sort order
    └──────────────────┴─────────┴───────────┴──────────┘    Move sort entry
          Space bar selects files for moving

    Re-sort    Move file(s)    Change sort order    Write changes to disk
    ═══════════════════════ Press F1 for Help ═══════════════════════
```

Figure 7-30 Directory Sort full screen display.

One major advantage of the interactive mode is that the changes do not become permanent until you specifically write the changes to the disk. This gives you a chance to change your mind before the directory is rewritten.

To sort all the files in a directory, you select the sort criterion by placing the cursor in the **Sort By** column. Enter

[Tab]

You can now select the sort order by entering N, E, D, T, or S, which correspond to name, extension, date, time, or size. The most common order is by extension. Enter

e

Extension is added to the sort order list. Note that a plus appears next to Extension indicating that the sort is to be in ascending order. To change the order to a descending order, enter

minus

To change it back to ascending order, enter

plus

You can add a second level of sort criteria. Suppose you want files with the same extension ranked within extension by name. Enter

n

Name is added to the sort order list. Note that the files have not been rearranged yet. To place the files in the order you have specified, enter

r

The files are rearranged into order by file extension as shown in Figure 7-31. Files with the same extension are grouped by name within each extension group. This is probably the most common way to arrange files. Note that directory entries always appear at the top of the list when extension or name is used as the criterion.

```
═════════════════════ Directory Sort ═════════════════════
┌──────────── A:\ ─────────────────────────────────────────┐
│   Name       │  Size  │  Date    │  Time   │                    │
│ DBASE        │ <DIR>  │ Sep 16 89│ 6:22 PM │  Sort by      Order│
│ LOTUS        │ <DIR>  │ Sep 16 89│ 6:22 PM │                    │
│ WP           │ <DIR>  │ Sep 16 89│ 6:22 PM │  Extension      +  │
│ mary         │    493 │ Oct 16 88│ 4:50 PM │  Name           +  │
│ bedemo   bat │    666 │ Sep  1 89│12:39 PM │                    │
│ make-tut bat │  2,980 │ Oct 16 88│ 4:50 PM │                    │
│ test     bat │    114 │ Aug 28 89│10:03 AM │                    │
│ make-tut bin │143,282 │ Oct 16 88│ 4:50 PM │ ───────────────────│
│ bedemo   dat │  7,641 │ Sep 16 89│ 3:20 PM │                    │
│ menu     dat │    850 │ Oct 16 88│ 4:50 PM │                    │
│ be       exe │ 22,426 │ Oct 16 88│ 4:50 PM │     Name           │
│ di       exe │  9,304 │ Oct 16 88│ 4:50 PM │     Extension      │
│ ds       exe │ 36,000 │ Oct 16 88│ 4:50 PM │     Date           │
│ dt       exe │ 21,080 │ Oct 16 88│ 4:50 PM │     Time           │
│ fa       exe │  9,300 │ Oct 16 88│ 4:50 PM │     Size           │
│ fd       exe │ 10,290 │ Oct 16 88│ 4:50 PM │                    │
│ ff       exe │  9,020 │ Oct 16 88│ 4:50 PM │  Clear sort order  │
│              │        │          │         │  Move sort entry   │
├──────────────────────────────────────────────────────────────┤
│  Re-sort    Move file(s)    Change sort order   Write changes to disk │
└══════════════════ Press F1 for Help ══════════════════════════┘
```

Figure 7-31 File arranged in extension and name order.

Keep in mind that these changes are not permanent because they have not yet been written to the disk. Entering [Esc] or [F10] will exit the program leaving the directory unchanged.

Another useful way to list files is by the date and time of creation. This order makes it easy to tell which files, if any, have been recently created. To start a new sequence, clear the existing sort order by using the Clear command. Enter

c

Sort by date and time by entering

d
t
r

The files are sorted in date and time order. Note that since all the Norton Utilities programs have the same date and time you might want to add a third criterion to the sort order. This time, add size. Enter

s

The normal order for date, time, and size is an ascending order, i.e., from low to high, or in the case of dates, from old to new. You can use descending sort order, which places the highest or newest files at the top of the list. Enter

```
c
d -
t -
s -
r
```

The files are arranged so that the most recent and largest files appear first (Figure 7-32). In this example the TREEINFO.NCD file should be at the top of the list because it was created while you were working with the NCD program earlier in this chapter.

```
════════════════════════ Directory Sort ════════════════════════
┌─────────────────── A:\ ──────────────────┐
│   Name        Size       Date        Time   │
│ DBASE        <DIR>    Sep 16 89    6:22 pm  │ Sort by            Order
│ WP           <DIR>    Sep 16 89    6:22 pm  │
│ LOTUS        <DIR>    Sep 16 89    6:22 pm  │ Date                -
│ treeinfo ncd   203    Sep 17 89   10:04 pm  │ Time                -
│ make-tut bin 143,282  Oct 16 88    4:50 pm  │ Size                -
│ nu       exe 140,616  Oct 16 88    4:50 pm  │
│ ndd      exe 116,276  Oct 16 88    4:50 pm  │
│ sd       exe  66,134  Oct 16 88    4:50 pm  │
│ ncc      exe  50,424  Oct 16 88    4:50 pm  │ ─────────────────────
│ format   exe  49,060  Oct 16 88    4:50 pm  │
│ sf       exe  49,060  Oct 16 88    4:50 pm  │ Name
│ fr       exe  44,244  Oct 16 88    4:50 pm  │ Extension
│ ni       exe  42,592  Oct 16 88    4:50 pm  │ Date
│ ds       exe  36,000  Oct 16 88    4:50 pm  │ Time
│ ncd      exe  35,200  Oct 16 88    4:50 pm  │ Size
│ be       exe  22,426  Oct 16 88    4:50 pm  │
│ dt       exe  21,080  Oct 16 88    4:50 pm  │ Clear sort order
│                                             │ Move sort entry

   Re-sort      Move file(s)     Change sort order    Write changes to disk
════════════════════════ Press F1 for Help ════════════════════════
```

Figure 7-32 Directory sorted in descending date, time, and size order.

Another feature of the interactive DS program is that you can manually change the location of any file or group of files that you like. For example, the directory names, if any, are always placed at the top of the directory listing. Suppose you want to place these names at the bottom of the directory. In order to accomplish this task you would have to manually position the names because the sort orders always place directories at the top.

To make a manual rearrangement, move the cursor into the file list window on the left side of the screen by entering

[Tab]

A highlight appears on the first name on the list. To change the position of a directory item you must first select the item or items and then move to the new position. Selection is accomplished by pressing the [space bar] while the item is highlighted. Select the first directory by entering

[space bar]

A triangle marks the item as selected for movement. Mark the next two items in the list by entering

↓ **[space bar]**
↓ **[space bar]**

To change the position of the items, move the highlight to the position in the list where you want them to appear. To skip to end of the directory, enter

[End]

Move the files by using the **Move Files** command. Enter

m

Note that the files are inserted **above** the last file in the list, as shown in Figure 7-33. The DS program always inserts the moved files above the highlighted position on.

```
══════════════════════ Directory Sort ══════════════════
                     ┌───── A:\ ─────┐
    ┌─────────────┬─────────┬──────────┬─────────┐
    │   Name      │  Size   │   Date   │  Time   │    Sort by        Order
    │ read    me  │  3,864  │ Oct 16 88│ 4:50 pm │
    │ tut-read me │  3,537  │ Oct 16 88│ 4:50 pm │    Date             -
    │ fileinfo fi │  3,217  │ Oct 16 88│ 4:50 pm │    Time             -
    │ mary        │    493  │ Oct 16 88│ 4:50 pm │    Size             -
    │ bedemo  dat │  7,641  │ Oct 16 88│ 3:19 pm │
    │ make-tut bat│  2,980  │ Oct 16 88│ 3:19 pm │
    │ menu    dat │    850  │ Oct 16 88│ 3:19 pm │
    │ DBASE       │  <DIR>  │ Sep 16 89│ 6:22 pm │
    │ WP          │  <DIR>  │ Sep 16 89│ 6:22 pm │    ───────────────────
    │ LOTUS       │  <DIR>  │ Sep 16 89│ 6:22 pm │
    │ bedemo  bat │    666  │ Oct 16 88│ 3:19 pm │        Name
    │             │         │          │         │        Extension
    │             │         │          │         │        Date
    │             │         │          │         │        Time
    │             │         │          │         │        Size
    │             │         │          │         │
    │             │         │          │         │        Clear sort order
    └─────────────┴─────────┴──────────┴─────────┘        Move sort entry
       Press <CR> when OK; <ESC> to cancel changes

    Re-sort     Move file(s)      Change sort order    Write changes to disk
══════════════════════ Press F1 for Help ═══════════════════
```

Figure 7-33 Directory items manually positioned.

If you want to make the directory entries you can move the highlighted block using the ↑ and ↓ keys. Enter

↓

The directories are now at the bottom of the directory list. If you don't like the changes you have made, enter [Esc] to undo the move. Entering ↵ will insert the change into the directory listing. Enter

↵

Keep in mind that the alterations in the directory order have not changed the actual disk directory yet. In order to change the disk directory to the order on the screen, you must explicitly execute the **W**rite changes to disk command. Enter

w

The disk directory is updated. This means that the DOS directory of the disk will now list the files in the specified order. The original order of the files has been overwritten and cannot be restored. Exit the program by entering

[space bar]
[F10]

List the files with the DOS DIR command.

DIR ↵

You can see that the files are listed in the same order as you selected in the DS program, as shown in Figure 7-34.

```
Volume in drive A has no label
 Directory of  A:\
TREEINFO NCD     203    9-17-89   10:04p
MAKE-TUT BIN  143282   10-16-88    4:50p
NU       EXE  140616   10-16-88    4:50p
NDD      EXE  116276   10-16-88    4:50p
SD       EXE   66134   10-16-88    4:50p
. . . . . . . . . . . . . . . . . . . . . . . . . . . . . . . . . . . .
BEDEMO   DAT    7641   10-16-88    3:19p
MAKE-TUT BAT    2980   10-16-88    3:19p
MENU     DAT     850   10-16-88    3:19p
BEDEMO   BAT     666   10-16-88    3:19p
DBASE         <DIR>     9-16-89    6:22p
WP            <DIR>     9-16-89    6:22p
LOTUS         <DIR>     9-16-89    6:22p
        42 File(s)    140288 bytes free
```

Figure 7-34 Sorted directory (abbreviated listing).

Directory Sort Command Line Execution

You can sort a directory without entering the full-screen display mode by running DS as a command line program. You can perform all the same sort orders as the full-screen mode but you cannot position individual files. Sort orders are specified using letter codes (Table 7-3).

Table 7-3 Directory Sort Codes

N	Name
E	Extension
D	Date
T	Time
S	Size
letter-	Sort descending order

The program will sort the current directory unless you enter the path name of a specific directory you want to sort. For example, suppose that you want to sort the current directory in ascending size order. Enter

DS S ↵

DIR ↵

The files are listed by size order from smallest to largest. You can perform multilevel sorts by using more than one letter. For example, to sort by name and extension, enter

DS NE ↵

DIR ↵

You can select descending sort order by adding - signs to the letters. Enter

DS N - E - ↵

DIR ↵

The DS command will also accept a subdirectory switch. The effect of this is to have DS sort all subdirectories included in the beginning directory. If you start at the root, you will be able to sort all the files on the hard disk with a single command. The command below arranges all the directories in order by extension and name. Note that the \ tells DS to begin at the root directory.

DS EN \S ↵

The program follows the tree structure and sorts the files in all the directories, as shown in Figure 7-35.

```
DS-Directory Sort, Advanced Edition 4.50, (C) Copr 1987-88, Peter Norton

  A:\ ... reading, sorting, writing, done.
  A:\DBASE ... reading, sorting, writing, done.
  A:\DBASE\CLIENTS ... reading, sorting, writing, done.
  A:\DBASE\CLIENTS\SALES ... reading, sorting, writing, done.
  A:\LOTUS ... reading, sorting, writing, done.
  A:\LOTUS\123 ... reading, sorting, writing, done.
  A:\LOTUS\123\ACCOUNTS ... reading, sorting, writing, done.
  A:\LOTUS\123\FINANCE ... reading, sorting, writing, done.
  A:\LOTUS\SYMPHONY ... reading, sorting, writing, done.
  A:\WP ... reading, sorting, writing, done.
  A:\WP\LETTERS ... reading, sorting, writing, done.
  A:\WP\MEMOS ... reading, sorting, writing, done.
```

Figure 7-35 Tree shows all directories on disk sorted.

Summary

This chapter discussed the Norton Utilities programs that help you organize and work with hard disks.

- **File Find.** The FF (File Find) program performs a search that can locate a file stored in any directory on the disk. This program will locate all the files that match a given wildcard and list the file and directory information for each match.

- **Text Search.** This program searches the contents of files to find matching words or phrases. The program displays the name of the files that contain the specified text, the context within the file in which it occurs, and the location in lines and byte offset. You can select to search files and/or unused disk space.

- **Main Norton Utilities Search.** The main Norton Utilities program, discussed in Chapter 2, has a search feature that can be used to locate both text and hex information. The search feature will locate data stored in files or in unused disk space, and display the disk clusters that contain the search information.

- **List Directories.** This program lists all the directories on a disk. The list can be text, or a graphics-tree representation.

- **Norton Change Directories.** This program provides a search facility which activates directories by searching the disk for a name matching the specified criterion. Unlike the DOS CD command, NCD does not require the full pathname to be used in order to activate a directory. NCD will search the directory tree for names that match the given criterion. In full-screen operation, the directory tree can be navigated using the arrow keys to select the desired directory.

- **Directory Sort.** This program rewrites the names of the files that appear in a directory by name, extension, date, time, or size order. The sorts can be ascending or descending. In full-screen mode you can manually arrange filenames in any order desired.

8

File Tasks

File Dates

When you list a directory you will notice that each file has a time and date listed. The time and date is stamped into the directory entry when the file is created or updated. When a file is duplicated with the COPY or XCOPY commands, DOS retains the time and date from the source file.

The date and time information are drawn from the operating system of the computer. Computers with internal clocks use the clock to place the correct time and date in the operating system.

Older models of computers, such as IBM PC and XT, were not originally designed to have internal clocks, but they could be added to the systems using expansion boards. However, because they were not part of the original design, these boards required the execution of a special program that would fetch the time and date from the internal clock and pass it to the operating system. In AT and 80386 computers the internal clock is part of the design and the date and time are automatically passed to the operating system each time the computer is booted.

Older computers not equipped with internal clocks will automatically use the same date, e.g., 01-01-80, each time the computer is booted. On those systems you can use the DOS commands DATE and TIME to set the clocks.

> On most AT and 80386 computers, you can use the Norton Control Center program's Time and Date option to adjust the internal clock to Daylight Saving Time, without having to run the diagnostics program.

The File Date program provides a means by which you can alter the time and date stamp on any file or group of files. By default the program will set the file date and time to the current system date and time. If you want to set the date and/or time to a specific value, you can use the /D and /T switches to specify the values you want to use.

Assuming that you have a disk in drive A which was used for Chapters 6 and 7, you can experiment a bit with the FD (File Date) program.

Suppose you want to change the date of the FF.EXE file to today's date. Enter the FD command followed by the name of the file.

FD ff.exe ⏎

The date and time of the file is changed to the current date and time, as shown in Figure 8-1

```
FD-File Date, Advanced Edition 4.50, (C) Copr 1987-88, Peter Norton


 A:\
    ff.exe            9-19-89    12:39 pm


 1 file updated
```

Figure 8-1 Current date stamped on FF.EXE file.

You can change the date and/or time to a specific date and time by using the /D and /T switches. Suppose you want the FF.EXE file to be dated 12/31/89. You can use the /D switch to stamp that specific date. Note that the date must be in *month-day-year* format. However, you can use either / or - characters as separators. It is also not necessary to enter leading zeros when you want single-digit values. For example, /D1-1-89 would be a valid date specification for January 1st, 1989. Enter

FD ff.exe/D12/31/89 ⏎

> *DOS 3.3 and 4.0 support the COUNTRY.SYS driver which is used in the CONFIG.SYS to set a country code for the system. This code is used to change aspects of the keyboard and the time and date displays. If you are running a country code which uses a different type of date sequence, e.g., France, code 033, uses dd-mm-yy dates, 31-12-89, you may find that the FD program will not operate properly with the /D switch.*

The date is changed to 12/31/89. When the /D or /T is used alone, the other portion of the date and time stamp is unaffected. In this example, the time of day remains the same as it was before the date was changed. Using both the /D and /T switches can change the date and the time. Note that time is entered in a hh:mm:ss format. You do not have to enter a value for minutes or seconds. The program assumes zero if they are not entered AM and PM as distinguished by entering the date in 24 hour format. For example, to set the date and time as 12/31/89 9:00 PM, enter

FD ff.exe/D12-31-89/T21

You can change the time stamp for a group of files by using a wildcard as the file specification. The next command sets all of the files that begin with the letter N to 1/1/90 12:15 PM. Enter

FD n*.*/D1/1/90/T12:15

By using \ (root directory) in combination with the /S switch (include subdirectories) you can change all the file dates on an entire disk with a single command. The example below changes all the file dates to 1/1/90.

FD \D1/1/90/S

Volume Label

DOS allows you to create a volume label for each disk when it is formatted.

> *The /V switch must be used with the FORMAT command if you want to enter a volume label.*

The volume label has little practical effect on the operation of the disk or the computer, but it does serve to identify the disk with a name rather than just a drive letter. The VL command allows you to insert a 1-11 character volume name on a disk.

> *Volume names are handy when running drives on a network since the drive letters may change depending on the workstation set-up. The volume labels would be the same no matter what letter was assigned to the drive. Note that if the disk is currently running under a network, the VL program will not work. To change a volume label, reboot the computer off the network.*

To create or modify the volume label of the current disk enter

VL ↵

The program displays the existing volume name, if any, and a prompt into which you can enter the new volume label (Figure 8-2). You can also delete the existing volume label by pressing the [Del] key.

```
VL-Volume Label, Advanced Edition 4.50, (C) Copr 1987-88, Peter Norton


Volume label in drive D: is now "Morgan_vol2"


  Press Enter to leave old label unchanged, or

  Press Delete to remove old label, or

  Enter new label: -----------
```

Figure 8-2 Change volume label display.

You can enter any alphanumeric character into the label but you cannot insert a space in the label. The underscore is often used to create a separation in the label. The label will accept and maintain both upper and lowercase characters. Unlike DOS filenames, the lowercase characters are not converted to uppercase. Enter

NU_TESTDISK ↵

The new volume label is set. When you list a directory the name will appear at the top of the display, as shown in Figure 8-3. Enter

DIR/W ↵

```
        Volume in drive A is NU_TESTDISK
        Directory of  A:\
```

Figure 8-3 New label appears in directory display.

The VL command can be used as a single-line command by specifying the label text as an argument for the command. The example below would create the volume label in a single step. Note the volume name must be enclosed in quotation marks.

"VL "NU_TESTDISK"

You can change the volume label of a different disk. The command shown below would set the label of disk C to *Fixed_Disk*.

VL c:"Fixed_Disk"

File Sizes

The List Directories program discussed in Chapter 7 is capable of calculating the total amount of space used by the files in a given directory. But what about other groups of files? Norton Utilities provides a program called FS (File Sizes) that calculates the size of a file or group of files.

This is a very handy program (a personal favorite). This program provides some useful information that can be invaluable in managing a computer system.

The basic operation of FS could not be simpler. FS functions like the DOS DIR command. For example, to list the files in the \DOS directory, enter

FS ↵

The command produces distinct pieces of information as shown in Figure 8-4.

1. **File List.** The FL (File List) displays the size of all the selected files. This is the same information that the DIR command provides, except that the FL formats the numbers with commas to make them easier to read.

2. **File Summary.** At the bottom of the file list, FS displays a summary of all the files listed. The first line contains a count of the files listed and the total size of all the files based on the size specification stored in the disk directory. The second line contains the total amount of disk space occupied by those files and an estimate of the amount of "slack" space.

3. **Disk Summary.** This occupies the last two lines of the display. It shows the total capacity of the disk. The amount still left for files is shown as a number of bytes and a percentage of the total disk space.

```
        qu.exe            18,448 bytes
        sd.exe            66,134 bytes
        sf.exe            49,060 bytes
        si.exe            16,484 bytes
        tm.exe             7,504 bytes
        ts.exe            19,126 bytes
        ud.exe            19,420 bytes
        vl.exe            11,120 bytes
        wipedisk.exe      13,410 bytes
        wipefile.exe      13,176 bytes
        fileinfo.fi        3,217 bytes
        nu.hlp            10,919 bytes
        read.me            3,864 bytes
        tut-read.me        3,537 bytes
        treeinfo.ncd         203 bytes
        p1.doc               279 bytes


     1,058,403 total bytes in 40 files
     1,068,544 bytes disk space occupied, 0% slack


 Drive usage
     1,213,952 bytes available on drive A:
       139,776 bytes unused on drive A:, 12% unused
```

Figure 8-4 File Size lists sizes and total space used.

> *When file lists exceed the screen length you can use the output by pressing any key while the information is scrolling. You can also set the program to automatically pause after each screen by using the /P switch with the list command, e.g., FS/P.*

There is one important difference between the list of files produced with FS and a DIR command. File Size does not include directory names in its listing. You might well prefer to use File Size to list only filenames in place of DIR which includes directories as well. This is particularly true when you are listing files in the root directory, which will contain a large number of directories.

The concept of *slack* space is discussed in Section I, but it might bear repeating since it is so closely related to the File Size program.

The size of the file listed in the directory represents the logical size of the file. "Logical size" refers to the number of bytes from the beginning of a file until the end of the file information. But that is not necessarily the same as the amount of disk space taken up by the file. The reason for the difference is that DOS assigns space to files using the data cluster as a minimum allocation unit. A minimum allocation is a familiar concept. When you go to the store you can't buy one aspirin or one egg. For efficient packaging, a minimum allocation unit, i.e., a dozen eggs, is established.

The file size listed in the directory may vary from the actual number of bytes stored in the file due to the way that some programs read and write blocks of data. For example, if you use WordStar to create a file with only one word, for instance, Hello, the file size listed in the directory will show 128, not 5 or 6. This is because WordStar reads and writes data in blocks of 128 characters at a time. This difference has no practical significance.

The data cluster is the minimum allocation unit used by DOS. It is interesting to note that the size of the cluster will vary with the type of disk being used and the version of DOS used to format the disk. Below is a table that shows the cluster sizes of various disks and formats.

Disk Type	DOS Version	Cluster Size
360K	3 or 2	1024
1.2 Meg	3	512
20 Meg	2	8192
20 Meg	3	2048

Slack space is created by the very natural fact that files do not always end at the exact end of a cluster. For example, a file with 1025 characters would require two data clusters on a 360K floppy disk because it, has one more character than would fit into a 1024 byte cluster. This causes 1023 bytes of slack space in the second cluster.

Cluster 1	Cluster 2	Cluster 3	Cluster 4	Cluster 5
File	Slack			

The next file to be added to the disk begins at the beginning of cluster #3. This means that the space at the end of the second cluster cannot be used by any other file. As chance will have it, a certain amount of slack will occur whenever a file is written.

Cluster 1	Cluster 2	Cluster 3	Cluster 4	Cluster 5
File	Slack	File	Slack	

Keep in mind that should the file expand, the file will use up the remainder of the cluster before allocating a new cluster to that file.

The table below shows the amount of disk space used by a 200 byte file on different disk formats.

Disk Type	DOS Version	Cluster Size	200 byte file	% Slack
360K(5 1/4)	3 or 2	1024	1024	80.5
720K(3 1/2)	3	1024	1024	80.5
1.2 Meg	3	512	512	60
20 Meg	2	8192	8192	98
20 Meg	3	2048	2048	90

The cluster size is always a trade-off. If the cluster size is too small, the slack space is cut down, but the disk works slower because it has to keep track of so many more clusters. Performance improves with larger clusters but the amount of slack space rises.

To find out the cluster size used on your hard disk, use the main Norton Utilities program (NU) and select Disk Information (D), then Technical Information (T). The fifth line under logical dimension will tell you the number of sectors in each cluster. To find the cluster size in bytes multiply the number of sectors by 512, i.e., 4 * 512 = 2048.

If all you are interested in is the summary totals, you can suppress the display of the individual filenames by using the /T switch. Suppose you wanted to find the total amount of space occupied by file in the root directory of the disk in drive A. Enter

FS /T ↵

The totals of the selected directory as well as a summary of the overall disk are produced by the command as shown in Figure 8-4.

```
FS-File Size, Advanced Edition 4.50, (C) Copr 1987-88, Peter Norton

  A:\
     1,058,403 total bytes in 40 files
     1,068,544 bytes disk space occupied, 0% slack

 Drive usage
     1,213,952 bytes available on drive A:
       139,776 bytes unused on drive A:, 12% unused
```

Figure 8-5 File Size program calculates totals.

File Size will also operate with a /S switch which will cause it to include subdirectories as well in its count. If you start with the root directory you can include the entire disk. Enter

FS VS/T ↵

The program will output a set of totals for each directory and the a summary for all the directories.

You can use DOS redirection to capture the data in a text file or send it directly to a printer. One handy listing is a summary of the space used on the hard disk. Since this listing might exceed a single page it would be best to capture the output in a text file and then use the LP program to make a page-formatted printout. Example:

FS VT/S >catalog
LP catalogue

Estimating Room

One of the main reasons for using the FS program is to estimate if you have enough room on a destination disk to copy a group of files. You can figure this out by running FS on the group of files you want to copy, then again on the disk that you want to copy to, and by comparing the amount of space the file takes up, with the empty space on the destination disk. But that effort is unnecessary. By specifying the destination disk, FS will make the comparison for you.

Suppose that you wanted to place another copy of files in the \NORTON directory into the \LOTUS directory of the floppy drive. The FS program can be used to determine if the selected files will fit onto the destination drive. By using FS you can avoid being surprised by an insufficient disk space message. This is accomplished by adding a destination drive specification to the FS command in a similar manner to the way a destination drive is specified in a COPY command. Enter

FS c:\norton a:/T ↵

The program summarizes the space required to copy the files, and the space available on the destination disk as shown in Figure 8-6. Note that the program calculates a value labeled *disk space needed to copy to*. This value takes into consideration the fact that when files are copied from one type of disk to another, a change in cluster size will alter the amount of space needed to store the files. In Figure 8-6 the files take up **1,155,072** bytes on the hard disk but require only **1,070,080** when copied to a 1.2 megabyte floppy disk which uses a smaller cluster size. This makes the file size estimate a very accurate reflection of what will actually fit onto the disk you are working with.

```
FS-File Size, Advanced Edition 4.50, (C) Copr 1987-88, Peter Norton

  C:\NORTON
    1,058,716 total bytes in 43 files
    1,155,072 bytes disk space occupied, 8% slack

    1,070,080 bytes disk space needed to copy to A:
      139,776 bytes available on A:, insufficient disk space

 Drive usage
   41,717,760 bytes available on drive C:
    1,486,848 bytes unused on drive C:, 4% unused
```

Figure 8-6 Files Size checks disk's capacity for new data.

The FS program allows you to quickly and clearly determine the amount of space used by or required for the storage a file or group of files.

File Attributes

The old expression "out of sight, out of mind" can be applied to files on the hard disk. In Chapter 1, the concept of hidden files was discussed in terms of the two system files, BIO and DOS, that are stored on the disk but hidden from display. Because the files are hidden they cannot be erased with the DEL or ERASE command and they do not clutter up the display when you list a directory.

As you work with your hard disk you may find there are a number of files you want to treat like the two hidden files that DOS places on the disk. These are files you do not want to erase but you don't need to be reminded of every time you list the root directory.

It has always been a personal preference to try to keep the root directory as uncluttered as possible. Ideally, the root directory might simply consist of the list of directories.

There are however, some files that absolutely must be placed in the root. They are COMMAND.COM, CONFIG.SYS, and AUTOEXEC.BAT. In addition, you may also have some batch files, such as the MENU batches discussed in Section II of this book. You might also have some device drivers stored in the root directory. Taken all together, the root appears pretty cluttered before you even begin.

> *It is not strictly necessary to place device driver files such as ANSI.SYS or VDISK.SYS in root directory. You can place these files in the any directory you like, e.g., DOS. The only file that must be in the root is CONFIG.SYS. The trick is to use the full pathname with the device driver in the CONFIG.SYS command. For example, suppose you placed the ANSI.SYS file in the \DOS directory. The line in the CONFIG.SYS file of that device drive should read: DEVICE=\DOS\ANSI.SYS. When the computer boots it will search the \DOS directory for the specified device driver. Remember that the CONFIG.SYS file is read after the IBMBIO.COM and IBMDOS.COM files have been loaded, which means the computer can search the drive for files. With this change you can remove the device drivers from the root directory. This does not apply to CONFIG.SYS, which must remain in the root directory of the boot disk.*

But DOS provides an opportunity, and Norton Utilities the means, to protect files from accidental erasure or modification. DOS reserves a byte in the directory entry for each file, for file attributes.

The concept of file attributes is borrowed from the systems used in larger computers. In those computer system files, directories and drives have levels of security that permit only certain operators to gain access to certain programs and files. But DOS was designed to operate a personal computer. The file attributes in DOS are not very complex. There are four attributes that can be changed with the FA program:

1. **Read-Only.** If a file is marked as read-only most of the commands issued by DOS or programs running under DOS will not erase or modify this file. If you attempt to copy a new file to a filename marked as read-only, DOS will display a "file creation" error and refuse to make the copy. Read-only files appear in normal directory listings and can be loaded into most programs.

2. **Hidden.** A hidden file is one that does not appear in the directory. For that reason commands like DEL and ERASE will not remove them. However, a hidden file is accessible to programs and can be modified or overwritten. For example, if a file is hidden and you copy a new file to the same name, DOS will overwrite the hidden file with the new file.

    If you modify a hidden file, DOS will write the modification to the disk. In the process, DOS also removes the hidden attribute and the file becomes visible again.

3. **Archive.** The archive attribute is automatically assigned to all files when they are first written. It is also applied to files that are revised. The attribute is used by the BACKUP, XCOPY, and RESTORE programs to determine which files need to be backed up, i.e., archived on floppy disks. For example, the BACKUP program removes the archive attribute from each file as it is backed up.

4. **System.** The SYSTEM attribute is not generally used by DOS commands. It was included in DOS for compatibility with other operating systems. Some of the Norton Utilities programs (e.g., Format Recover) will take advantage of this attribute to protect files they create because like **hidden** files **system** files do not appear in the directory listing and are ignored by the DEL command.

Files can be read-only, hidden, or both. You can use the attributes to hide or protect important files. The Norton Utilities program FA can be used to determine or modify the attributes of a file or group of files.

Begin by listing the attributes of the files on the floppy disk. Enter

FA ↵

The listing shown in Figure 8-7 is typical because new files added to a disk are automatically marked as *Archive*.

```
     ncc.exe      Archive
     ncd.exe      Archive
     ndd.exe      Archive
     ni.exe       Archive
     nu.exe       Archive
     qu.exe       Archive
     sd.exe       Archive
     sf.exe       Archive
     si.exe       Archive
     tm.exe       Archive
     ts.exe       Archive
     ud.exe       Archive
     vl.exe       Archive
     wipedisk.exe Archive
     wipefile.exe Archive
     fileinfo.fi  Archive
     nu.hlp       Archive
     read.me      Archive
     tut-read.me  Archive
     treeinfo.ncd Archive


    39 files shown
     0 files changed
```

Figure 8-7 File Attributes listing.

Use the FA command to display the attributes on the root directory of your hard disk. This is the **boot** directory since it is the one that the operating system is loaded from when the computer is booted. Enter

FA c:\P ↵

The screen will now show the first set of files from the root directory, as shown in Figure 8-8. The first three files listed will usually be the DOS systems files, in this case IO.SYS, MSDOS.SYS system, and COMMAND.COM. The IO.SYS, MSDOS.SYS are marked as hidden, system, and read-only.

The names used for the system files will differ according to which manufacturer's version of DOS you are running. IBM uses the names IBMBIO.COM and IBMDOS.COM for the DOS system files. One other small difference is that the IBM versions mark the DOS system files as hidden but not system files. The generic Microsoft version of DOS marks the files both as hidden and system.

```
FA-File Attributes, Advanced Edition 4.50, (C) Copr 1987-88, Peter Norton


C:\

    io.sys          Archive Read-only Hidden System
    msdos.sys       Archive Read-only Hidden System
    command.com     Archive
    autoexec.bat    Archive
    config.sys      Archive
```

Figure 8-8 File attributes listed for hard drive root directory.

This means they will not be accidentally erased or overwritten by another file. COMMAND.COM, the third of the MS-DOS files, is marked only as an archive file. Why isn't COMMAND.COM given the same attributes?

The answer lies in the intention of the designers that COMMAND.COM may be only one of a variety of command processors for DOS. The COMMAND.COM file is the program that translates resident DOS commands such as DIR, COPY, TYPE, and so on into operation. Many programs, e.g., Lotus 1-2-3, will remove COMMAND.COM from memory when they run in order to use that space for the application. When you exit the program, DOS reloads the COMMAND.COM file automatically. In this way the illusion is given that the COMMAND.COM command interpreter is always present. The designers of DOS anticipated that other people might design alternatives to COMMAND.COM that would replace commands like DIR and COPY.

As it turned out, very few alternative command processors were developed. Most DOS users employ COMMAND.COM as their exclusive command interpreter. In practice, COMMAND.COM is as much a part of the basic DOS system as the two hidden files. There is no reason that you cannot change the attributes of the COMMAND.COM file to match the other systems files. In doing so you accomplish two things.

1. You remove a file from the directory listing. Since seeing the filename is not necessary, this will reduce some of the clutter in the root directory.

2. This will also protect the COMMAND.COM file from accidental overwriting or erasure.

If the program is paused to display more files, terminate it by entering

[F10]

The FA program has four switches that can be used to find, set, and remove file attributes.

A	Archive
R	Read-only
HID	Hidden
SYS	System
U	Archive, read-only, hidden, or system
PLUS+	Add attribute to file
MINUS	Remove attribute from file

> *Since File Attribute produces a file list, it accepts the /P, /S, and /T switches used by other file listing programs. Do not confuse the /SYS switch, which operates on the system attribute, with /S which selects subdirectories for listing.*

One use of the switches is to list files that have specific attributes. For example, to list all of the files in the root directory of the hard dlsk that are **hidden** files enter

FA c:\HID ↵

The two hidden DOS files are listed, along with any other hidden files in the root directory, if any. You can list all of the hidden files on the entire hard disk by adding the /S switch. Enter

FA c:\HID/S ↵

The attribute switches can be used to change the attributes of a file. To add an attribute, add a plus sign (+) to the switch. To remove an attribute follow the switch with a minus sign (-). For example, the NCD command creates a file called TREEINFO.NCD that is treated as a normal file. This means that you could erase the file accidentally with the DOS DEL command. You might want to protect this file against such accidental erasures. Enter

FA treeinfo.ncd /HID+ ↵

The program adds the specified attribute to the specified file, as shown in Figure 8-9. The file now has the Archive and Hidden attributes.

```
FA-File Attributes, Advanced Edition 4.50, (C) Copr 1987-88, Peter Norton

A:\

    treeinfo.ncd  Archive          Hidden


    1 file changed
```

Figure 8-9 Hidden attribute added to file.

If you list the files in the directory that begin with the letter *T* you will see that the TREEINFO.NCD is not among them. Enter

DIR t*.* ↵

The file is still present and can be found by the NCD program, or others that read the disk directory. For example, the FS program ignores the hidden attribute. Enter

FS t*.* ↵

The TREEINFO.NCD file appears listed with the other files that begin with the letter *T*.

Another way to protect a file is to designate that file as **read-only**. When a file is designated as **read-only**, DOS and most applications running under DOS will refuse to overwrite the file. Files designated as **read-only** will appear in the directory unless you have also designated the files as hidden or system. A file marked with the read-only attribute is more secure than one that is simply hidden. Files that are hidden can be altered or erased by programs that ignore the hidden attribute (but not by the DOS DEL Command). Read-only files cannot be modified or erased unless the program first removes the read-only attribute.

> *The Norton Commander is such a program. If you attempt to delete a read-only file with the Commander, you are asked if you really want to overwrite or delete the read-only file. If you confirm your intention, the Commander will overwrite or delete the file.*

The TREEINFO.NCD file would not be a good file to make read-only. This is because the NCD program will have to update the file should you add, remove, or rename a directory. However, good candidates for read-only attributes are program files. In most cases, a program file is never rewritten once it is copied onto a disk. You can protect program files from erasure or overwriting, but allow them to be displayed in the directory by adding a read-only attribute to the file.

For example, suppose you want to protect all of the Norton Utility programs. This means you would want to add the read-only attribute to all of the files that have an EXE extension. Enter

FA *.exe/R+ ↵

If you are working with all of the Norton Utilities programs you will have protected some 28 files. If you attempt to overwrite or delete a read-only file, DOS will display the messsage **Access denied.** Enter

DEL ff.exe ↵

The message **Access denied** is displayed. If you ever see this message, it implies that the file you are attempting to overwrite or delete is marked as a read-only file.

Keep in mind that you can rename a read-only file. DOS protects the contents of read-only files, i.e., the data clusters that contain the information. However, you can change the name of the file as it appears in the disk directory even though it has a read-only attribute. Change the name of the FF.EXE file to FILEFIND.EXE by entering

RENAME ff.exe filefind.exe ↵

However, you cannot delete the file even with its new name. Enter

DEL filefind.exe ↵

The Access denied message appears again indicating that despite the change in name the file is still protected.

Using Files Protected by Attributes

The effect of file attributes will differ primarily based on the application that you are using. For example, DOS will run a program even though it has both a hidden and a read-only attribute. The FILEFIND.EXE file is currently a read-only file. Add the hidden attribute to that file with the following command.

FA filefind.exe/HID+ ↵

Execute the program by entering

FILEFIND ↵

DOS locates the program name in the disk directory and executes that program, even though many DOS commands ignore the file.

Other applications differ with respect to how they handle files with special attributes. For example, dBASE IV will load a database with a hidden attribute but Paradox3 will not. Some word processing programs, such as Microsoft Word or WordPerfect, will not load hidden files.

On the other hand, most applications will load read-only files. Word processing programs, for example, will load read-only files but will not save any changes made to the file. In those cases you can save the revised file under a new name, avoiding overwriting the original file.

Attributes in the Main Program

The main Norton Utilities program (NU) also allows you to change the attributes of a file. This is done by editing the directory display (discussed in Chapter 2). To see how the main Norton Utilities program can be used to change file attributes, load the main program. Enter

NU ↵

Display the contents of the root directory of the floppy disk by entering

↵ (4 times)
e

The Main Norton Utilities program displays the information stored in the root directory of the disk in the *Dir* format, shown in Figure 8-10. The column on the right side of the display label, **Arc**, **R/O**, **Sys**, and **Hid** corresponds to the Archive, Read-Only, System, and Hidden attributes.

```
┌ Root dir ══════════════════════════════════════ Directory format ═┐
│ Sector 15 in root directory                              Offset 0, hex 0 │
│                                                          Attributes │
│ Filename Ext     Size     Date       Time    Cluster  Arc R/O Sys Hid Dir Vol │
│ ══════════════════════════════════════════════════════════════════ │
│ DBASE                     9-16-89   6:22 pm      2                    Dir │
│ LOTUS                     9-16-89   6:22 pm      4                    Dir │
│ WP                        9-16-89   6:22 pm      3                    Dir │
│ MARY              493    10-16-88   4:50 pm   1690   Arc │
│ BEDEMO   BAT     666    10-16-88   3:19 pm   1691   Arc │
│ MAKE-TUT BAT    2980    10-16-88   3:19 pm   1990   Arc │
│ MAKE-TUT BIN  143282    10-16-88   4:50 pm   1710   Arc │
│ BEDEMO   DAT    7641    10-16-88   3:19 pm   1693   Arc │
│ MENU     DAT     850    10-16-88   3:19 pm   1708   Arc │
│ BE       EXE   22426    10-16-88   4:50 pm   1318   Arc R/O │
│ DI       EXE    9304    10-16-88   4:50 pm   1362   Arc R/O │
│ DS       EXE   36000    10-16-88   4:50 pm    634   Arc R/O │
│ DT       EXE   21080    10-16-88   4:50 pm    705   Arc R/O │
│ FA       EXE    9300    10-16-88   4:50 pm   1381   Arc R/O │
│ FD       EXE   10290    10-16-88   4:50 pm   1400   Arc R/O │
│ FILEFIND EXE    9020    12-31-89   9:00 pm    747   Arc R/O        Hid │
│ ══════════════════════════════════════════════════════════════════ │
│          Filenames beginning with 'σ' indicate erased entries │
│                   Press Enter to continue │
│ 1Help    2Hex    3Text  4Dir   5FAT   6Partn  7       8Choose 9Undo   10QuitNU │
```

Figure 8-10 Main Norton Utilities directory display.

In this display you can add or remove attributes from a file by using the [Tab] key to move the highlight to the column that contains the attribute you want to change. The [spacebar] can then be used to toggle the state of the attribute on and off. When the attribute is off, the column is blank.

For example, if you wanted to remove the hidden attribute from the FINDFILE.EXE file. Move the highlight to the file name FINDFILE.EXE. Enter

↓ *(until FINDFILE.EXE is highlighted)*

Position the highlight in the **Hid** column by entering

[Tab] *(13 times)*

The **Hid** in the column indicates that this file is currently a hidden file. To change the attribute (in this case to remove the hidden attribute) enter

[space bar]

The space becomes blank indicating that the file will no longer have the hidden attribute. Enter

[space bar]

The second [space bar] entry toggles the attribute back to the on position. You can toggle as many times are you desire. Set it to the off position once again by entering

[space bar]

In the Main Norton Utilities program changes made to a display screen are temporary until explicitly written to the disk.

[Esc]

The program asks if you want to write the changes to the disk or discard the changes leaving the disk sector as it was before you started, as shown in Figure 8-11.

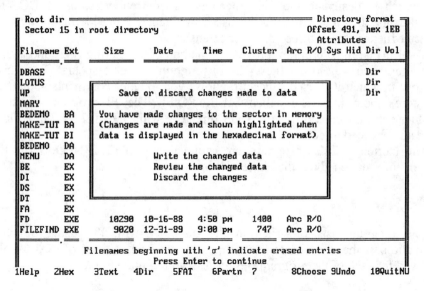

Figure 8-11 Windows asks if you want to save changes.

Save the changes by entering

w

Exit the main program by entering

[F10]

Enter

DIR f*.* ↵

The FILEFIND.EXE file appears in the directory listing. It is no longer a hidden file having had the hidden attribute removed in the Main Norton Utilities program.

File Info

The size of the filename used by DOS applications can be a source of frustration because it leaves so little room to identify the file. If the application you are working with reserves the extension, e.g., 1-2-3, you are left with eight characters with which to designate the file's meaning. All current versions of DOS are limited to the directory structure discussed in Chapter 2 that permits only eight character filenames and three character extensions.

The FI (File Info) program provides a method of annotating files, and is used as an alternative way to list files. The FI program creates a special file in each directory in which it is used. File Info allows you to enter comments about files and stores them in a file called FILEINFO.FI. The FI program works to coordinate the information in the DOS directory with the FILEINFO.FI file to create an enhanced directory display.

The Norton Utilities programs are supplied with a FILEINFO.FI file that contains information about the Norton Utilities programs. Enter

FI ↵

The program lists the files in the directory with the usual directory information, name, size, date, and time. In addition, a line of text is also displayed for each of the program files, as shown in Figure 8-12.

```
ncd       exe      35,200   1-01-90   12:15p  Graphic directory navigation
ndd       exe     116,276   1-01-90   12:15p  Automatic disk diagnosis and repair
ni        exe      42,592   1-01-90   12:15p  Norton Utilities "Command Post"
nu        exe     140,616   1-01-90   12:15p  Full-disk exploring and UnErasing
qu        exe      18,448  10-16-88    4:50p  Automatic recovery of erased files
sd        exe      66,134  10-16-88    4:50p  Reorganize disks to increase speed
sf        exe      49,060  10-16-88    4:50p  Format disks safely and quickly
si        exe      16,484  10-16-88    4:50p  Report computer technical info
tm        exe       7,504  10-16-88    4:50p  Automatic timing with 4 stopwatches
ts        exe      19,126  10-16-88    4:50p  Locate text in files or disks
ud        exe      19,420  10-16-88    4:50p  Recover removed directories
vl        exe      11,120  10-16-88    4:50p  Controls disk volume labels
wipedisk exe       13,410  10-16-88    4:50p  Overwrite disk, for maximum security
wipefile exe       13,176  10-16-88    4:50p  Obliterate files for security
fileinfo fi         3,217  10-16-88    4:50p  Contains all of the file comments
nu        hlp      10,919   1-01-90   12:15p  Help messages used by NU
read      me        3,864  10-16-88    4:50p  READ THESE ADDITIONS TO THE MANUAL
tut-read me         3,537  10-16-88    4:50p
treeinfo ncd          203   9-21-89    4:37p
42 files found       140,288 bytes free
```

Figure 8-12 File information displayed.

The program provides a switch, /C, that selects only those files that have a File Info comment. Files that do not have comments are skipped. Enter

FI/C ↵

This time only those files that actually have FI comments are displayed. You can use a normal file specification wildcard to select files for information display. The next command selects only those files that begin with WIPE. Enter

FI wipe*.* ↵

The program selects the two files that match the file specification.

File Comment Lists

Using the /S (subdirectories) switch you can create FI commands that display file information about all of the files on the disk. The command below is an example of a command that would display all of the files with comments on an entire hard or floppy disk.

FI \S/C/P

You can use the DOS redirection command to print the file information. Example:

FI/C > PRN

By combining /S with redirection you can print all of the comments on an entire hard disk.

FI \S/C > PRN

Keep in mind that the output is not formatted. In order to get a page-formatted output you can direct the FI output to a text file and then use LP to print that text. The following command could be used at DOS or in a batch file to print all of the commented files on a hard disk.

FI \S/C > fi.txt
LP fi.txt

Editing File Information

The information currently being displayed is a result of the comments supplied with the Norton Utilities programs. The FI program allows you to modify existing file comments or add your own comments to any file you select. If you want to revise or create file comments you must use the /E (edit) switch with the FI command. The /E places the program in the *edit* mode. In that mode each of the selected files is displayed one at a time inside an *editing box*. The box displays the name of the file and any file information currently stored for that file. You can edit the existing text or add a new comment.

The files selected for editing in the edit mode are determined by the file specification used with the FI command. If you want to edit or create a comment for one specific file use the full filename. If you want to edit the comments of a group of files, use a wildcard and the program will display editing boxes, one at a time, for each of the files selected. If you omit the file specification, the program will display an edit box for every file in that directory.

As an example of creating a new file comment, take the FILEFIND.EXE file. This file was originally named FF.EXE and, as such, had a corresponding comment in the file information supplied with the Norton Utilities. However, when the name of the file was changed, the FI program no longer associated the file comment with the new name. Suppose you wanted to create a comment for this file. Enter

FI filefind.exe/E ↵

The program displays a box with the name of the file and a blank entry area into which you can enter a comment up to 66 characters in length, as shown in Figure 8-13.

```
A:\>FI filefind.exe/E
FI-File Info, Advanced Edition 4.50, (C) Copr 1987-88, Peter Norton

Directory: A:\
File name: filefind.exe
  Comment: _
                        Press Esc to quit
```

Figure 8-13 File Info editing box.

You can now enter the text you want to use for a comment. Keep in mind that pressing ↵ saves the text as a file comment. To exit without saving enter [Esc] or [F10]. Enter

Program locates files in any directory, /A searches all drives ↵

The program confirms the creation of the file comment with the message **1 comment added.** Display the file with its comment by entering

FI filefind.exe ↵

The program displays the first 37 characters of the comment, as shown in Figure 8-14. The comment is truncated to enable the program to display the file size, time, and date information along with the comment.

```
FI-File Info, Advanced Edition 4.50, (C) Copr 1987-88, Peter Norton

 Directory of A:\

filefind exe     9,020  12-31-89   9:00p  Program locates files in any directo

1 file found    140,288 bytes free
```

Figure 8-14 First 37 characters of comment displayed.

If you want to display the full text of the file comments, which omit the size, date, and time, you would use the /L switch. Enter

FI filefind.exe/L ↵

The full text of the comment is now displayed but the size, time, and date of the file are suppressed, as shown in Figure 8-15.

```
FI-File Info, Advanced Edition 4.50, (C) Copr 1987-88, Peter Norton

 Directory of A:\

filefind exe  Program locates files in any directory, /A searches all drives

1 file found    140,288 bytes free
```

Figure 8-15 Full text of comment displayed.

The FI command can be used to add a comment to a file as a command line program. For example, suppose you wanted to change the comment used for the NU.EXE file to read *Main Norton Utilities program.* You could replace the current comment, if any, by entering

FI nu.exe Main Norton Utilities program ↵

The file comment is changed to the new text without entering the edit mode. Note that when you perform this operation any existing comment is overwritten.

If you want to alter an existing comment, use the /E switch to activate the edit mode.

You can add the same comment to a group of files by using a wildcard with the command. For example, suppose that you wanted to use the same comment, e.g. *Norton Utilities*, for all of the Norton Utilities program files. Enter

FI *.exe Norton Utilities ↵

All of the programs files now have the same comment.

Deleting File Information

The /D switch can be used to remove a comment from one or more files. Suppose that you want to remove the Norton Utilities comments you just added to the program files. Enter

FI *.exe/D ↵

The program removes all of the comments from the selected files.

The FILEINFO.FI File

As mentioned, the FI program stores the comments associated with the file names in a special file called FILEINFO.FI. There are some points to consider about how the FI program uses this file.

- When you create a file comment in a directory that does not contain any file comments, the program creates a new copy of the FILEINFO.FI in that directory. This means that there will be a FILEINFO.FI in each directory that contains commented files. If you delete this file from any of the directories, you will have deleted all of the comments for files in that directory.

- You may want to protect the FILEINFO.FI from accidental deletion by using the FA program to place a hidden attribute on the FILEINFO.FI file. Note that the FI program will be able to use the FILEINFO.FI file even if it is a hidden file. The following command will convert the file to a hidden file.

FA fileinfo.fi/HID+

If you want to hide all of the FILEINFO.FI files on an entire hard disk, you can do so with the following command.

FA \fileinfo.fi/S/HID+

- You can prevent modification to the file comments if you set the FILEINFO.FI files as read-only files. Attempts to edit, delete, or replace the comments will return an **Access denied** message. The following command would convert all FILEINFO.FI files to read-only files.

FA \fileinfo.fi/S/R+

- Deleting comments from a FILEINFO.FI will leave blank spaces within the FILEINFO.FI. If the FILEINFO.FI is large with a significant number of deletions you might want to compress the file so that the unused spaces are removed. Also, if you delete files from a directory the FILEINFO.FI file will retain the comments formerly associated with that file. On slower computers this may help speed up FI operations a bit. The /PACK switch will cause the FI program to rewrite and compress the FILEINFO.FI file. Example:

FI/PACK

- DOS does not recognize any link between the file comments in the FILEINFO.FI file and the filenames. Keep in mind that when a file is copied by DOS the file's comment is not copied with it. If you want to copy the comments you need to copy the FILEINFO.FI file as well. You should probably PACK the copied FILEINFO.FI to remove comments that do not apply to the new location.

The FI program provides a very important feature that DOS and most DOS applications lack. It enables you to attach comments that identify files much more clearly than you can with filenames alone.

Line Print

The LP (Line Print) program fills a significant gap left in the operating system's operations by DOS. There are three basic ways to print from the operating system.

1. Use the PrtSc command to dump the screen text to the printer.

2. Use [Ctrl/p] to echo the information displayed on the screen to the printer. This means that whatever you type and whatever text the computer responds with will be sent to the printer. A second [Ctrl/p] turns the printing off.

3. Use the redirection commands to send program output to the printer.

What is lacking in all three of these cases is page formatting. Page formatting refers to the process by which data is organized to print on pages of a specific size. This means that in addition to the raw text, margins, headers, footers, page numbers, and so on are added to the output. Unformatted output pays no attention to page breaks and margins.

If you intend to work with lists of files, it pays to print formatted information rather than unformatted text.

The LP program is provided to make that possible. Line Print will print text files with page formatting and is set with a series of default values that define the way the text will be placed on the page, as shown in Figure 8-16.

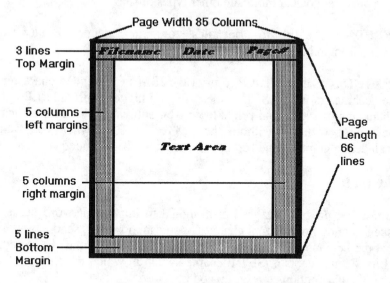

Figure 8-16 Line Print page layout.

The program automatically prints a header line in the top margin that prints out the name of the file being printed, the date of the printing, and the page numbers.

The program uses a number of switches to alter the page format. The table below lists the switches that can be used to alter the page formatting. The # stands for a number value such as /T10 for a ten-line top margin.

/T#	Top margin
/B#	Bottom margin
/L#	Left margin
/R#	Right margin
/H#	Page length (height)
/W#	Page width
/80	Page with 80 columns (Epson FX width)
/132	Page with 132 columns (wide carriage)
/S#	Line spacing (1 = single, 2 = double)
/P#	Starting page number
/N	Automatic line numbering
/HEADER#	Header format (0, 1, or 2)

The LP program assumes that you are printing a standard text file. However, two switches are provided to accommodate other types of files.

- **/EBCDIC.** Use this to print files stored in Extended Binary Coded Decimal Interchange Code.

- **/EXT.** This switch tells LP to print the IBM PC extended character set, i.e., characters with ASCII values 128 and higher. Normally LP ignores characters over 128 and prints their 7-bit equivalent. WordStar files can be printed with LP without the /EXT. Use EXT when you want to include the graphics and foreign characters in the extended character set.

Set-up Codes

As a line printing program, LP is not designed to implement word processing features such as underlines or font changes. You can, however, send a printer set-up string at the beginning of each printing. The set-up string must be stored in a text file. Line Print accepts a /SET:filename switch in which the filename is the name of the file that contains the set-up codes.

The LP program allows you to create printer code files in two formats:

1. **Lotus Format.** This format is one in which each character in the code sequence is expressed as a three digit decimal number equal to the ASCII decimal value for the character. Each character is preceded by a \

2. **Norton Format.** The LP program will recognize combinations of text and control characters. The \ is used to mark a character as a control character.

You can create set-up files by using EDLIN or any text editor. Below are examples of set-up strings. They begin by using EDLIN to create a file called PRTSETUP.STR.

edlin prtsetup.str ↵
i

The most common use of set-up strings is for compressed print. The IBM graphics and Epson printers can use:

Lotus format	\015
Norton format	\O

If you are using a Hewlett-Packard LaserJet printer, the set-up string is much more complex.

Lotus Format	\027E\027&l0O\027&k2S
Norton Format	\[E\[&l0O\[&k2S

Conclude the entry of the set up string with

↵
[Ctrl/c]
e ↵

\027 is the decimal value of [Esc]. [Esc] can also be implemented by a control code [Ctrl/[], expressed in Norton notation as \[.

The final step is to use the set-up string with LP. For example, suppose you wanted to print a file TEST.TXT using compressed printing, which would enable you to increase the line width to 132 characters. Enter

LP test.txt/132/SET:prtsetup.str ↵

If you use LP with a laser printer set for proportionally spaced font you will find that the text column will not line up. LP can only print in "monospaced" fonts in which all characters are allocated the same horizontal width value.

Norton Integrator

The Norton Integrator program was designed to provide a program that would coordinate the operations of all the Norton Utilities programs. The Norton Integrator program is a good way to learn about and experiment with the individual Norton Utilities programs that it coordinates. The Norton Integrator program does not provide any additional functionality but it does display a help screen that furnishes information about each of the Norton Utilities programs. The Norton Integrator program allows you to implement Norton Utilities commands directly from the program without having to return to DOS.

If you have worked through Section II on batch files you will see that the Norton Integrator program ties together all of the individual parts of the Norton Utilities package into a single menu operation.

Eventually you will find it easier to use the Norton Utilities programs without the Norton Integrator menu display. However, it is very helpful when your are learning how to use the programs, or when you want to use a program that you do not work with very often.

To start the Integrator, enter

NI ↵

The program divides the screen into three parts, as shown in Figure 8-17.

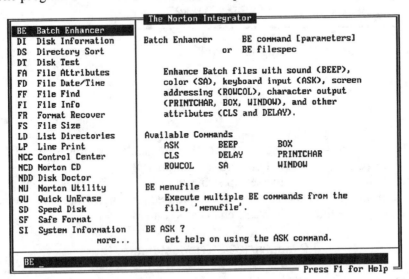

Figure 8-17 Norton Integrator display.

The left side of the display lists all the programs in the Norton Utilities package. The right panel is a help screen that displays a summary of information about the program that is currently being highlighted. The bottom window allows you to enter a command.

You can change the active command by using the up and down arrow keys to move the highlight to another command. Enter

$$\downarrow$$

The Disk Information command is highlighted. Note that the help screen changes to display information about the Disk Information program and the command on the command line now reads DI.

The Norton Integrator program features a speed search. If you want to move to the FI program, enter

[Tab]

The command line changes to a search line. Enter

f

The highlight jumps to the first program that begins with F,   Enter

i

The highlight moves to FI. If you want to execute the command, enter

$$\hookleftarrow$$

The Norton Integrator runs the FI program. The program pauses after it completes. Enter

$$\hookleftarrow$$

You return to the Norton Integrator menu. You can run any of the commands discussed in this section from the Norton Integrator menu system.

To exit the Norton Integrator program, enter

[F10]

Summary

The programs discussed in this chapter deal with Norton Utilities operations that help organize files.

- **File Date.** The File Date program allows you to modify the date and time stamp for a file or a group of files.

- **Volume Label.** Creates a volume label for the specified disk.

- **File Size.** The FS program will calculate the amount of space used by a file or group of files. The program takes into consideration any slack space precipitated by cluster size on the disk. The program can also estimate the space needed to store a file or group of files on another disk.

- **File Attributes.** The FA and Main Norton Utilities programs can be used to change the attributes of files. Files can be protected by assigning hidden, system, or read-only attributes to those files.

- **File Info.** The FI program allows you to create an annotated list for files. Comments are stored in a file called FILEINFO.FI in each directory.

- **Line Print.** The LP program will produce page formatted output from ASCII text files.

Section IV

Survival Skills

Section III of this book discussed operations that are performed in the course of everyday work on a computer. This section of the book is dedicated to a discussion of skills you may need from time to time to solve critical problems. These problems fall into two categories: user-created problems and disk errors.

User-created problems involve erasure of information, either by deleting files or formatting disks. Disk errors are errors that occur as a result of problems in the computer hardware or disk media, both hard and floppy disks.

It is important to keep in mind that even the methods discussed in this section cannot guarantee successful recovery of all lost data. Since no two disks or disk errors are ever exactly the same, you will have to apply the principles discussed here to the problems you encounter.

Some of the techniques discussed here are simple to perform, because they use the automated features supplied with the Norton Utilities programs. Others are more complicated and exotic because they use the general ability of the Main Norton Utilities program to change disk information, on a byte-by-byte basis.

Because the topics in this section involve errors and mistakes, not all the procedures can be discussed in the hands-on manner used throughout this book. For example, unformatting a hard disk is something that most people cannot practice because they don't have extra computers upon which they can experiment.

But there is no substitute for first-hand experience when dealing with unexpected problems. This section will attempt, as well as possible, to give you the background information that will aid in dealing with the small and large computer disasters that may arise.

Whenever possible, the chapter will use a hands-on approach to the subject so that you can recreate the operations on your own computer and experience the correction process.

The Norton Utilities programs covered in this section are:

Programs in Chapter 9-Recovering Data

Safe Format(SF.EXE)
Format Recover(FR.EXE)
Quick Unerase(QU.EXE)
Unerase Directory(UD.EXE)
WipeFile(WIPEFILE.EXE)
WipeDisk(WIPEDISK.EXE)

Programs in Chapter 10-Step by Step Unerasing

Main Norton Utilities(NU.EXE)

Programs in Chapter 11-Disk Errors

Disk Test
Norton Disk Doctor
Main Norton Utilities

9

Recovering Data

The subject of this chapter involves methods of recovering information that has been lost due to user error, i.e., accidental erasures and formatting of disks. The obvious question is, how can you recover something that is erased? The answer lies in understanding that *erase*, when applied to computer storage, has a specific technical meaning. The way data is treated when it is erased may be different from the way you expect it to be.

The Norton Utilities programs provide a means by which information that is normally unavailable to DOS, can, in some cases, be recovered in whole or part.

Format Protection

Because the operations in this chapter deal with recovering erased files, or files from a disk that was accidentally formatted, it makes sense to work with a floppy disk instead of a hard disk. Keep in mind that the principles discussed apply to both hard and floppy disks. The primary difference is the volume of information involved.

The first step in this chapter is to prepare a floppy disk for use. The assumption is made that you are working with a 360K disk in drive A, which is a 1.2 megabyte drive such as those found on AT-type computers.

> *If you have available only 1.2 megabyte or 3.5 inch 720K disks, notations will be made to indicate differences that occur with these disk sizes. The differences in disk size will be most significant in Chapter 10, where you use the main Norton Utilities program to piece together an erased file.*

The first step is to format a disk. Before you proceed, it is important to understand that the DOS format program treats hard and floppy disks differently. In Chapter 1 the concept of low-level and high-level formatting is discussed.

- **Low Level.** This type of formatting is **always** destructive. It obliterates all the data on the disk. The purpose of a low-level format is to organize

335

the disk for use by one or more operating systems. Note that low-level formatting is independent of the operating system used with your computer. You could place DOS, Unix, or OS/2 onto the disk in different partitions using the same low-level format structure. Also at the time of low-level formatting, any disk flaws, if they exist, are marked so that operating systems do not attempt to place data in that part of the disk.

- **High Level**. This type of formatting is done by the operating system to organize the disk as a data storage area. It is the high-level format that sets up a disk as one to be used by computers running DOS. What is significant about the high-level format, in terms of data recovery, is that the data stored in the data clusters is not destroyed by the high-level format process. The process does eliminate the directory information, however, which means that the disk appears to be empty because there are no filenames in the directory.

When the DOS format program is used to format a floppy disk, (5.25 inch or 3.5 inch) it performs both a high- and low-level format. Data formerly stored on floppy disks formatted with the DOS format program cannot be recovered, due to the low-level format performed by the command.

However, when a hard disk is formatted it performs only the high-level format. This means all the data clusters still maintain their data, even though the directory information about the file composed of the data clusters has been erased.

The Norton Utilities programs seek to prevent accidental loss of data due to formatting, in the following ways.

- **Safe Format.** The Safe Format program, discussed in Chapter 2, provides an alterative to the DOS format program. The program protects any disk formatted, hard or floppy, by performing a high-level format only. As part of the formatting process, the program stores information on the disk that can be used by the Format Recover program to recover the data that was on the disk before it was formatted.

- **Format Recover.** The /SAVE option of this program creates a file similar to that created by Safe Format, which enables you to recover a hard disk formatted with the DOS Format program. Note that FR/SAVE works only with hard disks. The DOS format program performs a low-level format on floppy disks that prevents the Format Recover from working.

The Volume Label command, which allows you to create or modify the disk volume label, can be used to create another level of protection against accidental reformatting of a hard disk. Beginning with DOS 3.1 and higher, the format command, when applied to a hard disk, displays the prompt "Enter current Volume Label for drive" before it will format the disk. If the volume has a label you must enter the exact name of the volume, or else the program will display "Invalid Volume ID, Format failure" and terminate without formatting the drive. Since it is unlikely that you can enter the exact volume name without realizing you are about to format the hard drive, this prompt helps prevent accidental formatting of hard disks. The Achilles' heel of this technique is that DOS does not require you to have a volume

label. If the disk has no volume label, entering ↵ at the "Enter current Volume Label for drive" will allow the drive to be reformatted. You can use the VL program to insert a volume label to add another layer of protection. Example: VL password.

You can use a floppy disk to learn more about how Safe Format and Format Recover work.

Begin by formatting the floppy disk. However, here, **do not** use the Safe Format method. Instead, use the /D switch to perform a DOS format (high- and low-level). This is done to create a disk that is completely blank, in case the disk you are using already has data on it. This allows you to see exactly how the commands in this section effect the disk.

In Chapter 2 the full screen of the Safe Format program is used. However, you can execute format operations using Safe Format as a command line program by adding the /A (automatic operation) to the command. Note the full-screen display will appear, but the program will run and terminate automatically. Enter

SF a:/4/D/A ↵

If you are using a 3.5 inch 720K disk, enter SF a:/720/D/A. If you are using a 1.2 megabyte disk, enter SF a:/D/A.

When the format is finished, a completely blank disk is ready for data. In this case, add some of the Norton Utilities files to the disk and place them in directories. This will create a simple model of a hard disk se-up that will allow you to experiment with data recovery techniques.

Begin by using the NCD program to create the directories. Enter

NCD a: ↵

Create three directories called FILES, CONTROL, and DISK. Enter

[F7]
files
← [F7]
control ↵
← [F7]
disk ↵

The directory tree looks like this:

Exit the NCD and return to the hard disk by entering

[F10]
c: ↵

Now copy Norton Utilities programs into the directories. Enter

COPY \norton\f?.exe a:\files ↵
COPY \norton\s?.exe a:\control ↵
COPY \norton*.exe a:\disk ↵

Before you work with Safe Format and Format Recover, use the Main Norton Utilities program to inspect the disk directory and the FAT (File Allocation Table). Enter

NU a: ↵
↵ (4 times)
e

The program displays the root directory of the disk. Note that the directory display, as shown in Figure 9-1, shows only the three subdirectories as entries. Switch to the FAT display by entering

[F8] ↵
↑ ↵

```
┌ Root dir ══════════════════════════════════════ Directory format ═┐
│ Sector 5 in root directory                             Offset 0, hex 0 │
│                                                           Attributes    │
│Filename Ext     Size      Date      Time    Cluster  Arc R/O Sys Hid Dir Vol│
│══════.══  ═══════  ═══════  ═══════  ═══════  ═══════  ═══════════════════│
│FILES                      9-23-89  12:59 pm     2                      Dir    │
│CONTROL                    9-23-89  12:59 pm     3                      Dir    │
│DISK                       9-23-89   1:00 pm     4                      Dir    │
│              unused directory entry                                           │
│              unused directory entry                                           │
│              unused directory entry                                           │
│              unused directory entry                                           │
│              unused directory entry                                           │
│              unused directory entry                                           │
│              unused directory entry                                           │
│              unused directory entry                                           │
│              unused directory entry                                           │
│              unused directory entry                                           │
│              unused directory entry                                           │
│              unused directory entry                                           │
│              unused directory entry                                           │
│══════.══  ═══════  ═══════  ═══════  ═══════  ═══════  ═══════════════════│
│         Filenames beginning with 'σ' indicate erased entries          │
│                   Press Enter to continue                             │
│1Help   2Hex    3Text   4Dir    5FAT    6Partn  7        8Choose 9Undo   10QuitNU│
└───────────────────────────────────────────────────────────────────────┘
```

Figure 9-1 Root directory of disk.

The program now displays the beginning of the FAT. Display the end of the FAT by entering

[Pg Dn]

The end of the FAT, shown in Figure 9-2, shows that the last cluster used for data is cluster 303. You will see later why this cluster number is significant.

```
┌─ FAT area ═══════════════════════════════════════════ FAT format ═┐
│ Sector 1 in 1st copy of FAT                         Cluster 230, hex E6│
│                                                                       │
│  231    232   233   234   235   236 <EOF>  238   239   240   241   242 │
│         243   244   245   246   247   248   249   250   251   252   253   254 │
│         255   256   257   258   259   260   261   262   263   264   265   266 │
│         267   268   269   270   271   272 <EOF>  274   275   276   277   278 │
│         279   280   281   282   283   284   285   286   287   288   289   290 │
│         291   292   293 <EOF>  295   296   297   298   299   300   301   302 │
│         303 <EOF>    0     0     0     0     0     0     0     0     0     0 │
│           0     0     0     0     0     0     0     0     0     0     0     0 │
│           0     0     0     0     0     0     0     0     0     0     0     0 │
│           0     0     0                                                 │
│                                                                       │
│                                                                       │
│                                                                       │
│                                                                       │
│                          Press Enter to continue                      │
│1Help   2Hex    3Text   4Dir    5FAT    6Partn  7       8Choose 9Undo   10QuitNU│
```

Figure 9-2 End of FAT displayed.

> *If you are using a 1.2 megabyte disk the cluster number of the last cluster will be 595
> in the bottom of the second sector in the FAT.*

Change the display format to the **Hex** format by entering

[F2]

The information on the left side of the screen, as shown in Figure 9-3, represents the actual hex values of the FAT. While the hex format is not generally used to display the FAT, this format will later be compared to parts of the disk following formatting.

```
FDFFFFFF FFFFFF6F 00078000 09A0000B C0000DE0 000F0001
11200113 40011560 01178001 19A0011B C0011DE0 011F0002
21200223 40022560 02278002 29A0022B C0022DE0 022F0003
FF2F0333 40033560 03378003 39F0FF3B C0033DE0 033F0004
41200443 F0FF4560 04478004 49A0044B C0044DE0 04FF0F05
51200553 40055560 05578005 59A0055B C0055DE0 055F0006
61F0FF63 40066560 06678006 69A006FF CF066DE0 066F0007
71200773 40077560 07778007 79A0077B C0077DE0 077F0008
81200883 40088560 08878008 89A0088B C0088DE0 088F0009
91200993 40099560 09978009 99A0099B C0099DE0 099F000A
A1200AA3 400AA560 0AA7800A A9A00AAB F0FFADE0 0AAF000B
B1200BB3 400BB560 0BB7800B B9A00BBB C00BBDE0 0BBF000C
C1200CC3 400CC560 0CC7800C C9A00CCB C00CCDE0 0CCF000D
D1200DD3 400DD560 0DD7800D D9A00DDB F0FFDDE0 0DDF000E
E1200EE3 400EE560 0EE7800E E9A00EEB C00EFFEF 0EEF000F
F1200FF3 400FF560 0FF7800F F9A00FFB C00FFDE0 0FFF0010
01211003 41100561 10078110 09A1100B C1100DE1 100F0111
FF2F1113 41111561 11178111 19A1111B C1111DE1 111F0112
21211223 411225F1 FF278112 29A1122B C1122DE1 122FF1FF
00000000 00000000 00000000 00000000 00000000 00000000
00000000 00000000 00000000 00000000 00000000 00000000
00000000 00000000
```

Figure 9-3 Hex values of FAT.

The directory and FAT summarize the state of the disk before it is formatted. You will want to compare that state to what happens to the disk after it has been formatted. Exit the program by entering

[F10]

Formatting with Safe Format

The Safe Format program will perform only a *high-level* format of the floppy disk. This is the same type of format operation that the DOS Format command carries out when it formats a hard disk. The format command does not actually wipe out the data in each disk sector. Instead, it modifies the directory and the FAT to make the disk appear as if all the files have been removed.

This means that the information on the disk can be reassembled into the same files that were on the disk prior to formatting. However, with the directory and FAT information, piecing together the data clusters into files can only be done indirectly by making intelligent guesses about how the files were stored before the formatting. For example, you might guess that all the clusters between two EOF (end of file) marks belong to the same file. This guess assumes the files are not fragmented. Although it is a good guess, it could be wrong. In such a case, the recovered data might contain only part of the original file. If the file consisted of text, it may be useful. If it were a program, it would not be useful because a program will not run if only part of it is recovered.

The Safe Format program takes another step to ensure a more accurate recovery of the disk's information. It copies information about the files into an unused area of the disk. This information can be accessed by the Format Recover program to reconstruct the directory and FAT for that disk.

To see how this actually works, use Safe Format to format the floppy disk you have been working with. Once again, save a few keystrokes by running Safe Format in the automatic mode. Keep in mind that by default Safe Format uses the Safe Format, not the DOS format method. Enter

SF a:/4/A ⏎

The program flashes a window that tells you the disk information is being saved, before it begins the formatting process.

What changes were actually made to the disk during the Safe Formatting process? You can answer that question by using the Main Norton Utilities program to inspect the disk. Enter

NU a: ⏎

Display the disk directory by entering

**⏎ *(4 times)*
e**

The directory, shown in Figure 9-4, reveals a number of things about what happens during the Safe Format process. First, the directory information has not been erased. Instead, the first letter of each entry has been changed to a special character, σ. DOS recognizes that character as an indication that the file or directory has been deleted. However, you can see that most of the information about the file or directory, in particular the remainder of its name, its size (for files) and the beginning cluster number, are all still intact. This information is very valuable when it comes to reconstructing the data that was stored on the disk prior to formatting.

> *The character at the beginning of each directory entry, σ , is the character displayed for character 229 (E5 in hex).*

```
┌ Root dir ═══════════════════════════════════════ Directory format ═┐
  Sector 5 in root directory                              Offset 0, hex 0
                                                          Attributes
 Filename Ext     Size     Date      Time    Cluster  Arc R/O Sys Hid Dir Vol
═══════════ ════════════ ════════════ ════════════ ══════ ═════════════════════
 σILES                  9-23-89   3:49 pm      2                           Dir
 σONTROL                9-23-89   3:49 pm      3                           Dir
 σISK                   9-23-89   3:49 pm      4                           Dir
 σRECOVER IDX     29    9-23-89   3:58 pm     355    Arc R/O Sys Hid
 σRECOVER DAT   5632    9-23-89   3:58 pm     304    Arc R/O
              unused directory entry
              unused directory entry
              unused directory entry
              unused directory entry
              unused directory entry
              unused directory entry
              unused directory entry
              unused directory entry
              unused directory entry
              unused directory entry
              unused directory entry
══════════ ════════════ ════════════ ════════════ ══════════════════════════════
         Filenames beginning with 'σ' indicate erased entries
                    Press Enter to continue
 1Help   2Hex    3Text    4Dir    5FAT    6Partn  7        8Choose 9Undo   10QuitNU
```

Figure 9-4 Directory of formatted disk.

There are also two filenames in the directory that were not there before the Safe Format program was run. The filenames are ?RECOVER.IDX and ?RECOVER.DAT. These files were written by the Safe Format program before it formatted the disk. The files contain the information needed to reconstruct the disk after formatting.

> *The actual names of the files as originally written on the disk were FRECOVER.IDX and FRECOVER.DAT. The FRECOVER.IDX is assigned the hidden attribute, which means it will not appear in the disk directory. The FRECOVER.DAT will appear in disk directories. Note that both files are protected with the read-only attribute.*

If you look at the cluster numbers of the two files you will notice an interesting pattern. The ?RECOVER.IDX file was stored in cluster 355. That is the last cluster on a 360K disk. The Safe Format places its file in that location so it is less likely to overwrite actual data.

> *If you are using a 720K disk the last cluster number will be 714, or on a 1.2 megabyte disk 2372.*

The other file placed on the disk is the ?RECOVER.DAT file. Its cluster number is 304. Recall that on this disk the last cluster used for data was 303. Safe Format placed this file in the first available cluster on the disk.

Display the FAT of the disk by entering

[F8] ↵

↑ ↵

The FAT table, shown in Figure 9-5, unlike the directory, has been wiped clear of data. There is nothing here that will help reconstruct the allocation of disk clusters.

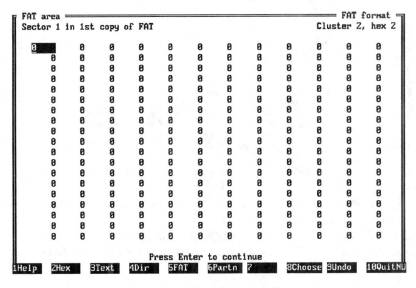

Figure 9-5 FAT of formatted disk.

However, it is exactly this information that the Safe Format program protects by making a copy of the FAT as part of the ?RECOVER.DAT file. Display the contents of this file by displaying cluster number 304. Enter

[F8]

L

304 ↵

↵

Sector 304 contains information that is part of the FRECOVER.DAT file created by the Safe Format process, as shown in Figure 9-6.

```
┌─ Cluster 304 ════════════════════════════════════════════ Hex format ═┐
│  Cluster 304, Sectors 616-617                          Offset 0, hex 0  │
│504E4349 4849424B 00410000 020A0001 00050002 02006200 PNCIHIBK.A..██.█.♦.██.b.│
│66000100 68020000 0917C507 151D6802 00000000 00000000 f.█.h█..o‡├·§⋅h█........│
│00000000 00000000 00000000 00000000 00000000 00000000 ......................│
│00000000 00000000 00000000 00000000 00000000 00000000 ......................│
│00006902 00000000 6A020000 01006B02 00000200 6C020000 ..i█....j█..█.k█..█.l█..│
│05006D02 00000600 6E020000 07006F02 00000800 70020000 ♦.m█..♦.n█..·.o█..█.p█..│
│09007102 00000A00 72020000 0B006B65 20697420 626F6F74 o.q█..█.r█..δ.ke it boot│
│61626C65 2C0D0A72 756E2074 68652044 4F532070 726F6772 able,♪run the DOS progr│
│616D2053 59532061 66746572 20746865 0D0A2020 20202073 am SYS after the♪█     s│
│79737465 6D206861 73206265 656E206C 6F616465 640D0A0D ystem has been loaded♪█♪│
│0A50606C 65617365 20696E73 65727420 6120444F 53206469 █Please insert a DOS dis│
│6B657474 6520696E 746F0D0A 20746865 20647269 76652061 kette into♪█ the drive a│
│6E642073 7472696B 6520616E 79206B65 792E2E2E 00000000 nd strike any key.......│
│00000000 00000000 00000000 00000000 00000000 00000000 ......................│
│00000000 00000000 00000000 00000000 00000000 00000000 ......................│
│00000000 00000000 00000000 00000000 00000000 00000000 ......................│
│00000000 00000000 00000000 00000000 00000000 00000000 ......................│
│00000000 00000000 00000000 00000000 00000000 00000000 ......................│
│00000000 00000000 00000000 00000000 00000000 00000000 ......................│
│00000000 00000000 00000000 00000000 00000000 00000000 ......................│
│00000000 00000000 00000000 00000000 00000000 00000000 ......................│
│00000000 000055AA           Press Enter to continue   ......U┐│
└────────────────────────────────────────────────────────────────────────┘
1Help   2Hex    3Text   4Dir    5FAT    6Partn  7       8Choose 9Undo    10QuitNU
```

Figure 9-6 Safe Format stores disk recovery information.

Enter

[Pg Dn]

This part of cluster 304 contains a copy of the Boot sector of the disk. Enter

[Pg Dn]

The information in the sector (Figure 9-7) may look like a series of hex values at first glance. But if you look more carefully you might recognize these values as an exact duplicate of the hex values contained in the original FAT of the disk. (See Figure 9-3.) With this information, the Format Recover program can restore the disk to its preformat state.

```
┌ Cluster 305 ═══════════════════════════════════════ Hex format ═┐
│ Cluster 305, Sectors 618-619                        Offset 0, hex 0│
│FDFFFFFF FFFFFF6F 00078000 09A0000B C0000DE0 000F0001 ᶻ......o.·G.◦â.δᴸ.♪α.✳.▯│
│11200113 40011560 01178001 19A0011B C0011DE0 011F0002 ◄ ▯!!◙◙⑤`▯↕Ç◙↓á◙←ᴸ◙→α◙▼.▯│
│21200223 40022560 02278002 29A0022B C0022DE0 022F0003 ! ▯#◙◙↕% ▯'Ç▯>á◙+ᴸ◙─α◙/.♥│
│FF2F0333 40033560 03378003 39F0FF3B C0033DE0 033F0004 ./♥3◙♥5`♥?Ç♥9≡.;↑=α♥?.♦│
│41200443 F0FF4560 04478004 49A0044B C0044DE0 04FF0F05 A ♦C≡.E`♦GÇ♦Iá♦Kᴸ♦Hx♦.♦♠│
│51200553 40055560 05578005 59A0055B C0055DE0 055F0006 Q ♦S◙♦U`♦UÇ♦Yá♦[ ᴸ♦]α♦_.♠│
│61F0FF63 40066560 06678006 69A006FF CF066DE0 066F0007 a≡.c◙↑e`↑gÇ↑iá↑.≞↑Hx↑o.·│
│71200773 40077560 07778007 79A0077B C0077DE0 077F0008 q ·s◙·u`·uÇ·yá·{ᴸ·}x·△.▯│
│81200883 40088560 08878008 89A0088B C0088DE0 088F0009 ü ▯á◙▯ ▯gÇ▯éá▯ïᴸ▯▯α▯▯. ◦│
│91200993 40099560 09978009 99A0099B C0099DE0 099F000A æ ◦â◙◦◦`◦↕Ç◦☼á◦↕Ç◦Lo♦¥x◦f.▯│
│A1200AA3 400AA560 0AA7800A A9A00AAB F0FFADE0 0AAF000B í ▯á◙Ç▯`▯°C▯-áᴾ↓=. i◙▯».δ│
│B1200BB3 400BB560 0BB7800B B9A00BBB C00BBDE0 0BBF000C ▯ δ| ◙δ|`δₙGδ|áδ∏ ᴸδ�

          ║α δ| .♀│
│C1200CC3 400CC560 0CC7800C C9A00CCB C00CCDE0 0CCF000D ⊥ ♀|◙♀|`♀|Ç♀|á♀∏ ᴸ♀═α♀=. ♪│
│D1200DD3 400DD560 0DD7800D D9A00DDB F0FFDDE0 0DDF000E ┬ ♪ᴸ◙|ᴾF ♪|Gᴺ|á|Ñ|≡.|α♪▀. ♫│
│E1200EE3 400EE560 0EE7800E E9A00EEB C00EFFEF 0EEF000F ♫ ♪m◙▯α`▯TÇ▯◙á▯◙5ᴸ♪.n♪n.✳│
│F1200FF3 400FF560 0FF7800F F9A00FFB C00FFDE0 0FFF0010 ± ✳<◙♦J`✳≈Ç♦·âᴬ√Lₓ²α♦..▶│
│01211003 41100561 10078110 09A1100B C1100DE1 100F0111 ◙!►♥↑►☻a▶·üᴸ►◦↑►δᴸ♪p►♦◙│
│FF2F1113 41111561 11178111 19A1111B C1111DE1 111F0112 ./◄|A◄§a◄↕ü◄↕¢ ←ᴸ←▶◄▼◙↕│
│21211223 411225F1 FF278112 29A1122B C1122DE1 122FF1FF !!‡!A‡%±.'ü‡)¢↑+ᴸ‡─p‡/±.│
│31211333 411335F1 FF000000 00000000 00000000 00000000 1!‼3A‼5±...............│
│00000000 00000000 00000000 00000000 00000000 00000000 ......................│
│00000000 00000000             Press Enter to continue    .......│
└─────────────────────────────────────────────────────────────────┘
1Help  2Hex   3Text   4Dir   5FAT   6Partn  7      8Choose 9Undo   10QuitNU
```

Figure 9-7 Safe Format copies FAT to unused area.

You may notice a slight difference between the FAT shown in Figure 9-3 and the one in Figure 9-7. The bottom of the table shows some additional values related to the recover files, which were not on the disk when Figure 9-3 was created.

Because this information is stored on the disk, you can recover the files and directories that are currently treated by DOS as erased. Exit the Main Norton Utilities program by entering

[F10]

Format Recover

The Format Recover program has two functions.

- **Recover Formatted Disks.** The Format Recover program will use the FRECOVER.DAT and FRECOVER.IDX files to restore the files and directories on the disk. The operation of the Format Recover program is automatic once recovery begins.

> *You can also apply the Format Recover program to a hard disk formatted with the DOS FORMAT command, which does not contain FRECOVER.DAT and FRECOVER.IDX file. In this case the program attempts to recreate the data by making a guess about the files and directories, based on the information left on the disk. This is a far less reliable way to attempt to recover a formatted disk. In most cases, complete recovery is unlikely, although it may be useful when recovering even part of the data or text file. Of course, the goal of the Norton Utilities programs is to ensure that you do not find yourself in this situation.*

* **Write Recovery Files.** If you have prepared a disk with the DOS FORMAT command you can use the Format Recover program to write the FRECOVER.DAT and FRECOVER.IDX files without having to actually reformat the entire disk. The command **FR/SAVE** creates the recovery files.

> *As part of its disk optimization process, the Speed Disk program will update the recovery files on the disk at the end of the optimization process. This is necessary because Speed Disk may have changed the position of files and directories. If Speed Disk is used on a disk without recovery files, it will create those files.*

The Format Recover program can therefore recover accurately two types of disks: those that have been formatted with the Norton Utilities Safe Format method and those disks on which the FR/SAVE command has been used to create recovery files without reformatting.

Suppose you want to recover the information on the formatted disk in drive A. Load the Format Recover program by entering

FR a: ↵

> *If your hard disk were accidentally formatted, you would need to have floppy disks that could supply the computer with the files necessary for operation, while you attempt to restore the hard disk. This means having a copy of DOS on floppy disk and a copy of the Format Recover program, as well as the other Norton Utilities programs on floppy disks. Since these files were erased from the hard disk during the format process, you **must** have a copy of DOS to boot the computer, and a copy of FREXE to recover formatted disk.*

The main menu of the program, shown in Figure 9-8, lists three operations.

* **Restore Disk Information.** This option should be used to recover the data on a disk that contained format recovery files before it was

formatted. The files could have been created by the Safe Format program (as in this example) or by the use of the FR/SAVE command.

- **Unformat Disk.** This option attempts to reconstruct the files and directories of a formatted disk without the aid of the recovery files by making intelligent guesses about the former structure of the disk.

- **Save Disk Information.** This option, which performs the same action as the /SAVE switch, creates format recovery files on the specified disk.

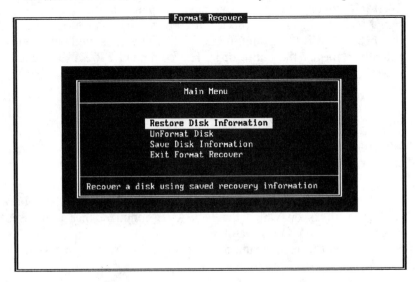

Figure 9-8 Main menu of Format Recover program.

To restore the formatted disk in drive A, enter

r

The program displays a window reminding you that recovery of a formatted disk depends upon the existence of the recovery files, which can be created with Safe Format, Format Recover, or Speed Disk. The window reminds you that if you are not sure if these files were placed on the disk you are trying to recover, you should try this option anyway, since it will cause no harm to the disk if you are wrong. Enter

y

Select the drive to recover. In this example, enter

a

Confirm your intention to recover the data by entering

y

The program displays a map of the disk, similar to the one used by the Main Norton Utilities program (see Chapter 2). The last block on the map is highlighted. The reason is that the Format Recover program always begins at the end of the disk because that is where the RECOVER.IDX file is always stored. When the file is located, the program displays the date and time that the recovery files were created, as shown in Figure 9-9.

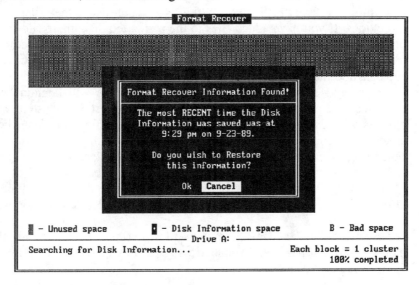

Figure 9-9 Format Recover locates recovery files.

You are asked if you want to restore the disk's information or not. Select OK to continue the recovery process. This window is significant because it tells you the last time the recovery files were updated. The ideal situation for recovery is one in which there have been no changes made to the disk since the last update of the recovery files. This ensures that all the lost data will be recovered. The Norton Utilities programs will automatically install a FR/SAVE command into the AUTOEXEC.BAT file, to ensure that the recovery files are updated each time you boot your computer (see Chapter 1).

However, even this action cannot always ensure complete recovery. It is quite common, in the case of an accidental format of a hard disk, that there were changes made to the disk subsequent to the recovery file update. Since recovery is based on the contents of the recovery files, changes not reflected in those files cannot be recovered. The date and time of the last update is important information for you to have when deciding whether or not to perform the recovery. Enter

o *(the letter O)*

The program displays yet another window with a warning (Figure 9-10). This warning involves the possible destructive aspect of restoring a formatted disk. The addition of new data to the disk **after** formatting will have two effects.

- **Unrecoverable Data.** The recovery of data from a formatted disk uses the directory and FAT information to reconstruct the files and directories. If you have added files to the formatted disk, these files may have, in most cases, overwritten some of the original data. Once this happens, there is no way to restore the information. When the recovery file data does not match the actual disk data, you will find problems with the recovered disk. For example, some of the files will contain both preformat and postformat data. You may also have lost disk clusters, i.e., clusters with data that cannot be assigned to an existing file. Your best chance of a complete recovery of the hard disk requires you to run the Format Recovery program before any new files are placed onto the disk. In the accidental formatting of a hard disk, if you have a copy of the FR.EXE program on a floppy disk **do not copy** it to the hard disk until after you have restored the hard disk. Execute FR.EXE from the floppy.

- **Overwriting Current Data.** Any new files that have been added to the hard disk **after** it has been formatted will probably be overwritten during the restoration process.

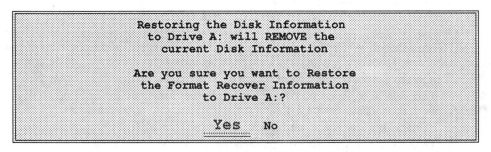

Figure 9-10 Warning about restoring disk data.

In this example, the recovery files are accurate and no files have been added to the disk. This means a complete, accurate recovery is possible. Enter

y

The program then proceeds to reconstruct the data, based on the information in the recovery files. When the process is complete, the program displays a window (Figure 9-10), telling you to run the NDD (Norton Disk Doctor) program on the recovered disk. This is a standard message displayed at the end of any recovery process and does not reflect the actual problem with the recovered disk. The purpose of NDD is to resolve disk problems that can occur when the recovery files do not exactly match the preformatted data. In this example such is not the case, so it is not necessary to perform the NDD/QUICK operation.

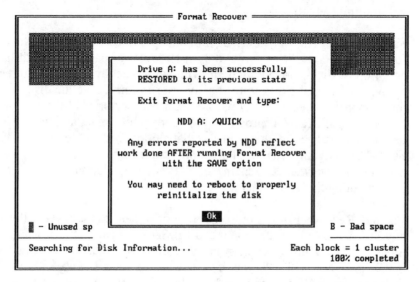

Figure 9-11 Reminder to use Norton Disk Doctor on recovered disk.

Exit the program by entering

[F10]

Limits of Format Recovery

Of course, it is preferable not to be put in a position of having to recover data from a formatted disk. But the best chance of recovering a formatted disk occurs when the recovery files have been updated just prior to the reformatting. If this is not the case, a discrepancy will exist between the recovered disk and the disk as it was before the formatting. The exact extent of the discrepancy is unpredictable because it depends on the exact changes made to the disk following the last update of the recovery files. Prevention is always preferable to recovery. Below is a summary of the tools provided by the Norton Utilities programs to prevent or recover from accidental formatting.

- **Volume Label.** You can make accidental formatting with the DOS Format command less likely by using the VL program to place a volume label on any of the hard disks in your system. DOS Versions 3.1 and higher require you to enter the exact volume name of the disk before they will reformat a hard disk.

- **Safe Format.** The Safe Format program provides a level of safety in formatting because it performs only high-level formatting on both hard and floppy disks. In addition, it will automatically update or create recovery files on the disk immediately prior to formatting the disk. Since the Norton Utilities Safe Format program can perform all the functions of the DOS FORMAT program and more while maintaining a safety factor, it is suggested that you use Safe Format in place of the DOS FORMAT program. The installation program for the Norton Utilities will ask you if you want to rename Safe Format as Format, as a way of implementing this safety factor.

- **Format Recover Files.** You can create or update the recovery files on any disk by executing the command FR/SAVE from DOS, or using the **Save Disk Information** option in the Format Recover main menu. The install program will ask you if you want to install FR/SAVE in the AUTOEXEC.BAT file of your hard disk. This will cause the recovery files to update each time the computer is booted.

> *You can go a step further for safety's sake and add a FR/SAVE command to your menu batch file, such as those discussed in Chapter 5. You can add FR/SAVE > NUL to the main menu portion of the batch file. A sample modification is shown in Chapter 10.*

- **Speed Disk.** The Speed Disk program, which is used to optimize disk performance by placing the directories and files in the most advantageous order, will also update or create format recovery at the end of its optimizing process.

- **Recovery by Guess.** If you have a hard disk formatted with the DOS FORMAT command that does not contain recovery files, the Recover

Format program will attempt to recover files by making intelligent guesses about the data. This method will create directories and files with generic names, such as DIR0000.

> *Certain formatting programs provided by computer manufacturers perform both a high-and a low-level format with a single command, on hard disks as well as floppy disks. The format command supplied with certain Compaq computers, e.g., DOS 3.1 version, will alter disk data, making unformatting impossible. It is best to use the Norton Utilities Safe Format program in place of the supplied version of FORMAT.*

Quick Unerase

The Format Recover program is used when you have wiped out an entire disk of data by accidentally formatting the disk. However, from time to time, you may create smaller disasters by erasing files from the disk, typically with the DOS DEL or ERASE commands.

The Norton Utilities provides the Quick Unerase program to enable you to recover files that have been erased. The Quick Unerase program takes advantage of the way DOS erases files. Recall the directory display shown in Figure 9-4. In this directory display you can see that when a file is erased DOS does not eradicate the directory information about that file. Instead, it simply places a special character, σ, as the first character of the filename. The rest of the information remains.

When a disk is formatted, the primary problem in putting the files back together is that the FAT is erased. The FAT is crucial for files that are larger than one data cluster. It is the FAT that contains the details connecting one cluster to another in the correct sequence. Recovery from an accidental format requires a copy of the FAT, such as that provided by the Format Recover recovery files.

However, when a file or group of files is erased, the FAT entries for that file, as well as the directory information, remain intact until overwritten by new information. This means that immediately after a file or group of files has been erased, the disk contains all the information necessary, with the exception of the first letter of the filename, to reconstruct the file. The critical word is **immediately**. Following an erasure, any new data added to the disk **may** be stored in all or part of the space formerly occupied by the erased files. If this new data overwrites the old data that belonged to the file you want to recover, recovery of the entire file is **not** possible.

> *However, partial recovery may be possible. With Quick Unerase, partial recovery is much more complicated to perform than is full recovery (see Chapter 10).*

The Quick Unerase program is designed to recover erased files that have not been over written. Note that overwriting can effect unerasing in two ways.

- **Directory Entries.** When DOS places the σ mark at the beginning of a directory entry, it does so to indicate that the space used by that file is now available to new files. If a new file name is placed into that section of the directory, the Quick Unerase program cannot recover the erased file because its directory entry has been obliterated.

- **Data Clusters.** The data clusters assigned to the erased file can be overwritten with data belonging to another file. This will also prevent unerasure of the file, even though the file's directory information may be intact.

The Quick Unerase program can be used to unerase files in several different modes.

- **Interactive.** In this mode, the Quick Unerase program attempts to unerase as many files in the current directory as possible. Each file that is potentially recoverable is displayed. You are asked if you want to recover that file or not. If you do, you are asked to enter the first letter of the filename. Recall that the first letter of the filename is overwritten when a file is erased.

- **Files Specification.** The Quick Unerase command allows you to select a file or group of files for recovery. This option allows you to concentrate on a file or files to recover when there are a large number of erased entries in a directory. For example, for unerasure, the command **QU *.exe** would select only files that have an EXE extension.

- **Automatic.** When set for automatic operation, the Quick Unerase command automatically fills in with the letter **A**, the missing letter of the filename. If a name conflict occurs with an existing file, the program changes the first letter to B, C, D, etc. until it creates a unique filename. The advantage of the automatic operation is that it is not necessary for you to approve each unerasure. You can later use the Rename command or the Norton Commander to alter the filenames that are not appropriate.

> *Using a wildcard that specifies the first letter of the filename has a special effect on the Quick Unerase program because it deals with erased files. Recall that erased filenames in the directory are missing the first character. When a first character is supplied, the program operates in the automatic mode, even though you have not used the /A switch. However, instead of replacing the missing letter of the filename with A, the letter specified in the wildcard is used. For example, the command QU m*.* would execute the Quick Unerase program in automatic mode. The first letter of every recoverable file would be written as M followed by the rest of the filename as found in the directory. This method can result in conflicting filenames since the program will not substitute a different letter for M. If a filename conflict occurs the automatic processing is halted and you are prompted to enter an alternative letter for the filename.*

The Quick Unerase program is designed to be an almost automatic way of recovering erased files. To learn about the abilities and limitations of QU, you can begin by easing some of the files on the disk in drive A. Enter

DEL a:\files\fa.exe ↵
DEL a:\control\sd.exe ↵
DEL a:\disk*.exe ↵

List the files on drive A using the File Size program.

FS a:\/S ↵

The display shows that there are only nine files remaining on the disk. At this point, all the erased files can be recovered using the Quick Unerase program because nothing has been added to the disk. The Quick Unerase program will search the specified directory for all entries that begin with the σ character. Enter

QU a:\files ↵

The program locates a file with the name **?A.EXE**, as shown in Figure 9-12. The top part of the display summarizes the disk information by telling you the number of unerased filenames found in the directory, and the total number of those files that can be fully recovered.

```
QU-Quick UnErase, Advanced Edition 4.50, (C) Copr 1987-88, Peter Norton


Using information from FRECOVER.DAT file


Directory of A:\FILES
   Erased file specification: *.*
   Number of erased files: 1
   Number that can be Quick-UnErased: 1


   Erased files lose the first character of their names.
   After selecting each file to Quick-UnErase, you will be
   asked to supply the missing character.


   ?a.exe           9,300 bytes     4:50 pm  Sun Oct 16 88
Quick-UnErase this file (Y/N) ?
```

Figure 9-12 Quick Unerase program displays recoverable file names.

Because the disk contains format recovery files, the Quick Unerase program takes advantage of the data to analyze the disk. However, Quick Unerase will function even when the recovery files are not present.

The program asks if you want to recover this file. Enter

y

The program then displays the prompt **"Enter the first character of the filename:"**. In this example you will recall that the original filename was FA.EXE. Enter

f

The program recovers the file. Enter

DIR a:\files ↵

The file is once again listed in the disk directory. Remember that it is not necessary to have recovery files on the disk in order to use the Quick Unerase program. Erase the FRECOVER.DAT file from the disk in drive A. Enter

DEL a:*.dat ↵

This time run the Quick Unerase program on the \CONTROL directory. Enter

QU a:\control ↵

The only difference here is that because there is no FRECOVER.DAT file available, it takes the Quick Unerase program a few moments longer to analyze the disk. Having the recovery files on the disk enables Quick Unerase to operate faster-a significant factor, when you are unerasing a large number of files.

In this instance, you will **not** unerase the file. Enter

n

The Automatic Mode

The automatic mode is useful when you want to unerase a large number of files and don't want to take the time to enter a specific first letter for each file. In this mode you allow the program to insert a first character, starting with **A**, automatically so that no user entry is necessary. If using the letter A creates a duplicate filename the program will try B, C, D, etc., until it has a unique filename to use.

As an example of the automatic mode, use the Quick Unerase program to recover the files erased from the \DISK directory. Enter

QU a:\disk/A ↵

The time the Quick Unerase program recovers the three erased file by inserting the letter **A** as the first letter of the file names. All three files are recovered without any user input, as shown in Figure 9-13.

```
Directory of A:\DISK
   Erased file specification: *.*
   Number of erased files: 3
   Number that can be Quick-UnErased: 3


   Erased files lose the first character of their names.
   Quick-UnErase will automatically replace them.

    ?i.exe             9,304 bytes      4:50 pm  Sun Oct 16 88
'ai.exe' Quick-UnErased

    ?t.exe            21,080 bytes      4:50 pm  Sun Oct 16 88
'at.exe' Quick-UnErased

    ?s.exe            36,000 bytes      4:50 pm  Sun Oct 16 88
'as.exe' Quick-UnErased
```

Figure 9-13 File unerased automatically.

Limits of Quick Unerase

It is important to keep in mind that any additions made to a disk can affect the ability of the Quick Unerase program to recover files. Add a new file to the \CONTROL directory by making a copy of the FI.EXE program. Enter

COPY a:\files\fi.exe a:\control ↵

This new file will have made changes to the disk that make file recovery impossible, in some cases. For example, recall that prior to this point the \CONTROL directory contained a file that could be recovered. Enter

QU a:\control ↵

The Quick Unerase program cannot find any files to unerase in that directory, as shown in Figure 9-14. When you copied the FI.EXE file, the new file entry overwrote the plot in the directory that had been used for the SD.EXE file before it was erased. Once overwritten, the Quick Unerase program could not restore the file.

```
QU-Quick UnErase, Advanced Edition 4.50, (C) Copr 1987-88, Peter Norton

Directory of A:\CONTROL
   Erased file specification: *.*
   Number of erased files: 0
```

Figure 9-14 No files found that can be recovered.

Another reason files cannot be recovered with the Quick Unerase program is because part of their data area has been overwritten. This means the erased file name is still in the directory, but the data clusters formerly used by that file are no longer free. This is also the result of writing information to the disk. It is important to note that overwriting data clusters can affect files that are in a different directories than the one into which the new file is copied.

Unerasing Directories

The Quick Unerase program recovers files from a specified directory when the file and its directory entry are intact. But suppose you delete an entire directory. In such a case, file recovery involves the recovery of the directory, as well as the files. The DOS command RD or the NCD program are capable of removing a directory from the disk.

In file recovery it may be necessary to recover a directory that was removed, in order to recover a file that was contained within that directory. The Quick Unerase program cannot recover a file if the directory is erased. The Unremove Directory program supplied with the Norton Utilities package is designed to unerase directories. This is often a prerequisite for using the Quick Unerase program.

To illustrate the use of the Unremove Directory program, delete one of the current directories on the disk in drive A. This requires two commands-one to remove the files and one to remove the directory. There is no a single command that removes both the files and the directory. Enter

DEL a:\disk*.* ↵
y ↵
a:
RD \disk ↵

List the directories on drive A. Enter

LD a:/G ↵

```
\———┬——CONTROL
└—FILES
```

The DISK directory has been erased.
The Unremove Directory program can be operated into two ways.

- **Prompted Search Mode.** If you do not specify a particular directory name to recover, the Unremove Directory program will search the disk and display any directory names, one by one, it finds that can be recovered. The program operates in a similar manner to the Quick Unerase program. You will be prompted to determine if you want to recover each directory.

- **Command Line Mode.** If you specify a particular directory pathname the program will attempt to recover just that specified directory.

You should note that like erased files, the first character of the directory name is also missing. As part of the recovery process you must supply the first letter for the restored directory. Enter

$$\text{UD} \hookleftarrow$$

The program searches the disk for directories that can be recovered. In this case it finds the DISK directory, minus the first letter, as shown in Figure 9-15.

```
UD-UnRemove Directory, Advanced Edition 4.50, (C) Copr 1987-88, Peter Norton

Directory of A:\
   Removed directory specification: *.*
   Number of removed directories: 1
   Number that can be UnRemoved: 1


   ?ISK              <DIR>        3:30 pm  Mon Sep 25 89
UnRemove this directory (Y/N) ?
```

Figure 9-15 Unremove Directory locates erased directory.

To restore the directory, enter

y

You need to supply the first letter of the directory name. Enter

d

The program then performs two actions. The first is to restore the directory to the disk. The second is to list all the filenames found in the restored directory, as shown in Figure 9-16. This is useful because it helps you determine if you want to use Quick Unerase to recover some or all of the files in the directory. Note that the Unremove Directory program does not verify whether the files it lists can be recovered with Quick Unerase. You need to run Quick Unerase to determine that.

```
A:\ ud
UD-UnRemove Directory, Advanced Edition 4.50, (C) Copr 1987-88, Peter Norton

Directory of A:\
   Removed directory specification: *.*
   Number of removed directories: 1
   Number that can be UnRemoved: 1


   ?ISK               <DIR>        3:30 pm  Mon Sep 25 89
Enter the first character of the filename: D


   ?s.exe           36,000 bytes   4:50 pm  Sun Oct 16 88
   ?t.exe           21,080 bytes   4:50 pm  Sun Oct 16 88
   ?i.exe            9,304 bytes   4:50 pm  Sun Oct 16 88


Files included in A:\DISK


'DISK' UnRemoved
```

Figure 9-16 Unremove Directory lists erased files in recovered directory.

Recover the files with the Quick Unerase program. This time, specify the first letter for the recovered files. This causes all the files to be recovered automatically, using the same first letter character. Enter

QU \disk\d*.* ↵

The files and directory have now been restored.

Wiping Data Clean

Much has been made of the fact that DOS takes a short cut when files are erased, making unerasing possible. Suppose you want to make sure that data was completely expunged from a file or an entire disk. The DOS DEL command would not accomplish this. The Norton Utilities program provides two programs, WIPEFILE and WIPEDISK, that actually write entire new sectors to the disk, containing all zero values. These commands eradicate the previous data by actually writing new information that replaces the old information. This type of operation would be used where security requires that erased information not be recovered by unauthorized personnel.

Both the WIPEFILE and WIPEDISK programs erase data by writing a value, by default 0, for each byte of the file or disk that is to be wiped clean.

> Note that the value is the hex value 0 called a "null" value, not the ASCII character zero, which has a hex value of 30 and a decimal value 48.

Since disk information is recorded magnetically, it is, in theory, possible to use special electronic equipment to try to construct the faint magnetic image of the value that had previously been placed on the disk. Remember the recovery effort made on the 18 minute gap in the Watergate tapes!

Both programs allow you to select different methods of wiping out data by using the following switches.

- /G#. This switch changes the wipe pattern to conform to the Department of Defense specifications (DID 5220.22-M) for media security. By default this option writes a 0/1 pattern on the wiped area, three times. If you want to perform more repetitions, replace the # with a value, e.g., 6 repeats the pattern 6 times.

- /R#. This switch sets the number of times the wipe area will be written over. The default is 1.

- /V#. This switch uses a value from 0 to 255 which represents the ASCII value of the character used to overwrite the data. For example, /V246 would place the ASCII character 246 (Hex F6) in each byte of the wiped area. This is the same character used by the DOS FORMAT command when it formats a floppy disk. Recall that the DOS FORMAT command will not overwrite disk sectors on hard disks.

- /LOG. The switch is used to format the output from the program for output to the printer or a text file.

As an example, suppose you want to wipe out the DI.EXE program in the \DISK directory. First, use the Main Norton Utilities to determine the exact cluster numbers used to store this file. You can take a shortcut when you want to display information from a specific file by entering the filename as an argument for the Main Norton Utilities program. Enter

NU \disk\di.exe ⏎

The program loads and automatically reads and displays that data from the specified file. If you look at the top of the display you will see the first cluster number for the file. In this example it is cluster 294. Note that if you are working with a different size disk, your number may differ. Move to the end of the file by entering

[End]

The cluster number is 303. Display the information about this file. Enter

[Esc]
i

The file information, as shown in Figure 9-17, shows that the file is stored in 10 consecutive clusters starting at 294 and ending at 303. If you were to use the WIPEFILE program on this file, this entire area would be overwritten with zeros.

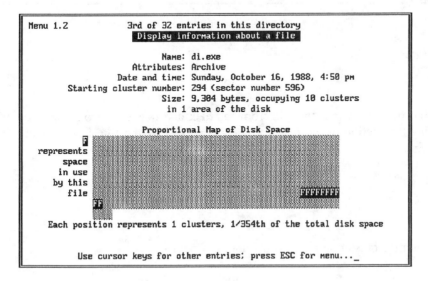

Figure 9-17 File information displayed.

Exit the program by entering

[F10]

Wipe out the file and its information by entering

WIPEFILE \disk\di.exe ↵

The program displays the parameters it will use for the operation, i.e., wipe count and wipe character, and then asks you to confirm your intention to wipe the specified file, as shown in Figure 9-18.

```
WF-Wipe Files, Advanced Edition 4.50, (C) Copr 1987-88, Peter Norton


         Action:  Wipe the file
       FileSpec:  A:\DISK\DI.EXE
Sub-directories:  No
     Wipe count:  1
     Wipe value:  0


Directory: A:\DISK
    di.exe       - Do you wish to wipe this file (Y/N) ?
```

Figure 9-18 Wipefile asks you to confirm operation.

Enter

y

The program wipes the file from the disk and deletes it from the directory. Display the section of the disk formerly occupied by the file, i.e., clusters 294-304. Enter

nu ↵
↵ ↵
L

Enter the cluster numbers you want to inspect.

294 ↵
303 ↵
e

The data area is filled with nothing but zeros as shown in Figure 9-19.

```
╔ Cluster 294-303 ════════════════════════════════════ Hex format ╗
║ Cluster 294, Sectors 596-597                         Offset 0, hex 0 ║
║00000000 00000000 00000000 00000000 00000000 00000000 █..................... ║
║00000000 00000000 00000000 00000000 00000000 00000000 ..................... ║
║00000000 00000000 00000000 00000000 00000000 00000000 ..................... ║
║00000000 00000000 00000000 00000000 00000000 00000000 ..................... ║
║00000000 00000000 00000000 00000000 00000000 00000000 ..................... ║
║00000000 00000000 00000000 00000000 00000000 00000000 ..................... ║
║00000000 00000000 00000000 00000000 00000000 00000000 ..................... ║
║00000000 00000000 00000000 00000000 00000000 00000000 ..................... ║
║00000000 00000000 00000000 00000000 00000000 00000000 ..................... ║
║00000000 00000000 00000000 00000000 00000000 00000000 ..................... ║
║00000000 00000000 00000000 00000000 00000000 00000000 ..................... ║
║00000000 00000000 00000000 00000000 00000000 00000000 ..................... ║
║00000000 00000000 00000000 00000000 00000000 00000000 ..................... ║
║00000000 00000000 00000000 00000000 00000000 00000000 ..................... ║
║00000000 00000000 00000000 00000000 00000000 00000000 ..................... ║
║00000000 00000000 00000000 00000000 00000000 00000000 ..................... ║
║00000000 00000000 00000000 00000000 00000000 00000000 ..................... ║
║00000000 00000000 00000000 00000000 00000000 00000000 ..................... ║
║00000000 00000000          Press Enter to continue    ....... ║
║1Help  2Hex   3Text  4Dir  5FAT  6Partn 7       8Choose 9Undo  10QuitNU║
```

Figure 9-19 Data wiped from disk.

Display the directory in which the file was stored. Enter

[F8]
d
[End]
↵

The directory display shows that in addition to wiping out the data, the directory entry is wiped clean as well (Figure 9-2). Recall that DOS merely inserts the σ character and leaves the remainder of the disk information intact. WIPEFILE has obliterated all the disk information about the DI.EXE file.

```
┌ Dir area ═══════════════════════════════════════ Directory format ═┐
│ Cluster 4, Sectors 16-17                          File offset 0, hex 0 │
│                                                        Attributes        │
│Filename Ext     Size      Date      Time     Cluster  Arc R/O Sys Hid Dir Vol│
│                                                                          │
│█████████          9-25-89   3:30 pm      4                        Dir   │
│..                 9-25-89   3:30 pm                               Dir   │
│DS       EXE   36000  10-16-88   4:50 pm    237   Arc                    │
│DT       EXE   21080  10-16-88   4:50 pm    273   Arc                    │
│σ                  0-00-80  12:00 am                                     │
│              unused directory entry                                     │
│              unused directory entry                                     │
│              unused directory entry                                     │
│              unused directory entry                                     │
│              unused directory entry                                     │
│              unused directory entry                                     │
│              unused directory entry                                     │
│              unused directory entry                                     │
│              unused directory entry                                     │
│              unused directory entry                                     │
│              unused directory entry                                     │
│                                                                          │
│         Filenames beginning with 'σ' indicate erased entries           │
│                    Press Enter to continue                             │
│1Help   2Hex   3Text   4Dir   5FAT   6Partn  7       8Choose 9Undo  10QuitNU│
```

Figure 9-20 Directory information is wiped clean.

Exit the program by entering

[F10]

You can wipe out more than one file at a time by using a wildcard as the file specification. For example, the command below would wipe out all EXE files in the root directory.

WIPEFILE *.exe

Note that when a wildcard is used, you will be asked if you want to confirm each file selected on a one-by-one basis, or allow the entire group to be wiped out without pausing.

Keep in mind that because these programs must write over each byte of data in the selected area, they work much more slowly than commands such as the DOS DEL or Safe Format commands.

Because of the destructive nature of these commands they are given long names instead of the short two or three character names used for the other utility programs. The long names are less likely to be entered by mistake.

Other Uses

If you are not interested in wiping out data for security reasons, there are two other uses for the WIPEFILE and WIPEDISK programs.

- **WIPEFILE/N/S.** This form of the WIPEFILE command can overcome a limitation in the DOS DEL command. The /N switch changes the action of the WIPEFILE command from wiping out the directory entry and data clusters associated with a file or group of files, to a command that duplicates the function of the DOS DEL command. The advantage of WIPEFILE lies in the fact that it can accept the /S (subdirectory) switch. This allows you to delete all the files beginning with a particular directory and include all the subdirectories. The DOS DEL command can erase only files in one directory at a tim**E.**

- **WIPEDISK/E.** The /E switch changes the focus of the WIPEDISK program from the entire disk to only those areas that contain erased files. You can use this command to clear the disk that is not currently in use for files of data. This operation is probably helpful if you find you need to recover an erased file from time to time. When you clear out all the unused space periodically, it makes it easier to locate the parts of an erased file since they will not be jumbled up with the remnants of files erased long ago.

You can delete all the files on drive A with a single WIPEFILE command. Enter

WIPEFILE *.*/N/S ↵

The program asks if you want to confirm each deletion. Enter

n ↵

The program searches through all the subdirectories and deletes all the files. To accomplish the same thing with the DOS DEL command, you would have to issue four separate commands, one for each directory. Note that the FRECOVER.IDX file is not affected by WIPEFILE because it is assigned a read-only attribute. To delete this file remove the attribute with the File Attribute command and then delete the file. Enter

FA a:*.*/R- ↵
WIPEFILE a:*.*/N ↵
n ↵

The /LOG option is used when you want to create a printed copy or a text file from the wipeout data that is generated by the program. However, you must keep in mind that whenever you use these commands you must enter a confirmation response. If you use >PRN or > *filename* to send the output to a printer or text file, the program will still pause for your confirmation. This is a problem because the question to which you must respond will not appear on the screen while the output is being redirected. You will have to remember to enter **n** and ↵ to a blank screen, or else the program will simply hang there waiting for your input. A better way to get the listing on the printer with this command is to enter [Ctrl/p] before you enter the command. [Ctrl/p] echoes all DOS input and output to the printer. The command is a toggle so that entering a second [Ctrl/p] will turn off the echo. This method is not as neat as the >PRN redirection but it works better with these particular programs. Example:

[Ctrl/p]
WIPEFILE *.*/N/S/LOG
[Ctrl/p]

The WIPEDISK/E will clear all the space on the disk that is not currently in use for files or directories. In this example the command will clear the entire disk but will leave the directory structure intact. Enter

WIPEDISK a:/E ↵

y ↵

Note that the data is wiped out starting with the last cluster on the disk and working its way forward. This is the opposite direction in which the data is stored. Assuming that the disk is not completely filled, starting at the end provides you with an opportunity of stopping the process by entering [Ctrl/c] or [Ctrl/break] before it reaches the front of the disk. Return to drive C by entering

c: ↵

Summary

This chapter discussed the Norton Utilities programs that are used to recover lost data. In addition, it also discussed the Wipefile and Wipedisk programs, which can obliterate erased data from a disk.

- **Safe Format.** The Safe Format program replaces the DOS FORMAT command with a formatting procedure that can be recovered in case the disk is formatted accidentally. The program will operate the same way on hard or floppy disks. Safe Format will create recovery files before it formats the disk. The Format Recover program can use the recovery files to restore the formatted disk.

- **Recover Format.** This program is used to reconstruct disk data based on the information in the recovery files stored on the disk. The recovery files can be created by the Safe Format program, the Speed Disk program, or the /SAVE switch of the Format Recovery program. If the disk does not contain recovery files the program will attempt to congregate files by grouping blocks of data into files.

- **Quick Unerase.** This command uses the information in the directory and FAT to recover files that have been erased with the DOS DEL command. The first letter of the erased files is always missing. The user can supply the missing characters or allow the program to run in an automatic mode in which the program selects the character. Quick Unerase will recover only erased files that have not been overwritten by new data. It cannot recover partial files.

- **Unremove Directory.** This command is used to restore a directory that has been removed with the DOS command RD or the NCD program. When the directory is restored a list of all of the erased files previously contained in that directory is produced.

- **WIPEFILE.** This program allows you to overwrite all data, including the directory entry of a file or group of files with a specific character, e.g., zero. This command is used to ensure that erased data cannot be recovered by unauthorized persons. Quick Unerase cannot be used on files wiped clean by this command. The /N switch changes the action to mere deletion, the same as the DOS DEL command.

- **WIPEDISK.** This program overwrites all of the directory, FAT, and data cluster information on a disk. You can use the /E switch to eradicate data only in areas marked as erased.

Sample Batch with Format Recovery

```
@ECHO OFF
:main_menu
FR/SAVE > NUL  ⇐
BE main.mnu
BE ROWCOL 19,25
BE ASK "Enter your choice:",lwdve,DEFAULT=e
IF ERRORLEVEL 5 GOTO exit
```

```
IF ERRORLEVEL 4 GOTO program4
IF ERRORLEVEL 3 GOTO program3
IF ERRORLEVEL 2 GOTO program2
IF ERRORLEVEL 1 GOTO program1

:program1
BE WINDOW 8,10,12,70 ZOOM
BE ROWCOL 10,22,"Loading Lotus 1-2-3 ..." BRIGHT WHITE
CD\lotus
123
BE WINDOW 8,10,12,70 ZOOM
BE ROWCOL 10,22,"Returning to Main menu ..." BRIGHT WHITE
CD\
GOTO main_menu

:exit
CLS
```

10

Advanced Unerasing

In Chapter 9 you learned how to recover information from formatted disks, and from files that have been erased. The programs used for this purpose--Quick Unerase, Format Recover, and Unremove Directory--all operate more or less automatically. The programs are designed to look for specific information or patterns of data as a guide to recovering the erased data.

However, the programs are limited to recovering data that has remained intact since it was erased. When you add data to a disk following an erasure, it is possible that you will overwrite part, or all, of the information that was formerly in the erased file.

The question this chapter addresses is how can you recover files that have been partially overwritten?

The answer lies in the broad capabilities of the Main Norton Utilities program. This program has the ability to read and write individual disk sectors. Its variety of display formats allow you to easily read the data contained in complicated structures, such as disk directories and FATs. Another powerful feature is the program's ability to cross-reference different ways of looking at the information on a disk. For example, the program can tell you what file, if any, a specific data cluster belongs to. On the other hand, you can determine which data clusters are used in a specific file.

These features and more make the Main Norton Utilities tool capable of solving many types of problems that can occur on a disk. However, the operation of the Main Norton Utilities is much less *automatic* than the programs discussed in Chapter 9. Using the Main Norton Utilities requires the user to make decisions about what they want to do, what the information means, and how they want to alter the disk. The program has the ability to help you recover data from erased files that have been partially overwritten. However, the program also has the potential of allowing the user to ruin an entire hard disk if they do not understand the implications of what they are doing.

The goal of this chapter is to show how the tools provided in the Main Norton Utilities can be used to recover partially overwritten files.

Which Files Can Be Recovered?

It is important to understand that it does not make sense to try to recover every type of file that may be partially overwritten. If the file is a program file, COM or EXE extension, you should probably not bother to attempt recovery. A partially recovered program will almost never execute correctly. Unless you can recover the entire file using Quick Unerase, there is not much point in trying partial recovery with the Main Norton Utilities program.

Other data stored in binary files is equally difficult to recover partially. Most spreadsheet programs store data in complicated mathematical formats that look nothing like the spreadsheet data displayed on the screen. Partial recovery of this type of file is not useful for several reasons. First, these files often contain special header information that is stored at the beginning of the file. Without this header, the remainder of the file cannot be loaded. The same is true of the end of some files. Without the proper ending sequence, any attempt to load the partial file will hang up the program. Finally, since the information is stored in a form you would not recognize, there is not much point in inspecting data clusters to determine if that cluster belonged to the erased file. This is one of the primary techniques for recovering partial files.

The type of information you should attempt to recover is text information. The simplest form of text information would be ASCII text files. Many word processors store text in files that are not pure ASCII text but contain sufficient text to be easily recognized. The same is true of many database programs. All dBASE versions store data in ASCII text format with a binary header on the file, making dBASE type files relatively easy to work with.

> Note that this lesson assumes you are working with a 360K or 720K floppy disk in drive A. If you are working with a 1.2 megabyte floppy the cluster numbers used in this chapter will not match your disk because the 1.2 megabyte format uses a 512 byte cluster size, in contrast to the 1024 cluster size used by the other formats. The cluster size is critical when performing manual unerasures.

Partial Recovery

There are two circumstances that prompt you to attempt partial recovery of an erased file.

- **Data Clusters Overwritten.** The Quick Unerase program will not attempt to unerase a file if one or more of the data clusters formerly belonging to that file are in use by another file. In this case, it may be that some of the data clusters in use by the original file are still intact. They could be recovered and gathered into a new file.

- **Directory Entry Overwritten.** If the directory entry for a file is overwritten, the Quick Unerase program will have no way of knowing anything about the erased file. However, even though the directory entry for a file has been erased, it is still possible that data clusters belonging to that file are still on the disk. These clusters could be gathered together to form a file. In this case you would actually be creating a new file composed of data stored in data clusters no longer in use by any files.

Keep in mind that the two situations are mutually exclusive. It is quite possible for a file to have its directory entry overwritten, as well as part of its data. In either case you would need to know something about the content of the files in order to recognize when you have located a cluster that belonged to the old file.

To begin exploring partial file recovery, place some text files onto the disk in drive A. The Norton Utilities programs are supplied with several text files in the form of batch and *readme* files. Begin by copying the BEDEMO.BAT, BEDEMO.BAT and MENU.DAT files to drive A. Enter

COPY \norton\bedemo.bat a: ↵
COPY \norton\bedemo.dat a: ↵
COPY \norton\menu.dat a: ↵

Drive A now has three text files in the root directory. Use the Main Norton Utilities program to examine the directory of the disk. Enter

NU a: ↵
↵ *(4 times)*
e

The three files you have just copied appear in the directory listing, as shown in Figure 10-1. In this instance, the values of most interest are the starting cluster numbers assigned to the files. The first file is placed into cluster 5. Since the cluster size of this disk is 1024 bytes and the file is only 659 bytes, the single cluster is sufficient to hold the entire file. The next file, BEDEMO.DAT, begins at cluster 6. This file is 7640 bytes in size requiring 8 data clusters, clusters 6 through 13. MENU.BAT is placed into cluster 14. It is small enough to fit in a single data cluster.

Filename	Ext	Size	Date	Time	Cluster
FILES			9-26-89	2:52 pm	2
CONTROL			9-26-89	2:53 pm	3
DISK			9-26-89	2:53 pm	4
BEDEMO	BAT	659	10-16-88	4:50 pm	5
BEDEMO	DAT	7640	10-16-88	4:50 pm	6
MENU	DAT	850	10-16-88	4:50 pm	14

Figure 10-1 Directory information about new files.

What would happen when you add another file to the disk? It would start in cluster 15, since this is the next available data cluster. But what if you erased the current list of files? The directory would indicate to DOS that the space formerly used by the files could now be used to store new data, i.e., the old data would be overwritten.

Exit the program and return to DOS by entering

[F10]

Delete all the files from the disk in drive A by entering

DEL a:*.* ↵
y ↵

Overwrite part of the disk by copying another of the Norton Utilities batch files to drive A. Enter

COPY \norton\make_tut.bat a: ↵

The data on drive A has been changed. What effect would this have on your ability to recover the files that you erased on drive A? You can get a quick check by using the Quick Unerase program. Enter

QU a: ↵

The summary presented by the Quick Unerase program tells you that there are two erased files listed in the directory, only one of which can be unerased. Of course this makes sense based on what you know about the disk directory. Recall that there had been three files listed in the directory before they were erased. When the new file MAKE_TUT.BAT was copied, it filled in one of the slots in the directory leaving only two erased filenames listed.

```
QU-Quick UnErase, Advanced Edition 4.50, (C) Copr 1987-88, Peter Norton

Directory of A:\
   Erased file specification: *.*
   Number of erased files: 2
   Number that can be Quick-UnErased: 1

   Erased files lose the first character of their names.
   After selecting each file to Quick-UnErase, you will be
   asked to supply the missing character.

   ?enu.dat          850 bytes     4:50 pm  Sun Oct 16 88
Quick-UnErase this file (Y/N) ?
```

Figure 10-2 Quick Unerase can recover only one file.

But why can't both files be unerased? To get a clear picture, exit the Quick Unerase program and load the Main Norton Utilities program again.

[F10]
NU a: ↵
↵ *(4 times)*
e

The directory information, shown in Figure 10-3, shows that the new file, MAKE-TUT.BAT, overwrote the BEDEMO.BAT entry in the directory. The first data cluster used for the MAKE-TUT.BAT is cluster 5. Recall that BEDEMO.BAT was stored in that cluster previously. This means that the old file and its directory entry have been completely overwritten.

Filename	Ext	Size	Date	Time	Cluster
FILES			9-26-89	2:52 pm	2
CONTROL			9-26-89	2:53 pm	3
DISK			9-26-89	2:53 pm	4
MAKE-TUT	BAT	2980	10-16-88	4:50 pm	5
σEDEMO	DAT	7640	10-16-88	4:50 pm	6
σENU	DAT	850	10-16-88	4:50 pm	14

Figure 10-3 Directory shows current and erased files.

However, the new file affects more than just the area previously used by the BEDEMO.BAT file. The directory entry shows that the new file is 2980 bytes in length. That means that the file requires 3 data clusters. If the file starts in cluster 5, it also is written into clusters 6 and 7. This means that the BEDEMO.DAT file that was stored in clusters 6 through 13 has been partially overwritten. The Quick Unerase program will not attempt to recover the file because it is no longer complete.

Unerasing a File

Suppose you decide to attempt to recover the remaining portion of erased file, BEDEMO.DAT. The first step is to begin with the Unerase option of the Main Norton Utilities program. This is found on the main menu of the program. Enter

[Esc]
r

The **Unerase** option is the second item on the main menu. Enter

u

The Unerase menu, Menu 2, is displayed as shown in Figure 10-4. Note that the **unerase menu** option is not currently available. That is because the program wants to force you to select a file to unerase before it allows you to begin manipulating disk clusters.

> Change drive or directory
>
> Select erased file
>
> (unerase menu)
>
> Return to main menu

Figure 10-4 Main Unerase menu.

The first step is to select a file to unerase. Enter

↵

The program displays a list of all the erased filenames that appear in the current directory, as shown in Figure 10-4. In addition to the filenames listed in that display, the first item is always **Create file.** This option is used when you want to recover data from a filename that has already been overwritten in the directory. You can enter a filename to use for any data clusters you recover.

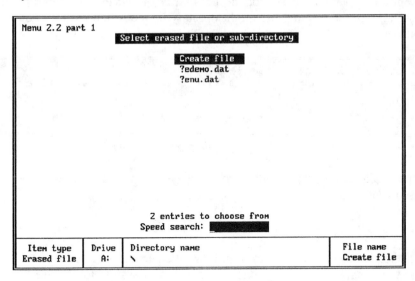

Figure 10-5 Erased file names listed.

In this case you can select one of the listed filenames, ?edemo.dat.

↓ ↵

When the filename is selected, the Main Norton Utilities program displays information about the file based on the current state of the directory and the FAT. The top part of the display, shown in Figure 10-6, is a summary of the information about the original file based on the directory information.

```
          Name: ?edemo.dat
    Attributes: Archive
 Date and time: Sunday, October 16, 1988, 4:50 pm
cluster number: 6 (sector number 20)
          Size: 7,640 bytes, occupying 8 clusters
```

Figure 10-6 Summary of directory information.`

The center of the screen, Figure 10-7, reports whether the recovery of the erased file is **Possible** or **Unlikely**, based on a comparison between the directory information and the current FAT. In this case the program sees that the original starting cluster of the erased file, cluster 6, is now allocated to another file. Thus the program displays **unlikely** for the possibility of successful unerasure. How much, if any, of the original file might possibly be recovered requires additional exploration.

```
   Successful UnErase: Unlikely
   The first cluster of this file is used by another file.


                        ?edemo.dat
```

Figure 10-7 Directory compared to current FAT.

One useful feature of this display is that you can scroll through the list of unerased files by using the ↓ or ↑ keys. Enter

↓

The screen display changes to summarize the current state of the **?ENU.DAT** file. The summary for this file concludes that it is **Possible** to unerase that file. Return to the previous file by entering

↑

Enter the first letter of the file name.

d

The filename is now complete. Exit this menu by entering

The Unerase Operations Menu

The program returns to Menu 2, but this time the Unerase menu is available. Enter

u

The Main Norton Utilities program displays the menu that controls all the unerase operations (Figure 10-8). The menu serves a dual purpose: (1) It lists the commands and operations available for unerasing files, and (2) it also displays information about the status of the file recovery operations. At the top of the display the program displays the number of clusters needed to recover the file. In this example that value is set at 8. The value is derived from the file size listed in the directory. Recall that the file was 7640 bytes, occupying eight clusters. Here, it is unlikely that you will be able to locate all 8 clusters because at least part of that group has been overwritten by another file.

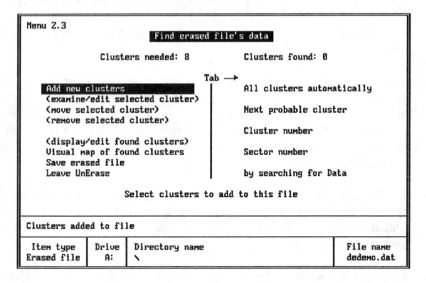

Figure 10-8 Unerase Operations menu.

The remainder of the screen lists the command options available for unerasing a file.

- **Add new clusters.** This option consists of a series of subcommands, each of which is designed to select data clusters to be added to the file you are trying to recover. The subcommands are listed in a column on the right side of the screen.

- **All Clusters Automatically.** This option allows the Norton Utilities program to automatically select the clusters that appear to belong with this file. This method is similar to that used by Quick Unerase, only this option accepts partial file recovery.

- **Next Probable Cluster**. This option is used when you suspect that the files may be, in part, overwritten. This option selects one cluster at a time. The assumption is that you will then inspect the contents of this cluster to decide if it really belongs with the file you are trying to recover.

- **Cluster number**. This command selects a specific data cluster by the specific cluster number. To use this option you must know the cluster number you want to add. You would normally use this option to add a cluster located by a search of the disk with the TS (Text Search) program.

- **Sector Number.** This option adds the cluster that contains the specific sector you request. Like the cluster number option, you need to know the exact sector number you want to add. Note that sector selection still adds the contents of the entire cluster. Clusters on a floppy disks usually contain two sectors, while hard disks will have between 4 and 16 sectors per cluster.

- **By Searching for Data**. This method locates clusters by searching for specific characters or hex values within the data clusters. Note this option requires you to know some of the information that was in the file you want to unerase.

- **Examine/Edit Selected Cluster**. This command displays the contents of a selected cluster. This option is used when you want to visually inspect the data to determine if it is really part of the file you want to recover.

- **Move selected sector**. This option is used to change the order in which the clusters selected for a file are arranged. In a simple case where there is only one cluster, you don't have to be concerned with sequence. But if you are assembling lost data, cluster by cluster, you may need to change the sequence of the data clusters to assemble the file correctly.

- **Remove Selected Cluster**. This option allows you to change your mind about clusters you have selected. If you don't want this cluster to be included with the file, it can be removed before the file is saved.

- **Display/Edit Found Clusters**. This option can be used to change the data in the selected clusters, as well as display it.

- **Visual Map Of Found Clusters**. The map shows you visually where on the disk the selected cluster is located.

- **Save Erased File.** This step saves all the selected clusters as the recovered file.

- **Leave Unerase**. Exits Unerase. Note that the selections will remain the same until you make a different selection.

When no clusters have been selected, as is the case at this point, examine, move, display, and save, are shown in parentheses to indicate they are not available. After you have selected one or more clusters you will be able to use these commands.

The first step is to select clusters. Enter

a

The highlight jumps to the right side of the screen to select **All** clusters.

In most cases it is a good idea to execute this option first. The clusters selected are the ones most likely to have been part of the file you are trying to recover. Enter

a

Norton Utilities automatically selects eight data clusters for the file, as shown in Figure 10-9. The numbers of the selected clusters are listed at the bottom of the screen in a box labeled **Clusters Added to File.** The highlight is automatically positioned on the **Save Erased File** option.

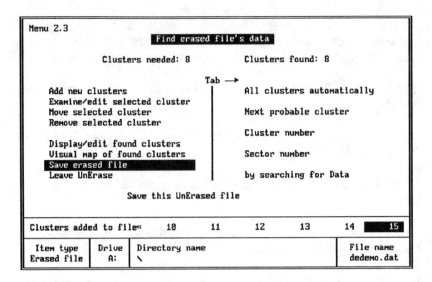

Figure 10-9 Automatic recovery selects data clusters.

Before you save this file, it is a good idea to inspect the selected clusters to see exactly what was automatically included in the file. One factor that indicates the automatic selection was not 100 percent accurate is the fact that eight clusters were selected. Since you know that at least the first cluster of the original file was overwritten by another file, it is not possible to recover all eight clusters. The automatic option must have selected one or more clusters that really don't belong to the file you are trying to recover.

A quick way to get an overview of what the automatic option has done is to use the option labeled **Visual Map of Found Clusters**. Enter

v

The programs display a map representing the location of the selected clusters on the disk, as shown in Figure 10-10. This map shows that the eight clusters selected automatically are consecutive clusters.

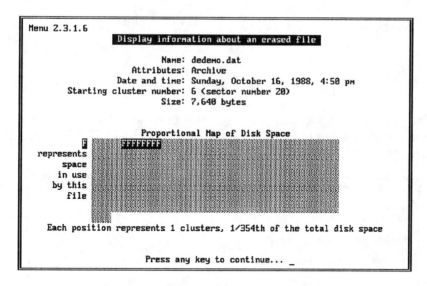

```
Menu 2.3.1.6
                  ┌─────────────────────────────────────────┐
                  │ Display information about an erased file │
                  └─────────────────────────────────────────┘
                           Name: dedemo.dat
                     Attributes: Archive
                  Date and time: Sunday, October 16, 1988, 4:50 pm
        Starting cluster number: 6 (sector number 20)
                           Size: 7,640 bytes


                      Proportional Map of Disk Space
            F
       represents
          space
          in use
          by this
           file

    Each position represents 1 clusters, 1/354th of the total disk space


                    Press any key to continue... _
```

Figure 10-10 Map display location of selected clusters.

The data at the top of the screen is the information stored in the directory listing for the selected file. It does not necessarily represent an accurate picture of the file you are recovering. For example, the size of the file listed as 7640 and the starting cluster 6 will not be accurate for the recovered file. The program will not update this information until you have saved the recovered file.

Return to the unerase operations menu by entering

↵

The next step is to inspect the contents of the selected clusters to determine if they contain information that belonged to the BEDEMO.DAT file. You have two ways of inspecting the data.

- **Examine/Edit Selected Cluster**. This option allows you to inspect a specific cluster from the selected cluster list. The currently selected cluster is 15. Note that 15 is highlighted in the cluster list. You can change the selected cluster number by moving the highlight with the ← and → keys.

- **Display/Edit Found Clusters.** This option allows you to browse through all of the selected clusters.

In this case choose the **Display** option by entering

d

The program changes to the sector display mode and shows the contents of the first selected cluster, cluster 8, as shown in Figure 10-11. The information is displayed in the text format.

```
 dedemo.dat ══════════════════════════════════ Text format ═
 Cluster 8, Sectors 24-25                       File offset 0, hex 0

  ►bri gre◄
  ►delay 1◄
  ►rowcol 2,2◄
  ►printchar " " 24◄
  ►◄
  ►rowcol 3,3 "Peter Norton presents..."  bri gre◄
  ►delay 1◄
  ►rowcol 3,3◄
  ►printchar " " 24◄
  ►◄
  ►rowcol 4,4 "Peter Norton presents..."  bri gre◄
  ►delay 1◄
  ►rowcol 4,4◄
  ►printchar " " 24 ◄
  ►◄
  ►rowcol 5,5 "Peter Norton presents..."  bri gre◄
  ►delay 1◄
  ►rowcol 5,5◄
  ►printchar " " 24 ◄
   ...more
                        Press Enter to continue
 1Help   2Hex   3Text  4Dir  5FAT  6Partn  7      8      9Undo  10QuitNU
```

Figure 10-11. Data from selected cluster displayed.

Does this cluster contain information that had been part of the BEDEMO.DAT file? The answer depends on your knowledge of what was stored in that file originally. In this example, you are trying to recover files that you did not create. In most cases, you would be attempting to locate data with which you are familiar. You would be able to easily recognize part of a word processing document or a database list you created. In this example the file BEDEMO.BAT was supplied with the Norton Utilities programs as an illustration of how the Batch Enhancer program could be used. The BEDEMO.DAT file is a Batch Enhancer subcommand file (see Chapter 5). The text in cluster 8 is clearly a list of Batch Enhancer subcommands. It is therefore quite likely that this cluster contains information that you want to recover.

Display the next five data clusters by entering

[Pg Dn] *(13 times)*

The screen should now display the data in cluster 13, as shown in Figure 10-12.

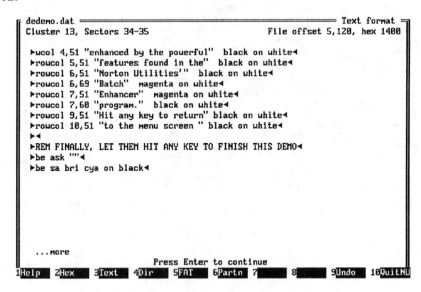

```
 dedemo.dat                                              Text format
 Cluster 13, Sectors 34-35                  File offset 5,120, hex 1400

     ►ucol 4,51 "enhanced by the powerful"  black on white◄
     ►rowcol 5,51 "features found in the"  black on white◄
     ►rowcol 6,51 "Norton Utilities'"  black on white◄
     ►rowcol 6,69 "Batch"  magenta on white◄
     ►rowcol 7,51 "Enhancer"  magenta on white◄
     ►rowcol 7,60 "program."  black on white◄
     ►rowcol 9,51 "Hit any key to return" black on white◄
     ►rowcol 10,51 "to the menu screen " black on white◄
     ►◄
     ►REM FINALLY, LET THEM HIT ANY KEY TO FINISH THIS DEMO◄
     ►be ask ""◄
     ►be sa bri cya on black◄




     ...more
                        Press Enter to continue
 1Help   2Hex   3Text   4Dir   5FAT   6Partn   7       8       9Undo   10QuitNU
```

Figure 10-12 Data cluster contains on text information.

If you read the contents of the last few lines on the screen you will see that this cluster actually contains the end of the text file. Below the last line is blank space. The blank space can be a bit misleading, since the currently active text display format will show all nontext values as blank spaces. Change the display to the hex mode to get a complete presentation of the cluster's contents by entering

[F2]

The end of the first sector of this cluster shows zeros. Enter

[Pg Dn]

The screen shows the end sector of the 13th cluster, as shown in Figure 10-13. What is the significance of this nontext area at the end of cluster 13? One conclusion you can draw is that you have reached the end of the text you are attempting to recover. The binary values, zeros or F6, are a pretty reliable indication that this area is the slack area at the end of a text file.

```
┌ dedemo.dat ═══════════════════════════════════════════════ Hex format ═┐
│ Cluster 13, Sectors 34-35                    File offset 6,143, hex 17FF │
│00000000 00000000 00000000 00000000 00000000 00000000 .......................│
│00000000 00000000 00000000 00000000 00000000 00000000 .......................│
│00000000 00000000 00000000 00000000 00000000 00000000 .......................│
│00000000 00000000 00000000 00000000 00000000 00000000 .......................│
│00000000 00000000 00000000 00000000 00000000 00000000 .......................│
│00000000 00000000 00000000 00000000 00000000 00000000 .......................│
│00000000 00000000 00000000 00000000 00000000 00000000 .......................│
│00000000 00000000 00000000 00000000 00000000 00000000 .......................│
│00000000 00000000 00000000 00000000 00000000 00000000 .......................│
│00000000 00000000 00000000 00000000 00000000 00000000 .......................│
│00000000 00000000 00000000 00000000 00000000 00000000 .......................│
│00000000 00000000 00000000 00000000 00000000 00000000 .......................│
│00000000 00000000 00000000 00000000 00000000 00000000 .......................│
│00000000 00000000 00000000 00000000 00000000 00000000 .......................│
│00000000 00000000 00000000 00000000 00000000 00000000 .......................│
│00000000 00000000 00000000 00000000 00000000 00000000 .......................│
│00000000 00000000 00000000 00000000 00000000 00000000 .......................│
│00000000 00000000 00000000 00000000 00000000 00000000 .......................│
│00000000 00000000 00000000 00000000 00000000 00000000 .......................│
│00000000 00000000         Press Enter to continue    .......│              │
│1Help  2Hex   3Text  4Dir   5FAT   6Partn  7      8      9Undo   10QuitNU│
```

Figure 10-13 Cluster contains empty values.

Since this cluster represents the actual end of the text file, it is obvious that the automatic unerase command has selected too many clusters. In order to recover only the text that belonged to the erased file you will need to remove clusters 14 and 15 from the selection.

Return to the unerase operations menu by entering

[Esc]

You can use the **Remove Selected Cluster** command to remove a cluster number from the selected cluster list. Enter

r

The highlighted cluster, #15, is removed from the list. The display shows that there are only seven clusters found. Remove cluster 14 by entering

r

You have now reduced the number of data clusters to 6, clusters 8 through 13. These clusters contain all of the data clusters that formerly belonged to the BEDEMO.DAT, file with the exception of clusters 6 and 7, which have been overwritten by another file.

You can now write the recovered file to the disk using the **Save Erased File** command. Enter

s

The program displays the Save Unerased File menu, as shown in Figure 10-14. This menu has two functions: (1) It allows you to confirm your intention to save the recovered data, or (2) to return to the unerase operations menu by selecting **Get More Data.**

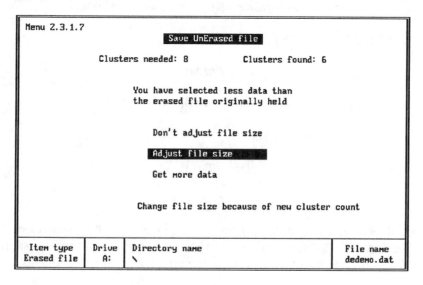

Figure 10-14 Save Unerased File menu.

The second function deals with the partial file recovery. In a partial file recovery the new file will contain fewer data clusters than the original file. In this case you are saving six clusters when the original file contained eight. You will have the option, in this instance, of adjusting the file size in the directory to match the size of the recovered file, or maintaining the original file size value in the directory. In most cases you will want to adjust the file size. Enter

a

The program now modifies the disk so that the selected clusters form a new file (Figure 10-15). In addition, the directory entry is adjusted to reflect the new file size.

```
                    Save UnErased file


          Saving record of file's data ... done

          Saving file's directory entry ... done


          UnErasing dedemo.dat is complete
```

Figure 10-15 Program confirms file recovery complete.

Display the disk directory by entering

↵ *(2 times)*

e

↵ *(2 times)*

Select the **Root dir** by entering

↑ *(4 times)*

↵

e

The directory, shown in Figure 10-16, displays the recovered file DEDEMO.DAT. Note that the file size has been changed to 6144 and the starting cluster is now 8. The program has retained the original date and time.

Filename	Ext	Size	Date	Time	Cluster
FILES			9-26-89	10:21 pm	2
CONTROL			9-26-89	10:21 pm	3
DISK			9-26-89	10:21 pm	4
MAKE-TUT	BAT	2980	10-16-88	4:50 pm	5
DEDEMO	DAT	6144	10-16-88	4:50 pm	8
◦ENU	DAT	850	10-16-88	4:50 pm	14

Figure 10-16 Directory shows recovered file.

You may have noticed that the filename of the recovered file is DEDEMO.BAT, when the original file was called BEDEMO.BAT. This was done to distinguish the partially recovered file from the full original file. This will serve as a reminder that this file is missing some of the original data and should not be mistaken for a complete recovery of the erased file. Exit the program by entering

[F10]

Unerasing Without a Directory Entry

The partial unerase operation performed in the previous section was facilitated by the fact that the directory entry for the erased file was intact. This entry provided information that made the recovery process semiautomatic.

However, this is not always the case. It is possible that all or part of a file's data can remain on the disk, but the directory entry for that file is overwritten. In this situation recovery is possible but it requires a more complicated method.

You can create this type of problem on drive A by entering the following commands.

DEL a:dedemo.dat ↵
COPY \norton\mary a: ↵
COPY \norton\bedemo.bat a: ↵
DIR a: ↵

The A drive now has three files listed in the root directory: MAKE-TUT.BAT, MARY, and BEDEMO.BAT. Recall that previously you copied the file MENU.DAT to drive A. Suppose you now realize that you do not have a copy of the MENU.DAT file. Can you recover that file from drive A?

It may indeed be possible to recover all or part of that file if the data has not been overwritten. Load the Main Norton Utilities program by entering

NU a: ↵

Select the Unerase option and display the list of erased files.

u
s

This time the list is blank. Does this mean that the data cannot be recovered? You may wonder why the unerased file list does not include the previously deleted files. Recall that DOS will overwrite directory entries marked as erased, with new file information. Here, the new files you copied overwrote the previous directory entries. Since there are no entries in the directory marked with the σ symbol, there are no names to show on the Unerase file list.

However, this does not mean you cannot recover some or even all of the data from the MENU.DAT file. It may be the case that the new files added have not overwritten the data clusters that were used for MENU.DAT file. It is likely that the data is still intact because the new files added to the disk, MARY and BEDEMO.BAT, are small files taking up only a single disk cluster each.

You can enter a filename for the file you are attempting to recover by entering

↵

recmenu.dat ↵

Display the Unerase operations menu by entering

↵

Searching for Data

The key to this recovery is to have some knowledge of what was contained in the file you want to recover. Without directory data you do not know where on the disk the file was initially stored. Below is a listing of the MENU.DAT file.

```
REM    FIRST PUT UP SOME WINDOWS ON THE SCREEN
window 0,0,24,79 bright yellow on blue explode
window 4,11,20,68 bright yellow on green explode shadow

REM    NOW PUT THE TEXT IN THE WINDOW FOR THE MENU CHOICES
rowcol 8,28 "Choose a program to run:" bright yellow
rowcol 10,25 "BE - More Batch Enhancer functions" bright white
rowcol 11 25 "NI - the Norton Integrator" bright white
rowcol 12,25 "DS - Directory Sort" bright white
rowcol 13,25 "SF - Norton Safe Format program" bright white
rowcol 14,25 "Quit" bright white

REM    AND MAKE THE CHOICE LETTERS A DIFFERENT COLOR.
rowcol 10,25 "B" bright yellow
rowcol 11,25 "N" bright yellow
rowcol 12,25 "D" bright yellow
```

rowcol 13,25 "S" bright yellow
rowcol 14,25 "Q" bright yellow

REM   PUT UP THE PROMPT FOR USER INPUT.
rowcol 18,25 "Press a letter to select program..." bright yellow

Activate the **Add New Clusters** menu by entering

a

In this instance you will need to use the **By Searching for Data** option to attempt to locate clusters that contain part of the data from the erased file. Enter

d

The program displays the search menu, Figure 10-17.

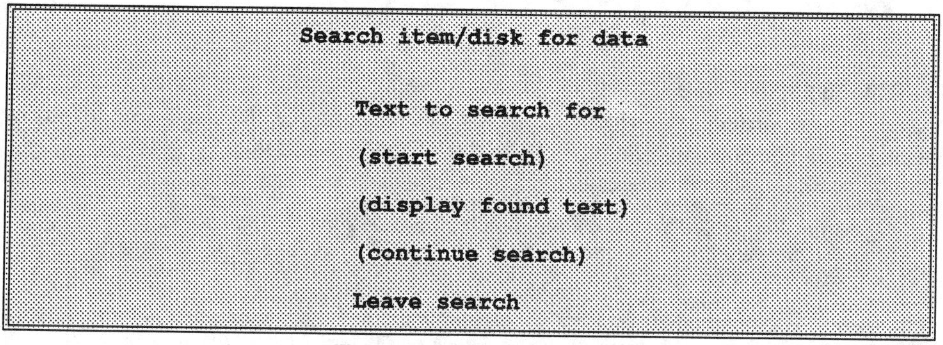

```
        Search item/disk for data


            Text to search for

            (start search)

            (display found text)

            (continue search)

        Leave search
```

Figure 10-17 Search menu.

The only option available is the **Text to Search For** option, which helps to locate the text. Enter

t

The next display (Figure 10-18) is the screen that allows you to enter the data to search for. The data can be entered as text characters or hex values by using the [tab] to shuttle the cursor between the entry areas.

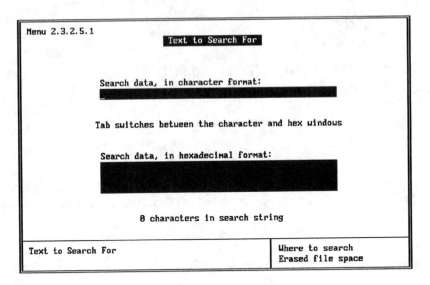

Figure 10-18 Enter search text.

Obviously, it is necessary to know something about the contents of the erased file in order to perform a search. For example, the first line of the MENU.DAT file contains the phrase *PUT UP SOME WINDOWS*.

> *The Main Norton Utilities search program is case-insensitive. This means that if the characters entered into the **search for** menu are ASCII text characters, the program will match the same characters, regardless of case, e.g., WINDOWS, Windows, or windows. If you want to make a case-sensitive search for text you can use the Text Search command with the ?CS switch. For example the command TS "Windows"/E/CS would perform a case sensitive search in the erased file area for the Windows and not WINDOWS or window.*

Enter

put up some windows

As you enter the characters the corresponding hex values for each are displayed in the bottom entry area (Figure 10-19).

```
                    Text to Search For


    Search data, in character format:
    put up some windows


    Tab switches between the character and hex window


    Search data, in hexadecimal format:
    70 75 74 20 75 70 20 73 6F 6D 65 20 77 69 6E 64
    6F 77 73


            19 characters in search string
```

Figure 10-19 Characters and hex values displayed.

Begin the search by entering

↵ *(2 times)*

The search begins at the first cluster on the disk that is not in use by a file. If the search encounters data that matches the *search for* data, it stops the search and displays a message (Figure 10-20) that tells you the cluster in which the text was located.

```
                    Searching for data

                  Searching cluster 14

                         Found!

            Press any key to continue...
```

Figure 10-21 Data located in erased area of the disk.

Continue by entering

↵

When the search program locates a data cluster that contains the text, the program switches to the **Review clusters** menu, as shown in Figure 10-21.

```
            Review cluster(s)

            Reviewing cluster 14

            Display/Edit cluster(s)

            Add cluster(s) to file

            Skip cluster(s)

            Examine the clusters
```

Figure 10-21 Review Clusters menu.

The menu has the following options:

- **Display/Edit Cluster(s).** Displays the cluster that has been located. This allows you to inspect the context in which the located text is stored.

- **Add Cluster(s) to File.** If you have determined that this cluster should be part of the recovered file, you can add this cluster to the recover list with this option. Note that this option always appends the current cluster to the end of cluster list. In some cases you will need to rearrange the clusters in a different order, using the unerase operation menu.

- **Skip Cluster(s).** Select this option if you do not want to add this cluster to the file you are recovering.

Display the cluster by entering

d

The cluster's data is displayed, and the search text is highlighted. You can see here that this cluster is the beginning of the data you are looking for. Add the cluster to the recovery file by entering

↵
a

The program returns to the search menu. From this menu you can continue the search for more matches, start a new search, or leave the search menu. In this instance you have found the beginning of the file. You might want to start a new search for the end of the file. The last words in the original file were *bright yellow*. Enter

t
bright yellow ↵

Note that you have two methods to perform the search. If you select **Start Search**, the search will begin at the first erased cluster on the disk. If you select **Continue Search**, the search will begin with the next available data cluster. Restart the search by entering

s

This time the program searches the entire disk without finding a match. In most examples this might indicate that the end of the file has been overwritten. However, there is one other possibility. Since there was no directory entry indicating the size of the file, it is possible that it would fit into a single cluster. If so, the program would not find *bright yellow* in any other clusters because the same cluster contained both the beginning and the end of the file. Note that once a data cluster is selected for recovery, the Unerase search command will skip that cluster.

To determine if this is such an instance, return to the Unerase operations menu by entering

↵
L

Display the contents of cluster 14 by entering

[Tab]
e

Move to the end of the cluster by entering

[End]

Figure 10-22 shows that the end of the file is contained in the selected cluster.

```
 recmenu.dat ════════════════════════════════ Text format ═╗
 Cluster 14, Sectors 36-37                    File offset 280, hex 118
 more...
   ►- More Batch Enhancer functions" bright white◄
   ►rowcol 11 25 "NI - the Norton Integrator" bright white◄
   ►rowcol 12,25 "DS - Directory Sort" bright white◄
   ►rowcol 13,25 "SF - Norton Safe Format program" bright white◄
   ►rowcol 14,25 "Quit" bright white◄
   ►◄
   ►REM AND MAKE THE CHOICE LETTERS A DIFFERENT COLOR.◄
   ►rowcol 10,25 "B" bright yellow◄
   ►rowcol 11,25 "N" bright yellow◄
   ►rowcol 12,25 "D" bright yellow◄
   ►rowcol 13,25 "S" bright yellow◄
   ►rowcol 14,25 "Q" bright yellow◄
   ►◄
   ►REM PUT UP THE PROMPT FOR USER INPUT.◄
   ►rowcol 18,25 "Press a letter to select program..." bright yellow◄
   ►◄
   ►×_..è.▓ü⊔4⊔05F  EXE ._..δ.≡}⊔4⊔05T  EXE ╱_..¢. Ç⊔4⊔06F  EXE Z_..Ñ.É\⊔4⊔06
   T  EXE 3_..¬.0q⊔4⊔10F  EXE ╘a..▓.≡]

   ...more
                        Press Enter to continue
 1Help   2Hex    3Text   4Dir   5FAT   6Partn  7       8       9Undo  10QuitNU
```

Figure 10-22 End of data cluster displayed.

Return to the menu by entering

↵

You now have all the data you need to restore the file. You are ready to save the restored file. Enter

s

Since no previous file size exists for this file, select to adjust the directory entry size by entering

a

The file has now been recovered. Exit the program by entering

↵
[F10]

List the directory for drive A by entering

DIR a: ↵

The directory now shows the recovered file in the directory.

```
Volume in drive A has no label
Directory of  A:\


FILES         <DIR>        9-26-89   10:21p
CONTROL       <DIR>        9-26-89   10:21p
DISK          <DIR>        9-26-89   10:21p
MAKE-TUT BAT    2980     10-16-88    4:50p
MARY             494      8-30-89    7:54p
BEDEMO   BAT     659     10-16-88    4:50p
RECMENU  DAT    1024      9-27-89   11:24a
        7 File(s)     353280 bytes free
```

The file size entered for the RECMENU.DAT file is 1024, the total number of bytes in the recovered cluster. However, only part of that cluster is actually occupied by the text file. The end of the cluster, about 400 bytes, is slack space. The inclusion of this slack space in the file size can cause problems in some instances. When the file is loaded into a program, the end of the file is determined in one of two ways: (1) an end of file character (ASCII 26, [Ctrl/z], 1A hex) is encountered, or (2) the program had loaded the total number of bytes indicated by the file size value. In this example, the recovered file does not contain an end of file character. Any program loading this file would depend upon the file size to determine the location of the end of the file. However, since the file size is set at the cluster size, the program would load the data at the end of the file that is not really part of the text file. This would result in what appears to be garbage at the end of the file. You can resolve this problem by using the editor or word processor to delete the unwanted text. When the file is saved, the program will write the correct file size into the directory.

Copying Data Clusters

One of the most powerful features of the Main Norton Utilities program is its ability to copy data clusters from one location to another. This feature allows you to copy a data cluster or select list of clusters into a new file on the same or a different disk. There are also options that let you write data into a specific cluster, sector, or absolute sector location. This feature can be used to solve a number of disk problems, some related to erased files, and others related to disk errors.

In this chapter the topic is erased files. In the previous sections data clusters from erased files were recovered. In this section you will look at a how you can recover part of a cluster when the beginning is in use by another file. Set up the disk by copying and then deleting a text file. Enter

COPY \norton\bedemo.dat a: ↵
DEL a:bedemo.dat ↵

Create a new file on drive A using the EDLIN program. Enter

EDLIN a:sample.txt ↵

Enter a single line of text into this file and save it.

i
This is a text. ↵
[Ctrl/c] e ↵

Display the new file using the Main Norton Utilities program.

NU a:sample.txt ↵

The program loads and displays cluster 10. You can see the text you have just entered at the top of the right-hand column. The text occupies only a small portion of this data cluster. Move the display to the end of cluster 10. Enter

[End]

The end of cluster 10 contains information that belonged to another file. Suppose this data was information you wanted to recover. You would not be able to unerase this cluster because it is currently in use for the SAMPLE.TXT file.

When this type of situation arises you can resolve the conflict by using the Norton Utilities program to copy the data to another location, such as an unused portion of this, or another disk.

The ability to copy data from any disk cluster or sector is a very powerful tool. In this case you will want to make a copy of the bottom half of cluster 10. Note that on a 360K disk, each cluster is composed of two sectors. In this example, cluster 10 is composed of sectors 28 and 29. Sector 29 contains the text you want to copy.

Before you copy the data, you should decide where you are going to place it. Most appropriately, that is usually in a cluster on this disk or another currently empty disk in the system. Since you have been unerasing, you might want to make sure that the cluster is empty, not just marked as erased. The most likely place to look for unused clusters is at the end of the disk. Since the Norton Utilities programs like to place the FRECOVER.IDX file in the very last cluster, 355 on 360K disk, display cluster 354. Enter

[F8]

L

354 ↵ ↵

This cluster is completely empty, as shown in Figure 10-23. Note that the beginning sector for cluster 354 is sector 716.

```
┌ Cluster 354 ══════════════════════════════════════ Hex format ═┐
│ Cluster 354, Sectors 716-717                        Offset 0, hex 0 │
│00000000 00000000 00000000 00000000 00000000 00000000 .....................│
│00000000 00000000 00000000 00000000 00000000 00000000 .....................│
│00000000 00000000 00000000 00000000 00000000 00000000 .....................│
│00000000 00000000 00000000 00000000 00000000 00000000 .....................│
│00000000 00000000 00000000 00000000 00000000 00000000 .....................│
│00000000 00000000 00000000 00000000 00000000 00000000 .....................│
│00000000 00000000 00000000 00000000 00000000 00000000 .....................│
│00000000 00000000 00000000 00000000 00000000 00000000 .....................│
│00000000 00000000 00000000 00000000 00000000 00000000 .....................│
│00000000 00000000 00000000 00000000 00000000 00000000 .....................│
│00000000 00000000 00000000 00000000 00000000 00000000 .....................│
│00000000 00000000 00000000 00000000 00000000 00000000 .....................│
│00000000 00000000 00000000 00000000 00000000 00000000 .....................│
│00000000 00000000 00000000 00000000 00000000 00000000 .....................│
│00000000 00000000 00000000 00000000 00000000 00000000 .....................│
│00000000 00000000 00000000 00000000 00000000 00000000 .....................│
│00000000 00000000 00000000 00000000 00000000 00000000 .....................│
│00000000 00000000 00000000 00000000 00000000 00000000 .....................│
│00000000 00000000 00000000 00000000 00000000 00000000 .....................│
│00000000 00000000 00000000 00000000 00000000 00000000 .....................│
│00000000 00000000 00000000 00000000 00000000 00000000 .....................│
│00000000 00000000          Press Enter to continue   ........│
│1Help   2Hex    3Text   4Dir   5FAT   6Partn  7       8Choose 9Undo   10QuitNU│
```

Figure 10-23 Empty disk cluster located.

Now that you have established this cluster is empty, feel free to copy the data into this area of the disk without having to worry about overwriting current or erased data.

The procedure to perform requires you to copy the data in sector 29, into sector 716. Note that you are using sectors to perform this operation because it is only the second 512 bytes in cluster 10 that you want to copy.

The first step in the copying process is to select the item, file, cluster or sector, that will be the source of the data you want to copy. In this case, you should copy sector 29. Enter

[F8]

s

29 ↵ ↵

The program displays the data in sector 29. Return to the Explore Disk menu by entering

[Esc]

The command to use is the **Write Item to Disk** command. This command allows you to duplicate the current item, which is displayed in a box at the bottom of the screen. Enter

w

The **Write Item to Disk** menu appears (Figure 10-24). The menu has three options.

- **File Mode.** This mode copies the selected item into a file. You can specify the filename and the drive on which it is written. This mode has the advantage of creating a file out of the information selected, in a single step. The disadvantage is that you do not have direct control over what clusters the new file will be written in. As with any file added to a disk, you run the risk of overwriting erased data.

- **Cluster Mode.** This mode allows you to specify a cluster on a specific disk where you will write the data into consecutive clusters, beginning at a specified location. Note that this method will overwrite any data at the specified location, regardless of what information it contains.

- **Sector Mode** The sector mode writes the selected item into consecutive sectors beginning at the specified disk sector. This option will overwrite any information in the disk sectors.

```
    File mode

    Cluster mode

    Sector mode

    Absolute sector mode
```

Figure 10-24 Write to disk menu.

The safest option is the file mode. If you use the sector or cluster modes, you must be certain of the effect you will have on the disk. These modes are destructive and will overwrite any data already in those locations. Keep in mind that in this case, you checked the disk to find a sector into which the data could be written, without overwriting other information.

Another very important point is that data copied with the cluster or sector modes is placed onto the disk without modifying the directory or FAT. This means that if the data is written into the erased area of the disk, it will not belong to a file and is subject to overwriting. If the data is written to disk locations that are already parts of files, those areas will be treated by DOS as if they are part of the files that use that location. All this indicates that using these methods incorrectly can cause damage to the disk.

Since you are copying only a single sector, you can choose either the cluster or sector mode. Note that when you copy a sector into a cluster, the first sector is placed into the first sector of the new cluster. In this example this is exactly what you would like to happen. Enter

c

The program asks you to select a drive on which to write the file. By default the program will select a different disk than the one you are using as the source. Select drive A.

a

Enter the cluster number-here, cluster 354.

+*-*+
- 354 ↵

Before the operation is carried out, the program displays a screen that summarizes what you have selected to do, as shown in Figure 10-25.

```
                        Warning!
        You may be destroying information by writing
      +  the selected item out in cluster mode

              Are you sure you want to write

                        Sector 29

                           to

           Cluster 354 on drive A:
```

Figure 10-25 Message displays disk write selection.

Proceed by entering

y

The program writes a copy of the specified sector into the cluster location.
Enter

↵

Creating a File From a Cluster

The final step in recovering the data is to create a file out of the cluster (or
clusters) you have just written. This can be done with the Unerase section of the
Main Norton Utilities program. Enter

r
u

Create a new file by entering

s ↵
copy.txt ↵

Use the Unerase operations menu to select cluster 354. Enter

↵
a
c

Enter the cluster number.

354 ↵ ↵

Display the contents of the cluster by entering

d

The display shows you have successfully copied the data from sector 29 into
this cluster, as shown in Figure 10-26.

```
┌ copy.txt ══════════════════════════════════════════ Hex format ═┐
│ Cluster 354, Sectors 716-717                            Offset 0, hex 0 │
│20202020 20202020 20202020 20202020 20207072 6573656E █        presen│
│74732E2E 2E202020 20202220 0D0A6465 6C617920 310D0A72 ts...     " ♪█delay 1♪█r│
│6F77636F 6C203130 2C302022 50657465 72204E6F 72746F6E oucol 10,0 "Peter Norton│
│20202020 20202020 20202020 20202020 20202020 20202020 │
│20202070 72657365 6E74732E 2E2E2020 20202022 200D0A64     presents...     " ♪█d│
│656C6179 20310D0A 726F7763 6F6C2031 302C3020 22506574 elay 1♪█roucol 10,0 "Pet│
│6572204E 6F72746F 6E202020 20202020 20202020 20202020 er Norton│
│20202020 20202020 70726573 656E7473 2E2E2E20 20202020        presents...│
│22200D0A 64656C61 7920310D 0A726F77 636F6C20 31302C30 " ♪█delay 1♪█roucol 10,0│
│20225065 74657220 4E6F7274 6F6E2020 20202020 20202020 "Peter Norton│
│20202020 20202020 20707265 73656E74 732E2E2E 20202020        presents...│
│2022200D 0A64656C 61792031 0D0A726F 77636F6C 2031302C " ♪█delay 10,│
│30202250 65746572 204E6F72 746F6E20 20202020 20202020 0 "Peter Norton│
│20202020 20207072 6573656E 74732E2E 2E202020 20202220        presents...     "│
│0D0A6465 6C617920 310D0A72 6F77636F 6C203130 2C302022 ♪█delay 1♪█roucol 10,0 "│
│50657465 72204E6F 72746F6E 20202020 20202070 Peter Norton          p│
│72657365 6E74732E 2E2E2020 20202022 200D0A64 656C6179 resents...     " ♪█delay│
│20310D0A 726F7763 6F6C2031 302C3020 22506574 6572204E 1♪█roucol 10,0 "Peter N│
│6F72746F 6E202020 20202020 70726573 656E7473 2E2E2E20 orton          presents...│
│20202020 22200D0A 64656C61 7920310D 0A726F77 636F6C20 " ♪█delay 1♪█roucol│
│31302C30 20225065 74657220 4E6F7274 6F6E2020 20207265 10,0 "Peter Norton    pre│
│73656E74 732E2E2E        Press Enter to continue   sents...│
│1Help  2Hex   3Text   4Dir   5FAT   6Partn  7     8     9Undo  10QuitNU│
```

Figure 10-26 Cluster 354 contains a copy of the data contained in sector 29.

Complete the process of creating a file out of this cluster by entering

[Esc]
a
[Tab]
s

Adjust the file size by entering

a

The file has now been written to the disk (Figure 10-27).

```
┌─────────────────────────────────────────────────────────┐
│                                                           │
│         Saving record of file's data ... done            │
│                                                           │
│         Saving file's directory entry ... done            │
│                                                           │
│                                                           │
│            UnErasing copy.txt is complete                 │
│                                                           │
│                                                           │
│                                                           │
│             Press any key to continue...                  │
│                                                           │
└─────────────────────────────────────────────────────────┘
```

Figure 10-27 Cluster written to the file COPY.TXT.

Exit the program by entering

[F10]

You can use the Speed Disk program to collect the scatter files on the disk into contiguous files at the beginning of the disk.

At times, the process of file recovery is as complex as the system of file storage. To recover a file you have to be part detective and part programmer. But the process is interesting, and when needed, a lifesaver.

The key to locating files is to have some salient character in mind that will identify the data in an erased cluster as belonging to a particular file.

If the file is a text file, the contents of the file can be used as they were in the previous illustration. Text files are easy to recover because their contents are visually identifiable and even partial recovery is helpful. For example, the file can usually be loaded into the word processor and the missing information can be reentered.

Other types of files are more difficult. Spreadsheet files are usually very hard to recover because they are not stored in text format. In Section III under Searching, the file header used for a 1-2-3 Release 2 worksheet was shown to be the hex sequence **0000020006040600**. This is important since 1-2-3 will not load a partial file if the beginning sector is missing. If you can locate the beginning of a worksheet, 1-2-3 will load the file. If the correct file ending is missing, an error will be produced but the portion of the file recovered will appear on the spreadsheet. If you save the file under a new name, 1-2-3 will place the correct end of file information into the new file.

The same problem exists with dBASE III files. If the header section is missing the data portion of the file will not load. Since dBASE III files are mostly ASCII text files, you might be able to load them into a word processor. Not all word processing programs will allow this because the ASCII portion of a dBASE III file does not contain LF/CR characters after each record. WordStar will only load a portion of such a file. Microsoft Word and the Norton Editor will load as much of the file as will fit into memory.

Once you have loaded the file you can recover the data through a rather laborious process. First, edit the file by placing a ↵ at the end of each record. Count the exact number of characters, including spaces, that make up each field. Then create a new structure for the text in dBASE III Plus that matches the exact character count for each field in the text file. Finally, use the APPEND FROM filename SDF to load the text into a new dBASE III structure.

The main Norton Utilities program provides a means of examining the patterns of the file structure produced by various programs. By looking at correctly written files you may find a clue as to the type of patterns that identify the lost data.

One of the most common types of recovery that requires the use of the main Norton Utilities program, rather than QU, is a program crash during a file save. In a floppy disk system this is caused often by disk-full problems. I have also seen this same problem in many applications. When saving a file, the program appears to be working, the disk light goes on indicating writing is taking place, but the program crashes before the saving is complete.

The usual symptom is a file with zero bytes showing in the directory. This entry is caused by a problem that has taken place as a file is being updated. In most cases, part or all of the affected file is still on the disk. The zero bytes size shows that the program crashed before the new file size could be written into the directory. Naturally, writing the size of the file is the last part of the file saving process. It may well be that all the data has been safely stored in clusters before the crash.

The key is to find the first cluster of that file by searching for data or header information. When you find that header, make a best guess, as shown in the previous section, to allocate consecutive data clusters to the file. Most programs will recover from bad file endings if the file begins correctly.

The Norton Utilities programs provide a means by which you can make at least a valiant attempt to recover from disaster. If nothing else, you can learn a lot about your computer in the attempt.

Summary

This chapter discussed the use of the Main Norton Utilities program for recovering erased data that Quick Unerase cannot recover.

- **Unerase Operations.** The Main Norton Utilities program allows you to manipulate the data on the disk directly, so you can recover data from erased files that have been partially overwritten by new data. The program allows you to select, display, and arrange data clusters into recovered files.

- **Adding Clusters.** The main task in partial recovery of files is the cluster selection process. If directory information is available the program can automatically select likely data cluster.

- **Searching.** You can select clusters or sectors by number, using the search facility to locate clusters that contain specific text items or hex information.

- **Copying Data.** The Write to Disk option allows you to duplicate file, cluster, or sector information. You can create new files, or place the data into specific disk clusters or sectors on any of the disks in the system.

11

Disk Errors

Both hard and floppy disks operate on the principles of magnetic storage. The storage is accomplished by placing small magnetic charges onto the surface coating of the disk. The coating is a special metallic oxide that is highly sensitive to changes in magnetic fields. While the reliability of these coatings is quite remarkable, it is impossible to create a completely flawless coating. There will always be minute fluctuations in the thickness of the coating, which in some cases can create weak spots that will eventually fail to retain the magnetic data placed on the disk. Some of these weak spots appear right away while others may take years of use to show up. When a weak spot develops, it may operate correctly sometimes and fail at other times. As time goes on, these intermittent failures tend to become worse.

The Norton Utilities supplies two programs, Disk Test and the Norton Disk Doctor, that are designed to help prevent or fix disk errors. Also, the Main Norton Utilities program can be used to recover data effected by disk errors.

In general, the best policy is to use the Disk Test and NDD programs as preventative measures.

Because this chapter deals with disk errors, it is not possible to write about the programs in the *work-along* style used previously throughout this book.

Error Reading Drive

The most dreaded message that your DOS can display about your hard disk is **Error reading drive C.** This error indicates that DOS has been unable to read the data stored in one of the sectors on the hard disk. The media on hard disks and floppy disks alike are vulnerable to failure; i.e., the recording surface can contain a flaw that prevents the computer from reading the data contained in that sector. Since the coating of a disk is a magnetic medium, minute variations in the density of the coating can cause fluctuations in the intensity of the magnetic signals placed there by the disk drive. A flaw may be such that the computer can read the sector sometimes, and not read it other times.

When such an error is encountered, DOS displays three alternatives:

A   **Abort.** This cancels the command or the program that caused DOS to attempt the disk operation. Choosing Abort may result in the loss of the data you were trying to save, since most programs are not prepared to deal with this type of error.

R   **Retry.** This tells DOS to attempt the disk operation again. Sometimes, when the flaw is marginal, retrying will be successful. If it works you should quit the application as soon as possible and make a copy of the file. You should always Retry at least once. If it doesn't work, you are no worse off then you were before.

I   **Ignore.** This option tells DOS to simply skip over that sector and continue with the next step in its operation. This will often allow you to complete the operation. But remember that the file you have just read or written may still contain the flawed sector. The next time you use the file, the same problem may arise.

DOS attempts to prevent this type of error by blocking out bad clusters that contain bad sectors when the disk is formatted. It is not unusual to have some bad sectors on a hard disk.

Bad sectors are usually blocked out during the low level format of the hard disk. If any new problems arise while the high level formatting takes place, FORMAT C:, DOS marks those clusters as bad and reports the number of characters lost to bad sectors at the end of the formatting.

Soft Errors and Hard Errors

When disk errors occur, they can fall into two basic classifications.

- **Soft Errors.** A soft error is a disruption in the formatted structure of the disk, often caused by inconsistencies in the magnetic field on the disk. When a soft error occurs, DOS will attempt to reaccess the area in 30 to 150 attempts, before it displays the *Abort, Retry, or Ignore* message. In many cases the soft error will be corrected by this retry process. When a disk area begins to exhibit numerous soft errors, it is usually a sign that the data storage capacity of that part of the hard disk is failing.

> *For example, when a computer is turned off, the read/write heads in the hard drive will often settle to the disk at their current position. It is claimed that when the computer restarts, a surge of power will flow through the heads, corrupting the data in the spot where the heads were last positioned. The recommended solution is to park the disk drive heads. Parking refers to moving the heads to a safety zone, usually the last track on the disk, before the computer is turned off.*

- **Hard Errors.** Hard errors are disk flaws that cannot be corrected even with a low-level format. These areas are usually marked off so that the operating system will ignore the areas. The goal of disk maintenance programs is to locate and mark off hard error locations **before** a unrecoverable data loss occurs.

  Of course, from a user's point of view, hard and soft errors behave the same way in some circumstances. For example, you might encounter an *Abort, Retry, or Ignore* message each time you try to access a certain file. However, the next day when you try to show someone what the problem is, the file loads perfectly. In this example the error acted like a hard error but turned out to be soft. Keep in mind that soft errors will usually continue to degrade, becoming harder and harder for the disk to read. Part of this process is exacerbated by the computer trying 50, 100, or 150 times to access the file each time.

DOS, Controllers, and Error Correction Code

You might wonder why special programs, such as the ones discussed in this chapter, are necessary. The reason for these programs is similar to the reason for all of the Norton Utilities programs. While DOS is important, it does not cover every conceivable situation or need.

Reading data from the disk is an operation that combines DOS commands with the operations built into the hard disk controller. When DOS or some application run through DOS, requests data from the disk, a special program on the controller card carries out the request.

With disk errors, most versions of DOS are primarily concerned with reading the data and returning it to the application that requested the information. For example, DOS does not report or record the number of attempts performed by the controller card needed to read a particular disk sector. DOS is satisfied to get the data and makes no distinction between 1 and 100 attempts. While getting the data is important for the application to complete its task, the fact that a particular sector requires a significant number of retries can be a warning of future problems.

The first visible sign that DOS is encountering a problem is the *Abort, Retry, or Ignore* message, which can often come too late to save the data. When this message appears, the controller will activate its ECC (error correction code) program to attempt to recover the data. If successful, DOS takes the data but still does nothing about the source of the problem.

The Disk Test and NDD programs, discussed in this chapter, are designed to detect problems with disks by analyzing the data reading process, to see if parts of the disk exhibit unusually high error rates. The program also attempts to fix the problem by moving what data can be recovered to another location and marking off the flawed area for further use. Unlike DOS, these programs are not concerned about using the data, but in the quality of the data reading process.

Disk Test

The DT (disk test) program is designed to help you handle problems that arise on your disks. DT cannot solve all the problems, but it is a valuable tool. DT has three uses.

1. **Analysis.** The DT program performs tests on the disk data that will report to you the condition of the disk clusters and files.

2. **Recovery.** The DT program can be used to recover files corrupted by disk errors.

3. **Prevention.** Running DT can help to locate and isolate bad sectors before they corrupt files.

DT can be run on either hard or floppy disks. The test performed by DT is different than that done by CHKDSK. In CHKDSK the test is one in which the data in the directory and the file allocation table are cross-correlated to locate any inconsistencies. The DT program actually attempts to read the information stored on the disk. For that reason the DT program takes much longer to operate.

The DT program can be run in one of two modes.

- **File.** In the file mode the DT program tests only the space currently shown to be used by files. This test is generally shorter than a full-disk test because it skips the root directory and FAT and any clusters not currently assigned to files.

  An important aspect of the file test is that it will report the names of the files that contain problem sectors. By reading the name you can decide if you need to try to recover this file. For example, if the NU.EXE program reported an error you would probably not be concerned since you would have a copy of the program on the original floppy disk.

On the other hand, if the error was reported from a document or data file, you would face the prospect of a loss of unique data if the file had not been copied or backed up.

- **Disk.** In the Disk Test mode, all the sectors on the disk including the boot, root directory, file allocation table, and unused clusters, are tested. The primary advantage of this mode is to locate potential problems before they are allocated to a file. When you locate a bad cluster, the program reports if the cluster is in use by a file or not.

The Disk Test program also provides an option in which both tests, disk then file, are performed consecutively.

It is a good idea to run a Disk Test at least once a month or more. To perform both tests, enter

DT/B

The Disk Test program will first test the entire disk, sector by sector. It will display the number of clusters checked, as it works through the disk. Remember, these tests will take some time. For example, a 20 megabyte hard disk will have 10,355 clusters to check.

After the overall disk test, the program will then follow the directory tree and test all the files on the hard disk. The test will proceed, directory by directory, displaying each filename as it does so. This part of the test should be shorter than the entire disk test, but not always. The disk test proceeds in a straight path through all the sectors. The file test must jump around and test the clusters in the order in which they are used by the files, which is slower than going straight through the disk. The program displays messages as it progresses with the disk test, as shown on Figure 11-1.

```
DT-Disk Test, Advanced Edition 4.50, (C) Copr 1987-88, Peter Norton

During the scan of the disk, you may press
BREAK (Control-C) to interrupt Disk Test

Test reading the entire disk C:, system area and data area
   The system area consists of boot, FAT, and directory
      No errors reading system area

   The data area consists of clusters numbered 2 - 236
      106th cluster read error: already marked as bad; no danger
      178th cluster read error: already marked as bad; no danger

Test reading files
   Directory C:\
   Directory C:\LANTASTI
   Directory C:\LANTASTI.NET
   Directory C:\LANTASTI.NET\SYSTEM.NET
   Directory C:\LANTASTI.NET\SPOOL.NET
   Directory C:\LANTASTI.NET\MORGAN
   Directory C:\LANTASTI.NET\FLOPPY
      No errors reading files
```

Figure 11-1 Disk Text displays messages during operation.

You can stop the test at any time by entering [Ctrl/c] or [Ctrl/Scroll Lock].

If you are lucky, the only messages from Disk Test that you will see are the ones illustrated above. Below is an illustration of the type of messages that would be reported if errors were encountered during a total disk test. The command used for this test would be

DT/D

Note that because the clusters are allocated to files, the Disk Test program warns that there is **DANGER NOW!**, as shown in Figure 11-2.

```
No errors reading system area

The data area consists of clusters numbered 2 - 355
    130th cluster read error: in use by a file -- DANGER NOW
    134th cluster read error: in use by a file -- DANGER NOW
    139th cluster read error: in use by a file -- DANGER NOW
    143rd cluster read error: in use by a file -- DANGER NOW
    148th cluster read error: in use by a file -- DANGER NOW
    152nd cluster read error: in use by a file -- DANGER NOW      DT reports
    157th cluster read error: in use by a file -- DANGER NOW      errors in
    161st cluster read error: in use by a file -- DANGER NOW      clusters
    166th cluster read error: in use by a file -- DANGER NOW◄──── already
    170th cluster read error: in use by a file -- DANGER NOW      allocated to
    175th cluster read error: in use by a file -- DANGER NOW      files.
    179th cluster read error: in use by a file -- DANGER NOW
    184th cluster read error: in use by a file -- DANGER NOW
    188th cluster read error: in use by a file -- DANGER NOW
    193rd cluster read error: in use by a file -- DANGER NOW
    197th cluster read error: in use by a file -- DANGER NOW
    202nd cluster read error: in use by a file -- DANGER NOW
    206th cluster read error: in use by a file -- DANGER NOW
    211th cluster read error: in use by a file -- DANGER NOW
    215th cluster read error: in use by a file -- DANGER NOW
    220th cluster read error: in use by a file -- DANGER NOW
 _ 221
```

Figure 11-2 Files with disk errors listed.

The program is telling you that part or all of the data in the cluster is not readable. The disk test does not display the names of the files to which the cluster are allocated. That information can be found by running a File Test, the results of which are shown below. Example:

DT/F

This test lists the names of the files that contain the flawed clusters, Figure 11-3.

```
The data area consists of clusters numbered 2 - 355
    130th cluster read error: in use by a file -- DANGER NOW
    139th cluster read error: in use by a file -- DANGER NOW
    143rd cluster read error: in use by a file -- DANGER NOW
    148th cluster read error: in use by a file -- DANGER NOW   Bad Clusters not
    152nd cluster read error: in use by a file -- DANGER NOW   allocated to
    157th cluster read error: in use by a file -- DANGER NOW   existing files.
    161st cluster read error: not currently in use -- DANGER
    166th cluster read error: not currently in use -- DANGER TO COME
    170th cluster read error: not currently in use -- DANGER TO COME
    175th cluster read error: not currently in use -- DANGER TO COME
    179th cluster read error: not currently in use -- DANGER TO COME
    184th cluster read error: not currently in use -- DANGER TO COME
    188th cluster read error: not currently in use -- DANGER TO COME
    193rd cluster read error: not currently in use -- DANGER TO COME
    197th cluster read error: not currently in use -- DANGER TO COME
    202nd cluster read error: not currently in use -- DANGER TO COME
    206th cluster read error: in use by a file -- DANGER NOW
    211th cluster read error: not currently in use -- DANGER TO COME
    215th cluster read error: not currently in use -- DANGER TO COME
    220th cluster read error: not currently in use -- DANGER TO COME
    224th cluster read error: not currently in use -- DANGER TO COME
    229th cluster read error: not currently in use -- DANGER TO COME
    238th cluster read error: not currently in use -- DANGER TO COME
    239
```

Figure 11-3 Bad cluster not allocated to files identified.

Once you have established where the bad clusters are, there are two ways to handle the problems.

1. If the files are ones for which you have duplicates, you are not concerned with recovering the files. The files can simply be deleted. Remember that to delete a file, DOS does not have to read its contents, only the entries in the directory and the FAT.

    However, you want to make sure that no new files are placed into the bad clusters. In this case, use Disk Test to mark those clusters as unusable.

2. If the files represent valuable data, you want to attempt to recover the files, as well as block out those areas for future use. The Disk Test program has an option that attempts to move the data to a usable cluster area.

Look at what both operations would consist of. Begin with the files you don't want to recover. For example, on the sample test shown above, some of the files were EXE program files. Suppose you have copies of these programs on another disk, such as the original program disks supplied by the manufacturer. There is no point in wasting effort trying to recover the programs.

The first step would be to delete the programs from the disk. Keep in mind that deleting simply removes the allocation for these clusters from the directory and the FAT. The commands below are samples of how you would delete the files you had copies of.

del b:mergeprd.exe
del word_dca.exe

Now that the files have been removed from the directory, you would run the Disk Test program again for the disk space. You want to specify the disk, not the files in this. The reason is that you want to locate those bad clusters that used to belong to those deleted files. At this point you do not know which of the bad clusters belonged to **mergeprd.exe** and **word_dca.exe**. Enter

DT/D

Note that this time when the program encounters the bad clusters, some of them are shown to be DANGER TO COME. This means that you have the opportunity of marking these clusters as unusable. This will prevent DOS from attempting to write data into these clusters. Once blocked out, these clusters will no longer pose a danger, (Figure 11-4).

```
148th cluster read error: in use by a file -- DANGER NOW
152nd cluster read error: in use by a file -- DANGER NOW
157th cluster read error: in use by a file -- DANGER NOW
161st cluster read error: not currently in use -- DANGER TO COME
166th cluster read error: not currently in use -- DANGER TO COME
170th cluster read error: not currently in use -- DANGER TO COME
175th cluster read error: not currently in use -- DANGER TO COME
179th cluster read error: not currently in use -- DANGER TO COME
184th cluster read error: not currently in use -- DANGER TO COME
188th cluster read error: not currently in use -- DANGER TO COME
193rd cluster read error: not currently in use -- DANGER TO COME
197th cluster read error: not currently in use -- DANGER TO COME
202nd cluster read error: not currently in use -- DANGER TO COME
206th cluster read error: in use by a file -- DANGER NOW
211th cluster read error: not currently in use -- DANGER TO COME
215th cluster read error: not currently in use -- DANGER TO COME
220th cluster read error: not currently in use -- DANGER TO COME
224th cluster read error: not currently in use -- DANGER TO COME
229th cluster read error: not currently in use -- DANGER TO COME
238th cluster read error: not currently in use -- DANGER TO COME

During this operation, do not press
BREAK (Control-C) to interrupt Disk Test      Program will mark
Errors found in disk areas not currently in use  ← ba clusters.
Mark them as bad sectors, to prevent use (Y/N) ? _
```

Figure 11-4 Program will mark bad clusters.

Once the entire disk is tested, the program will ask if you want the bad sectors and the clusters that contain them, marked. Enter

y

Since the Disk Test program found errors in the file area, it will automatically display the name of the files that still are in danger after it has marked the DANGER TO COME clusters as unusable.

How should you handle the files that you do want to recover? For example, the file SEMI.STY on the sample disk might represent a user-file for which there is no duplicate. The Disk Test program recognizes a /M switch. /M is used to tell Disk Test to attempt to move the data contained in the file with the bad sector to another location on the disk.

You can use Disk Test/M to recover all the files, or select a specific file by entering its name, or group of files by using a DOS wildcard. In this case, the command will be aimed at a specific file that you want to recover. Enter

DT semi.sty/M

The Disk Test program will attempt to read the file and place its contents into a new area of the disk. If successful, it will display a message indicating that the file is safely moved, as shown in Figure 11-5.

```
During this operation, do not press
BREAK (Control-C) to interrupt Disk Test
Errors found in disk areas not currently in use
Mark them as bad sectors, to prevent use (Y/N) ? Y

Disk errors found in data area; now checking files

You may again press BREAK (Control-C) to interrupt Disk Test
   Directory B:\
     File mu.hlp: error reading file in the used area -- DANGER NOW
     File hyph.dat: error reading file in the used area -- DANGER NOW
     File semi.sty: error reading file in the used area -- DANGER NOW

[C:\]dt b:semi.sty/m
DT-Disk Test, Advanced Edition, (C) Copr 1987, Peter Norton

During the scan of the disk, you may press
BREAK (Control-C) to interrupt Disk Test              ┌──┤File moved to new location│
                                                      │
Test reading files                                    │
                                                      ▼
    │ File semi.sty: error reading file. Moved to safe area.      │

[C:\]_
```

Figure 11-5 Disk Test moves file to a new location.

You can enter a general form of DISK TEST to attempt to move any file that appears to be in danger. Enter

DT/M/F

The program will automatically attempt to recover any endangered files it encounters, (Figure 11-6).

```
      238th cluster read error: already marked as bad; no danger

Disk errors found in data area; now checking files
   Directory B:\
      File mw.hlp: error reading file in the used area -- DANGER NOW
      File hyph.dat: error reading file in the used area -- DANGER NOW

[C:\]dt b:/m
DT-Disk Test, Advanced Edition, (C) Copr 1987, Peter Norton

Select DISK test, FILE test, or BOTH
Press D, F, or B ...

[C:\]dt b:/m/f
DT-Disk Test, Advanced Edition, (C) Copr 1987, Peter Norton

During the scan of the disk, you may press
BREAK (Control-C) to interrupt Disk Test

Test reading files

 ┌─────────────────────────────────────────────────────────┐
 │   File mw.hlp: error reading file. Moved to safe area.    │
 │   File hyph.dat: error reading file. Moved to safe area.  │
 └─────────────────────────────────────────────────────────┘

[C:\]_
```

Figure 11-6 Endangered files automatically relocated.

If you perform a Disk Test on the disk, the program will report the bad clusters that have been marked, (Figure 11-7).

DT/D

```
130th cluster read error: already marked as bad; no danger
139th cluster read error: already marked as bad; no danger
148th cluster read error: already marked as bad; no danger
152nd cluster read error: already marked as bad; no danger
157th cluster read error: already marked as bad; no danger
161st cluster read error: already marked as bad; no danger
166th cluster read error: already marked as bad; no danger
170th cluster read error: already marked as bad; no danger
175th cluster read error: already marked as bad; no danger
179th cluster read error: already marked as bad; no danger
184th cluster read error: already marked as bad; no danger
188th cluster read error: already marked as bad; no danger
193rd cluster read error: already marked as bad; no danger
197th cluster read error: already marked as bad; no danger
202nd cluster read error: already marked as bad; no danger
206th cluster read error: already marked as bad; no danger
211th cluster read error: already marked as bad; no danger
215th cluster read error: already marked as bad; no danger
220th cluster read error: already marked as bad; no danger
224th cluster read error: already marked as bad; no danger
229th cluster read error: already marked as bad; no danger
238th cluster read error: already marked as bad; no danger


[C:\]_
```

Figure 11-7 Program lists clusters already marked as bad.

If you were to display a map of the disk usage with the main Norton Utilities program, the bad clusters would appear marked with **B**, as shown in Figure 11-8. Example:

nu
d
m

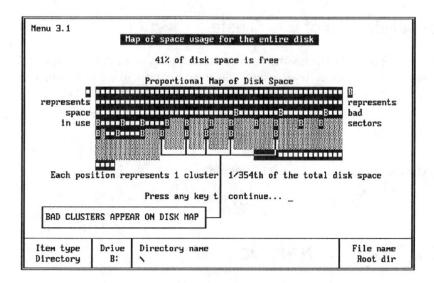

Figure 11-8 Disk map shows bad clusters.

On a large disk you may want to print the output of the DISK TEST program, rather than simply have it displayed on the screen. The usual DOS redirection technique can be applied to the DISK TEST command. Note that you should use the /LOG switch to suppress the portions of the display that are not appropriate for printer output. Below is an example of a page formatted report on disk integrity.

DT /B/LOG > diskstat
LP diskstat

You might want to create a batch file for this operation, and perform it on a regular basis.

If bad sectors are encountered as part of the Disk Test command when the redirection is set to redirect the output to a file, the program will appear to hangup. The reason is that the program has paused to ask you if you want to mark the bad clusters. But because you have redirected the output to the disk, the question does not appear on the screen. If this happens, break the program with [Ctrl/c] and run the test again with the output displayed on the screen. Note that the /LOG switch, which is normally used to suppress interactive dialogue in a program, does not work in this case.

Manual Marking of Bad Clusters

The Disk Test program has the facility for marking or unmarking specific data clusters. This feature is used when you have reason to suspect that a cluster should not be used. Suppose you want to mark cluster 555 as bad. You would enter

DT/C555

The mark could be removed by entering

DT/C555-

The Norton Disk Doctor

The NDD is designed to find and correct a number of problems that can occur on both hard and floppy disks.

The tests and fixes provided by the NDD cover a greater variety of disk problems than does the Disk Test program. However, the complete disk analysis performed by the NDD takes much more time than the analysis performed by Disk Test. The NDD program will carry out a sector-by-sector analysis of the disk, while Disk Test works data cluster by data cluster. For example, testing a 1 megabyte partition on a hard disk would take the Disk Test program about 10-15 seconds, while the NDD program would take 30-45 seconds. The larger the disk, the longer the test will take.

Keep in mind that since disk integrity is crucial, the extra time required by the NDD program is well worth the effort.

Running Norton Disk Doctor

The program can be run in either a full-screen or command-line mode. To start the program in full-screen mode, enter the following command at the DOS prompt:

NDD

In the full-screen mode, the program displays a menu that has two basic options, as shown in Figure 11-9.

- **Diagnose Disk.** This option is the primary activity of the NDD program. When selected, this option will analyze all the sectors on the selected disk on both the logical level, i.e., DOS files and directories, and on the physical level, i.e., soft errors that occur in individual disk sectors.

- **Common Solutions.** This option allows you to perform three special disk tasks not available with the standard DOS tools. You can create a bootable disk, perform a nondestructive low-level format on a **floppy** disk, or correct problems caused by the mistaken use of the DOS RECOVER program.

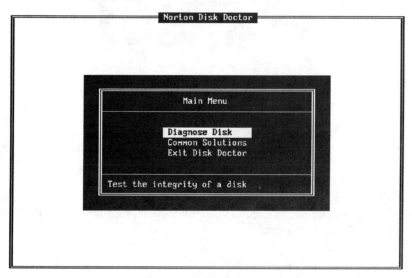

Figure 11-9 Norton Disk Doctor main menu.

Disk Diagnosis

The disk diagnosis is the main function of the NDD program. Its purpose is to check the performance of the selected disk to determine if there are any problems, and mark those sectors if there are.

When the **Diagnose** option is selected, the program displays a window listing the disk available for analysis, as shown in Figure 11-10.

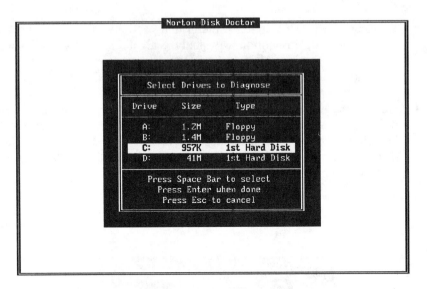

Figure 11-10 Available disks listed.

When you select a disk, the program displays a screen that shows information about the logical and physical structure of the disk, see Figure 11-11. The logical information refers to the way the disk is viewed by DOS. They include the drive letter, size, media description code, FAT type, total sectors and clusters, bytes per sector, sectors per cluster, and number of copies of the FAT stored on the disk (Figure 11-11).

```
        Drive Letter:  C:
                Size:  957K
   Media Description:  F8h
     Large Partition:  No
            FAT Type:  12-bit
       Total Sectors:  1,921
      Total Clusters:  235
     Bytes Per Sector: 512
   Sectors Per Cluster: 8
      Number of FATs:  2
```

Figure 11-11 Logical Disk data.

The physical information describes the disk as the disk controller pictures it. The data includes the number of heads, cylinders, sectors per track, the starting head, cylinder and sector, and the ending head, cylinder and sector (Figure 11-12).

```
        Drive Number:   80h
               Heads:   6
           Cylinders:   19
    Sectors Per Track:   17
       Starting Head:   1
    Starting Cylinder:   0
      Starting Sector:   1
          Ending Head:   5
      Ending Cylinder:   18
       Ending Sector:   17
```

Figure 11-12 Physical disk data.

At the top of the screen, a window is displayed that shows three automatic tests that will be performed: Analyzing DOS Boot Record, Analyzing File Allocation Tables, and Analyzing Directory Structure.

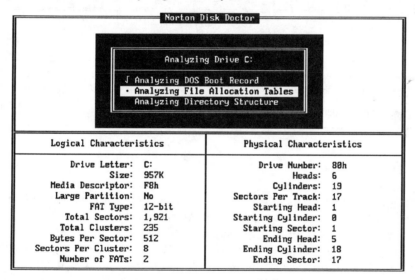

Figure 11-13 Disk analysis display.

Following the examination of the boot record, the program will scan the directory tree of the disk, as shown on Figure 11-14.

```
                    Scanning Directory Structure

                              CFAX
```

Figure 11-14 Searching directory tree.

The program then proceeds to analyze the File Allocation Table, searching for lost chains of data clusters (Figure 11-15).

```
                    Searching for Lost Chains

                              7,953
```

Figure 11-15 Search for lost clusters.

> *The three tests performed in this part of the program make up the \QUICK option. When NDD is executed as a command line program, the \QUICK switch will cause the program to terminate after the boot, directory, and lost cluster analysis, eliminating the defective sector test.*

Lost Clusters

The program will automatically search the directory tree of the disk and analyze the FAT for problems, such as lost chains (also called lost clusters). A *lost cluster* is a cluster whose number appears in the FAT, but does not actually belong to any of the files in any of the directories. Lost clusters are typically created when an error occurs during the writing of a file. For example, if an application hangs up while writing a file, it will usually leave some lost clusters.

If the program encounters any lost clusters, it displays a window that explains the amount of lost clusters and the number of chains found in the FAT (Figure 11-16).

A chain is a series of lost clusters that are stored in consecutive disk clusters. They are called a chain because the assumption is made that since they are consecutive, they are related, possibly as part of the same file.

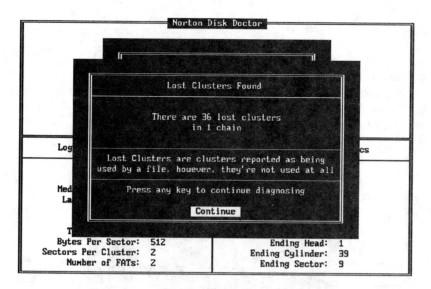

Figure 11-16 Warning about lost clusters.

The program then displays a window that asks if you want to correct these errors, as shown in Figure 11-17. Correcting refers to a process in which all the lost clusters are recovered by assigning filenames to the chains. Each chain is assigned a unique file name. The process is similar to the way the automatic mode works in Quick Unerase. The names used for the recovered files are FILE0000._DD, FILE0001._DD, etc. These files are always stored in the root directory of the disk.

The files created by the recovery of lost clusters resolve the anomalies between the FAT and the directories. In most cases, the data in the recovered clusters is not important and you can delete those files in order to free up the space to be used for new data files. If you are not sure, you can inspect the file with the Main Norton Utilities to determine if the recovered clusters contain usable information.

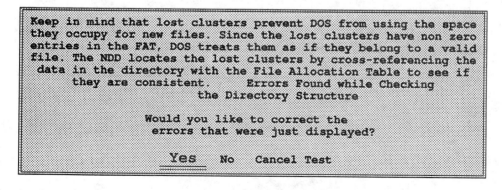

Figure 11-17 Correct or ignore lost clusters.

Hard Disk Partitions

If you are using versions of DOS newer than 4.0, and a hard disk larger than 32 megabytes, your hard disk will be partitioned into two or more logical drives. If you attempt to run the NDD on one of the nonbooting partitions (usually drives D, E, F, etc.) the program will display a window with a message that refers to an invalid *Boot Record Program* (Figure 11-18).

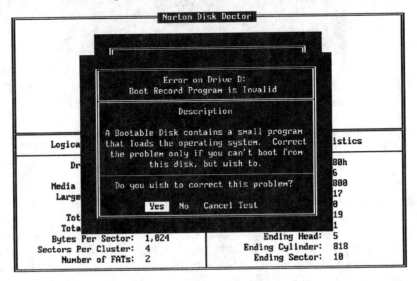

Figure 11-18 Boot record error window.

The *Boot Record Program* is the information stored in sector zero of the disk. If software other than the DOS FDISK program is used to create disk partitions, the first sector in the partition, which the NDD assumes should be the disk boot sector, may not contain an actual boot program. Since the computer does not boot from the partition, there is really nothing wrong. Select **No** and proceed with the rest of the test.

Complete Sector Analysis

The most comprehensive part of the NDD program's operation is the Defective Sector test. This test examines all the sectors on the disk and analyzes their performance.

Following the boot record, directory, and lost cluster analysis, the program will display a window asking if you want to perform the Defective Sector test, as shown in Figure 11-19.

```
                        Analyzing Drive D:

                Would you like to test ALL of Drive D:
                        for Defective Sectors?

                            Yes   No
```

Figure 11-19 Select defective sector test.

The Defective Sector test will scan the entire hard disk (or partition) and examine the sectors to determine if they can be read correctly. If a sector exhibits errors, the program can be used to mark that cluster as bad. If the bad sector occurs in a cluster that is in use by a file, the program will copy the readable sectors of the file to an unused cluster and adjust the file to the modification.

> *The ability to copy data to an unused sector assumes that there is still unused space available on the disk. If the program is unable to find an unused cluster into which the data can be copied, it will display a window explaining the problem and skip the sector. The solution is to copy and then remove some of the files unaffected by the bad sectors, making room for the data to be moved.*

These changes can be made in a manual or automatic mode, as shown in Figure 11-20.

- **Manual.** In the manual mode the program will stop whenever a bad sector is encountered, and display a window. The window will tell you what sector is defective, and offer you the option of correcting the problem, ignoring the problem, or terminating the sector test.

- **Automatic.** In the automatic mode, bad sectors are automatically corrected without user intervention. If the sector is in an unused cluster, it is marked as bad. If the sector falls within an existing file, the program attempts to copy the data into an unused cluster somewhere else on the disk.

> *The only exception to the automatic mode is if there is no more room on the disk for copying data from bad clusters. In that event the program will pause even in the automatic mode, to display a message window.*

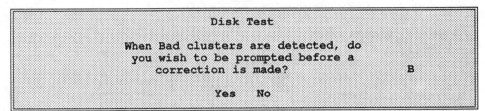

Figure 11-20 Automatic or manual correction mode.

When the sector test is operating the program, it displays a map of the disk (Figure 11-21), that represents the current state of the disk sectors. The map shows the clusters as blocks that represent a number of sectors. The ratio of sectors to blocks is based on the total number of sectors on the disk. Sectors that are marked as bad appear with a B.

> *Since a block usually represents more than one sector, a B is displayed when one or more sectors in that block are marked bad. Keep in mind that a B does not necessarily mean that all the sectors in that block are bad.*

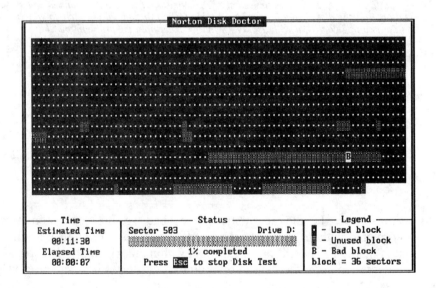

Figure 11-21 Sector test displays map of disk while operating.

At the bottom of the display the program shows the estimated time it will take to complete the entire defective sector test and the amount of time that has elapsed so far. If a large number of bad sectors are encountered, the program will lengthen the estimated time accordingly. The time estimate is useful if you want to run the test in the automatic mode while you do something else, since it gives you a rough idea of how long the computer will be tied up.

The center of the bottom panel represents the amount of the test completed by a white bar and a percentage. You can stop the test at any time by pressing [Esc].

Bad Sectors

When the defective sector test encounters a bad sector, the program has two options that it can use to correct the problem. If the sector is not part of a cluster that is part of an active file, it can simply mark the cluster as unusable. This prevents future files from using this cluster, thus avoiding data loss.

If you are operating in the manual mode, the program displays a window, such as the one in Figure 11-22 The window allows you to choose whether you want to mark the cluster as bad, ignore the problem, or mark the cluster as bad and continue in the automatic mode.

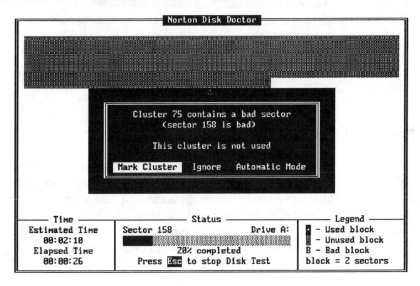

Figure 11-22 Bad sector in unused cluster.

If the data cluster is currently in use by a file, the program displays a window, such as the one in Figure 11-23, which tells you the name of the file involved, as well as the cluster and sector numbers.

In this case, you have the option of allowing the program to copy as much of the cluster's data as possible, to an unused cluster on the disk. You also have the option of skipping this sector, leaving the endangered cluster as it is. You might select to ignore the error so you can exit the program and examine the cluster with the Main Norton Utilities. This will give you a detailed idea of exactly what data has been lost.

If you select the automatic mode, this cluster and any others with errors will be automatically corrected.

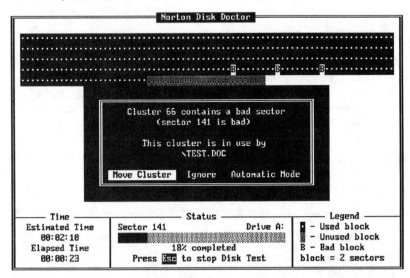

Figure 11-23 Bad sector in cluster use by file.

The Norton Disk Doctor Report

When the defective sector report has been completed (or terminated by pressing [Esc], the program will display a window that asks if you want to generate a report (Figure 11-24). The report is important because it summarizes all the tests and corrections taken by the NDD program during this session.

If you select to create a report, you can choose to send the data to the printer or to a text file. A a general rule, you should always create a report if the program has had to make corrections.

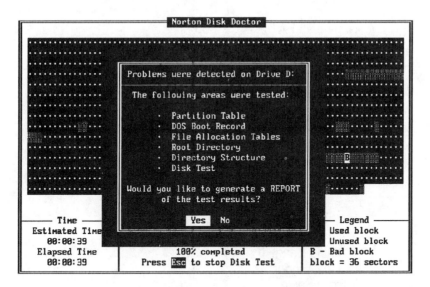

Figure 11-24 Report generation option.

Below is a sample report that contains examples of the information reported from a NDD session.

Norton Disk Doctor
Advanced Edition 4.50
Thursday, September 28, 1989 3:29 pm
****

* Report for Drive A: *
****

DISK TOTALS

362,496 bytes Total Disk Space
9,216 bytes in Bad Sectors
353,280 bytes Available on the Disk
LOGICAL DISK INFORMATION

Media Description: FDh
Large Partition: No
FAT Type: 12-bit
Total Sectors: 720
Total Clusters: 354
Bytes Per Sector: 512
Sectors Per Cluster: 2
Bytes Per Cluster: 1,024

Number of FATs: 2
First Sector of FAT: 1
Number of Sectors Per FAT: 2
First Sector of Root Dir: 5
Number of Sectors in Root Dir: 7
Maximum Root Dir File Entries: 112
First Sector of Data Area: 12

PHYSICAL DISK INFORMATION

Drive Number: 0h
Heads: 2
Cylinders: 40
Sectors Per Track: 9
Starting Head: 0
Starting Cylinder: 0
Starting Sector: 1
Ending Head: 1
Ending Cylinder: 39
Ending Sector: 9

SYSTEM AREA STATUS

No Errors in the System Area

FILE STRUCTURE STATUS

No Errors in the File Structure

DISK TEST STATUS

Error reading Sector 158 in Cluster 75
Cluster 75 currently not in use
Status: NOT Corrected; Skipped

Error reading Sector 365 in Cluster 178
Cluster 178 was not used
Status: Corrected; Marked as Unusable

Error reading Sector 303 in Cluster 147
Cluster 147 was used by file: \TEST.DOC
  Contents relocated to cluster 343
Status: Corrected; Marked as Unusable

Error reading Sector 330 in Cluster 161
Cluster 161 was used by file: \TEST.DOC
  Contents relocated to cluster 346
Status: Corrected; Marked as Unusable

Error reading Sector 438 in Cluster 215
  Cluster in use by file: \TEST.DOC
  Status: NOT Corrected; Skipped

Command Line Operation

The NDD program can be used in the command line mode to perform disk analysis automatically. When executing the NDD in the command line mode, you must use one of two switches.

- **Quick.** This switch limits the operations of the program to the boot record, directory, and lost clusters tests.

- **Complete.** This option includes the defective sector test, along with the boot record, directory, and lost clusters tests. The program runs in the automatic correction mode. No report is issued.

The command below executes the NDD, running a complete set of tests on drive C.

NDD c:/COMPLETE

Keep in mind that errors encountered in the Directory/FAT test will cause the program to pause and display a message window.

The NDD is unusual in that it can accept more than one drive specification at a time, allowing you to test more than one drive with a single command. The example below performs a quick test on drives C, D, and E.

NDD c: d: e:/QUICK

Other Norton Disk Doctor Options

The second option on the Norton Disk Doctor main menu is labeled **Common Solutions.** This option contains three operations that fix some specific disk problems. The menu is shown in Figure 11-25.

- **Make a Disk Bootable.** A bootable diskette is one that can be used to start an MS-DOS system. To be bootable, a disk must contain the three files that comprise the basic DOS system: IO.SYS, MSDOS.SYS, and COMMAND.COM.

> *The names of the files may be different under different manufacturers versions of DOS.*

> However, it is not sufficient that these files be on the disk. In order to function in the boot-up procedure, the IO.SYS and MSDOS.SYS files must be in a specific location on the disk. Unlike almost all other files, these files are position-sensitive. They must be stored as the first two files on the disk. Note that COMMAND.COM is an exception. It is treated like a normal DOS file. It can reside anywhere on the disk.
>
> If a disk is empty, then you can use the DOS SYS command to transfer the system files to the correct locations on the disk. However, if there is a file already using any of the clusters at the beginning of the disk, SYS will fail.
>
> The NDD option solves this problem by automatically moving any data store in the clusters required by DOS to another disk location, and then copying the three files needed to make a bootable disk to the correct locations.

> *The Safe Format program can be used to create a disk that leaves room for the system files at the beginning of the disk, without actually copying the files. This option is used when you want to distribute programs on a disk that can be made bootable because you do not have a license to distribute MS-DOS along with your program or data.*

- **Recover from DOS's RECOVER.** The DOS RECOVER command often creates a problem because it is used by people who do not know how it works and what it will or will not do. The program's name gives users the incorrect impression that it performs data recovery operations, like those performed by the Norton Disk Doctor or Quick Unerase programs. This is not the case. Recover does not diagnose bad sectors, nor does it recover erased files.

RECOVER was designed to group together data chains into files. The program can be applied to a file, group of files, or an entire disk. The program will look through the FAT and create a file out of every group of consecutive data clusters, called chains, and write a directory entry for each chain. The filenames in the directory will be FILE0000.REC, FILE0001.REC, and so on.

The problem with RECOVER is that it is not designed to discriminate between valid files and lost cluster chains. For example, suppose drive A contained a normal disk and you entered the command **RECOVER a:**.

The RECOVER command would erase all the filenames and directories and rewrite a list of files, FILE####.REC, into the root directory. Each file would contain a single chain of data clusters. In this case, RECOVER would destroy a perfectly fine disk. This would not happen with the Norton Utilities Disk Test or NDD program because they would respect the normal files.

If RECOVER is so bad why is it included? RECOVER was designed to provide a way to access a file in parts, if a bad cluster occurred within the file. For example, suppose the file MEMO.DOC used 15 consecutive data clusters. In attempting to read the file, the seventh cluster was unreadable. In most applications the program would simply stop at that cluster even though cluster 8 through 15 might be readable. If RECOVER was used on that file it would create two new files, FILE0000.REC containing clusters 1 through 6, and FILE0001.REC containing clusters 8 through 15. By loading file FILE0001.REC you could gain access to the end of the file.

The Norton Utilities programs provide far better tools than RECOVER for dealing with disk problems. In general, you should avoid RECOVER. However, if a disk is accidentally decimated by RECOVER, this option will be able to repair some or all of the damage. Note that this option cannot restore the original filenames to files stored in the root directory of the disk. Files stored in subdirectories can usually be recovered more successfully.

- **Revive a Defective Disk.** This option can be used only with floppy disks. It performs roughly the same operation as the defective sectors test run in the automatic mode. The operation rewrites the low-level format of the floppy disk while marking and where necessary moving bad clusters.

A similar result can be obtained by using the Safe Format program to format the disk and restoring the data with the Format Recover program.

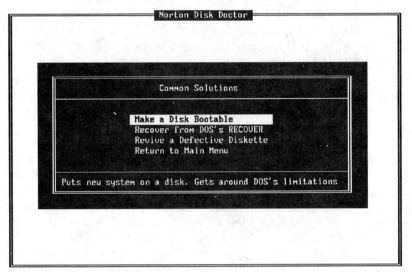

Figure 11-25 Common Solutions menu.

Main Norton Utilities Maintenance Mode

Most data errors can be handled by the more or less automatic operation of the NDD Disk Test programs. However, you can use the Main Norton Utilities program to access directly the information stored in sectors that are marked as bad or that create errors, even if the disk directory is bad.

The Main Norton Utilities program can be operated in the *maintenance* mode. In this mode the program does not attempt to read the logical information from the disk, such as the directory or File Allocation Table. This allows the program to operate on a disk that has an unreadable directory. If you ran the Main Norton Utilities program in the normal mode, an error in reading the disk directory would cause the program to terminate.

In the *maintenance* mode, options that require logical disk information such as the Unerase options are not available. The program is basically reduced to one that allows you to display disk data by selecting a sector or cluster by number.

As an example, suppose that in running the Disk Test or NDD program you discover that cluster 75 shows up as having a disk error. If the information in that cluster is of particular importance you might want to see the exact extent of the damage, on a byte-by-byte basis. Load the Main Norton Utilities program in the maintenance mode by using the /M switch.

NU/M

Use the Explore Disk options to select cluster 75 for display. When the program attempts to read the bad cluster, it will display an error message (Figure 11-26).

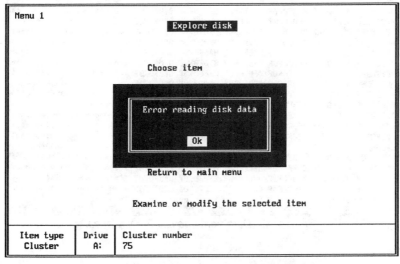

Figure 11-26 Error encountered when reading cluster.

The message tells you that the data you are about to see is corrupted. In order to make a clear illustration of what happens to a disk when errors occur, the disk used for Figure 11-27 was set up with the WIPEDISK program so that every byte contained the value for the letter A. This was done with the following command:

WIPEDISK a:/V65

The disk error was created by placing a small magnet very close to the disk surface. The Disk Test program was run to determine which disk clusters were corrupted by the magnet.

When the cluster is loaded you can see in Figure 11-27 that the first 27 bytes contain the letter A. This means that this section of the sector is not affected by the error. However, at byte 27 characters that were not part of the data originally placed on the disk begin to appear. The majority of the sector shows the wrong values, 0F, where there should have been A.

It is interesting to note that the disk errors may create a slightly different display each time it is loaded.

Once inspected, you might want to preserve the part of the cluster that you observed. You can use the **Write to Disk** option to copy the data into a file, preferably on another disk.

```
┌ Cluster 75 ══════════════════════════════════════ Hex format ═┐
│ Cluster 75, Sectors 158-159                          Offset 511, hex 1FF
│41414141 41414141 41414141 41414141 41414141 41414141 AAAAAAAAAAAAAAAAAAAAAAAA
│41414141 41414141 41414140 41410249 AC439E20 8F0F0F0F AAAAAAAAAAA@AABI¼CR Å•••
│0F0F0F0F 0F0F0F0F 0F0F0F0F 0F0F0F0F 0F0F0F0F 0F0F0F0F ••••••••••••••••••••••••
│0F0F0F0F 0F0F0F0F 0F0F0F0F 0F0F0F0F 0F0F0F0F 0F0F0F0F ••••••••••••••••••••••••
│0F0F0F0F 0F0F0F0F 0F0F0F0F 0F0F0F0F 0F0F0F0F 0F0F0F0F ••••••••••••••••••••••••
│0F0F0F0F 0F0F0F0F 0F0F0F0F 0F0F0F0F 0F0F0F0F 0F0F0F0F ••••••••••••••••••••••••
│0F0F0F0F 0F0F0F0F 0F0F0F0F 0F0F0F0F 0F0F0F0F 0F0F0F0F ••••••••••••••••••••••••
│0F0F0F0F 0F0F0F0F 0F0F0F0F 0F0F0F0F 0F0F0F0F 0F0F0F0F ••••••••••••••••••••••••
│0F0F0F0F 0F0F0F0F 0F0F0F0F 0F0F0F0F 0F0F0F0F 0F0F0F0F ••••••••••••••••••••••••
│0F0F0F0F 0F0F0F0F 0F0F0F0F 0F0F0F0F 0F0F0F0F 0F0F0F0F ••••••••••••••••••••••••
│0F0F0F0F 0F0F0F0F 0F0F0F0F 0F0F0F0F 0F0F0F0F 0F0F0F0F ••••••••••••••••••••••••
│0F0F0F0F 0F0F0F0F 0F0F0F0F 0F0F0F0F 0F0F0F0F 0F0F0F0F ••••••••••••••••••••••••
│0F0F0F0F 0F0F0F0F 0F0F0F0F 0F0F0F0F 0F0F0F0F 0F0F0F0F ••••••••••••••••••••••••
│0F0F0F0F 0F0F0F0F 0F0F0F0F 0F0F0F0F 0F0F0F0F 0F0F0F0F ••••••••••••••••••••••••
│0F0F0F0F 0F0F0F0F 0F0F0F0F 0F0F0F0F 0F0F0F0F 0F0F0F0F ••••••••••••••••••••••••
│0F0F0F0F 0F0F0F0F 0F0F0F0F 0F0F0F0F 0F0F0F0F 0F0F0F0F ••••••••••••••••••••••••
│0F0F0F0F 0F0F0F0F 0F0F0F0F 0F0F0F0F 0F0F0F0F 0F0F0F0F ••••••••••••••••••••••••
│0F0F0F0F 0F0F0F0F 0F0F0F0F 0F0F0F0F 0F0F0F0F 0F0F0F0F ••••••••••••••••••••••••
│0F0F0F0F 0F0F0F0F 0F0F0F0F 0F0F0F0F 0F0F0F0F 0F0F0F0F ••••••••••••••••••••••••
│0F0F0F0F 0F0F0F0F         Press Enter to continue     •••••••□
│1Help   2Hex   3Text   4Dir   5FAT   6Partn  7      8Choose 9Undo  10QuitNU
```
Figure 11-27 Data from bad cluster displayed.

Summary

The programs discussed in this chapter provide a means of finding and correcting disk errors.

- **Disk Text.** This program examines the disk to determine if any of the clusters contain disk errors. The program can search by disk cluster and/or file order. Bad clusters that fall in the unused area of the disk are marked as bad. If the /M switch is used, bad clusters that are in use by a file are copied as correctly as possible to a good, unused data cluster.

- **Norton Disk Doctor.** This program performs a variety of tests to find and correct disk problems. The program will handle logical problems, such as lost cluster chains, and physical problems, such as unreadable sectors. The program can be used to mark clusters with unreadable sectors as bad, or move the data if the bad sector falls the active file area. The program also has the ability to recover disks ruined by the DOS

RECOVER program, create a bootable disk from a disk that already contains data, or reformat a floppy disk without erasing the data.

- **Maintenance Mode Main Norton Utilities.** The maintenance mode can be used to access clusters or sectors, even on disks that have errors in the directory and FAT areas.

Section V

Additional Programs

In addition to the programs included in the Norton Utilities package, Version 4.5, Peter Norton Computing also publishes three programs that can help you improve and enhance your computing environment. This section of the book describes these additional programs:

Chapter 12-The Norton Commander
Chapter 13-The Norton Editor
Chapter 14-The Norton Guides

12

The Norton Commander

The Norton Commander is a program that falls into the classification of an operating system *shell* program. *Shell* programs provide the user with an alternative environment to the interface presented by the DOS program COMMAND.COM. When the Norton Commander is running you can carry out common operations such as listing directories, copying, or deleting files with *point and shoot* methods rather than by entering DOS command lines. The Norton Commander provides an interactive, visual display in which files and file operations can be selected using function keys or pull-down menus.

In addition to standard DOS operations, the Norton Commander provides other functions that go far beyond what can be performed with DOS commands. Many of the design and functional elements found in the Norton Commander are drawn from parts of the Norton Utilities programs. If you have used the Norton Utilities you will find that you understand and know how to use many of the Norton Commander's features already.

For many users the Norton Commander can replace the DOS interface so that they may never have to enter another DOS command. In this chapter the main features of Version 3.0 of the Norton Commander will be described and illustrated.

The Philosophy of the Commander

The purpose of the Norton Commander is to provide an alternative way in which PC users can perform operations that need to be carried out on a daily basis. The DOS interface created by the COMMAND.COM program provided with DOS has a number of limitations.

- **Directory Listings.** One of the primary functions of the user interface of any operating system is the management of files. However, DOS is extremely limited in the amount and style of information it can provide about files. A shell program that supersedes DOS should provide more and more varied ways of looking at the files and directories available to the user.

- **Access to Files.** While DOS lists the names of files, it provides only limited ways in which you can look at the contents of those files. A shell program should provide additional means by which you can inspect the contents of files without having to load them into an application.

- **Linking Data Files with Applications.** The limited directory structure of DOS does not permit the recording of links between applications and the data files they create. For example, files with WK1 extensions are usually spreadsheet files created with Lotus 1-2-3 Version 2, 2.01, or 2.2. It would be useful if you could load and execute a program by selecting a data file created by that program.

- **Mouse Support.** DOS Versions 3.3 and earlier do not provide support for the use of a mouse. Mouse operations could greatly aid file management tasks.

The Norton Commander program addresses these basic concerns, along with a number of other useful features that can dramatically improve the productivity of anyone using a DOS-based computer.

Visual Display Interface

One of the most obvious and important structures in the Norton Commander is the use of *visual display panels*. The *panels* are used to display and select files and/or directories. When the Norton Commander is first loaded, it displays a single panel, (Figure 12-1) which occupies most of the right half of the screen. The panel lists the directory names (uppercase letters) and files (lowercase letters) stored in the current directory.

In adition to the file display panel, the Norton Commander has three other elements that contribute to the information provided by the display.

- **Mini Status.** At the bottom of the file display panel is the mini status box. The box shows information (size, date, and time) about the file or directory currently highlighted.

- **DOS prompt and cursor.** The Norton Commander also displays the DOS prompt with a cursor, at the bottomleft corner of the screen. This prompt functions just as the standard DOS prompt does. You can enter and execute any valid DOS command here. The Commander thus is able to combine standard DOS operations with the interactive panel display.

- **Function key bar.** The bottom line of the display is a bar listing the Norton Commander operations that can be executed with the ten function keys.

Table 12-1 Function Bar Commands

[F1]	On screen help
[F2]	Activate user-defined menu
[F3]	View highlighted file
[F4]	Edit highlighted file
[F5]	Copy files
[F6]	Move or rename files
[F7]	Create a new directory
[F8]	Delete files or directories
[F9]	Activate pull down menus
[F10]	Exit Norton Commander

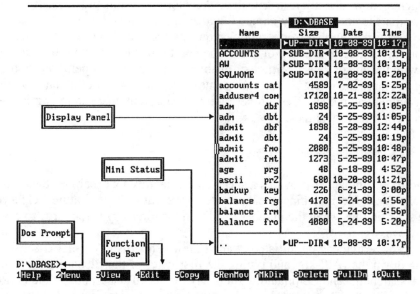

Figure 12-1 Norton Commander single panel display.

Selecting Items

The Norton Commander display is not simply a list of files and directories, but an interactive display in which the highlight in the panel can be used to scroll through the file and directory names. The primary advantage of the panel display is that it will remain on the screen, even when you execute a Norton Commander or DOS operation.

You can change the active directory by selecting any of the directory names. Selection can be done in two ways.

- **Cursor keys.** The $\uparrow$, $\downarrow$, $\leftarrow$, $\rightarrow$, Pg Up, Pg Dn, Home, and End keys can be used to position the highlight on the name of a directory or the [..] symbol (parent directory). Pressing $\hookleftarrow$ will activate the highlighted directory.

- **Mouse.** If you are using a mouse, you can select a directory by double-clicking the directory name or the [..] symbol to activate the parent directory.

When a new directory is selected, the Norton Commander reads it and displays the file and directory names found in it. The interactive display can be used to perform a number of operations requiring the specifications of filenames, directory names, or of a group of files. The ability to select an item by pointing, either with the cursor keys or a mouse, enables you to perform operations without having to enter file, directory, or path names. Selecting items eliminates a great deal of typing and reduces the number of errors caused by inaccurate or mistyped filenames or directory names.

Speed Search

The Norton Commander provides a speed search facility that searches the current directory for a file matching the characters you enter. This feature helps you locate specific files when the number of files in the directory is too large to easily scan by eye.

A speed search can be initiated at any time when a display panel is active by holding down the [Alt] key and typing the first letter of the filenames for which you are searching. The Command will display the speed search box at the bottom panel, showing the character or characters you are searching for, and at the same time, position the highlight to the firstfile name in the directory that matches the search character or characters. If there are no matches, the Command will not display the character in the speed search box. If you want to narrow the search, you can enter more characters, e.g., in Figure 12-2 the letters *cu* are used to locate the first file in the directory that matches those characters. You can include file extensions as part of the speed search by following the DOS convention of entering a period followed by the extension.

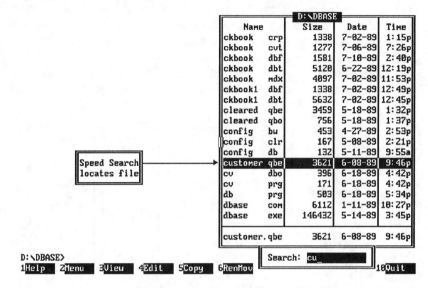

Figure 12-2 Speed search locates matching file.

Alternative Display

The visual display created by the display panels is a central theme in the organization of the Norton Commander interface. In order to afford the user the greatest possible functionality, the Norton Commander provides a number of alternative ways in which the display panels can be used.

Dual Panels

The initial Norton Commander display, which is set up when the program is installed, uses a single panel that covers the right half of the screen. However, you can select to display a second panel on the left side of the screen.

There are two ways in which you can take advantage of the program's ability to display more than one panel. You can use the [Tab] key to switch between panels.

- **Different Directories.** The Norton Commander can display information from different disk directories in each panel. The directories can even be on different disks. If you are operating on a network, the Norton Commander will allow you to select from any of the logical drives currently active on the system. Figure 12-3 shows the root directories of two different drives, drive E in the left panel and drive D in the right panel. In addition to displaying the contents of two different directories, the Norton Commander can use panels to copy or move files between the directories indicated by the panels, using one panel as the source directory and the other as the destination directory. This allows you to perform operations such as copying files without having to manually enter any drive or file names.

```
┌─────────────── E:\ ───────────────┐┌─────────────── D:\ ───────────────┐
│   Name   │   Name    │   Name     ││   Name    │   Name    │    Name    │
│CC        │WINDOWS    │mn      bat ││123        │treeinfo ncd│           │
│DBASE     │WORD5      │mouse   sys ││CAM        │           │           │
│DBNETCTL 300│WORKS    │move    bat ││CFAX       │           │           │
│DOS       │WP50       │move1   bat ││DBASE      │           │           │
│DU        │Frecover idx│move2  bat ││DBNETCTL 300│          │           │
│DUC       │appoint app│movefile bat││DOS        │           │           │
│HSG       │buzzer  snd│moveit  bat ││FW         │           │           │
│LANTASTI  │cl      bat│movex   bat ││HSG        │           │           │
│LANTASTI NET│clock dat│movexx  bat ││IN         │           │           │
│LOTUS     │config  one│mw      ini ││NORTON     │           │           │
│MSWORD    │du      bat│mx      bat ││NU         │           │           │
│NG        │filelist bat│net_inco prt││PARADOX3  │           │           │
│NU        │frecover bak│net_inco tbl││SCAN      │           │           │
│PAGE      │frecover dat│net_inco txt││SIERRA    │           │           │
│PH        │himem   sys│net_inco uks││TOM       │           │           │
│TOM       │loan_pay txt│notes      ││TU         │           │           │
│TYPESET   │main    bat│notes   bak ││WINDOWS    │           │           │
│VENTURA   │main    mnu│phone   bak ││WORD5      │           │           │
├──────────┴───────────┴────────────┤├───────────┴───────────┴───────────┤
│NU        ►SUB-DIR◄ 10-08-89 10:26p ││123       ►SUB-DIR◄ 10-12-89 10:34p│
└────────────────────────────────────┘└────────────────────────────────────┘
E:\>
1Left  2Right  3View..  4Edit..  5      6      7Find  8Histry  9EGA Ln  10Tree
```

Figure 12-3 Dual panels shows different directories.

- **Different Views.** Another use for dual panels is to display different information in one or the other panel. The panels can differ in two respects. One is the order in which files and directories are displayed. You can select to display items by name, extension, time and date, size, or the actual order in which they appear in the disk directory. This means you might select to display one panel by date and time order, while the other panel lists items by name order. The time order is useful in determining which files have been most recently added to the directory.

  In addition to changes in the order of listing, the Norton Commander allows you to select a different type of panel display: brief, full, info, tree, or quick view.

Display Panel Types

You can select one of five different types of display modes to use in either of the
display panels. Each different view displays the disk data in a different manner.

- **Brief**. The *brief display* mode is the default mode used by the Norton
  Commander. In this mode the panel is divided into three columns. The
  columns are filled with the names of the directories and files listed in the
  active directory. This display has the advantage of showing the largest
  number of items at one time.

Name	Name		Name	
CC	WINDOWS		mn	bat
DBASE	WORD5		mouse	sys
DBNETCTL 300	WORKS		move	bat
DOS	WP50		move1	bat
DU	Frecover	idx	move2	bat
DUC	appoint	app	movefile	bat
HSG	buzzer	snd	moveit	bat
LANTASTI	cl	bat	movex	bat
LANTASTI NET	clock	dat	movexx	bat
LOTUS	config	one	mw	ini
MSWORD	du	bat	mx	bat
NG	filelist	bat	net_inco	prt
NU	frecover	bak	net_inco	tbl
PAGE	frecover	dat	net_inco	txt
PH	himem	sys	net_inco	wks
TOM	loan_pay	txt	notes	
TYPESET	main	bat	notes	bak
VENTURA	main	mnu	phone	bak
NU	▶SUB-DIR◀ 10-08-89 10:26p			

Figure 12-4 Brief panel display.

- **Full**. The full-display mode divides the panel into four columns. The first
  column displays the name of the file or directory. The other columns
  show the size, date, and time for that file, as shown in Figure 12-5. This
  display provides you with more data about each file or directory, but
  reduces the number of items that can be displayed at one time.

Name		Size	Date	Time
..		►UP--DIR◄	10-08-89	10:17p
ACCOUNTS		►SUB-DIR◄	10-08-89	10:19p
AW		►SUB-DIR◄	10-08-89	10:19p
SQLHOME		►SUB-DIR◄	10-08-89	10:20p
accounts	cat	4589	7-02-89	5:25p
adduser4	com	17120	10-21-88	12:22a
adm	dbf	1898	5-25-89	11:05p
adm	dbt	24	5-25-89	11:05p
admit	dbf	1898	5-28-89	12:44p
admit	dbt	24	5-25-89	10:19p
admit	fmo	2080	5-25-89	10:48p
admit	fmt	1273	5-25-89	10:47p
age	prg	48	6-18-89	4:52p
ascii	pr2	680	10-20-88	11:21p
backup	key	226	6-21-89	9:00p
balance	frg	4178	5-24-89	4:56p
balance	frm	1634	5-24-89	4:56p
balance	fro	4080	5-24-89	5:20p
..		►UP--DIR◄	10-08-89	10:17p

Figure 12-5 Full panel display.

- **Info.** This display mode presents a statistical summary of memory and disk usage, as shown in Figure 12-6. The summary includes:

      Total conventional memory
      Total conventional memory free
      Total disk space on current drive
      Total unused space on current drive
      Total number of files in current directory
      Total bytes used by current directory's files
      Name of current directory

```
╔═════════════════ D:\DBASE\SQLHOME ══════════╗╔═══════════════ Info ══════════════╗
║     Name      │ Size │  Date   │  Time  ║║ The Norton Commander, Version 3.0 ║
║..             │►UP--DIR◄│10-08-89│10:20p║║ Copyright (C) 1986-9 by Peter Norton║
║catalog   cat  │   607│ 4-19-89│ 2:30p║║                                    ║
║dirinfo        │   187│10-18-89│ 5:34p║║     655,360 Bytes Memory           ║
║sqldbase  str  │   194│10-20-88│11:22p║║       433,872 Bytes Free           ║
║sysauth   dbf  │  1156│10-20-88│11:22p║║ 78,020,608 total bytes on drive D: ║
║syscolau  dbf  │   226│10-20-88│11:22p║║ 17,137,664 bytes free on drive D:  ║
║syscols   dbf  │  5586│10-20-88│11:22p║║   17 files use 131,072 bytes in    ║
║sysdbs    dbf  │   254│ 5-26-89│10:29a║║        D:\DBASE\SQLHOME            ║
║sysidxs   dbf  │   418│10-20-88│11:22p║║                                    ║
║syskeys   dbf  │   226│10-20-88│11:22p║║ SQLHOME directory:                 ║
║syssyns   dbf  │   163│10-20-88│11:22p║║                                    ║
║systabls  dbf  │  1094│10-20-88│11:22p║║ Used by dBASE IV to store databases║
║systime   mem  │    41│10-20-88│11:22p║║ that function as SQL system tables ║
║systimes  dbf  │   427│10-20-88│11:22p║║ for dBASE IV SQL.                  ║
║sysvdeps  dbf  │   270│10-20-88│11:22p║║                                    ║
║sysviews  dbf  │   258│10-20-88│11:22p║║ SYSCOLS.DBF  - holds all field specs║
║untitled  cat  │  2417│ 4-19-89│ 2:33p║║ SYSTABLS.DBF - holds tables names  ║
║                                       ║║                                    ║
║..             │►UP--DIR◄ 10-08-89 10:20p║                                    ║
╚═══════════════════════════════════════╝╚═══════════════════════════════════╝
D:\DBASE\SQLHOME>
1Left   2Right  3View.. 4Edit.. 5      6      7Find  8Histry 9EGA Ln 10Tree
```

Figure 12-6 Info display panel mode.

Another feature of the Info mode is the display of a directory **information** text. The text appears in the bottom portion of the Info panel. The info text, such as that appearing in Figure 12-6, is drawn from a text file called DIRINFO. The text is used to identify the contents of the displayed directory.

This file can be created in the Norton Commander by using the Edit command, [F4], while the Info panel is selected. You can then type in as much comment text as desired. The Norton Commander will automatically store it in a DIRINFO file in the current directory. The file is a standard ASCII text file, which can be created with any ASCII editor or word processor.

If there is no DIRINFO file in a directory, the program will display the message **No dirinfo file in this directory** in the bottom half of the info panel. A DIRINFO file should be placed in each directory for which you want to display Info text.

Note that when dual panels are active, an Info panel is synchronized with the directory shown in the other panel. This means that both panels will always reflect information about the same directory when one of the panels is in the Info display mode. If the directory is changed in one panel, the Info panel automatically updates for the new directory.

> *The Brief and Full modes allow you to view data from different directories at the same time.*

- **Tree.** The tree mode displays a directory tree, shown in Figure 12-7, similar to the tree display created by the Norton Change Directory program. When the Tree panel is active, you can use the ↑ and ↓ keys to move the highlight to any branch of the directory tree. As you highlight the directory names on the tree, the Norton Commander automatically activates that directory. This means if there is another panel active in the Brief, Full, or Info modes, the panel will display the information for the selected directory.

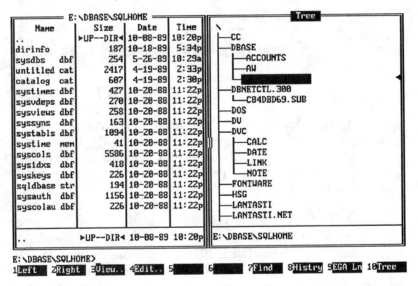

Figure 12-7 Tree structure panel display.

As with the Info display mode, the Tree mode panel is always synchronized with the other panel. Changes in the selected directory in either panel will be reflected in both panel displays.

- **Quick View.** The Quick View mode links the file names highlighted in a Brief or Full mode panel, with the display of their contents in an adjacent Quick View panel, as shown in Figure 12-8. The Quick View mode uses the Norton Commander's view feature, discussed on page 456, to format data created by database, spreadsheet, or word processing applications, as well as ASCII text files. Files with EXE or COM extension and graphics files are not automatically displayed.

```
┌──────────────── E:\DBASE\SQLHOME ──────────┬───────────── dBASE View ═══════════╗
│    Name     │  Size   │  Date   │  Time    ║  Colname  TBNAME                    ║
│ ..          │►UP--DIR◄│10-08-89 │10:20p    ║    Tbname  SYSTABLS                 ║
│dirinfo      │     187 │10-18-89 │ 5:34p    ║  Tbcreator  SYSTEM                  ║
│sysdbs   dbf │     254 │ 5-26-89 │10:29a    ║    Colno    1                       ║
│untitled cat │    2417 │ 4-19-89 │ 2:33p    ║   Coltype  C                        ║
│catalog  cat │     607 │ 4-19-89 │ 2:30p    ║   Collen   10                       ║
│systimes dbf │     427 │10-20-88 │11:22p    ║   Colscale  0                       ║
│sysvdeps dbf │     270 │10-20-88 │11:22p    ║     Nulls N                         ║
│sysviews dbf │     258 │10-20-88 │11:22p    ║   Colcard            0              ║
│syssyns  dbf │     163 │10-20-88 │11:22p    ║   Updates N                         ║
│systabls dbf │    1094 │10-20-88 │11:22p    ║  High2key          0                ║
│systime  mem │      41 │10-20-88 │11:22p    ║   Low2key          0                ║
│syscols  dbf │    5586 │10-20-88 │11:22p    ║                                     ║
│sysidxs  dbf │     418 │10-20-88 │11:22p    ║                                     ║
│syskeys  dbf │     226 │10-20-88 │11:22p    ║                                     ║
│sqldbase str │     194 │10-20-88 │11:22p    ║                                     ║
│sysauth  dbf │    1156 │10-20-88 │11:22p    ║                                     ║
│syscolau dbf │     226 │10-20-88 │11:22p    ║                                     ║
│                                            ║                                     ║
├────────────────────────────────────────── ╠═════════════════════════════════════╣
│syscols.dbf       5586 10-20-88 11:22p      ║syscols.dbf        5,586       1 / 76 ║
└────────────────────────────────────────── ╚═════════════════════════════════════╝
E:\DBASE\SQLHOME>
 1Left   2Right  3View.. 4Edit.. 5       6         7Find  8Histry 9EGA Ln 10Tree
```

Figure 12-8 Quick View panel.

The Quick View panel makes it possible to scroll through a list of files and inspect their contents at the same time. You would not need to run the database, spreadsheet, or word processing program in order to inspect the contents of the data files. Note that the [F3] key can be used to zoom the Quick View display to the Full-Screen View mode.

The five panel types can be mixed and matched to display a variety of different types of information about the disk, directory, and files you are working with. By using the panels effectively you can obtain a wide scope of information without having to run other applications.

Controlling the Panels

The Norton Commander provides two methods by which you can control the display panels.

- **Pull Down Menu.** The commands [F9] L or [F9] R can be used to display pull-down menus for the left or right panels, respectively, as shown in Figure 12-9. The menu allows you to select both the type of panel display and the order in which files should be listed. You can also change drives or reread the current drive to update the display. This feature is used primarily when you change floppy disks.

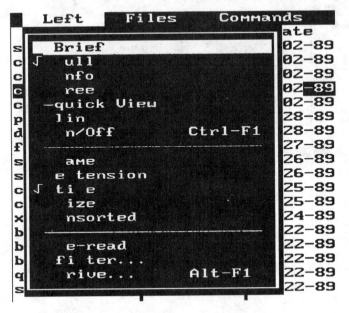

Figure 12-9 Pull-down menu for left panel.

- **Shortcut Command Keys.** The following special key commands are provided to speed panel operations.

Table 12-2 Panel Control Keys

[Alt/F1]	Select drive, left panel
[Ctrl/F1]	On/off left panel
[Alt/F2]	Select drive, right panel
[Ctrl/F2]	On/off right
[Ctrl/r]	Reread current drive
[Tab]	Switch active panels
[Ctrl/L]	On/off Info, inactive panel
[Ctrl/o]	On/off both panels, show DOS screen
[Ctrl/p]	On/off inactive panel
[Ctrl/q]	On/off Quick View, inactive panel
[Ctrl/u]	Swap left/right panels

Filtering Files

The Norton Commander allows you to *filter* the files used in panel displays. You can create two types of filters.

- **Executable Files.** This option limits the files used by the Brief, Full, or Info panels to program files, those with EXE or COM extensions, or DOS batch files with BAT extensions.

- **Custom Wildcard.** Files are selected on the basis of a DOS wildcard file specification, such as you would use with DOS or Norton Utilities commands, e.g., ***.DOC** would select only the files with a DOC extension.

The filter setting is selected by using the commands [F9] **L**eft fi**L**ter or the [F9] **R**ight fi**L**ter for the left or right panels, respectively. The command displays a dialog box, shown in Figure 12-10, which allows you to select among **All files**, the default setting, or the other specialized file filters.

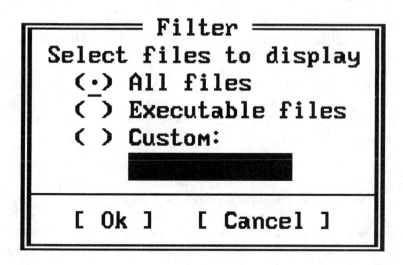

Figure 12-10 Select file filter dialog box.

Once a filter is selected, it will be maintained until specifically changed to another filter, or the normal setting, **All files**. With a filter set you can scan all the disk directories for only the selected files. This makes it much easier to find files because you have concentrated the display on a particular group of files.

Viewing File Contents

One area of file operations barely addressed by DOS is access to a file's contents. Since files can be created by any number of applications, DOS provides no way to quickly inspect the **contents** files. The only command related to this problem is the TYPE command, which will scroll the contents of an ASCII text file on the screen. However, most programs, even word processing programs, do not store data in standard ASCII text files with CR/LF characters at the end of each line.

This would not be a very significant problem if DOS filenames were not limited to 11 characters (including extensions). However, lists of 11 character file names make it very difficult for anyone to accurately remember what is contained in those files.

In most cases the only way to access the contents of the files is to load the application and load the file or files you are interested in inspecting. This process can be quite slow and tedious.

The Norton Commander provides extensive file view interpreters, which allow you to view, but not change, the data stored in files created by the most popular word processing, spreadsheet, and database programs. You can view file contents in two ways.

- **View File.** The command [F3] displays the contents of the file currently highlighted in the Full or Brief display modes.

- **Quick View.** In a dual panel display you can set one panel to the Quick View display mode. In this mode the first part of the contents of the highlighted file is displayed in the Quick View panel as you scroll through the file list.

With either method, the Norton Commander will attempt to automatically attempt to translate the data stored in the selected file into the proper word processing, spreadsheet, or database format.

The program uses the file extension and/or the structure of the file to determine how to display the information. The Norton Commander is supplied with library programs called 123VIEW.EXE, DBVIEW.EXE, PARAVIEW.EXE, PCXVIEW.EXE, RBVIEW.EXE, REFVIEW.EXE, and WPVIEW.EXE. These programs are invoked as needed to interpret the data stored in the file which has been selected for viewing. In most cases this process is automatic and the Norton Commander will select the correct format for viewing the file.

Text Files and Word Processing Files

The View command can be used to display files that store data in the ASCII text format. If the Norton Commander cannot identify the file or its format it will displays the contents as a standard text file.

The View mode can also display text from files created with the following word processing programs:

Table 12-3 View Word Processing Files

WordPerfect	Versions 4.2, 5.0
Microsoft Word	Versions 4.0, 5.0
Windows Write	All versions
Microsoft Works	All versions
XyWrite	All versions
WordStar Pro	All versions
WordStar 2000	All versions
Multimate	All versions

It is important to understand that the Norton Commander will display the text of the documents. However, all formatting codes, bold, underline, indents, centering, page breaks, etc. that appear in the original word processing document will not appear in the Norton Commander view display. The program simply ignores all the idiosyncratic formatting codes and picks out the text for display. The text lines are wrapped to the width of the screen to make reading easier.

Keep in mind that program files, EXE and COM extensions, will be treated as text files, even though they contain binary information. When displayed in the text mode, they will appear to display an incoherent series of characters.

The View display has four options.

- **Unwrap.** This option turns on/off the line wrapping feature of the Text View mode. In most cases, you want to leave the line wrap on so that long paragraphs are wrapped in lines, making the text easier to read. Some type of files, such as program source codes that use extensive indenting to indicate logical structures in the program code, may be easier to read if long lines are not wrapped. In this case you can use the [F2] key to toggle the line wrap feature off.

- **Hex.** You can display the file's contents in a hex number display similar to that used in the Main Norton Utilities program. The [F4] key toggles the display between text and hex formats.

- **Search.** The [F7] allows you to initiate a text search to locate a group of characters within the text file.

- **Viewer.** In cases where the Norton Commander does not select the correct display mode, you can select a different word processing format by pressing [F8]. Using the dialog box (Figure 12-11), you can select a view format that better suits the data being displayed.

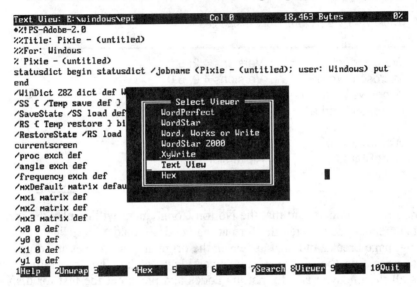

Figure 12-11 Select word processor format.

Spreadsheet Files

The Norton Commander can display spreadsheet data stored in files in a simulated spreadsheet display. You can scroll though the display from cells to cell. The status line will display the current value of the cell. If the cell value is the result of a formula, **(Formula)** will appear on the status line, along with the value to its maximum precision, as shown in Figure 12-12.

The Norton Commander can display spreadsheets stored in the following formats.

Table 12-4 Spreadsheet Formats for View

Lotus 1-2-3	Release 1.0 - 2.2
Symphony	Release 1.0 - 2.0

Excel   Version 1.0 - 2.2
Multiplan   Version 4.0
Quattro   All versions
Microsoft Works   All versions
Mosaic Twin   All versions
Words & Figures   All versions
VP-Planner   All versions

If you are using programs such as PFS Plan or Framework, you can convert spreadsheets to a 123 format, which can be displayed by the Norton Commander using the 123 format.

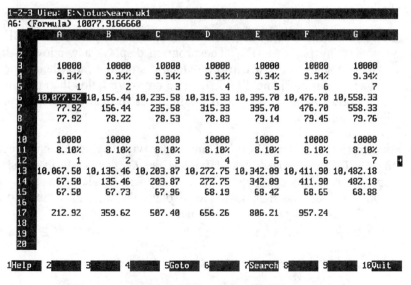

Figure 12-12 1-2-3 file viewed by Norton Commander.

The Spreadsheet View mode offers you the option of moving to a specific cell location, [F5] GOTO, or performing a search for data, [F7] Search. Note that since only data is displayed, you cannot search for formulas.

Database Files

The Norton Commander can provide you with the ability to display the data stored in database files created with a number of popular applications.

Table 12-5 Database Formats for View

dBASE	II, III, III+, IV
Foxbase	All versions
Clipper	All versions
Paradox	All versions
R:BASE	All versions
Microsoft Works	All versions
dBXL	All versions
Reflex	All versions

In addition to the [F5] Goto Record and [F7] Search commands, the database display includes:

- **Fields.** You can display the file structure, or in the case of R:BASE, file attributes, by pressing [F2]. The program displays a window over the database listing the fields in the database structure, and their type and size, as shown in Figure 12-13. If there are more fields than can fit into the window, the program scrolls the field list vertically to display all the file structure data.

- **Browse/Record.** The Norton Commander will display database records in two different modes. The default is the *Record* mode in which one record at a time is displayed. The [F4] key will toggle the display to the *Browse* mode. The *Browse* mode displays the data in a table format, revealing up to 20 records at one time.

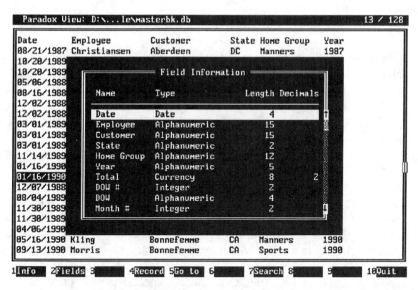

Figure 12-13 Database field window over browse display.

Editing Files

The Norton Commander can also be used to edit or create ASCII text files. This feature allows you to easily modify text files, such as the CONFIG.SYS, AUTOEXEC.BAT, or other batch files, without having to load a special editing or word processing program.

The editor is activated by highlighting the file you want to edit, then pressing [F4]. The editor can work with files that are up to 25,000 bytes in size. This should accommodate most batch files and many program language source code files.

> *The Edit command will attempt to load whatever file is highlighted, when you press [F4]. If the file is not an ASCII text file, the screen will display the data found in a text format, so far as that is possible. In most cases you would want to simply exit, [F10], without making any changes.*

When a file is loaded you can insert and delete text up to the file size limit of 25,000 bytes. In addition to editing, you can use the following commands.

- **[F2], Save.** Saves the edited file. The original file is overwritten.

- **[Shift/F2], Save New Name.** This option allows you to save the edited file under a new name. The original file remains unchanged.

- **[F7], Search.** Initiates a search within the text file.

- **[F10], Quit.** This command exits the Edit mode. If you have made changes but not saved the file, the program will prompt you to determine if you want to save or discard the changes.

- **[Shift/F10], Quit and Save.** This command saves the current text file and exits in a single step.

- **[Ctrl/q].** The **[Ctrl/q]** command is used to insert control or other nonkeyboard characters into a text file. Normally, [Ctrl] key combinations or the [Esc] key entered in the Edit mode are taken by the Norton Commander as commands. For example, [Esc] has the same effect as [F10], i.e., a command to exit the editor. However, there are special circumstances in which it is necessary to store [Ctrl], [Esc], or other nonkeyboard characters as part of a text file. The [Esc] character is typically used in text files that contain special printer code sequences used to implement special printer effects, such as bold or italic printing. For example, the character sequence [Esc]E turns on bold printing on many Epson or compatible dot matrix printers. If you wanted to include those characters as part of a text file you would need to find a way to enter [Esc] as a character instead of an instruction. This can be accomplished by using [Ctrl/q]. Following the entry of [Ctrl/q] the Norton Commander editor will allow you to enter a [Ctrl] character or [Esc] as part of the text. The keystrokes below insert [Esc]E into text.

[Ctrl/q][Esc]E

The [Esc] character is represented by a ← symbol in the text.

Using an External Editor

The editor built into the Norton Commander is adequate for most users needs. However, some users, might find the need for a more powerful editor. For example, if you are writing source code files in a computer language such as BASIC, dBASE, or Pascal, you would probably want an editor that has features like search and replace, copy and move text, and the ability to edit more than one file at a time-features found in the Norton Editor.

The Norton Commander allows you to integrate an external editor with the Norton Commander. An external editor is a word processing or text editing program.

To select an external editor, use the command [F9] **O**ptions **E**ditor:

e[F9] o e

The program displays the dialog box shown in Figure 12-14. The default setting is the internal editor. When you select an external editor, it is necessary to enter the name of the program you want to use as the external editor. In this example the Norton Editor is specified as the external editor by entering NE for NE.COM.

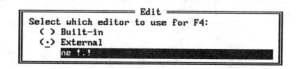

```
============ Edit ============
Select which editor to use for F4:
   ( ) Built-in
   (.) External
   ne !.!
```

Figure 12-14 Select external editing program.

Once you have selected an external editing program, that program will be invoked each time you use the [F4] Edit command. Since most external editors can handle files larger than 25,000 bytes (the Norton Editor can handle files of up to 256,000 bytes), the use of an external editor circumvents that limitation. Note that in order for the external editor to function there must be sufficient memory for both the Norton Commander and the external editor to be resident at the same time.

You can switch back to using the internal Norton Commander editor at any time by using the command **[F9] O E B**.

File Maintenance

The Norton Commander's panel display interface is more than just a display. It is an interactive operational mode in which the files and directories displayed in the panels (Brief and Full-mode displays) can be used to carry out file maintenance operations such as copy, move, and delete.

Copy

You can select a file to be copied from the Brief or Full-panel displays by highlighting the filename and pressing the [F5] key. The program will display a dialog box that allows you to specify how you would like the copying process to proceed. The contents of the dialog box vary, depending upon whether or not you have dual panels displayed in the Brief or Full modes.

- **One-Panel Copying.** When only one panel is in the Brief or Full display modes, the program inserts the current drive and directory name as the destination for the copy (Figure 12-15). Of course it would not make sense to attempt to copy a file into itself. You would need to edit the destination specification by changing the drive and/or the directory name. If you want to change the name of the file when it is copied, enter the new filename as well.

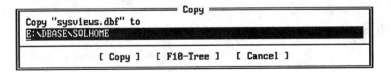

Figure 12-15 Copy file dialog box.

As an aid in selecting a directory name, you can press [F10] to display a directory tree of the current disk, as shown in Figure 12-16. You can select a destination directory by using the ↑ and ↓ keys, or the speed search to locate the desired directory. The Norton Commander will display a warning dialog box if the copying process threatens to overwrite an existing file.

> *The tree option will display only the tree of the source disk when a single-panel display is used.*

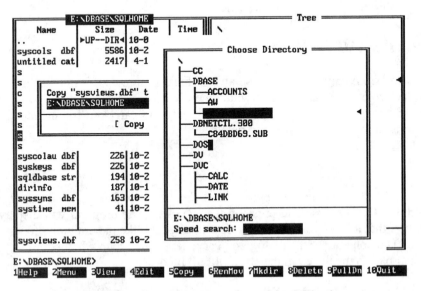

Figure 12-16 Directory tree used to select destination.

- **Dual-Panel Copying.** When two panels are used, the inactive panel is automatically selected as the destination. Using the active panel to select the source file and the inactive panel to indicate the destination, eliminates the need to make any manual entry. This is the fastest and most mistake-proof way to copy a file. The tree command, [F10], will display the directory tree of the destination drive so that you can easily select a different directory as the destination, if necessary.

Move and Rename

The move and rename functions are both executed using the command [F6]. The Norton Commander assumes that you want to rename a file if there is only one Brief or Full-display mode panel. If there are two panels displayed in the Brief or Full modes, the program assumes that you want to move the file to the location indicated by the inactive panel.

If the remaining or moving process would cause an existing file to be overwritten, the program will warn you with a dialog box that allows you to continue or terminate the operation.

- **Rename.** The rename operation changes the filename of the selected file but has no effect on its contents. The Norton Commander rename operation is much less cumbersome than the DOS RENAME command because you do not have to enter the full names of the source and destination files. If the new name is similar to the old name you can simply edit the current filename in the rename dialog box.

- **Move.** The move operation takes place when you select a different drive and/or directory for the destination. When a file is moved, it is deleted from its original location and placed into a new location.

> *Although it looks the same to the user, moving a file to a different drive requires a very different operation than does moving a file to a different directory on the same drive. When moving files on the same drive, the directory information about the file is copied into a different directory. The file itself remains in exactly the same location on the disk and no alterations are made to the File Allocation Table. When you move a file to a different disk, the Norton Commander actually performs two operations: a copy operation and delete operation. The file is first copied to the new disk and then deleted from the old disk. Unlike a move operation on a single disk, moving to a new disk actually requires the file itself to be rewritten. One significant result of this difference is that it takes much longer to move files between drives than it does to move files between directories on the same drive. Also keep in mind that when files are moved on the same drive you will never encounter a problem with disk space. However, when files are moved to a different disk, it is possible that you will not have sufficient disk space available on the destination disk to complete the operation.*

Delete

You can use the Norton Commander to delete the selected file using the command [F8]. If empty, you can also delete directories. Since files with hidden attributes appear in the panels marked with a ▓ character, you can also delete hidden files.

Tagging Files

The major file operations (copy, move, rename, and delete) can operate on groups of selected files. A group is determined by tagging files that appear in the panel display. There are two ways to tag files.

- **One by One.** You can tag or untag individual file names using the [Ins] key. The key toggles the selection status of the highlighted file from tagged to untagged each time it is pressed.

- **Logical groups.** The gray [+] allows you to tag all of the files in the current directory that match a wildcard specification. The gray [-] key will untag files according to a wildcard specification. The keystrokes shown below would select all of the batch files in the current directory.

[+]
*.bat ↵

> *Keep in mind that you can include or exclude individual files manually using the [Ins] after a group has been tagged or untagged.*

When you have completed the tagging operation, pressing [F5], [F6], or [F8] will perform the specified operation on all the tagged files.

If the operation requires an existing file to be overwritten, a dialog box will appear allowing you to select to overwrite the file, skip that file, or automatically overwrite all files.

Copying or Moving Files to Floppy Disks

The Norton Commander file copy procedure has a special advantage when you are copying files to a floppy disk. You can perform the same function with the DOS COPY command. However, if during the copying process the floppy disk gets filled, you are left with a problem. If you put another disk into the floppy drive, you do not know which of the files has already been copied to the first disk and which file remains to be copied.

If you run out of floppy disk space while using the Norton Commander Copy command, the panel will reflect all of the selected files that have not been copied yet. The files that have been successfully copied are automatically untagged. If you replace the disk in the floppy drive, you can continue copying the remaining files using [F5]. This makes it convenient to copy groups of files to a series of floppy disks, a task that would be very difficult with the DOS copy command.

Creating and Deleting Directories

The display panels can be used to create and delete directories as well as files. The [F7] command allows you to create a new directory as a subdirectory of the current directory.

You can also delete a directory by highlighting the directory name in the panel and using [F8]. Keep in mind that the directory **must** be empty in order to be able to complete a deletion. If the directory contains any files or other directories, a message will be displayed warning you that the directory is not empty and cannot be deleted.

You can only delete one directory at a time since the [Ins] key has no effect on a directory name.

Program Execution

The Norton Commander can use its panel displays to execute programs, as well as to perform file maintenance operations.

The Norton Commander provides two ways in which applications can be launched directly from the panel displays.

- **Executable Files.** You can execute any EXE, COM, or BAT file displayed in a Brief or Full-display panel by positioning the highlight to that file and pressing ↵. Keep in mind that when an application is loaded from the Norton Commander, there is about 13-16K less memory available for the application than there would be if you loaded the program directly from DOS.

- **Related Data Files.** The Norton Commander allows you to relate file extensions to the application that created those data files. You can execute an application by highlighting a data file and entering ↵. In order to take advantage of this feature you must create an *extension* file that specifies the data files which are deleted to the applications.

The Extension File

The Norton Commander has the ability to execute an application by selecting data files related to that application with the panel highlight, and pressing ↵. The programs that can be executed in this manner fall into two varieties.

- **Programs that Accept a File Argument.** A program that accepts a file *argument* will automatically load a specified file as soon as the program is loaded. This is quite common in the word processing field. WordStar, WordStar 2000, WordPerfect, and Micro SoftWord all accept file arguments. Multimate does not. For example, the commands listed below will run the specified programs and load the file, TEXT.DOC.

    ws text.doc
    ws2 text.doc
    wp text.doc
    word text.doc

    Among database programs, dBASE, Foxbase, and dBXL are some that will accept a program name as an argument. The following command will load dBASE and run a program named MENU.

    dbase menu

    Keep in mind that the argument for a database program is the name of an application, not the name of a data file. This implies that only users writing programs can take advantage of point and shoot execution.

    In the spreadsheet area, 1-2-3 does not accept an argument; however, Excel does. The command below loads Excel with the worksheet BUDGET.

    excel budget

- **Programs that do not accept file arguments.** Lotus 1-2-3 will not accept a filename as an argument. For example, the command below will **not** start 1-2-3 and load the SAMPLE.WK1 worksheet.

    123 sample

    In fact, the SAMPLE will be taken for a driver set name and the program will fail to load. Driver sets are used in 1-2-3 to specify hardware options such as screen displays.

If you are running an application that accepts a filename argument, you can tell the Commander to run the program and load the file, whenever you point at a data file with the correct extension and press ⏎.

If the related application does not accept a file argument, you can still run the program by pointing at a data file, but the application will not automatically load the file.

This effect is achieved by a special text file called **NC.EXT**. This file contains a list of file extensions and the DOS execution commands that should be related to those extensions. For example, files with a WK1 extension would be related to 123 Release 2.0, 2.01, and 2.2. The DOC extension is used by Microsoft Word, and the PRG extension is used by dBASE program files.

The NC.EXT file is a normal text file. It contains a list of extensions and the instructions for what program to run if the highlighted file matches one of the extensions. You can create the file by using a text editor or directly in the Norton Commander using the command **[F9]**. This command allows you to create a new extension file if none exists, or edit the existing extension file. Example:

[F9] c e

The command invokes a special mode of the Norton Commander editor. The file name NC.EXE is automatically assigned to the file and a special help screen appears at the bottom of the screen, as shown in Figure 12-17.

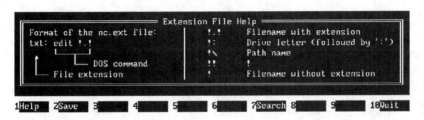

Figure 12-17 Extension file loaded into editor.

The extension file consists of a series of loading instructions. Each instruction relates a specific file extension to a loading instruction that tells the Norton Commander what program to execute when a file with the specified extension is selected. A loading instruction has the following form.

extension: program filespec

- **Extension**. The extension tells the Commander what files are related to which loading instructions. You can enter any three character file extensions or use DOS wildcards, * or ?, to represent characters.

- **Program.** The program is the name of an EXE, COM, or BAT file that is used to execute the application that is related to the specified extension.

- **Filespec.** The most unusual part of the loading instruction is the *filespec*. The extension file uses the ! as a special symbol to indicate how the file argument should be used.

The filespec can be used five different ways:

!   The ! used by itself tells the Norton Commander to insert the filename portion of the highlighted file as part of the file argument.

.!   This form causes the program to insert the file extension as part of the file argument.

!:   Inserts the current drive into the file argument.

!\   Inserts the current directory name into the file argument.

!!   Inserts the character ! into the file argument.

There is a wide variety of ways in which you can use these elements to create point and shoot execution. As a first example, take Lotus 1-2-3. This program does not accept a file argument, but you can still load the application from any of its data files, using the Norton Commander. 1-2-3 Version 1A uses the file extension WKS for all its files. A loading instruction for that program might look like this:

wks:123

The extension and the program name are separated by a colon. Release 2.01 and 2.2 of 1-2-3 can load files with extensions WKS and WK1. To accommodate both of those file types you might use a DOS wildcard character, ? or *, in the loading instruction. The following instruction would execute 123 if you select a file with an extension that begins with WK.

wk?:123

If the program is capable of accepting a file argument, you can use ! symbols to indicate how the highlighted file name should be used as an argument.

The most common type of file argument is one that uses the name of the file without a file extension. The application assumes that the file has the default file extension: DOC for Word, XLS for Excel, PRG for dBASE, etc. For example, dBASE assumes that any loading argument will have the standard dBASE program extension, PRG. A loading command for that program would look like this:

prg:dbase !

When a file with a PRG extension is selected, the Commander substitutes the filename, without the extension, into the loading command.

Highlighted filename	Commander loading instruction	Command passed to DOS
menu prg	PRG:dbase !	dbase menu

Some loading instructions require the file argument to include the file extension as well as the filename. For example, dBASE IV expects a PRG extension for a program file. However, dBASE IV query files, with QBE extensions, can be executed in a similar manner as a dBASE IV program. In order to load the QBE file, you must include the file extension in the loading instruction. Example:

qbe:dbase !.!

Files that have no extensions in their filenames can pose a special problem. For example, Microsoft Word expects a DOC file extension but can load ASCII text files even if they have no extension at all. However, you need to include a period after the filename to indicate that the file does not have an extension. Example:

:word !.

WordPerfect poses a different kind of problem. Since WordPerfect does not require any file extensions to be used with its files, the only extension references that could be used are ones that you decide to use. If you assume that files without extensions are probably WordPerfect documents you would enter an empty extension as the criterion for WordPerfect.

:wp

Keep in mind that the Commander will search the extension file sequentially. This means that you can create a final option that will operate if no other matches are found. The specification below would display the message *Cannot be selected for auto loading* as a default message for all nonspecified extension.

*:Echo Cannot be selected for auto loading

Some applications require the complete pathname of the file in order to load the program and data file. Ventura, Desktop Publisher is an example of such a program. Normally Ventura is loaded through a batch file VP.BAT (or VPPROF.BAT for the professional extension). If you want to load a chapter file, CHP extension, along with the program you must specify the drive and directory as well as the filename. The example below would load Ventura by selecting CHP files.

chp:vp !:!\!

When you have created the loading instruction, save the file with [Shift/F10]. You can immediately use the specifications to point and execute.

DOS History

The Norton Commander allows you to integrate DOS commands along with Norton Commander operations. The DOS prompt is always available at the bottom of the screen. You can enter DOS commands without having to exit the Norton Commander. When the DOS command terminates, the Norton Commander is reloaded and the panel display returns to its previous form.

In addition, the Norton Commander stores the last 15 DOS commands you have entered so that you can recall them. The commands can be executed again or modified and executed without having to enter the entire command.

There are two ways in which you can access the commands stored in the DOS history area:

- **[Ctrl/e], [Ctrl/x].** The command [Ctrl/e] causes the Norton Commander to display the previous DOS commands on the DOS prompt line. You can display the last 15 DOS command one at a time using [Ctrl/e]. The command [Ctrl/x] moves you forward in the list.

  When a command is displayed next to the DOS prompt, you can execute it again by entering ↵. You can also use the ← and → keys to position the cursor to edit the command. Any new characters entered are added to the command and characters can be removed with the [Del] command. The edited command can be executed by pressing ↵. Note that the editing cursor need not be at the end of the line in order to execute the command.

- **History Windows.** The command [Alt/F8] displays a window, shown in Figure 12-18, that lists the previous DOS commands. You can use the ↑ and ↓ keys to scroll through the list and execute the highlighted command by entering ↵. You cannot edit the commands displayed in the history window.

Programs executed by the point and shoot method are stored as part of the DOS history.

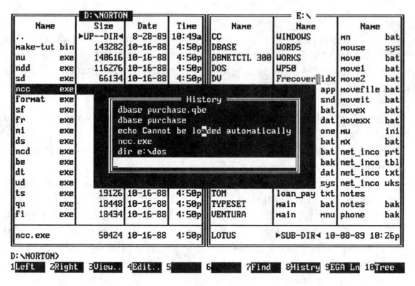

Figure 12-18 History Window displays previous commands.

Another way to combine the Norton Commander with DOS is through the use of the [Ctrl/↵] combination. [Ctrl/↵] inserts the currently highlighted filename or directory name onto the DOS command line. Filenames are inserted with the extension, if any. Directory names are inserted as they appear in the panel display without the full pathname. For example, suppose you wanted to copy an entire directory from one disk to another. You could use the DOS XCOPY command because it operates faster than either the DOS COPY command or the Norton Commander Copy command. Begin by positioning the panel highlight on the name of the directory that you want to copy. Enter

**xcopy **

Instead of entering the directory name, use the [Ctrl/↵] command to copy it from the panel. Enter

[Ctrl/↵]
[space]
a:

Insert the directory name a second time by entering

[Ctrl/↵]
/s

If the highlighted directory was called LOTUS the command would read:

xcopy \LOTUS a:\LOTUS/s

Pressing ⏎ would execute the XCOPY command as if you had manually entered all of the text yourself.

The XCOPY command appears in DOS Version 3.2 and higher. When the COPY command is used to copy files it read and writes one file at a time. XCOPY reads as many files as can fit into memory and then writes all of those files. XCOPY will also accept a directory name as a source without requiring the *.*. The program assumes that you want to copy all of the files in the directory. The /S switch tell XCOPY to copy any subdirectories found in the source directory.

User-Defined Menus

The Commander has the ability to display user-defined menus. These menus can be superimposed over the display panels or displayed by themselves with the panels and function key bar suppressed. The key to user menus are files called **NC.MNU**. When **[F2]** is pressed, the Commander searches for a **NC.MNU** file and use it to control menu display and operation. If there is a **NC.MNU** file in the current directory the menu specified in that file is displayed. If no menu is found in the current directory the Norton Commander displays the main menu, which is the one stored in the same directory as the Norton Commander.

The Commander program is supplied with a sample menu file. When you press [F2], the program will display the sample menu shown in Figure 12-19. The sample menu lists three operations. To select an item from the menu you can position the highlight with the ↑ and ↓ keys and press ⏎.

A second method is to use the shortcut keys. The first two operations on the list are preceded by the names of the keys, D and [F1], which can be used to select the respective options. Note that the third item, **Check free disk space**, does not have a shortcut key and can only be executed by highlighting.

Figure 12-19 Sample Norton Commander menu.

You can exit the menu by entering [Esc].

Norton Commander Menu Structure

You can create your own system of menus by creating NC.MNU files of your own design. The NC.MNU files are ASCII text files that could be created by any text editor or ASCII compatible word processor. However, the Norton Commander has a special editor mode that is designed to simplify the creation of menus.

You can access the Norton Commander menu editor using the command **[F9]** Commands **M**enu file edit.

[F9] c m

When you enter this command the program displays a dialog box, Figure 12-20, that asks if you want to edit the main menu or a local menu.

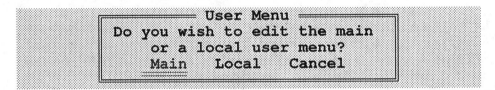

Figure 12-20 Select menu to edit.

- **Main Menu.** The main menu is the NC.MNU file stored in the same directory as the Norton Commander program. This is the menu that is displayed when you press [F2] unless there is a menu file, NC.MNU, in the current directory.

- **Local Menu.** A local menu is a menu specified by a NC.MNU file in any directory other than the directory in which the Norton Commander is stored. When the [F2] key is pressed, a local menu, i.e., a NC.MNU file in the current directory, will take precedence over the main menu.

If you select to edit the main menu the Norton Commander will display the text of the sample menu file in the special edit mode for menus (Figure 12-20)

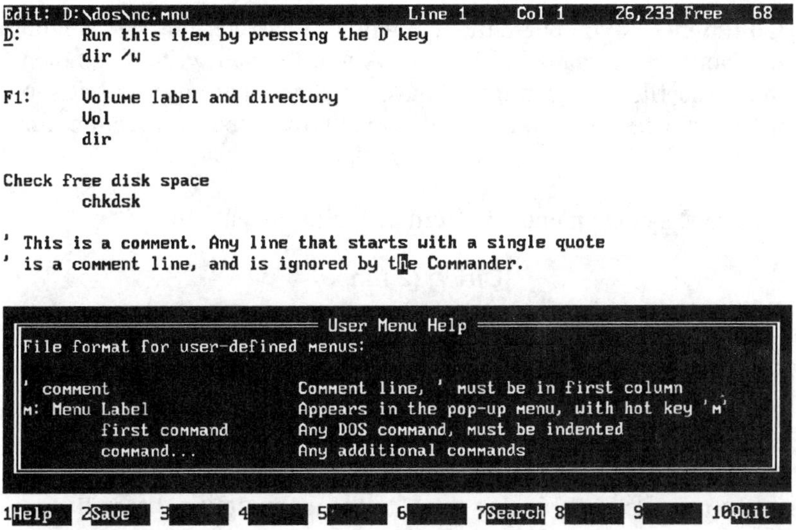

```
Edit: D:\dos\nc.mnu                    Line 1      Col 1      26,233 Free     68
D:       Run this item by pressing the D key
         dir /w

F1:      Volume label and directory
         Vol
         dir

Check free disk space
         chkdsk

' This is a comment. Any line that starts with a single quote
' is a comment line, and is ignored by the Commander.


┌══════════════════ User Menu Help ══════════════════┐
│File format for user-defined menus:                 │
│                                                    │
│' comment              Comment line, ' must be in first column
│M: Menu Label          Appears in the pop-up menu, with hot key 'M'
│     first command     Any DOS command, must be indented
│     command...        Any additional commands
└════════════════════════════════════════════════════┘


1Help  2Save  3      4      5      6      7Search 8      9      10Quit
```

Figure 12-21 Sample menu in edit mode display.

A menu file must follow a specific structure. The structure allows you to enter three types of items.

- **Menu Items.** A menu item is a single line of text that contains the name of the shortcut key, if any, used to activate the menu item, followed by a colon. After the colon, you can enter the text you want displayed in the menu window for that item. Note that the shortcut key is optional. It is not necessary that a menu option be assigned keystroke commands. If no keystroke command is assigned, the option can be executed by moving the highlight to the desired item and pressing ↵.

  All menu items **must** begin at the left margins of the document.

  The command keys can be letters, numbers, function keys, or [Ctrl] characters. Function keys are entered as **F1, F2, F3**, and so on. [Ctrl] characters are entered as **^A, ^B, ^C**, and so forth. A menu can display up to 20 menu items at one time.

- **DOS Instructions**. Following each menu item should be a list of the DOS commands needed to carry out the operation indicated by the menu item. You can list as many commands as needed after each item. There is a 25,000 character limit on the size of the NC.MNU file.

  All of the DOS commands that are related to a given menu item **must** be indented from the left margin with at least one space or tab character. The indent identifies the line as a DOS command and not a menu item.

- **Comments**. If you begin the line with a ' character, the line is ignored by the Norton Commander. This allows you to enter written comments into the menu file. The comments have no functional purpose but should be included when you want to document the menu's structure for other users.

You can clear the sample menu text from the editor by entering

[Ctrl/y] *(2 times)*

Creating a Menu

Suppose you want to create a menu that would run three applications, Lotus 1-2-3, dBASE IV Plus, and WordPerfect.

Begin the text file by assigning the **L** to the menu option that will load Lotus 1-2-3. Enter

L:
[Tab]
Lotus 1-2-3 Release 2.01 ↵

A space or a [Tab] **must** precede each of the DOS commands so that the program can distinguish them from menu items. Enter the commands you want to execute when this item is selected. Enter

[Tab]CD\lotus ↵
[Tab] 123 ↵
[Tab] CD\norton ↵

Notice the last command in the sequence, **cd\norton**. This command is used to return the program to the directory that contains the NC.MNU file. The assumption is made that the Norton Commander program is stored in a directory called NORTON. The return to the original directory is important if you intend to create local menus in addition to the main menu.

Using Norton Utilities Features in Menus

In Section II of this book you learned how to use Norton Utilities programs, such as Batch Enhancer and Time Mark, to create menu programs through DOS batch files. The Norton Commander menu system simplifies menu creation because it eliminates the need to use complicated DOS commands, such as ERRORLEVEL and GOTO, in order to create a menu item selection routine. However, you can add Batch Enhancer and TM commands to a Norton Commander command listing in just about the same way that you did in batch files.

Suppose you want to display the elapsed time after each use of WordPerfect. You can use the TM and Batch Enhancer commands as part of a Norton Commander menu. Create the menu item for WordPerfect.

W: [Tab]
WordPerfect 5.0 ↵

The first command under this option is a TM command that will start a timer clock.

[Tab] TM START /N >NUL↵

Next load and execute the WordPerfect program.

[Tab] CD\wp50 ↵
[Tab] WP ↵
[Tab] CD\norton ↵

The next part of the command section will display the time elapsed since WordPerfect was loaded. The Batch Enhancer program is used to create a pause before the Norton Commander panels are redisplayed.

[Tab] CLS
[Tab] TM STOP "WordPerfect in use for"/N/L ↵
[Tab] BE DELAY 100 ↵

The menu file now looks like this:

```
L:      Lotus 1-2-3 Release 2.01
        CD\lotus
        123
        CD\norton
W:      WordPerfect 5.0
        TM START/N >NUL
        CD\wp50
        WP
        CD\norton
        CLS
```

TM STOP "WordPerfect in use for"/N/L
BE DELAY 100

The current menu file would create a menu that looks like Figure 12-22.

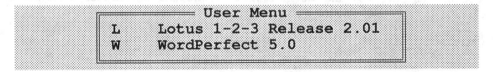

Figure 12-22 User defined menu..

Automatic Menu Display

The Norton Commander will display the main menu, or a local menu if one exists, when you press [F2]. When you have made your selection from the menu and the associated DOS commands have been executed, the Norton Commander will normally return to the panel display.

If you want the Norton Commander to automatically display the menu, you must select the **Auto Menus** option from the Options menu.

[F9] O A

This option will ensure that the menu is always displayed when the Norton Commander is loaded, and is redisplayed after a menu selection has been completed.

If you want to use the Norton Commander as a turnkey menu system, you need to make the following adjustments.

1. Place a command at the end of your AUTOEXEC.BAT file that loads the Norton Commander.

CD\norton
nc

2. Turn off the panel displays.

[Ctrl/o]

3. Turn off the function key bar display.

[Ctrl/b]

4. Make sure that the Auto Menu setting on the Options menu is ON.

[F9] O A

5. Save the current set up by entering.

[Shift/F9]

> *The settings options used by the Norton Commander as default settings are stored in a file called NC.INI. By default the Norton Commander will automatically save the current settings into the NC.INI file each time you exit the Norton Commander. This means that the next time you load the program it will have the same settings and panels that were active when you last exited. If you do not want the NC.INI file automatically updated, each time you exit you must make sure that the **Auto save set-up** option on the **Configuration** dialog box is not selected. When **Auto save set-up** is not in use the NC.INI file will be updated only when you enter the [Shift/F9] command. Otherwise the Norton Commander retains the same default values each time it is loaded regardless of what was done in the previous session.*

Local Menus

The concept of user menus can be extended beyond a single menu into a system of local menus. Local menus are menus that display options that are related to the file in a particular directory. For example, some programs can be executed in more than one way. Microsoft Word can be loaded using WORD, which displays a blank document screen, or WORD/L which automatically displays the last document used. dBASE II, III, and IV can be started with a program name as an argument causing immediate execution of the program when dBASE is loaded. For example, DBASE SALES would load dBASE and run the Sales program.

Suppose you want to have a menu that lists four ways to start dBASE.

dBASE running the Sales program
dBASE running the Clients program
dBASE running the Accounts program
Standard dBASE.

It would be better to create a local dBASE menu rather than crowd your main menu with these options. The creation of the local dBASE menu requires two types of modifications.

- **Link Between Main and Local Menu.** The link between the main and the local menu is an option in the main menu that is associated with a CD (Change Directory) command. The CD command is important because the Norton Commander will display the text of a local menu, if one exists, when that menu is in the active directory. If you store a NC.MNU file in the dBASE directory, changing to the dBASE directory will cause that menu to be displayed instead of the main menu.

- **Local Menu.** A local menu is simply a NC.MNU text file stored in a directory other than the directory in which the Norton Commander is stored.

The menu file listed below shows a link between the main menu and a menu in the DBASE directory.

```
L:      Lotus 1-2-3 Release 2.01
        CD\lotus
        123
        CD\norton
W:      WordPerfect 5.0
        TM START/N >NUL
        CD\wp50
        WP
        CD\norton
        CLS
        TM STOP "WordPerfect in use for"/N/L
        BE DELAY 100
D:      dBASE IV
        CD\dbase
```

The local menu is created by activating the directory in which it is to be stored and select the **local** option from the **Menu file edit** dialog box.

CD\dbase
[F9] m l

Selecting Local causes the Norton Commander to store the NC.MNU file in the current directory, thus creating a local menu.

The text listed below shows the dBASE local menu. Note that the last option completes the link back to the main menu by using the CD command to activate the directory, assumed to be called NORTON, in which the Norton Commander and the main menu are stored. The menu that results from this file is displayed in Figure 12-23.

D: dBASE IV
        DBASE
S: The Sales program
        DBASE sales
C: dBASE Client Management Program
        DBASE clients
A: dBASE Accounting Program
        DBASE accounts
[F1]   Return to Main Menu
        CD\norton

When the Auto Menu option is on, selection of dBASE IV from the main menu will cause the local dBASE menu to appear. The menu will remain active until you select to return to the main menu or press [F10] to turn off the menu display.

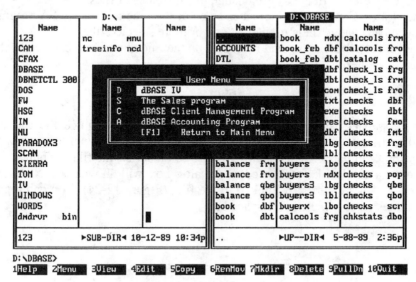

Figure 12-23 Local menu displayed.

Norton Utilities Functions

The Norton Commander also incorporates some of the Norton Utilities features discussed in Section III of this book. The Norton Commander includes the File Find program, the NCD program, and part of the FA program.

Table 12-6 Norton Utilities Features in Norton Commander

[F9] F A	File Attributes
[Alt/F7]	File Find Window
[F9] C F	
[Alt/F10]	Norton Change Directory Windows
[F9] C N	

File Attributes

In Chapter 8 the Norton Utilities File Attribute program was discussed. DOS recognizes four *file attributes*: read-only, archive, hidden, and system. The File Attribute program provided with the Norton Utilities allows you to manipulate files based on their attributes, or to change the attributes of files.

The Norton Commander duplicates some of the functions of the FA program in that you can change file attributes of one or more selected files.

The **File attribute** command is located on the File menu. You can access this command by entering

[F9] f a

The command should be entered when you have highlighted the file you want to work with, or selected a group of filenames from a panel to work with. The Norton Commander will display a dialog box that lists the file attributes.

If only a single file is selected, the dialog box will show a **x** next to any attributes which are currently applied to the file, (Figure 12-24). You can toggle the attributes on or off, using the space bar.

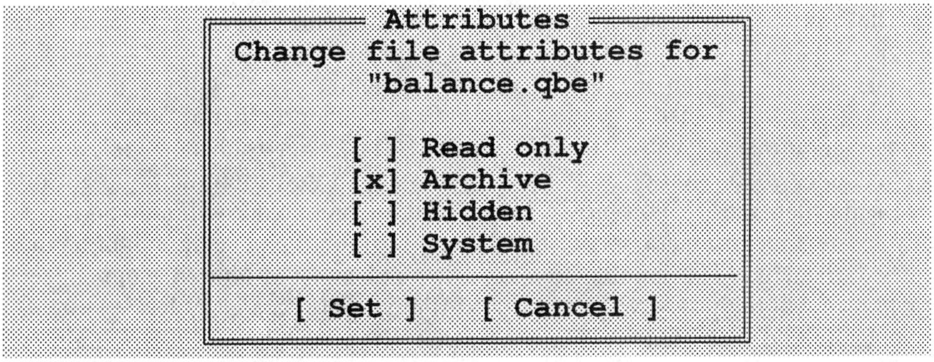

```
╔══════════════ Attributes ══════════════╗
║ Change file attributes for             ║
║         "balance.qbe"                  ║
║                                        ║
║      [ ]  Read only                    ║
║      [x]  Archive                      ║
║      [ ]  Hidden                       ║
║      [ ]  System                       ║
║                                        ║
║     [ Set ]      [ Cancel ]            ║
╚════════════════════════════════════════╝
```

Figure 12-24 File attribute dialog box, single file.

If more than one filename from the panel has been selected, the dialog box will list two columns: one for setting, the other for clearing an attribute, as shown in Figure 12-25.

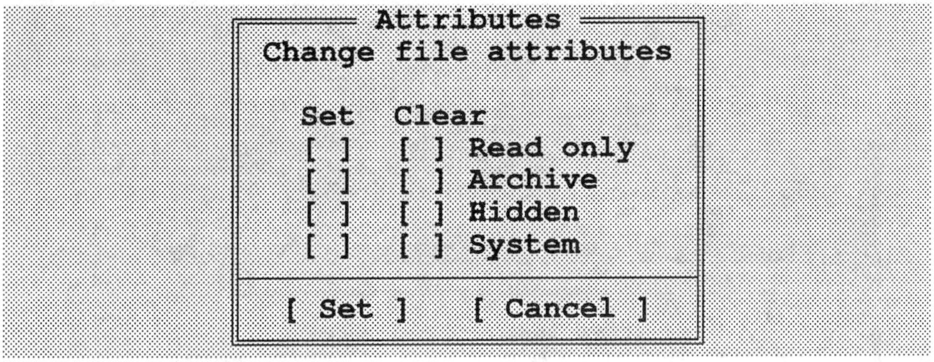

```
╔══════════════ Attributes ══════════════╗
║ Change file attributes                 ║
║                                        ║
║   Set  Clear                           ║
║   [ ]   [ ]  Read only                 ║
║   [ ]   [ ]  Archive                   ║
║   [ ]   [ ]  Hidden                    ║
║   [ ]   [ ]  System                    ║
║                                        ║
║     [ Set ]      [ Cancel ]            ║
╚════════════════════════════════════════╝
```

Figure 12-25 File attribute dialog box, multiple files.

File Find

The Norton Utilities File Find program, discussed in Chapter 7, is used to search all the directories on a disk in order to find files. A similar feature is built into the Norton Commander program and can be accessed from the menus using the command [F9] Commands File or through the [Alt/F7] key combination.

When you enter the FF command you are allowed to enter a wildcard file specification which will be used to find matching files. When you press ⏎ the program scans the current disk and locates all of the files in any of the directories that match the wildcard.

The Norton Commander version of FF is a bit different from the Norton Utilities version with respect to how the list of matching files can be used. In the Norton Utilities version the list of files is a standard DOS output placed by default on the screen display. In the Norton Commander the list of files becomes an interactive display within the FF window. The result is that in the Norton Commander version you can use the ↑ and ↓ keys to position the highlight on one of the filenames. If you press ↵, the Norton Commander will automatically activate the directory that contains the file and position the panel highlight on the selected filename. The combination of File Find and the Norton Commander provides one of the fastest ways to locate a file possible on a DOS-based system. If you combine these features with a **Quick View** panel you will be able to quickly inspect the contents of the file when you select it from the file find display. Since File Find ill search all disk directories it is a much faster way to find files than displaying directory by directory in panel views.

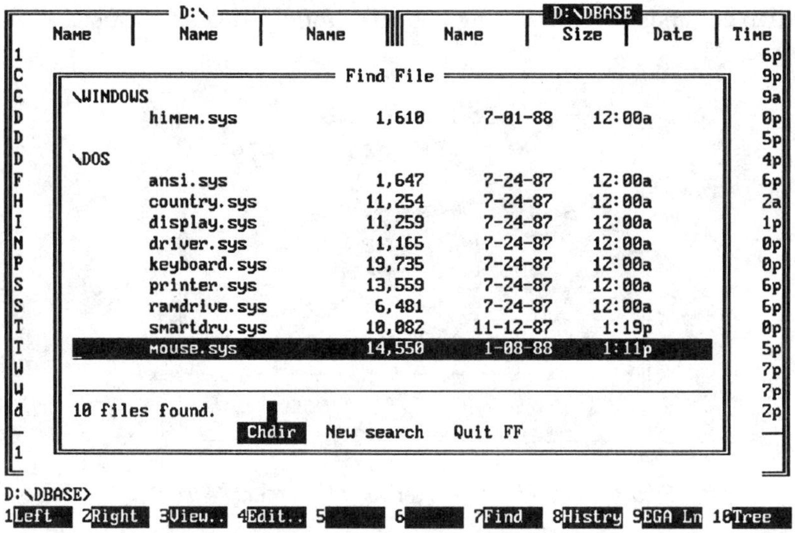

```
┌──────────── D:\ ─────────────┐┌───────[ D:\DBASE ]───────┐
│ Name  │  Name   │   Name   │││ Name    │  Size │ Date │ Time │
│1                                                        6p│
│c ═══════════════════ Find File ═════════════════        9p│
│c \WINDOWS                                                9a│
│D        himem.sys        1,610      7-01-88    12:00a    0p│
│D                                                        5p│
│D \DOS                                                    4p│
│F        ansi.sys         1,647      7-24-87    12:00a    6p│
│H        country.sys     11,254      7-24-87    12:00a    2a│
│I        display.sys     11,259      7-24-87    12:00a    1p│
│N        driver.sys       1,165      7-24-87    12:00a    0p│
│P        keyboard.sys    19,735      7-24-87    12:00a    0p│
│S        printer.sys     13,559      7-24-87    12:00a    6p│
│S        ramdrive.sys     6,481      7-24-87    12:00a    6p│
│T        smartdrv.sys    10,082     11-12-87     1:19p    0p│
│T       ▓mouse.sys▓      ▓14,550▓   ▓1-08-88▓   ▓1:11p▓   5p│
│W                                                        7p│
│W                                                        7p│
│d 10 files found.        ▓                                2p│
│           ┌──────┐                                        │
│           │ Chdir │  New search    Quit FF               │
│1          └──────┘                                        │
└───────────────────────────────────────────────────────────┘
D:\DBASE>
1Left  2Right  3View..  4Edit..  5     6     7Find  8Histry  9EGA Ln  10Tree
```

Figure 12-26 File Find window.

Norton Change Directory

The NCD program, discussed in Chapter 7, provides an alternative to DOS for accessing directories. The NCD contains a version of the NCD interactive tree display that provides a high, speed way to locate and activate a specific directory.

The NCD window can be activated by entering [Alt/F10]. The Norton Commander will look for the **TREEINFO.NCD** file in the root directory of the current drive. The Norton Commander will use an existing **TREEINFO.NCD** created by the Norton Utilities version of NCD. If no **TREEINFO.NCD** file is found then the program will create one by scanning the disk directory tree.

The directory tree display shown in Figure 12-27 is similar to the tree display in the tree-type panel. The primary advantage of the NCD window is that it offers a speed search option that will locate the directories in the tree automatically, in contrast to simply scrolling through the tree with the arrow keys.

Like other speed search options, it will locate the first item in the directory that matches the character or characters entered into the speed search box. The [Ctrl/↵] combination will move to the next match, if any. Pressing ↵ will activate the highlighted directory.

While the NCD window is active you can also use Norton Change Directory commands to add [F7], remove [F8], or rename [F6] directories. The [F2] will update the TREEINFO.NCD file.

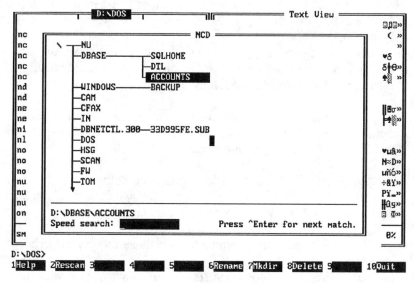

Figure 12-27 Norton Change Directory window.

Special Features

Finally, the Norton Commander contains some special features that have no direct equivalents in either DOS or the Norton Utilities. They are:

Table 12-7 Special Norton Commander Features

[F9] C C	Compare Directory Panels
[F9] C L	Commander MCI Mail commands
[F9] C R	
[F9] F S	
[F9] L K	Link to another computer
[F9] R K	

Compare Directories

The Compare Directories command is used to automatically determine differences in filenames between two panels. In order to perform this operation you must have a dual-panel display in which both panels are in the Brief or the Full display modes.

When you use command **[F9] C C**, the Norton Commander the program compares the files in the two active panels. The program will automatically select files if it finds one of two possible conditions.

- **Unique FileNames.** Any filenames that appear in one panel but not the other are marked as if you had manually used the [Ins] to mark the files. The effect covers files in both panels.

- **Updated Files.** If the same file appears in both panels but with a different time and date, the file with the most recent date and time is selected regardless of which panel it appears in.

Conversely, all the files that remain unmarked are those that match an identical file in the other panel.

The compare directories operation is useful when you want to find differences between directories on different disks. Since the command marks files you can quickly update the directories by copying the files with the [F5] command or deleting marked files with [F8].

Linking Computers

The introduction of laptop computers and IBM PS/2s that use 3.5 inch floppy disks, created incompatibility between computers that otherwise would be 100 percent compatible. One solution to this problem was to add disk drives so that every computer had both a 3.5 inch and a 5.25 inch drive. Of course, this solution was expensive, clumsy, and in many cases, impossible to implement.

The solution most commonly used is a technique called *null modem* transfer. A *null modem* is a connection between the serial ports on two computers. The term *null modem* is used because data transfer between the computers mimics the way data would be transferred using a modem over telecommunications connects. In this case there is no actual modem but a direct cable link between the computers.

Null modem transfers provide an end run around different disk sizes and formats, since the data is transferred from computer to computer. Each computer can write the data into files using its own disk formats. This method is the most popular way of transferring data from a laptop computer to a desktop computer, but it works just as well when two desktop computers are used. In this case, you can quickly transfer data from the hard disk on one computer to the hard disk on another without having to place the files on a floppy disk. Null modem transfers are simpler and faster than using floppy disks. You can also transfer large files-- files too large to fit onto a single floppy disk-- via a null modem connection.

To perform null modem transfers you need:

- **A null modem cable.** A null modem cable is one that can connect two computers through the serial interface ports, referred to by DOS as COM1 or COM2. This means that both of the computers you want to link must have at least one serial port free to accept the null modem cable. The cable required is one designed for use with null modem communications. These cables typically have 25-pin female connectors on both ends. However, standard series cables such as those used for modems will not work as null modem connectors. Null modem communications requires that the connections between pins on either end of the cable be crossed in a special way.

> *The proper null modem cable can be acquired from Peter Norton Computing.*

- **Null Modem Software.** Once the hardware, i.e., serial ports connected with the proper cable, is in place, you need to run a program on both computers which will use the null modem connections to transfer data. The Norton Commander provides a null modem transfer program in the form of the **Link** display panels. Link can be selected from the Left or Right pull down menus.

[F9] L K
[F9] R K

When you select a Link panel display, the program displays a dialog box, as shown in Figure 12-28, that contains the settings needed to connect the two computers.

- **Mode.** Null modem transfer operations usually require the designation of one computer as the *master* and the other as the *slave*. The master computer is the one that issues commands as to what files to transfer. The slave computer is the passive partner in the transfer, reacting to the operations executed on the master computer. Keep in mind that the distinction between master and slave does not limit the way that data can be transferred. Files can be copied to or from either of the computers. Once a link has been established, you can control both computers from the master computer keyboard.

   If you are working with a desktop and laptop computer, you would select the desktop computer as the master because it usually has a better keyboard and screen display than the laptop. However the choice is a personal one.

   Note that to establish a link between computers you must bring up and use the link dialog box on each computer from its own keyboard. Once the link is made you can return to the master computer and complete the operations from that keyboard.

- **Port.** You can select COM1 or COM2 as the port over which the communications will take place.

- **Turbo Link.** Some computers will experience problems in transferring data over a null modem link, which can be corrected by using a slower transfer method. If you have problems linking computers, turn off the **Turbo mode** option. This may correct the problem. Note that with the turbo mode inactive, file transfers will take longer.

- **Link.** Select link to activate the link using the current settings in the dialog box.

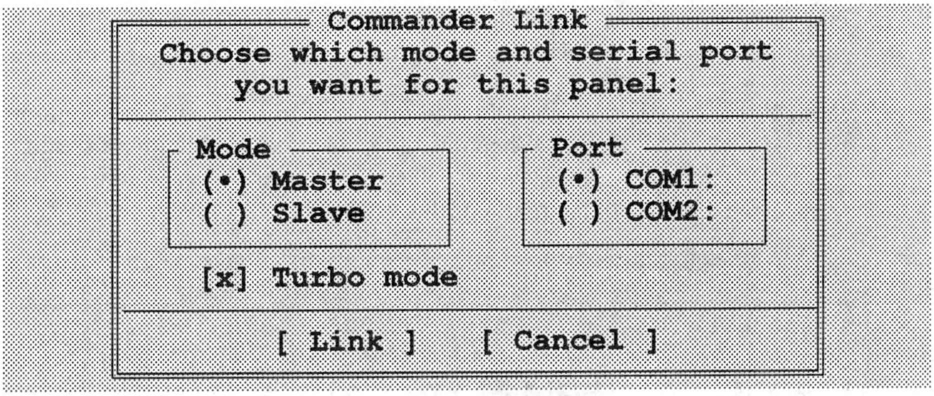

```
╔══════════════════ Commander Link ══════════════════╗
║        Choose which mode and serial port           ║
║            you want for this panel:                ║
║                                                    ║
║   ┌─ Mode ─────────────┐   ┌─ Port ─────────────┐  ║
║   │  (•) Master        │   │  (•) COM1:         │  ║
║   │  ( ) Slave         │   │  ( ) COM2:         │  ║
║   └────────────────────┘   └────────────────────┘  ║
║                                                    ║
║      [x] Turbo mode                                ║
║                                                    ║
║          [ Link ]      [ Cancel ]                  ║
╚════════════════════════════════════════════════════╝
```

Figure 12-28 Link dialog box.

Once the link has been established between the two computers, the link panel on the master computer will display the directory of the **slave** computer. In a dual-panel display you can use the copy, move, and delete commands to transfer or remove files from either computer.

Electronic MCI Mail

The Norton Commander supports the use of MCI electronic mail thorough the MCI.EXE and MCIDRIVR.EXE programs it supplies. These program integrate the Norton Commander display panel system with MCI electronic mail (Figure 12-29). Keep in mind that this feature requires that you have telecommunications hardware, typically an internal or external modem, and a valid MCI mail account. MCI mail allows you to send and receive messages, computer files, or Fax transmissions.

The Norton Commander allows you to use MCI mail in the following ways.

- **Commander Mail.** Selecting the **Commander Mail** option from the Commands pull-down menu executes the MCI.EXE program and begins an MCI mail session.

[F9] C L

You can use this session to set up your MCI account, send MCI mail, or check your MCI mailbox for messages.

- **Send/Receive Mail.** This option is also located on the Commands menu. It down loadswaiting MCI mail and uploads outgoing messages directly from the Norton Commander panel interface. This features uses the IN and OUT directories established during the MCI mail set up to store incoming messages or locate outgoing mail.

- **Send Files.** This option is used when you want to send a file or group of marked files as MCI mail. When this option is used the MCI mail session allows you to enter a message, an electronic cover letter, which is then transferred along with the marked files via MCI.

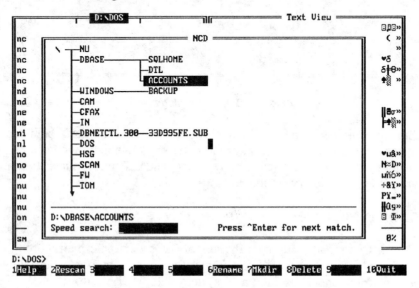

Figure 12-29 Commander MCI mail setup window.

Summary

The Norton Commander is a shell-type program that provides an alternative user interface to DOS, as well as furnishing unique features that aid in the daily task of managing a computer system.

- **Panel Display Interface.** The heart of the Norton Commander is the interactive screen panel displays. You can display one or two panels. Each panel can be used to display a different disk directory or the directory information in one or more alternative display modes. The panel displays that list file and directory information are the basis for all other Norton Commander operations. You can select items by moving the highlight within or between the panels. You can mark files as part of a group manually, or use wildcard specifications. The program will also mark unique files based on a comparison of two directories.

- **View Files.** The Norton Commander has the ability to display the data files produced by many popular word processing, spreadsheet, or database programs directly without having to load the applications that created them. You can also select a Quick View panel which will display the highlighted files in a panel automatically as you scroll through a directory listing.

- **File Operations.** The panel interface can be used to select files and directories for standard DOS operations, such as copying, moving, renaming, or deleting files or directories. You can also create new directories. When dual panels are used, the active panel will serve as the source directory and the inactive panel as the destination directory.

- **DOS Operations.** You can enter and execute DOS commands while the Norton Commander is active. To aid in entry, you can transfer the name of the highlighted directory or file with the [Ctrl/↵] command.

- **Point and Shoot Program Execution.** You can execute programs by using the data files related to those program with a point and shoot method. The applications and data files are linked through an extension file, NC.EXT, which lists the file extensions that match the various application programs.

- **User-Defined Menus.** The Norton Commander can support a system of menus that can be used to execute DOS operations, such as program execu tion or backup procedures. Menu files-NC.MNU-can be used to create menu windows. The menu stored in the same directory as the Norton Commander is the main menu. Local menus are created by storing NC.MNU files in other directories.

- **Norton Utilities Features.** Features found in the Norton Utilities programs FF, NCD, and FA, are integrated into the Norton Commander.

- **Null Modem Transfers.** The panel display system can be used to transfer data via a null modem connection between two computers running the Norton Commander.

- **MCI Mail.** The Norton Commander integrates an MCI mail program, MCI.EXE, into the Norton Commander pull-down menu system. You can access MCI mail directly from the Norton Commander panel display through the Send/Receive mail option.

13

The Norton Editor

The primary difference between an editor and a word processor is that an editor is concerned with creating text files, while a word processing program is concerned with printing text.

An editor is useful for creating text files intended to be used as source code for computer programs, or for DOS batch files. DOS operations often entail the creation and editing of text files.

An editor is concerned merely with the features that aid in the entry and revision of text. They are simpler programs than word processors because they do not need features and commands that apply to the paragraph and page formatting requirements of printing.

Editors create standard ASCII text files. Word processing programs will usually add special formatting codes to the text that deviates from standard ASCII text format.

The most popular word processing programs, WordStar, WordPerfect, and Microsoft Word, have the ability to store text in an ASCII format if you select the proper option. WordStar uses the N command to place the program in a nontext editing mode, WordPerfect uses [Ctrl/F5] to load and save text files, and Microsoft Word requires that you turn OFF the Formatted option on the Transfer Save menu to create a text file.

The advantage of using a text editor over a word processor is one of speed and compactness. Because the editor is not burdened with all the overhead needed in a full-powered word processor, it can provide the necessary editing tools in a simpler, faster, and smaller program. Since the program is smaller it takes up less memory, leaving more memory to use for text, which also enhances the performance. The Norton Editor consists of a single file, NE.COM, which is 32,375 bytes in size. Compare that to word processing programs that are supplied on six or more disks.

The Norton Editor fills a gap that exists between primitive editing programs like EDLIN and full-powered word processing programs. The Editor is a small, fast, text editing program that contains a variety of handy features, all designed to help you produce computer programs or text files as quickly and easily as possible.

In addition, the Editor is one of the few text editing or word processing programs on the PC to offer support for a mouse, another great advantage when editing.

The Norton Editor Features

The Norton Editor is designed specifically to meet the needs of people who are creating computer programs or other types of structured text files, such as DOS batch files.

It makes sense that the features contained in an editor will differ somewhat from those found in a word processing program.

The following section explains some of the features that make the Norton Editor a unique text editing environment.

Editing Features

The Norton Editor contains all of the usual editing features found in word processing programs. The Editor is an **insert**-oriented editor. This means that any text that is typed is automatically added to the file. Insert-oriented editors are the safest type because you cannot accidentally overtype existing information.

Editing in an insert-oriented program consists of deleting, moving, and copying text.

Of the major word processing programs, only Multimate defaults to an overtype mode. Insert-oriented editing has become the accepted norm, although there is still a core of word processors that prefer overtype mode.

- **Delete**. The Editor provides the following delete commands. Note that [Ctrl] combinations will delete to the left while [Alt] combinations delete to the right.

Table 13-1 Delete Commands in Norton Editor

Backspace and Delete	[backspace]
Delete current character	[Del]
Delete word, left	[Ctrl/w]
Delete word, right	[Alt/w]
Delete rest of line, left	[Ctrl/L]
Delete rest of line, right	[Alt/L]
Delete entire line, left and right	[Alt/k]
Delete marked block	[F4] d

- **Undelete**. The Editor also includes a simple undelete feature that restores the previous deletion. Note that moving the cursor following a delete clears the undelete buffer. This means that undelete works only immediately after a deletion. Undelete does not work with a block deletion, [F4] d. Undelete Commands are [Ctrl/u] or [Alt/u].

- **Copy and Move**. Text can be moved or copied by the use of block markers. Once a block is set, the text can be copied, moved, or deleted from the file. Block markers can be set automatically for an entire line, or manually for blocks of any size. To mark a block manually you must set two markers; all the text between the markers is the block. As with WordStar, there can be only one block set at a time.

Table 13-2 Copy and Move Commands

Mark a line as a block	[F4] L
Mark from cursor to end of line	[F4] e
Set individual block marker	[F4] s
Remove block markers	[F4] r
Copy block	[F4] c
Move block	[F4] m
Delete block	[F4] d
Move cursor to block marker	[F4] f

- **Search and Replace**. The Editor provides full search and replace functions, features a programmer cannot be without. The search and replace commands are the same command key. If you enter a second command following the search text, the command becomes a search and replace.

Table 13-3 Search and Replace Commands

Search/Replace toward top of file	[Ctrl/f]
Search/Replace toward bottom of file	[Alt/f]
Continue backward search	[Ctrl/c]
Continue forward search	[Alt/c]

- **Windows.** The Editor has the ability to operate in a split-screen mode, as shown in Figure 13-1. The split screen allows you to edit two files at the same time. This is an invaluable aid when working since you can refer to one file without having to save or remove the other. The editor allows you to move or copy text from one window to another. The illustration below shows two dBASE programs being edited at the same time.

```
@ 21,13 Say  "Please Enter number ......" get CHOICE picture "9"
read
DO CASE
        case CHOICE="0"
                EXIT
        case CHOICE="1"
                clear
                menunumber="  "
                ppause="  "
                @ 10,10 to 15,70 double
                @ 11,15 Say "Enter Menu Number or ^Q-I of Main Menu " get menun»
                read
Line=28    Col=8                    A:MNUBAT.PRG                Insert      WW=Off
@ 21,13 Say  "Please Enter number ......" get CHOICE picture "9"
read
DO CASE
        case CHOICE="0"
                EXIT
        case CHOICE="1"
                clear
                menunumber="  "
                ppause="  "
                @ 10,10 to 15,70 double
                @ 11,15 Say "Enter Menu Number or ^Q-I of Main Menu " get menun»
                read
```

Figure 13-1 Split-screen editing.

You can split the display by entering **[F3] x**. Once the display is split, the **[F3] x** command will move the cursor between windows. The Compare command is an interesting one and very useful. The command tells the editor to compare the text in the current window to the text in the other window. This feature enables you to find differences in files that are very close in content. This method is much better than trying to visually inspect a program.

Table 13-4 Window Commands

Copy block from other window	[F4] w
Compare text between windows	[F6] t

- **Formatting**. As an added feature, the Editor does have some simple formatting features. You can turn on **wordwrap**, which allows the editor to create paragraph-oriented text.

Table 13-5 Formatting Commands

Turn on wordwrap, paragraph entry mode	[F5] w
Set line length, i.e., right margin	[F5] L
Reformat paragraph	[F5] f

- **Files**. The [F3] key is used to implement file related commands. The Editor can also edit files that are larger than the available memory. This is done by loading part of the file, saving that part and loading additional text. In this way the Editor can handle files of almost any size.

    The Editor can also append text from one file into the current file being edited. Note that Append always places the next text at the **end** of the current file regardless of the cursor position at the time of the appending. This feature is not as flexible as file-merge functions in most word processing programs, in which the text is inserted at the cursor position

Table 13-6 File Commands

Save current file and exit editor	[F3] e
Exit without editing	[F3] q
Save text without exiting	[F3] s
Load a new file	[F3] n
Rename current file	[F3] c
Write current portion of file	[F3] w
Load next portion of file	[F3] l
Append text file to current file	[F3] a

- **Printing**. While the Editor is designed primarily for editing text files, it does contain printer commands that can produce hard copy.

Table 13-7 Print Commands

Print file	[F7] p
Print marked block	[F7] b
Eject remainder of page	[F7] e
Set page length, in lines	[F7] s
Set left margin for printing only	[F7] m

> *Note that if you want to print a program and have line numbers automatically inserted, use the Norton Utilities program LP with the /N switch. You can run LP without exiting the Editor by using [F9], the DOS access command. First save the current text file: [F3] s y. Then access DOS: [F9]. Run the LP command: LP*
>
> *sample.bat/N, and return to the Editor by entering.* ↵

- **Mouse Support.** The Editor supports the use of a mouse for cursor location and scrolling. If you have a three button mouse, you can use the middle button to set block markers.

Programmers' Aids

The Editor contains a number of features of special interest to people writing programs, macros, batch files, or other types of text files.

- **GOTO Line.** The Editor can locate specific lines in a text file. Most word processing programs cannot carry out this function. This command is useful when you want to find a specific line. For example, the Norton Utilities TS (Text Search) program will supply the line number of matching text found during a text search. With the line number you can use the **[F6] g** to move to that line.

    In addition, the Editor will accept a line number as part of the command line when loading a file. Example:

NE +15 sample.bat

    The previous command will load the file **SAMPLE.BAT** and place the cursor on line #15.

- **Switch Case.** The Editor uses [Ctrl/v] and [Alt/v] to change the case of the left or right portions of a line. In most programming languages case is not significant when entering commands. But good form often dictates that certain parts of a command appear in uppercase or lowercase to improve the readability.

For example, when I publish dBASE programs I always place command verbs, functions, and other reserved words, in uppercase and user defined terms in lowercase. The Editor allows me to quickly change the case of items without having to retype. WordPerfect has a similar feature, [Shift/F3], but it operates only in the block mode. The Editor's method is much simpler.

- **DOS Access.** [F9] allows you to access DOS without having to exit the Editor. You can use this access to run DOS commands, DIR, COPY, and so forth, or Norton Utilities programs.

- **Insert Control Characters.** Because of the need to use [Ctrl] characters in batch files, the Editor uses a method similar to EDLIN to insert special characters.

To enter a [Ctrl] character or [Esc], enter **[Ctrl/p]** followed by the [Ctrl] character or [Esc]. For example, to enter an [Esc] character, enter

[Ctrl/p][Esc]

The character appears as ^[in the document. You can also use **[Ctrl/p]** in conjunction with the [Alt]-keypad method to enter control characters by their ASCII decimal value. For example, the following is an alternative method of inserting an [Esc] character.

[Ctrl/p][Alt/27]

- **Extended Characters.** You can use the [Alt]-keypad method to enter extended ASCII characters into a text file. Note the characters should be 128 or higher. Characters lower than 128 must be preceded by [Ctrl/p].

The editor will not insert character 255 into a text file. The use of this character with the DOS ECHO command, discussed in Section II, is a method by which blank lines can be inserted into a batch file. EDLIN does allow you to enter this character.

However, blank lines can also be created using the ANSI command [Esc][#B, where # is the number of blank lines to insert.

5. **Find Matching Brackets**. This is a feature that can be a lifesaver if you write programs or macros that require the use of matching sets of (), [], { }, or <>.

For example, the illustration below contains a line taken from a dBASE program. The purpose of the command is to index names written as first name and last name, in the order of last name then first name. The AT() function searches for spaces to create substring SUBS() that reverse the order of last and first names. What is wrong with this command?

```
INDEX ON SUBS(name,AT(SPACE(1),name)+1)+SUBS(name,1,AT(SPACE(1),name-1 TO TEST
```

The answer is that one of the parentheses is missing. But which one? The Norton Editor has a unique feature that locates the matching bracket to any one that you place the cursor on. For example, place the cursor on any (and enter **[F6] M**. The Editor will search for the) that logically matches the highlighted (. This feature makes it much easier to locate missing brackets.

In the example, the missing bracket could be located by testing each opening parenthesis wth [F6] M, as shown in Figure 13-2.

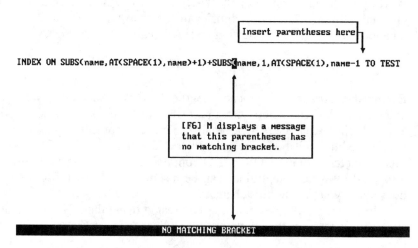

Figure 13-2 Missing bracket located by program.

- **Auto-Indent**. Indenting programs properly is considered good programming because it makes your programs more readable and easier to understand. The Editor has an auto-indent mode, in which successive lines will be indented to the same level following a ↵ instead of placing the cursor at the left margin each time. To increase the indent level, enter [tab]. To decrease the level, enter [backspace].

Like the matching feature, this one can save you countless keystrokes and speed the process of creating well-structured programs.

- **Suppress Details.** The **[F6] C** command causes the Editor to suppress the display of all lines that do not begin with a letter. This means that all intended lines will be suppressed. This feature is a convenient way of suppressing some of the detail in a computer program. The effect of this command will differ with the way the programs are written.

Figure 13-3 shows a section of a dBASE program in the normal display mode.

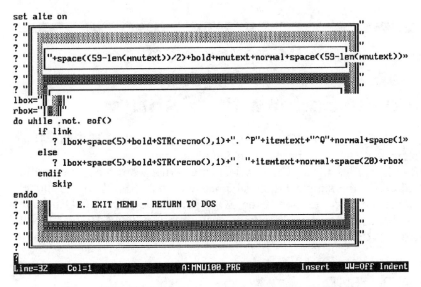

Figure 13-3 dBASE program code in normal display mode.

If the **[F6] C** command is used to suppress lines, the display is reduced to those commands that begin with a letter, as shown in Figure 13-4. In this example, that allows you to check the DO WHILE and ENDDO loops to see that each pair is correctly matched. Note lines that begin with a space, [tab], or ? are suppressed.

```
Set alte on
lbox="|| ▓ ||"
rbox="|▓▓||"
do while .not. eof()◄─────────────┐
enddo◄                            │
close alte
use &mnuname
SET ALTE TO &batch
set alte on
do while .not. eof()◄─────────────┐
enddo◄                            │
close alte
set console on
close database
return
```

┌─────────────────────────────┐
│ Compressed Display Mode   │
└─────────────────────────────┘

```
Condensed display mode, press RETURN to exit
```

Figure 13-4 Compressed program code display.

Using the Editor with dBASE

If you work with dBASE III Plus you will find that the Norton Editor is an ideal way to create dBASE programs, or to edit memo fields.

dBASE III Plus allows you to select an external word processing program as a substitute for the simple Editor supplied with dBASE. To make this change, you can use the Editor to modify the CONFIG.DB file. CONFIG.DB is a text file that dBASE reads for default settings each time it is loaded. The CONFIG.DB supplied with dBASE III Plus reads:

STATUS=ON
COMMAND=ASSIST

These two commands turn on the status line and run the Assist command each time dBASE is loaded.

To install the Norton Editor as the dBASE text editor, add the following lines to the CONFIG.DB file.

TEDIT=ne
WP=ne

Make sure that the NE.COM file is accessible when dBASE is running. This can be done by opening a path to the directory in which NE.COM is stored, or placing a copy in the same directory as dBASE.

DOS Editor

The Norton Editor program disk also contains a program called the Norton DOS Editor. The file is stored in a directory on the Norton Editor disk called **\NDE**.

The program is included, as well as its source code. The program is designed to enhance the command editing template built into DOS. When the Norton DOS Editor is active, you can use the [up arrow] and [down arrow] keys to scroll through a list of previous DOS commands. You can edit the commands and reexecute them. The normal DOS template stores only the last command you entered, while the Norton DOS Editor stores the last 1000 characters worth of DOS commands.

The Norton DOS Editor is a memory-resident program that uses about 3K of memory. It uses many of the same editing commands as the Norton Editor to alter commands stored in the memory buffer.

14

The Norton Guides

The Norton Guides program is really a series of programs like the utilities programs, which enables you to run and create on-line **informational databases**. An **informational database** should not be confused with a "database program," which is a computer application that allows you to enter and retrieve data. An **informational database** is one that contains a fixed set of information that is referenced, but not altered. It is like a reference book that is implemented as a computer-based source of information as opposed to the conventional printed reference text.

The guides were originally conceived as aids for programmers who needed to remember the specific syntax for commands and functions in a programming language. But most computer users require help in remembering commands, functions, and usages, even if they never write a computer program.

Informational databases, fairly common in today's applications, are usually encountered in the form of help screens built into various applications. The NORTON GUIDES programs are designed to provide additional means of this type of on-line help. The Norton Guides programs can be used in one of two ways.

- The Norton Guides programs are currently sold in conjunction with a database, which provides on-line help in a specific programming language, such as BASIC, Pascal, or 8088 Assembly Language.

- You can use the Norton Guides programs to create and run your own online databases.

This chapter will discuss how the Norton Guides programs can be used to create databases of your own design.

Why Custom-Informational Databases?

If the Norton Guides programs provide a form of help-screen display, why are they needed? Aren't the help-screen displays provided with the specific applications sufficient?

There are three reasons to create a custom-informational database.

- **Inadequate Help**. Even the best help-screen displays provided with standard applications such as word processing or spreadsheets, cover only a fraction of the information that you might want or need. This is especially true of powerful and complex programs such as 1-2-3, dBASE III Plus, WordPerfect, and other major applications. In addition, the quality and quantity of these screens will vary greatly from product to product. In the end, help screens are viewed as a necessary evil by most software vendors. The Norton Guides programs allow you to purchase or develop professional-level reference guides just as you would purchase reference books about applications.

- **No Help Available**. Not all applications provide on-line help. Many special-use programs have no help facility at all. This is true of many programming environments like Turbo Pascal or Quick-Basic.

  Another problem is that important information is often hidden while you are working on a different part of the application. For example, most accounting programs assume that you know the chart of an account number when you are entering transactions. The common practice is to print out a chart of accounts and keep it by the computer as you are working. The same thing is true for vendor and customer numbers. The Norton Guides programs provide a means by which you can place that information into an on-line database.

  You can create a supporting database for these applications with the Norton Guides programs. This is helpful to programmers who are developing custom applications. You can create a Norton Guides database to provide help for those applications without having to write the code for that help into your applications.

- **Local Information**. In any computer installation there are many choices about how the computers and the applications that are supposed to run on it will be set up. It is not uncommon to see Post-it notes tagged on computer monitors to remind users of certain names or commands that are needed to find their way around the system.

  In addition, you may want to create a database with explanations about how your business uses a specific application. For example, you may have an established method of calculating a customer's credit rating. Creating a database explaining that method for a user who was working on a spreadsheet that requires this procedure would be useful.

A Norton Guides database can be designed that will contain all of this idiosyncratic information.

The Norton Guides programs provide a means by which you can place a large volume of information about the computer, the application, or a specific office procedure, in one place. The databases can be as simple as a list of customers and account numbers, or a full reference guide about the difference between Version 1A of 1-2-3 and Release 2.

The Norton Guides programs literally provide a window by which MS-DOS computers can access large amounts of information while running standard applications. Their potential cannot be underestimated. Creating and using on-line guides can be one of the most rewarding ways to better organize your computer usage.

How the Guides Work

The Norton Guides programs fall into three separate types.

- **The Engine**. The engine refers to the NG.EXE program. This program is a memory-resident application that takes up 65K of memory. The application stays in memory and is activated by a **hot key**. This **hot key** prompts a window to be displayed on the screen that shows information from a specific database file.

    The engine is designed to load and unload information from the database, which is a disk-based file. This means that the engine will use only 65K no matter how large a database is being referenced. It also means that the engine can switch database files while still on-line. You can select from several databases stored on the disk without having to reload the engine.

    The engine is also designed to be removed from memory if the user desires, without having to reboot the computer.

- **Databases**. Databases refer to special files that actually contain the information that the engine will display. The size of the database is limited only by disk space, since the engine loads the section of the database requested for viewing. Databases can contain menus and cross-references as well as data.

- • **Development Tools**. If you want to create your own databases, the Norton
  Guides programs contains two programs, NGC (Norton Guides
  Compiler) and NGML (Norton Guides Menu Linker), which will create a
  database from a series of text files. Like a programming language, the
  basic information is entered as a text file with special commands inserted
  into the text. The NGC and NGML programs convert and assemble the
  text files into a Norton Guides database.

If you have the Norton Guides programs you have all the tools you need to create
custom databases. The text files can be prepared by any program that produces
standard ASCII text files, such as the Norton Editor or Microsoft Word.

If you use a word processing program you will have to use a special
technique, covered later in this chapter, to carry your formatting over to the text
files.

Features of Databases

The on-line informational databases that can be created and run with the Norton
Guides programs have a number of special features. Like other memory-resident
programs, the Norton Guides programs overlay the screen but do not disturb the
application with which you are working. When you exit the guide, you return to
the application you were working with at the exact point where you left it.

Figure 14-1 is a illustration that shows a database for WordPerfect 4.2, called
Krumm On-Line WordPerfect 4.2. It will illustrate some of the features of the
Norton Guides programs.

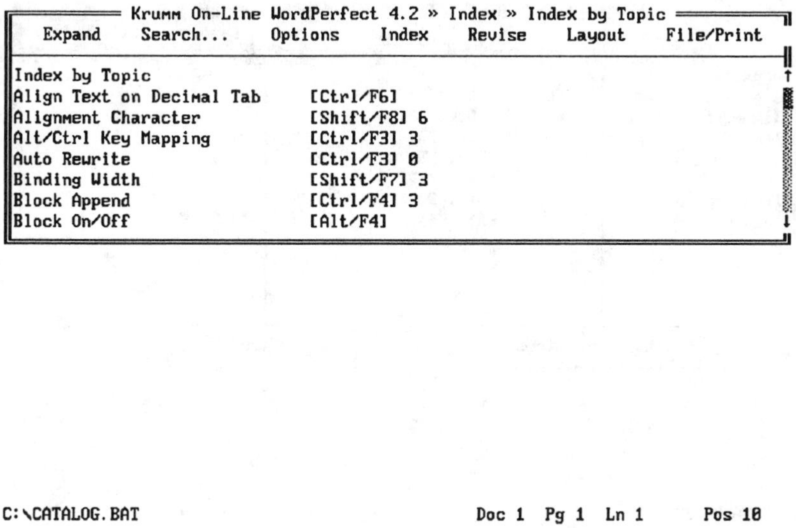

```
╔══════════ Krumm On-Line WordPerfect 4.2 » Index » Index by Topic ══════════╗
║   Expand      Search...    Options    Index    Revise    Layout    File/Print ║
╠══════════════════════════════════════════════════════════════════════════════╣
║Index by Topic                                                                ↑
║Align Text on Decimal Tab      [Ctrl/F6]                                       ▓
║Alignment Character            [Shift/F8] 6                                    ▓
║Alt/Ctrl Key Mapping           [Ctrl/F3] 3                                     ▓
║Auto Rewrite                   [Ctrl/F3] 0                                     ▓
║Binding Width                  [Shift/F7] 3                                    ▓
║Block Append                   [Ctrl/F4] 3                                     ▓
║Block On/Off                   [Alt/F4]                                        ↓
╚══════════════════════════════════════════════════════════════════════════════╝
```

C:\CATALOG.BAT   Doc 1 Pg 1 Ln 1   Pos 10

Figure 14-1 Sample WordPerfect database.

- **Pull-Down Menus.** The Norton Guides shows a menu bar at the top of the window, which displays a series of pull down menus. The first three options, Expand, Search, and Options, are built into the Norton Guides programs engine, as shown in Figure 14-2. The last four are user defined menus and will change with each database that you load. The menus are displayed by moving the highlight with the left or right arrow keys.

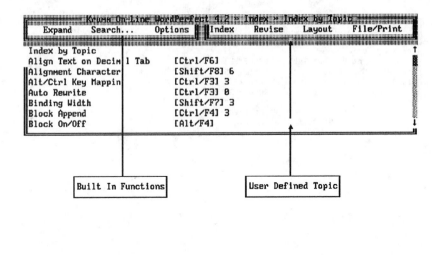

Figure 14-2 Main menu bar.

A user-defined, pull-down menu can list eight more topics, Figure 14-3.

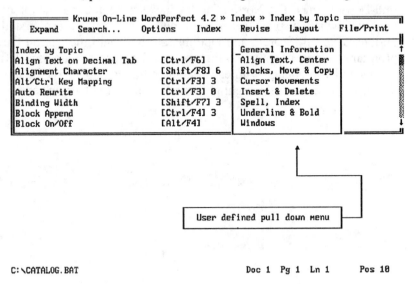

Figure 14-3 User-defined pull-down menu.

- **Short Topic Listing.** Short topics are the headings for full text
  discussions. These headings form a list within the window, as shown in

Figure 14-4. The highlight can be moved from heading to heading using the up and down arrow keys.

On the right side of the window is a vertical bar with a highlight. This bar indicates your position in the list of topics. This is helpful in browsing a list of topics that is longer than can be displayed in the window at any one time.

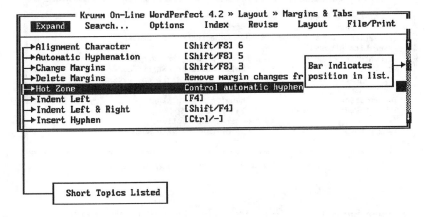

Figure 14-4 Short topics listed.

- **Full-Screen Display.** The [F9] keys toggles the display between half-screen, the default, and full-screen display, (Figure 14-5).

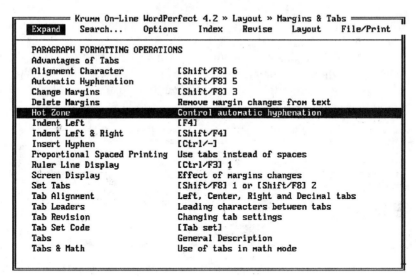

Figure 14-5 Full-screen display of short topics.

- **Expand Short Topics.** Short topics headings displayed in the windows can be expanded to display a full-text entry using the **Expand** command. Expand can be entered by pressing ↵ when you have highlighted the short topic heading of your choice as shown in Figure 14-6.

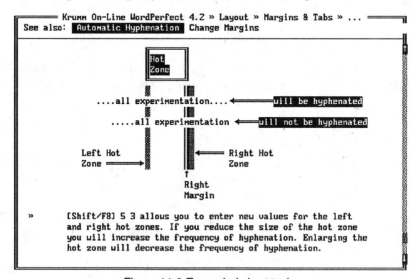

Figure 14-6 Expanded short topic.

- **Search Short Topics.** You can use the **Search** option to locate a key word or text string in the list of short topics, as shown in Figure 14-7.

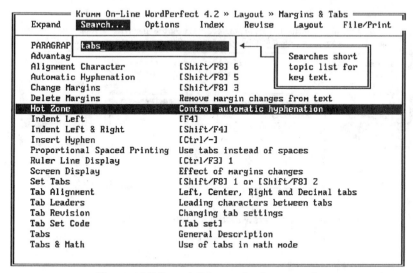

Figure 14-7 Search box used to locate topic.

The program moves the highlight to the first short topic that matches the key (Figure 14-8).

```
======= Krumm On-Line WordPerfect 4.2 » Layout » Margins & Tabs =======
 Expand    Search...    Options    Index    Revise    Layout    File/Print

 PARAGRAPH FORMATTING OPERATIONS
 Advantages of Tabs
 Alignment Character           [Shift/F8] 6
 Automatic Hyphenation         [Shift/F8] 5
 Change Margins                [Shift/F8] 3
 Delete Margins                Remove margin changes from text
 Hot Zone                      Control automatic hyphenation
 Indent Left                   [F4]
 Indent Left & Right           [Shift/F4]
 Insert Hyphen                 [Ctrl/-]
 Proportional Spaced Printing  Use tabs instead of spaces
 Ruler Line Display            [Ctrl/F3] 1
 Screen Display                Effect of margins changes
 Set Tabs                      [Shift/F8] 1 or [Shift/F8] 2
 Tab Alignment                 Left, Center, Right and Decimal tabs
 Tab Leaders                   Leading characters between tabs
 Tab Revision                  Changing tab settings
 Tab Set Code                  [Tab set]
 Tabs                          General Description
 Tabs & Math                   Use of tabs in math mode
```

Figure 14-8 Search highlights short topic.

- **Select Database.** You can display a list of on-line databases to select. Use this option to switch back and forth between different topics (Figure 14-9).

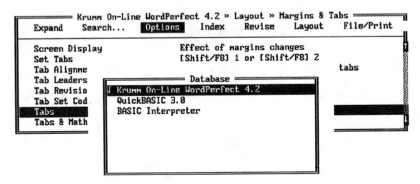

Figure 14-9 Window dispays alternative databases.

- **Hot Key Selection.** The hot key used to activate and deactivate the guide display can be changed at any time. The default hot hey is [SHIFT/F1]. The Krumm On-Line WordPerfect database hot key is set to [~], the tilde key, because [Alt/F1] is used in WordPerfect for Super/Subscript (Figure 14-10).

- **See Also References.** An expanded entry can contain a list of other topic headings that are related to the displayed topic. The list of topics appears at the top of the window display. You can select a cross-referenced topic by highlighting the topic you want, and pressing ↵. The program then displays the expanded entry for that topic. If the cross-referenced topic also contains cross-references they appear at the top of the window. This system allows the reader to move through all the related entries in a large database in a few moments. It is a much more efficient way to locate data than using an index in a book, since the computer takes care of locating the data for you (Figure 14-11).

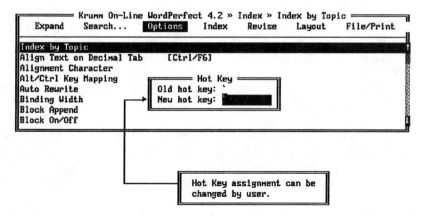

Figure 14-10 Define hot key.

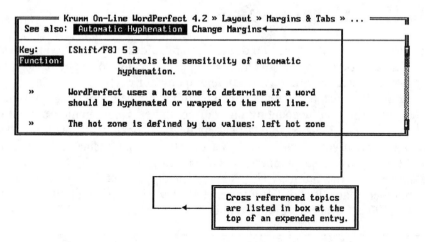

Figure 14-11 Cross reference topics listed at top of screen.

- **Automatic Lookup.** This option causes the Norton Guides programs to highlight the word at the cursor position on the screen when the hot key is pressed. The program then automatically searches the current list of topics to locate a matching entry.

This option is useful for command-driven programs such as dBASE III Plus, or programming languages in which the word you are typing might be a command or function that would be listed as a heading in the database.

The option doesn't work very well with applications like word processing in which the text on the screen is not usually related to the topic you want to look up.

Another advantage of Auto-Lookup is that the Norton Guides window will display in the top or bottom of the screen, opposite the half in which the program cursor is located. This means that the text near the cursor will always be visible when the guide window is displayed.

The Norton Guides programs presents a new medium in which information can be brought to the people who need it. Keep in mind that there is no reason to restrict a database to computer-related topics. For example, you might create a database on standard accounting procedures to run in the background of an accounting program.

Creating Databases

In order to realize the full potential of the Norton Guides programs you may want to create a database of your own. Databases can be created for many reasons and the look of the database will vary depending upon your goal.

To learn about database creation, begin with a simple example. Suppose that you are doing financial accounting on your computer. One common problem is that accounting programs or spreadsheet applications deal mostly with numbers. For instance, when you create a chart of accounts for your business, the accounts are traditionally assigned numbers; when you enter items into your inventory, you assign each item a number. This is very efficient, except that it is not the way you remember things. It is difficult to remember when entering a transaction that account 50100 is Legal Fees or that Walter La Fish is customer # 1034.

> *The One-Write accounting system from Great American Software is one accounting program that will display windows that allow you to list account and vendor numbers.*

If you have the Norton Guides programs you can create a database or databases that will display the lists whenever you need them. A list-type database is the simplest type you can create for the Norton Guides programs. Even though they are simple, most people will find many uses for these list displays. Remember that the Norton Guides programs have a search function that will search the list database to locate an entry.

Preparing a List Database

Norton Guides databases begin with text files. The basic text file is one that contains the data to be displayed in the window when the Norton Guides program is activated. Suppose you need to create three lists for your accounting work: a chart of accounts, a list of vendors, and a list of customers. Your goal would be to pop-up the Norton Guides database if you couldn't remember an account, vendor, or customer number while using your accounting software.

To prepare a text file for the Norton Guides you need a word processor or text editor that will create ASCII text files. You could use the DOS EDLIN program, or better yet, the Norton Editor.

If you are making an extensive database you will probably need to use a full-powered word processing program. The use of word processors is discussed later in this chapter. For now, the assumption is made that you are using a standard editor, such as the Norton Editor.

Short Topics

The list database that you want to create will end up looking like the database pictured in Figure 14-12. The window displays the list of information that you need.

```
═══════════════ Accounting Lists » Lists » Chart of Accounts ═══════════════╗
   Expand      Search...     Options     Lists                              ║
╔════════════════════════════════════════════════════════════════════════╗
║CASH - CHECKING ACCOUNT                1000                              ↑║
║CASH-CHECKING ACCOUNT                  1040                               ║
║CASH-SAVINGS ACCOUNT                   1050                               ║
║CASH-PAYROLL ACCOUNT                   1060                               ║
║PETTY CASH                             1080                               ║
║CASH TRANSFERS                         1099                               ║
║ACCOUNTS RECEIVABLE                    1100                               ║
║ALLOWANCE FOR BAD DEBTS                1190                              ↓║
╚════════════════════════════════════════════════════════════════════════╝
```

Figure 14-12 Accounting database example.

The list database that you are creating will consist of a series of "short entries." Each short entry will show up in the window as a single line of text.

The Norton Guides programs uses the exclamation point (!) as the beginning of all Norton Guides commands. If the program encounters a ! as the first character on a line, it expects a command to follow. Note that ! used in other locations in the text will be treated as a normal character.

Begin by creating a text file. In this example the file will be called COA.TXT (chart of accounts text).

The first line in the database is the one that creates the first line in the display window, **CASH -- CHECKING ACCOUNT 1000.** You would enter

!SHORT:CASH -- CHECKING ACCOUNT   1000

This line consists of two parts:

```
Command
word                    Text to display


    !SHORT: CASH - CHECKING ACCOUNT                 1000
```

Keep in mind that the **!SHORT:** will not be displayed on the screen. The entire chart of accounts display will consist of a series of **!SHORT:** entries, one for each item in the list. Below is an example of such a file.

Listing 14-1 COA.TXT file listing

```
!SHORT:CASH - CHECKING ACCOUNT               1000
!SHORT:CASH-CHECKING ACCOUNT                 1040
!SHORT:CASH-SAVINGS ACCOUNT                  1050
!SHORT:CASH-PAYROLL ACCOUNT                  1060
!SHORT:ACCOUNTS RECEIVABLE                   1100
!SHORT:ALLOWANCE FOR BAD DEBTS               1190
!SHORT:INVENTORY                             1200
!SHORT:PREPAID EXPENSES                      1350
!SHORT:LOANS AND EXCHANGES                   1400
!SHORT:LAND                                  1500
!SHORT:BUILDING                              1510
!SHORT:ACCUM DEPR-BUILDING                   1511
!SHORT:EQUIPMENT                             1570
!SHORT:ACCUM DEPR-EQUIPMENT                  1571
!SHORT:FURNITURE AND FIXTURES                1580
!SHORT:ACCUM DEPR-FURN & FIX                 1581
!SHORT:OTHER FIXED ASSETS                    1680
```

```
!SHORT:ACCUM DEPR-OTH FIX ASSETS                        1681
!SHORT:GOODWILL                                         1850
```

Notice that in this file the lines begin with the name of the account. This is because the search feature in the Norton Guides programs will search the beginning of each short entry for match text. Therefore, you should try to place the key word in each entry at the beginning of the line. For example, the key word in CASH-**SAVINGS** ACCOUNT is the word **SAVINGS**, it might be better to enter it as **SAVINGS** ACCOUNT-CASH. That way, searching for **SAVINGS** would locate the correct item. If the item was left as CASH-**SAVINGS** ACCOUNT, a search for **SAVINGS** would skip that entry.

The order in which the items appear in the text file is the order in which they will appear in the database. If you want the names of the accounts to appear alphabetically you would rearrange the text in the correct order. For example, you might enter the chart of accounts as:

Listing 14-2 COA.TXT file listing sorted alphbetically.

```
!SHORT:ACCOUNTS RECEIVABLE                              1100
!SHORT:ACCUM DEPR-BUILDING                              1511
!SHORT:ACCUM DEPR-EQUIPMENT                             1571
!SHORT:ACCUM DEPR-FURN & FIX                            1581
!SHORT:ACCUM DEPR-OTH FIX ASSETS                        1681
!SHORT:ALLOWANCE FOR BAD DEBTS                          1190
!SHORT:BUILDING                                         1510
!SHORT:CASH - CHECKING ACCOUNT                          1000
!SHORT:CASH-PAYROLL ACCOUNT                             1060
!SHORT:CASH-SAVINGS ACCOUNT                             1050
!SHORT:EQUIPMENT                                        1570
!SHORT:FURNITURE AND FIXTURES                           1580
!SHORT:GOODWILL                                         1850
!SHORT:INVENTORY                                        1200
!SHORT:LAND                                             1500
!SHORT:LOANS AND EXCHANGES                              1400
!SHORT:OTHER FIXED ASSETS                               1680
!SHORT:PREPAID EXPENSES                                 1350
```

> *If you were using a word processor, such as WordPerfect or Word, that performs sorting, you can get lists sequenced automatically.*

Once you have created this file, you can create similar files for other lists you want to include. Below are two more short sample files, one for vendors and one for customers.

Listing 14-3 VEND.TXT file listing

```
!SHORT:ACE MACHINING                          147
!SHORT:COMMUNICATIONS SYSTEMS INC             148
!SHORT:DEES EXPORTS                           144
!SHORT:OAKS HARDWARE                          143
!SHORT:PHOTO FAST                             142
!SHORT:R & B TRAVEL                           145
!SHORT:STAMPS & COINS                         146
!SHORT:WORLD EDUCATION CENTER                 149
```

Listing 14-4 CUST.TXT file listing

```
!SHORT:ANDERSON, VAL             1011
!SHORT:BLADES, SUZANNE           1012
!SHORT:DEMPSEY, PAUL             1013
!SHORT:DEMTROLOPULOS, LLOYD      1014
!SHORT:DIAS, KEITH               1015
!SHORT:FEHR, JAMES               1016
!SHORT:HAGAN, CHUCK              1017
!SHORT:KEANE, BILL               1018
!SHORT:LAIO, BEV                 1019
!SHORT:TOMPKINS, ALEX            1020
```

This part of the process can continue with the creation of additional lists. At this point, each list is a separate text file. As of yet no relationship between the various lists has been created. That will come in the next stage.

The Menu-Link File

Once you have created the files that contain the short entries that you want to include in your database you need to create an additional text file called the "menu-link." The **menu-link** file is used by the Norton Guides programs to combine all of the individual text files into a single database. The menu link file establishes the following for the database:

- **Database Name.** Each database **must** have a name. This name is the one that appears in the list of databases when you select a database for loading, and appears at the top of the window to identify which database is being displayed. Remember that the databases are not listed by their filenames in the selection window, but by the database name. This means that your database name can be up to 40 characters in length.

- **Pull-Down Menus.** This file also contains the name of the pull-down menus that appear on the menu bar at the top of the screen. You must have at least one menu name. You can have as many as four. Keep in mind that these names are the ones that appear at the top of the display. Each pull-down menu name can contain entries for as many as eight items. Each item in a pull-down menu refers to an entire file of !SHORT entries. This means that you have room to coordinate up to 32 text files worth of data in a single database.

  Note that the one to four pull-down menu names can be accessed by typing the first letter of the menu item. To allow this system to work with all menus, make sure that no two menu names begin with the same first letter.

  Also keep in mind that since the options Expand, Search, and Options are always displayed, avoid menu names that begin with E, S, or O.

- **Pull-Down Items**. When a pull-down menu is selected, the Norton Guides programs display a box with one to eight topics. The topics and their order are determined in the menu-link file. If you want the items in the pull-down box in a specific order-alphabetical or some other order-you must place them in that order in the menu-link file.

  Each item in the pull-down box refers to a file of !SHORT entries. However, the name that appears in the pull-down menu box is not the filename of the text file. The menu-link file allows you to assign a description. The description should be between 1 and 65 characters.

Like the !SHORT entry files, the menu-link file is a text file. In this example a file called **LISTS.TXT** will be created as the menu-link file for the accounting information list file COA.TXT, VEND.TXT, and CUST.TXT.

The menu-link file contains only a few lines. The first line is always the **!NAME** command, which assigns the name to the database. For example, you might call this database **Accounting Lists**. Remember that the name can be up to 40 characters in length. Enter

!NAME:Accounting Lists

Following the !NAME command, which names the entire database, you will enter a **!MENU** command. This command creates the name of the pull-down menu. It is not restricted by the program but is limited by the display width of your computer. If you create pull-down menu names that are too wide for the screen, the database will function correctly but the menu displays will be off the screen. As a general rule, the total length of all the menu items should not exceed 40 characters, including spaces. In this case the name **Lists** should be sufficient.

> *As mentioned before, it is best to begin each pull-down menu name with a unique first letter. This enables the person using the database to simply type the letter of the menu to display the option box. Avoid E, S, and O as first letters because they would conflict with Expand, Search, and Options, which are always part of the menu bar.*

Enter

!MENU:Lists

Following the menu you can list up to eight items. Each item represents a text file that contains your **!SHORT** entries. For example, suppose you wanted the chart of accounts list to appear as the first item on this pull-down menu. Enter the name of the menu item and the name of the file that contains the entries.

There is one small change that must be made at this point. In the example, the file that contains the chart of accounts information is COA.TXT. But the name you need to enter is COA.NGO. What is COA.NGO? The answer is that the Norton Guides programs cannot directly incorporate text files into a database. There is an intermediate step in which the text files are converted into NGO (Norton Guides Object) files. It is these NGO files that are linked with the NGML program, not your original text files. When you prepare a menu-link file you need to remember that it will be NGO, not TXT, files that are linked.

To place the chart of accounts as the first item in the Lists menu, enter

Chart of Accounts coa.ngo

> *Keep in mind that there is no basic restriction on the size of the menu item entry. However, as a practical matter, entries over 65 characters will cause the text not to be displayed properly. It is advised that these entries be kept under 65 characters, which will not impose too great a design limitation.*

Note that this item is not preceded by a special command. The NGML program assumes that all items listed following a **!MENU** command belong to the same menu. The assumption continues until another **!MENU** is encountered.

> *The first item in the first pull-down menu has a special significance in the Norton Guides system. This item will, in effect, become the default display item. When a database is first loaded, the program automatically displays this item in the window. If you are creating a complex database, it might be a good idea to create a table of contents or index file and place it as the first item in the first menu. When the database is loaded the user is automatically presented with this table of contents list, which can serve as a guide to rest of the database. This is the technique used in the Krumm On-Line databases. If you have a small database, select the most commonly used menu item as the default.*

Next, enter the item names and filename of the other two lists. Enter

Vendor List vend.ngo
Customer Lists cust.ngo

The file now looks like Listing 14-5.

Listing 14-5 Menu file listing.

```
!NAME:Accounting Lists
!menu:Lists
Chart of Accounts coa.ngo
Vendor List vend.ngo
Customer List cust.ngo
```

As with the menu bar, you might want to consider starting each menu item with a unique letter. If this is done, you can type the first letter of the entry to activate the option instead of using the highlight. In this case you have two items, Chart of Accounts and Customer List, that begin with the first letter C. The Norton Guides program will always activate the first C, Chart of Accounts, if C is pressed. You might want to change the first entry to read **Accounts List** to take advantage of the unique letter feature, as shown in Listing 14-6.

Listing 14-6 Menu File Listing rearranged.

```
!NAME:Accounting Lists
!menu:Lists
Accounts List coa.ngo
Vendor List vend.ngo
Customer List cust.ngo
```

If you find that you simply cannot use items with unique letters, you can fudge the difference by adding letters to the menu choice. For example, you might label three entries with the same first letter with A, B, C. Example:

```
!menu:Formatting
A. Margins mar.ngo
B. Macros mac.ngo
C. Merge mer.ngo
```

The final step is the compiling and linking of these text files. Before you reach that step, the illustration below relates the text files and commands to the final use in the displayed database, Figure 14-13.

```
!NAME       Creates name of database.
!MENU       Creates pull-down menu names
!SHORT      Creates short topics lists that appear
            in data window.
```

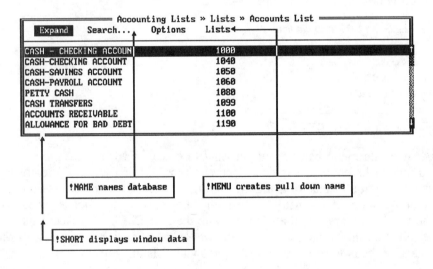

Figure 14-13 Database created by sample listings.

Compiling Text Files

Now that you have created the required text files, you can perform the steps necessary to create a database. First you must convert the files that contain the **!SHORT** commands into NGO (Norton Guide Object) files.

The term "object file" is used in programming to represent a binary file produced from a text file. The program is usually written as a text file, referred to as the "source" file or "source code" file. The compiler program converts each "source code" file, i.e., text, to an "object" file, i.e., binary. In programming source files are compiled to object files. The object files are then linked to form the final program. A similar process takes place in the Norton Guides programs.

The NGC program is used to change text files into NGO files. The program does not change your original text files but creates a new file with the same name, and an NGO extension. For example, to convert the COA.TXT file to an NGO file, enter

NGC coa.txt ↵

The program displays a list of items showing what it found while compiling the text file.

```
The Norton Guides Compiler, Copyright (C) 1987 by Peter Norton Computing
    Compiling `coa.txt'
        Scanning...
        Writing list...
        Writing longs...
        Cross referencing...

32 entries processed
```

If there were problems with the text file, the program would display information about those problems. The most common dilemmas concern cross-referencing, which is covered under the heading Cross-References, later in this chapter.

You can compile more than one file at a time by using several filenames as parameters. Example:

NGC vend.txt cust.txt ↵

The program will output the statistics for each of the selected files.

```
    Compiling `vend.txt'
        Scanning...
        Writing list...
        Writing longs...
        Cross referencing...

 8 entries processed


    Compiling `cust.txt'
        Scanning...
        Writing list...
        Writing longs...
        Cross referencing...

10 entries processed
```

If you have a very large number of files to compile (more than eight), you should not place all the names as parameters on a single command. The best solution would be to limit each command to five or six files and create a batch file with a series of NGC commands. When you want to compile your entire database, enter the name of the batch file that contains the NGC commands. You might also add the NGML linking command to the file to compile and link with a single command.

The final step is to use the menu-link file with the NGML program. Notice that the menu-link file is not compiled like the files with the !SHORT commands. Enter

NGML lists.txt ↵

The program displays a list of the NGO files used in the database. Any files that could not be located would also be displayed. Note that the NGML will not write a database, NG file, if one of the specified NGO files cannot be found. All of the NGO files referenced in the menu-link file must exist for a database file, NG, to be produced.

```
    Building `Accounting Lists'

        coa.ngo...

        vend.ngo...

        cust.ngo...

    Cross referencing...


Created lists.ng
```

You can now load the database into the NG program. Use the **Options Database** command to display the list of databases (Figure 14-14).

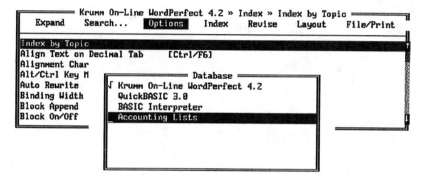

Figure 14-14 New database is listed in database window.

Load the database by highlighting the name, and pressing ↵. Pressing **L** displays the pull-down menu, **LISTS**, which displays three items on the menu, as seen in Figure 14-15.

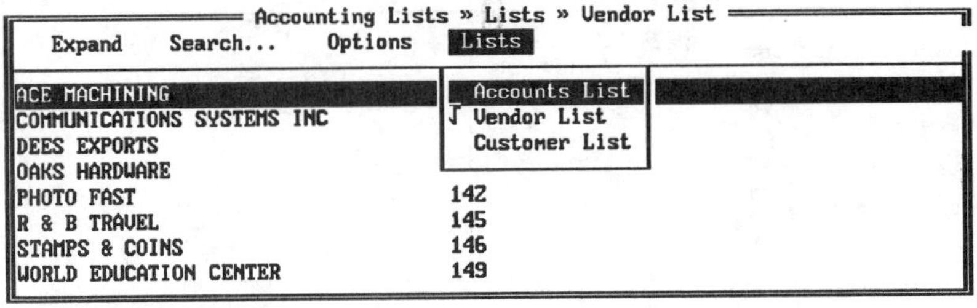

```
╔═══════════════ Accounting Lists » Lists » Vendor List ═══════════════╗
║   Expand      Search...     Options     Lists                         ║
╠══════════════════════════════════╤═══════════════════╤═══════════════╣
║ ACE MACHINING                    │   Accounts List   │               ║
║ COMMUNICATIONS SYSTEMS INC       │ √ Vendor List     │               ║
║ DEES EXPORTS                     │   Customer List   │               ║
║ OAKS HARDWARE                    └───────────────────┘               ║
║ PHOTO FAST                         142                                ║
║ R & B TRAVEL                       145                                ║
║ STAMPS & COINS                     146                                ║
║ WORLD EDUCATION CENTER             149                                ║
╚══════════════════════════════════════════════════════════════════════╝
```

Figure 14-15 Main topics of accounting database listed.

To load the vendor file, simply enter V. You can use the search command to locate a specific vendor. Example:

v
s
stamps ↵

The highlight locates STAMPS & COINS (Figure 14-16).

```
══════════════ Accounting Lists » Lists » Vendor List ══════════════
┌──────────────────────────────────────────────────────────────────┐
│  │ Expand │   Search...    Options    Lists                        │
│ ACE MACHINING                      147                             │
│ COMMUNICATIONS SYSTEMS INC         148                             │
│ DEES EXPORTS                       144                             │
│ OAKS HARDWARE                      143                             │
│ PHOTO FAST                         142                             │
│ R & B TRAVEL                       145                             │
│ STAMPS & COINS                     146                             │
│ WORLD EDUCATION CENTER             149                             │
└──────────────────────────────────────────────────────────────────┘
```

Figure 14-16 Search locates short topic.

The database that was created in this section was the simplest type, a list database. But the Norton Guides programs can accommodate much more complicated databases. In the next section you will see how the basic list database you have created can be expanded.

Long Entries and Cross-Referencing

The simple list database you have just created functions quite well. However, this type of database can be viewed as an outline. The Norton Guides allows you to create **long** entries for one or more of the short entries in your text files.

A **long** entry is simply any type of text you want to associate with a short entry. The only limit on a long entry is a size limit of 12,000 characters for each long entry.

If you use an editor or word processor that allows you to enter the extended IBM character set you can create diagrams and drawings as part of your long entry.

Below is a modified version of the VEND.TXT file (Listing 14-7). Notice that text has been entered below the !SHORT entry for DEES EXPORTS, which represents the long entry for DEES EXPORTS. The text will not be displayed unless DEES EXPORTS is expanded.

Listing 14-7 VEND.TXT with expanded entry.

```
!SHORT:ACE MACHINING                                       147
!SHORT:COMMUNICATIONS SYSTEMS INC                          148
!SHORT:DEES EXPORTS                                        144
^uProduct:^u
                Women's Shoes
                Goose Down Pillows
^bTerms:^b       Net 30 Days
^rOrders:^r      Call in, 800-555-9292
                Ask for Dave Preston
                Account Number 666-99999
!SHORT:OAKS HARDWARE                                       143
!SHORT:PHOTO FAST                                          142
!SHORT:R & B TRAVEL                                        145
!SHORT:STAMPS & COINS                                      146
!SHORT:WORLD EDUCATION CENTER                              149
```

The Norton Guides programs allow you to enhance the text of a long or short entry by using special symbols to indicate different display attributes.

^u   Changes the display to underlined text

^b   Changes the text to bold display

^r   Changes the text to reverse display

The commands are toggles. This means that the first display code turns the attribute on while the next occurrence of the same code turns it off. Make sure that the codes are entered in pairs that bracket the text you want to affect.

> *Note that the underline command will be translated as a change in color on a Color/Graphics Adapter running a color display. The underline applies only to monochrome displays.*

It is important to note that the use of the attribute codes makes it more difficult to judge column alignment. If you look at the text of the long entry the items do not appear to line up vertically.

```
^uProduct:^u
                Women's Shoes
                Goose Down Pillows
^bTerms:^b       Net 30 Days
```

```
^rOrders:^r      Call in, 800-555-9292
                 Ask for Dave Preston
                 Account Number 666-99999
```

But when the text is compiled the attribute commands are converted from text to non-printing instructions. The space they took up as text items is also removed and the final alignment on the database display is correct.

```
Product:
                 | Women's Shoes
                 | Goose Down Pillows
Terms:           | Net 30 Days
Orders:          | Call in, 800-555-9292
                 | Ask for Dave Preston
                 | Account Number 666-99999
```

If you want to use these attribute codes, you will have to be content with the alignment problems they cause. A good method is to enter all the text first and get the proper alignment, then add the codes after you are sure that the alignment is correct.

Cross References

A long entry can be cross-referenced to other long entries by using the !SEEALSO command, which should be the last line of a long entry. Its purpose is to list the names of other long entries that are logically related to the currently displayed long entry.

For example, suppose that there was information in the entries for **OAKS HARDWARE** and under **CHUCK HAGAN** (in the customer file) that was related to **DEES EXPORTS**. A !SEEALSO command could be created that would display those two items for cross-referencing at the top of the display when DEES EXPORTS was expanded.

A **!SEEALSO** command sets up an automatic search for a short entry that matches the **!SEEALSO** reference. If you highlight the reference and press ↵, the program will automatically locate the matching **!SHORT** reference and display the text of the long entry. Note that cross-referencing will only work when the cross-referenced item **!SHORT** entry has long entry text associated with it. This makes sense because there would be little purpose in making a cross-reference if all you saw was the short entry topic. The basic purpose of cross-referencing is to eliminate redundant information by linking related items.

The **!SEEALSO** commands can have one or more references to other **!SHORT** topics. You can reference any **!SHORT** topic in the same text file or you can specify a !**SHORT** topic in some other file in the database. This means that a cross reference can jump to another topic in any menu in the database.

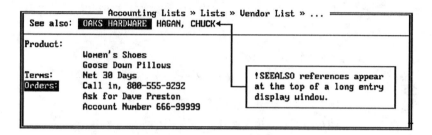

Figure 14-17 SEEALSO cross references.

The Form of Cross References

The !**SEEALSO** syntax is a bit more complicated than the other ! commands. The simplest form of !**SEEALSO** is shown below:

!SEEALSO:OAKS

This reference will link the current long entry with a !**SHORT** entry in the same file that begins with the letters **OAKS**.

Keep in mind that a !**SEEALSO** will search for a match in the same way that a Search command from the menu bar will search a list of short topics. The match will assume that the !**SHORT** entry begins the letters **OAKS**. The case of the text, upper or lower, is not important. But OAKS will not match **SHERMAN OAKS** because the !**SHORT** entry begins with **SHERMAN**, not **OAKS**.

To create a !**SEEALSO** for more than one item, simply add that next item to the list. For example, to cross-reference **OAKS** and **PHOTO** you would enter

!SEEALSO:OAKS PHOTO

Note that the cross-references appear in the order in which they are entered. If you want the reference to have a particular order you must enter them in that order.

You can create references that contain more than one word by enclosing the reference in quotations. The command shown below refers to three short entries: Oaks, Photo Fast, and Stamps. Note that the case of the characters is not significant.

!SEEALSO:OAKS "Photo Fast" Stamps

> *If you use a multiword reference, take care that you have left only a single space between the word in your reference and your !SHORT entry. If you have accidentally entered two spaces (a common word processing mistake) in either the reference or the !SORT entry, the program will not locate the cross-reference.*

To reference a **!SHORT** entry in another file, you must precede the reference with the name of the NGO file that contains the **!SHORT** entry. For example, suppose you wanted to create a cross-reference to a specific customer, CHUCK HAGAN, who has a short entry in the **CUST** file. You would enter both the filename and the reference text, separated by a colon. Note that the name is entered as HAGAN, CHUCK because that is the way it is entered in the **!SHORT** entry in the CUST file.

> *Remember that at the time the cross-reference is actually made, the text files will have been compiled into NGO (object) files. The cross-reference must contain a reference to the NGO (object) file, not the original text file.*

!SEEALSO:cust.ngo:"HAGAN, CHUCK"

You can combine cross-references from the same file in the same **!SEEALSO**, with references to **!SHORT** entries in the same file. The command below refers to OAKS, in the same file, and HAGAN, CHUCK in the cust file.

!SEEALSO:cust.ngo:"HAGAN, CHUCK" OAKS

The order is not significant. You can also make references to additional **!SHORT** entries in other files. The command below refers to an entry in the same file and entries in CUST and COA.

!SEEALSO:cust.ngo:"HAGAN, CHUCK" OAKS coa.ngo:LAND

As with other entries, you are not limited in the number of cross references you enter. There are some points to consider when creating a **!SEEALSO** reference.

- If the text of cross-reference items is wider than can be displayed on a single line, the reference will not appear on the screen display. Note that the length of the displayed references will not include the filenames or other delimiters entered in the **!SEEALSO** command.

- When a long entry is displayed, you can move the highlight to a specific cross-reference by typing the first letter of the reference. Note this does not activate the cross-reference. You still must press ─″.

- If you must place more cross-references in an entry than can be displayed on one line. Those references can be activated by typing the first letter of entry and pressing ─″. Since the reader cannot see the name of the reference on the top line, you can include a note in the text of the long entry indicating which letters will activate additional cross-reference items.

- It is not necessary to include a backward reference to return to the calling reference. For example, if you jump from DEES to OAKS, you would probably want to have a reference that would return you to DEES, which was the original entry you expanded. If you do not place a reference in OAKS for DEES, the program will automatically display a reference called **Previous**. Selecting this option returns the reader to the last **!SHORT** entry that was expanded.

Below are samples of the file VEND.TXT and CUST.TXT, which now include cross-references.

Listing 14-8 VEND.TXT listing.

```
!SHORT:ACE MACHINING                              147
!SHORT:COMMUNICATIONS SYSTEMS INC                 148
!SHORT:DEES EXPORTS                               144
^uProduct:^u
            Women's Shoes
            Goose Down Pillows
^bTerms:^b    Net 30 Days
^rOrders:^r    Call in, 800-555-9292
            Ask for Dave Preston
            Account Number 666-99999
```

```
!SEEALSO:"OAKS HARDWARE" CUST.NGO:"HAGAN, CHUCK"
!SHORT:OAKS HARDWARE                            143
^AF0Note:^A07 This company is a branch of DEES
EXPORTS. Please refer
all business to DEES EXPORTS.
!SEEALSO:CUST.NGO:"HAGAN, CHUCK"
!SHORT:PHOTO FAST                               142
!SHORT:R & B TRAVEL                             145
!SHORT:STAMPS & COINS                           146
!SHORT:WORLD EDUCATION CENTER                   149
```

Listing 14-9 CUST.TXT listing.

```
!SHORT:ANDERSON, VAL                1011
!SHORT:BLADES, SUZANNE              1012
!SHORT:DEMPSEY, PAUL                1013
!SHORT:DEMTROLOPULOS, LLOYD         1014
!SHORT:DIAS, KEITH                  1015
!SHORT:FEHR, JAMES                  1016
!SHORT:HAGAN, CHUCK                 1017
This customer does not like shoes from Dee's.
Send him Dee's but tell him you got it somewhere
else.
He will never know the difference.
!SHORT:KEANE, BILL                  1018
!SHORT:LAIO, BEV                    1019
!SHORT:TOMPKINS, ALEX               1020
```

In the VEND.TXT a different type of attribute command was used, ^A. The ^A is employed to insert a hexadecimal value, which will be used to affect the screen display. This command allows you to implement some video effects other than the ones possible with ^B, ^U and ^R. If you are using a monochrome system, then you can implement blinking text in normal, bold, or reverse video. If you have a color display you can change the color of the foreground and background of the text.

The IBM PC and compatible display adapters use a system in which each bit is assigned a specific meaning, in terms of the effect it will have on the video display. (This is similar to the way individual bits are used to determine the file attributes for each file, as discussed in Section IV.)

On monochrome displays, the highest bit controls blinking, the next three the background, then bold, and three more for the foreground. A value of 000 produces black, while 111 produces white. Note that a foreground color of 001 will create underlined text.

Suppose you wanted to create a warning that would catch the readers attention. You could use black letters blinking on a white background. The bit settings would be as shown in Figure 14-18).

Blink	Background			Bold	Foreground		– Under
1	1	1	1	0	0	0	0

Figure 14-18 Setting for blinking black on white.

But this is a binary number. To use it with the ^A command it must be converted to hexadecimal notation. (See Chapter 1.) The 1111 in binary coverts to the hex number F, and 0000 converts simply to 0 hex. Thus, to change to black letters blinking on a white background the value hex F0 should be used. Remember that you must explicitly enter another ^A command to return the screen to normal text or else the attribute will continue. The bits for normal white on black text are shown in Figure 14-19.

Blink	Background			Bold	Foreground		– Under
0	0	0	0	0	1	1	1

Figure 14-19 Settings for white on black.

Since 0000 is hex 0 and 0111 is hex 7, the value to return to normal text is hex 07. In the example the word **Note:** will appear flashing black letters in a white background because it is entered as:

^AF0Note:^A07

Keep in mind that the ^A07 is used to return the rest of the text to normal video.

On a color display, you can control the individual red, green and blue components to create the full eight color palate available on the Color/Graphics Adapter (CGA). To create blinking red letters on a white background you would need to set the bits in the following way (note that in additive color systems, such as CGA, turning on red, green and blue creates white; green and blue create cyan; green, and red, yellow-brown; and red and blue, magenta)

	Background				Foreground		
Blink	Red	Green	Blue	Bold	Red	Green	Blue
1	1	1	1	0	1	0	0

Figure 14-20 Settings for blinking red on white.

This translates to hex F4. To create the warning you would enter

^AF4Note:^A07

Note that white on black text is 07 for color and monochrome systems.

> *The color operations are complicated by the fact that the Norton Guides programs provide a color option that automatically selects specific colors for the text, highlights, and menus. If you are running a database under the color option, and you enter a specific color combination, like the one above (red on white), you will want to return to normal color use by the color option, which is cyan letters on a blue background, not white on black. The value for the cyan on blue is binary 00011011, which is 1B hex. Instead of ^A07 you would use ^A1B to return to normal text. Running hex color 1B on monochrome will produce bold white on black text.*

To alter the database, all the altered files must be recompiled and relinked. When that is done you can try out the cross-referencing feature you placed in the database. To compile, enter

NGC vend.txt cust.tct ↵
NGML lists.txt ↵

> *Note that the Norton Guides programs will automatically load the new version of the database if you replace the file, LISTS.NG, with a new file of the same name.*

If you display DEES on the vendor list you will see the cross references appear at the top of the window, as shown in Figure 14-21.

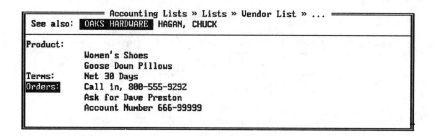

Figure 14-21 Cross References displayed.

You can access the HAGAN entry by entering

h ↵

The text of the entry now appears in the window. If you look at the top line of the display you will see that the current menu topic has changed to the Customer List. The Norton Guides automatically insert a **Previous** cross-reference that will take you back to the calling topic.

Nesting Lists

The Norton Guides programs also contain a feature that allows you to have a **!SHORT** entry expand into another file instead of a long text entry. This is very useful when the information that falls under a given **!SHORT** can be presented better as a list than a text entry. The advantage of lists of **!SHORT** entries over long text entries is that they can be searched quickly to find specific data.

When a list entry calls a list rather than a long text entry, it is called "nesting."

Nesting lists within lists allows you to create an outline structure in which a short entry is a category and the file that it displays contains a list of subtopics.

For example, the current chart of accounts listing contains four cash account entries.

```
!SHORT:CASH - CHECKING ACCOUNT                        1000
!SHORT:CASH-CHECKING ACCOUNT                          1040
!SHORT:CASH-SAVINGS ACCOUNT                           1050
!SHORT:CASH-PAYROLL ACCOUNT                           1060
```

You might consider storing this detail in a separate file and showing only a general topic in the display called CASH ACCOUNTS (Figure 14-22).

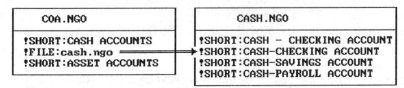

Figure 14-22 Settings for white on black.

The **!FILE** command is used to link a **!SHORT** entry with another file that contains an additional list of **!SHORT** entries, creating the expanding outline effects.

As an example, create a file called CASH.TXT that contains the first four lines of the COA.TXT file. If you are using a word processor you can simply copy those lines to a new file.

Then alter the COA.TXT file to read as below. Note that the cash accounts are replaced by a single **!SHORT** entry, which is then followed by a **!FILE** reference to the CASH.NGO file. Note that the NGO extension is used, not TXT, because the link will be created after the compiling process creates the object files.

Listing 14-5 CASH.TXT listing.

```
!SHORT:CASH - CHECKING ACCOUNT                        1000
!SHORT:CASH-CHECKING ACCOUNT                          1040
!SHORT:CASH-SAVINGS ACCOUNT                           1050
!SHORT:CASH-PAYROLL ACCOUNT                           1060
```

Listing 14-11 Revised COA.TXT listing.

```
!SHORT:CASH ACCOUNTS
!FILE:cash.ngo
!SHORT:ACCOUNTS RECEIVABLE                            1100
!SHORT:ALLOWANCE FOR BAD DEBTS                        1190
!SHORT:INVENTORY                                      1200
!SHORT:PREPAID EXPENSES                               1350
```

```
!SHORT:LOANS AND EXCHANGES                       1400
!SHORT:LAND                                      1500
!SHORT:BUILDING                                  1510
!SHORT:ACCUM DEPR-BUILDING                       1511
!SHORT:EQUIPMENT                                 1570
!SHORT:ACCUM DEPR-EQUIPMENT                      1571
!SHORT:FURNITURE AND FIXTURES                    1580
!SHORT:ACCUM DEPR-FURN & FIX                     1581
!SHORT:OTHER FIXED ASSETS                        1680
!SHORT:ACCUM DEPR-OTH FIX ASSETS                 1681
!SHORT:GOODWILL                                  1850
```

Compile and link the new files into a revised database. Remember that you must compile all files that have been changed, COA.TXT and CASH.TXT.

When you load the new database you will see the entry for CASH ACCOUNTS (Figure 14-23).

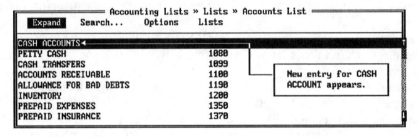

Figure 14-23 New CASH ACCOUNT short entry appears.

Enter

↵

The entry expands to display the sublist from the CASH file (Figure 14-24).

```
========== Accounting Lists » Lists » Accounts List » ... ==========
  Expand     Search...    Options    Lists

CASH - CHECKING ACCOUNT             1000
CASH-CHECKING ACCOUNT               1040
CASH-SAVINGS ACCOUNT                1050
CASH-PAYROLL ACCOUNT                1060



```

Figure 14-24 Entry links to short file listings.

The Norton Guides programs provide a few simple but powerful tools. If you plan to construct a database it is probably a good idea to sit down and create an outline of the files and the names that you will use. An outlining program like Ready or Think-Tank, or an outlining word processor like Word are helpful. Remember that good planning makes it much easier to write **!SEEALSO** commands since your plan contains the names of the files and key reference words you will need to cross-reference the database.

Word Processing And Text Files

If you are going to be creating large databases that contain a great deal of text, you will want to create the text files in a word processing program, as opposed to a text editor like the Norton Editor. Word processing programs such as WordPerfect and Word provide spelling checking and synonym help that is always useful in writing text.

In addition, word processing programs can help you quickly format text by setting margins, indents, centering, and other special effects that will enhance the look of your database display. For example, you can set the margins on your word processor to 80 columns wide to allow you to type lines that are as wide as the screen display. Remember that this text is not destined for the printer, but the screen.

Most of the popular word processing programs, including WordPerfect and Word, provide a means to save text in ASCII text format. But you should remember what that option actually means in terms of the specific word processor you are using.

When you save a file as text, the word processor will strip out all the formatting codes that are contained in the file. This includes settings for margins, centering, indents, and overhangs.

When you are creating text for the long entries in a database these formatting features allow you to create more readable text. But if you save the text as a text file, the word processor will remove those indent, and margin changes.

The [Ctrl/F5] command used in WordPerfect, and the Transfer Save option in Word, create text files that lose the formatting displayed on the word processing screen. However, there is another way to create the ASCII text file and retain all of the formatting advantages displayed on the word processing screen.

This method involves the use of a printer file rather than a text file. A printer file is one that captures the output that would normally be sent to the printer. This output would contain the formatting shown on the screen because that is the way the word processor would print it. Not all word processing programs have this option. Word and WordPerfect do because they use printer description files to assign formatting techniques specific for each printer. The trick is to select a printer that changes the formatted word processed text into ASCII standard text, in which all of the margin, indents, and overhangs are implemented with spaces. The effect is that the text will look the same in the Norton Guides display as it does on the word processor screen.

Printing Text to a File with Word

To create a formatted text file with Word you will need to locate a file called **PLAIN.PRD**, provided on one of the printer disks. This file implements a standard ASCII output when text is printed. Once you have this file, use the **Print Options** command to select **PLAIN** printer name.

Then use the **Print File** command to create a printer file from the text. Enter an appropriate filename, for instance, xxxx.txt, and Word will create a standard ASCII text file in which margins, centering, indents, and overhangs will be implemented as space characters. This will create a formatted text file that can be compiled with the Norton Guides programs into a database.

If you are using Word 4.0, this procedure will include any line drawings or paragraph boxes displayed on the screen. Word 4.0 is my personal choice for editing text for databases. Its outline and style sheet features make it easy to print out databases in one style for the printer and another for the text file.

Printing Text to a File with WordPerfect

WordPerfect also allows you to create formatted files but its method of doing so is more limited than Word.

WordPerfect contains two default printer definitions that will create standard text output. You can display a list of WordPerfect printer definitions by entering [Shift/F7] 4 3.

Select **DOS Text Printer** as the printer. For example, enter 2 ↵. This will display options for the printer port to use. To direct the text to a text file rather than a printer, select 8, then enter the name of a file, i.e., TEST.TXT.

When you want to print, use [Shift/F7] 1 to select the printer assigned to the **DOS Text Printer/Text File** definition.

This creates a text file that contains the centering and margin formats. Note that WordPerfect does not implement line drawing with these printer definitions so that line-drawn items will not be included in these files.

Summary

The Norton Guides programs are one of the most exciting utilities developed for the PC in recent years. They provide a fascinating and accessible means by which information can be placed into a computer system and recalled when and where it is needed. It provides a link between the necessary reference material and the computer user who needs it.

The commands used in database text files are:

- **!NAME.** This command is used to create the name of the database that will appear in the database selection menu. It also appears at the top of the menu window.

- **!MENU.** Creates a pull-down menu on the main menu bar. You can usually create four pull-down menus, each one containing eight menu items. Menu items should begin with unique letters avoiding E, S, and O.

- **!SHORT.** Creates a short, one-line entry in the database window. The short entry can be followed by up to 12,000 characters of text called a long entry.

- **!SEEALSO.** Use this as the last line of a long entry. It creates a cross-reference to the text of a another short entry. The short entry can be in the same file or any other file used in the database.

- **!FILE.** This command can be used to substitute a list of short entries for a long entry. Following a short entry with !FILE causes the specific short entry file to be displayed when the current short entry is expanded.

Index

The Classic Definitive IBM PC Reference

Inside the IBM PC, Third Edition is now revised to cover every generation of the IBM personal computer family — from the original PC to the latest PS/2 models. Page after page provides Peter Norton's easy-to-understand coverage of:

- how the 8088, 80286, and 80386 microprocessors work;
- DOS commands and operations from version 1.1 to 4.0;
- the operation of the BIOS system;
- programming techniques and examples in BASIC, Pascal, and assembly language;
- disk drive operation and data storage techniques;
- how ROM is allocated; and more.

Throughout you'll find next examples and applications that pass on Norton's expertise. Whether you're a novice or an experienced user, *Inside the IBM PC, Third Edition* is the book to use.

ISBN: 0-13467317-4
Price: $24.95

Look for this an other Brady titles at your local book or computer store.
To order directly
call 1 (800) 624-0023,
in New Jersey 1 (800) 624-0024
Visa/MC accepted